The Ethics of Philodemus

Voula Tsouna presents a comprehensive study of the ethics of the Epicurean philosopher Philodemus, who taught Virgil, influenced Horace, and was praised by Cicero. His works have only recently become available to modern readers, through the decipherment of a papyrus carbonized by the eruption of Vesuvius in 79 AD.

Tsouna examines Philodemus' theoretical principles in ethics, his contributions to moral psychology, his method, his conception of therapy, and his therapeutic techniques. Part I begins with an outline of the fundamental principles of Philodemus' ethics in connection with the canonical views of the Epicurean school and highlights his own original contributions. In addition to examining central features of Philodemus' hedonism, Tsouna analyses central concepts in his moral psychology: notably, his conception of vices, which she compares with that of the virtues; his account of harmful or unacceptable emotions or passions; and his theory of corresponding acceptable emotions or 'bites'. She then turns to an investigation of Philodemus' conception of philosophy as medicine and of the philosopher as a kind of doctor for the soul. By surveying his methods of treatment, Tsouna determines the place that they occupy in the therapeutics of the Hellenistic era. Part II uses the theoretical framework provided in Part I to analyse Philodemus' main ethical writings. The works considered include: *On Characters and Ways of Life*, *On Vices and the Opposite Virtues*, and *On the Passions*.

Voula Tsouna is Professor of Philosophy at the University of California, Santa Barbara.

The Ethics of Philodemus

Voula Tsouna

OXFORD
UNIVERSITY PRESS

OXFORD
UNIVERSITY PRESS

Great Clarendon Street, Oxford OX2 6DP

Oxford University Press is a department of the University of Oxford.
It furthers the University's objective of excellence in research, scholarship,
and education by publishing worldwide in

Oxford New York

Auckland Cape Town Dar es Salaam Hong Kong Karachi
Kuala Lumpur Madrid Melbourne Mexico City Nairobi
New Delhi Shanghai Taipei Toronto

With offices in

Argentina Austria Brazil Chile Czech Republic France Greece
Guatemala Hungary Italy Japan Poland Portugal Singapore
South Korea Switzerland Thailand Turkey Ukraine Vietnam

Oxford is a registered trade mark of Oxford University Press
in the UK and in certain other countries

Published in the United States
by Oxford University Press Inc., New York

First published 2007
First published in paperback 2011

British Library Cataloguing in Publication Data

Data available

Library of Congress Cataloging in Publication Data

Data available

Typeset by Laserwords Private Limited, Chennai, India
Printed in the United Kingdom by
Lightning Source UK Ltd., Milton Keynes

ISBN 978–0–19–929217–2 (Hbk)
ISBN 978–0–19–964012–6 (Pbk)

In memory of my father, Kostas Tsounas,
and for my mother, Richard, and Eleni

Acknowledgements

The Ethics of Philodemus took about a decade to write. During this period I had the privilege and pleasure to interact frequently with several scholars who have been working on the Herculaneum papyri, in particular on Philodemus' extant remains. My first thanks are addressed to David Sedley, who read earlier drafts of my manuscript and whose detailed comments led to substantial improvements. I owe an important debt as well to the late Marcello Gigante from whose learning and encouragement I have often benefited. I think of him with respect and affection. Warm thanks also to all the members of the Centro Internazionale per lo Studio dei Papiri Ercolanesi in Naples for their hospitality and their help with difficult readings. My research on the book was aided by participation in conferences, seminars, and workshops on Philodemus, many of them hosted by members of the Philodemus Translation Project and funded by the National Endowment for the Humanities. I am very grateful to my fellow participants, many of whom are valued friends, for their input, and to the institutions that sponsored these events. A special word of thanks is due to David Armstrong and Ben Henry for making available to me their unpublished text and translation of the extant remains of Philodemus' *On Anger* and *On Death*. My chapters on these topics reveal how indebted I am to their work. Moreover, I should like to acknowledge the friendly assistance of Daniel and Joelle Delattre on numerous occasions.

I presented drafts of some material of the book at University College London, the London Institute of Classical Studies, the University of Cambridge, the École Normale de Hautes Études, the Institut de Papyrologie and the Université de Paris IV—René Descartes, the Université de Lille III, the Symposium Hellenisticum 2004 held at the University of Rome, the University of Athens, the Central European University (Budapest), the

University of Texas at Austin, and Stanford University. I have benefited enormously from the reactions of these audiences and would like to extend to them my sincerest thanks. Although I do not acknowledge here my debts individually, most of them, I hope, are recorded in particular chapters and in the bibliography. Other debts are more difficult to pin down—a stimulating conversation, insights into a philosophical perplexity, a tough question, a fetching suggestion, the copy of a book hard to find, and so on. I have received these forms of help and many more, and I am grateful to the people who provided them—papyrologists, classicists, and philosophers, including my own colleagues and students at UCSB. Also, I would like to thank OUP, its staff and collaborators, for an exemplary process of reviewing and publication. The criticisms and comments of the four readers for the press have been invaluable. I am, of course, solely responsible for the errors that remain.

I dedicate the book to the memory of my father, Kostas Tsounas. I have confidently relied on his intelligence, kindness, and generosity, and most of all his unconditional love. I shall always be grateful to him for these reasons, and also for having taught me something about myself and about the complexities of the human heart. I also dedicate the book to my mother, Zoe Tsouna, Richard McKirahan, and our daughter, Eleni, for their love and patience and for times of happiness. Richard's forbearance was put to the test over the years, as he read and commented on many drafts of the manuscript and often debated with me what the texts actually say. I prepared the final version of the book during a sabbatical year 2005–6 in Athens, my native city. It was a kind of magical homecoming, and I should like to express my thankfulness and my love to those that made it so.

Athens, January 2007 V T

Contents

Abbreviations

Ancient Sources

Anonymous in Theaet. = *Anonymi Commentarius in Platonis Theaetetum*

Aristotle

De an. = *De anima*
Eth. Eud. = *Ethica Eudemia*
Eth. Nic. = *Ethica Nicomachea*
Pol. = *Politica*
Rhet. = *Rhetorica*

St Augustine

Doct. Chr. = *De doctrina Christiana*

Cicero

ad Pis. = *ad Pisonem*
De fin. = *De finibus bonorum et malorum*
De nat. deor. = *De natura deorum*
De off. = *De officiis*
Tusc. = *Tusculanae Disputationes*

Dem. Lac. = Demetrius of Laconia

D.L. = Diogenes Laertius

Epicurus

ad Herod. = *ad Herodotum*
ad Pyth. = *ad Pythoclem*
ad Men. = *ad Menoeceum*
De nat. = *De natura*
KD = *Kyriai Doxai*
SV = *Sententiae Vaticanae*

Erotian

gloss. Hippocr. praef. = *Vocum (glossarium) Hippocraticarum collectio*

Galen

Comp. Med. = *De compositione medicamentorum*
PHP = *De placitis Hippocratis et Platonis*
Sub. emp. = *Subfiguratio empirica*

Homer

Od. = *Odyssea*

Lucretius

DRN = *De rerum natura*

PHerc. = Papyrus Herculanensis

Philodemus

De adul. = *De adulatione*
De conv. = *De conversatione*
De div. = *De divitiis*
De elect. = *De electionibus et fugis*
De Epic. = *De Epicuro*
De grat. = *De gratitudine*
De inv. = *De invidia*
De ir. = *De ira*
De lib. dic. = *De libertate dicendi*
De mort. = *De morte*
De mus. = *De musica*
De oec. = *De oeconomia*
De piet. = *De pietate*
De poem. = *De poematis*
De sign. = *De signis*
De superb. = *De superbia*
De vit. = *De vitiis*
Rhet. = *De rhetorica*

Plato

Leg. = *Leges*
Phdr. = *Phaedrus*
Rep. = *Respublica*

Plutarch

Adul. = *De adulatore et amico*
Adv. Col. = *Adversus Colotem*
De coh. ir. = *De cohibenda ira*
De se ipsum = *De se ipsum citra invidiam laudando*
Non posse = *Non posse suaviter vivi secundum Epicurum*

Porph. = Porphyry

Ad Marc. = *Ad Marcellam*

Proclus

In Eucl. Elem. = *In primum Euclidis librum commentarius*

Pseudo-Aristotle (cf. Theophrastus)

Oik. = *Oeconomica*

Pseudo-Plutarch

De libid. et aegr. = *De libidine et aegritudine*

Quintilian

Inst. or. = *Institutio oratoria*

Seneca

De ir. = *De ira*
Ep. = *Epistula*
ad Marc. = *ad Marciam*

Sextus Empiricus

adv. phys. = *Adversus physicos*
M = *Adversus mathematicos*

SVF = *Stoicorum Veterum Fragmenta*

Theophrastus

Char. = *Characteres*
Oik. (cf. Pseudo-Aristotle) = *Oeconomica*

Thucydides

Hist. = *Historiae*

Xenophon

Oec. = *Oeconomicus*

Journals

APQ	*American Philosophical Quarterly*
BCPE	*Bolletino del Centro Internazionale per lo studio dei papiri ercolanesi*
CErc	*Cronache Ercolanesi*
CP	*Classical Philology*
JP	*Journal of Philosophy*
OSAP	*Oxford Studies in Ancient Philosophy*
PPA	*Philosophy and Public Affairs*
PPQ	*Pacific Philosophical Quarterly*
RIGI	*Rivista Indo-Greca-Italica di Filologia, antichità*

Introduction

I

Philodemus was an Epicurean philosopher of the first century BC (*c.*110–*c.*40/early 30s BC). Born in Gadara, a small town in the Middle East, he spent his formative years as a student of the Garden of Athens and was taught philosophy by the Epicurean scholarch Zeno of Sidon (*c.*150–70s BC) and by Demetrius Lacon, Zeno's younger contemporary. Then, perhaps during the Mithridatic War,[1] he left Athens in search of better conditions of life and work, and took up residence in Italy. Under the patronage of a patrician philhellene, Lucius Calpurnius Piso Caesoninus, he settled in the so-called Villa of the Papyri in the resort of Herculaneum in Campania, and formed around him a genuine Epicurean community of pupils and friends.[2] His works constitute the largest portion of the library of the Villa, which was buried beneath the mud and ashes of Vesuvius in AD 79 and was excavated in the mid-eighteenth century. They count among the most difficult Greek texts to edit, translate, and understand. For the papyri on which they are written are charred and blackened, and they are preserved in various states of fragmentation and corruption. Therefore, for a long while, many of these writings were not available in usable form. This accounts for the fact that they were sadly neglected, despite their historical and philosophical importance. For, in truth, Philodemus was a major figure of late Epicureanism, who elaborated and even transformed Epicurus'

[1] Like many other intellectuals, Philodemus left Athens probably during the crucial years 88–86 BC: see Sedley 2003.

[2] See Marcello Gigante's discussion of Philodemus' epigrams as autobiography in Gigante 1995: 49–61.

system in ways that deserve our attention and study. Moreover, many of his contributions (especially in aesthetics and ethics) have considerable philosophical merit in their own right.

In recent years Philodemus' writings have become more accessible, for many reasons. Among them are the use of new scientific techniques, the discovery of a method for recovering the original structure of book-rolls, and the coordinated efforts of international teams of scholars who were able to work on the papyri, in the *Officina dei Papiri* in Naples, from different but mutually complementary angles. In particular, much attention has been devoted to Philodemus' literary and aesthetic theory, which is developed chiefly in his works *On Poems*, *On Rhetoric*, and *On Music*, but also in the treatise *On the Good King According to Homer* and in passages of *On Piety*. The brilliant editions of the first part of *On Piety* and the first book of *On Poems*, by Dirk Obbink and Richard Janko respectively, have considerably contributed to the appreciation of Philodemus' artistic theory and practice in their totality.

Important work has been done on Philodemus' ethics as well. In that domain, however, discussion has been restricted chiefly to particulars, and has not led to integral accounts of Philodemus' ethical doctrine. One reason for this is practical: while Philodemus' aesthetics has had the benefit of many years of work by various experts, his ethical writings have been relatively overlooked. Another reason is that the systematic connections which hold between Philodemus' ethical writings are not easy to trace. In any case, the fact is that there is a major gap in the scholarly literature concerning Philodemus, which has to do with the absence of a book-length comprehensive study of his ethical works. It is important to fill that gap for both historical and philosophical reasons. For, in addition to every classicist's wish to piece together the contents of the Philodemean corpus, philosophers need to become aware of Philodemus' contributions to ethics and moral psychology.

My book is a first attempt to achieve these aims. Its claims are rather modest, and it might be useful at the outset to explain what they are. The editions by Obbink and Janko are based on exhaustive papyrological, paleographical, and philological analyses of the relevant papyri, and they establish authoritative versions of their texts. On the other hand, the project in which I am engaged, and which deals with the entire corpus of Philodemus' ethical writings, precludes such detailed textual scrutiny.

My discussion is inevitably based on the available editions, even though several of them may be superseded in the future. I occasionally propose new textual readings and reconstructions, which I have checked to the best of my ability; but my principle has been to keep technical concerns to the barest minimum. Thus, regarding the texts, there is nothing definitive in my own book, although, I hope, there is much that is plausible and is likely to withstand the test of time. Regarding content, fifteen years of work on Philodemus, as well as on Greek and Roman ethics in general, has given me an understanding of Philodemus' arguments in individual treatises, and also has led me to an overall interpretation of his doctrine. Even allowing for future improvements in the texts, I think it is unlikely that its main lines will be shown to be substantially incorrect. However, one should bear in mind that there are many ways of piecing together the various parts of Philodemus' doctrine, and that the peculiar condition of the texts leaves ample room for disagreement among reasonable people.

In any event, I have pursued in this book several main goals. I have given a general account of Philodemus' theoretical principles in ethics, his contributions to moral psychology, his method, his conception of therapy, and his therapeutic techniques. I have discussed significant aspects of his ethical treatises not as a series of isolated fragments, but as belonging to a larger conceptual whole. I have provided a kind of running commentary for these treatises. And I have tried to highlight aspects of his analyses which are of genuine philosophical importance. To an extent, some of these goals compete with each other. Meticulous exposition may occasionally divert attention from the philosophically interesting points, but also philosophical focus can make the discussion of less exciting parts of the writings seem redundant. I have tried to strike a balance between these concerns. And although it may be virtually impossible to please two masters, I hope that both classical scholars and philosophers will find in this book at least some of the things that they are looking for.

II

I shall now explain briefly the conventions that I have followed and other related matters. Every one of Philodemus' ethical treatises is contained in one or more Herculaneum papyri and is identified in scholarship in many different ways: by translating its title into some modern language, by mentioning its title in Greek or in transliteration, by translating the title into Latin (usually abbreviated in accordance with scholarly convention), and by citing the relevant Herculaneum papyri numbers (e.g., PHerc. 1251). Usually, when I give the full title of a book, I give its English translation, whereas when I give the reference of a passage in parentheses, I use the Latin abbreviated form.

In the next section, which outlines the contents of the book, I identify each treatise by giving its title in English translation and, in parentheses, the Latin abbreviated form and the relevant papyri numbers: for example, *On Frank Speech* (*De lib. dic.*; PHerc. 1471), *On Arrogance* (*De superb.*; PHerc. 1008), *On Flattery* (*De adul.*; PHerc. 222, 223, 1082, 1089, 1457, 1643, 1675). Near the beginning of each chapter, I use all three ways, as well as the Greek title(s), when referring for the first time to the treatise or treatises that constitute that chapter's principal object of study. This practice should help non-specialists identify correctly every time the work cited. I have used Greek words and short phrases, especially for the sake of classical readers. For Greek words which occur frequently (e.g., *τέχνη*, *παρρησία*, *οἰκονομία*, *ὀργή*, *θυμός*), most of the time I use their transliterated form. As a rule, I do not use Greek words and phrases or transliterated words in the main text without also translating them at least at their first occurrence. I indicate the columns by roman numerals and the line numbers by arabic numerals (e.g., *De ir.* XXVI. 11). I indicate both the fragments and their line numbers by arabic numerals (e.g., *De lib. dic.* 49. 2–5).

As mentioned, I have kept down the technical aspects of Philodemus' texts and have treated them as philosophical writings to the extent that this is possible. However, there are limitations to that effort which are set by the peculiar nature of the evidence and, especially, by the fact that many passages are fragmentary, and their restorations partly conjectural. I have tried to avoid the phenomenon that David Sedley was the first to characterize as 'bracket blindness': i.e., the tendency to overlook the brackets surrounding editorial restorations of a word or passage and thus develop interpretations based on slim or even non-existent evidence. But sometimes I have taken the liberty to interpret heavily supplemented passages when the interpretation that I propose finds support in the context.

I have used square brackets in my translations to indicate those places in which a given passage has been heavily restored, and hence its translation and interpretation are largely conjectural. On the other hand, I have not marked with square brackets supplementations where I have a high degree of confidence in their correctness. Overall, I have indicated that not everything in Philodemus is at the same level of certainty, and, moreover, I have demarcated places in which the evidence is particularly precarious. But I have not undertaken to show systematically here the special difficulties and pleasures of working with the texts of the Herculaneum papyri, although I hope that I have conveyed to my readers some sense of that too. For Philodemus' parenthetical phrases I use dashes unless I indicate otherwise. In my translations of Philodemus' texts, I have occasionally used parentheses. Their purpose is to clarify or to complete the meaning of a word or phrase. Neither the parentheses nor what is included in them correspond to anything in the Greek text.

In the second part of the book, I have given in translation considerable stretches of the writings under discussion. I have made that choice not only in order to present a broad textual basis for my arguments, but also in order to facilitate physical and conceptual access to these texts. As the matter stands, the relevant editions can be found in few university libraries of the anglophone world. Even then, they can be used only by scholars who read Greek. In fact, most of Philodemus' ethical writings have not yet been translated into English, and some of them have not been translated into any modern language at all. But persons who read Greek may also find difficulties, unless they are used to Philodemus' style of writing and to his various modes of argumentation. For example, it has often proved difficult to distinguish between Philodemus' own views and those of his opponents and to recognize arguments that he advances in his own behalf as opposed to others that he develops for dialectical reasons. My translations accompanied by exegeses should prove useful for such purposes.

I suggest below that Philodemus' approach to the vices and passions exhibits a general methodological pattern, albeit with variations, and that we find support for that suggestion in individual treatises. All I mean is that, perhaps despite appearances, the treatises in question are composed with a fair degree of systematicity, and that their surviving parts indicate that Philodemus has in mind a model of analysis marked by certain general features. However, the elements of that model do not appear in any particular sequence. For example, the description of a character trait does not necessarily come before its comparison with other traits, and the pragmatic consequences of a vice are not enumerated always at the same stage of the analysis. Also, any outline of Philodemus' methodological steps is necessarily incomplete, since it emerges not from entire works, but only their surviving portions. And although, for example, the final third of a given book gives a good enough idea about Philodemus' procedure, the hypothesis that he followed a similar procedure in the missing beginning of the same writing is only tentative. Regarding the sequence of topics in my own discussion of individual treatises, it often reflects not the order of the Greek text, but rather what seems to me a natural way of developing Philodemus' exposition and argument.

When we deal with texts belonging to the Herculaneum papyri collection, we usually move from passages which are better preserved to those that are least well preserved. However, it has seemed best for systematic reasons to begin several chapters at or near the beginning of the extant texts that they discuss, although beginnings are typically more damaged than the columns that follow. When I proceed in this manner, I try to remain aware of the highly conjectural parts and, if possible, I interpret them in the light of better-known passages. Finally, my discussion of extremely fragmentary works—for instance, *On Flattery*—is informed by my understanding of texts which are in better shape and preferably belong to the same ensemble: for example, several continuous columns of *On Arrogance*. Even so, I should stress once more the tentative character of such interpretations.

III

The book is divided into two parts. They are unequal in length, study Philodemus' writings from different angles, and, regrettably, overlap to a small extent. The first part is more theoretical than the second and consists of the following chapters.

Chapter 1 ('First Things') outlines the fundamental principles of Philodemus' ethics in connection with the canonical views of the Epicurean school, and points to his own original contributions. I examine central features of Philodemus' hedonism, which sometimes are stated but often merely presupposed, and also elements of his approach to the virtues and friendship. I draw evidence from the text [*On Choices and Avoidances*] (*De elect.*; PHerc. 1251) and from the eulogy *On Epicurus* (*De Epic.*; PHerc. 1232,

1289b) both of which can confidently be attributed to Philodemus, and also from the first and the second books of Cicero's *De finibus*. Chapter 2 ('Vices, Emotions, and "Bites"') concerns central concepts of Philodemus' moral psychology: notably, his conception of vices, which is compared with that of the virtues, of harmful and unacceptable emotions or passions, and of corresponding acceptable emotions, or 'bites'. Chapter 3 ('Analysis and Treatment: Methodological and Epistemological Prolegomena') outlines a general pattern of analysis that Philodemus seems to follow from one ethical treatise to another, and then points to certain epistemological features of that pattern, including the empirical elements that mark Philodemus' conception of the medical metaphor: i.e., of philosophy as medicine and of the philosopher as a kind of doctor for the soul. Chapter 4 ('Therapeutic Tactics') offers a rapid survey of Philodemus' methods of treatment and determines the place that they occupy in the therapeutics of the Hellenistic era.

The second part of the book relies on the theoretical framework provided in the first part. It is devoted to several chapters dealing individually with Philodemus' main ethical writings or groups of writings and, pragmatically, can be used as a guide to that territory. I have divided it into three subsections that correspond roughly to three ensembles of works: namely, *On Characters and Ways of Life*, *On Vices and the Opposite Virtues and the People in whom they occur and the Situations in which they are found* (henceforth *On Vices and the Opposite Virtues*, or simply *On Vices*), and *On the Passions*.

The central piece of the group *On Characters and Ways of Life* may be Philodemus' treatise *On Frank Speech* (*De lib. dic.*; PHerc. 1471), which is based on the lectures of Zeno of Sidon in Athens. Chapter 5 ('Frank Speech') studies in detail the practice of frank speech or candid criticism (παρρησία, translit. *parrhēsia*), the principal educational method of late Epicurean schools and a major tool of moral and psychological therapy. Topics include the nature, scope, forms, and circumstances of application of *parrhēsia*; the types of characters of the students and their reactions to parrhesiastic criticism; the dispositions of the teachers and the ways in which these dispositions affect the use of frank speech; the confessional practices used at every level of hierarchy of the Epicurean school, including the sages; and the role of *parrhēsia* in securing the cohesion and solidarity of Epicurean communities. There are three appendices to Chapter 5. The first discusses the slender evidence on good will, benevolence, and gratitude found in the fragments of the treatise *On Gratitude* (*De grat.*; PHerc. 1414). The second concerns Philodemus' views on the importance of appropriate conversation and silence as they can be surmised from the remnants of *On Conversation* (*De conv.*; PHerc. 873). Both these works probably belong to the project *On Characters and Ways of Life*. In the third appendix I try to piece together Philodemus' views about envy and malicious joy in the few extant remains of a treatise which may have borne the title *On Envy* (*De inv.*; PHerc. 1678), and which may have been part of the ensemble *On the Passions* or of the project *On Vices and the Opposite Virtues*.

The surviving treatises of this last work are the subject of the next three chapters. Chapter 6 ('Flattery and the Desire to Please') tries to piece together the extant remains of *On Flattery* (*De adul.*; PHerc. 222, 223, 1082, 1089, 1457, 1643, 1675) and give a sense of what Philodemus' arguments might be. Chapter 7 ('Arrogance and Related Vices') concerns Philodemus' book *On Arrogance* (*De superb.*; PHerc. 1008). Chapter 8 ('Wealth and Property Management') focuses primarily on the treatise *On Property Management* (*De oec.*; PHerc. 1424), but also discusses passages of *On Wealth* (*De div.*; PHerc. 163)—a fragmentary work that probably does not belong to *On Vices*.

The last two chapters are devoted to the ensemble *On the Passions* and the work *On Death*, which is conceptually related to that ensemble. The books *On Folly*, *On Lack of Proper Measure*, and *On Erotic Love* also belong to *On the Passions*, but there is very little evidence about them. *On Envy* too is part of the same group, but is discussed earlier (in Appendix III to Chapter 5) for organizational reasons. Thus, Chapter 9 ('Anger and the Desire for Revenge') examines Philodemus' diatribe *On Anger* (*De ir.*; PHerc. 182), a principal piece of *On the Passions* and an important contribution to the philosophical literature on that subject. Chapter 10 ('The Fear of Death') is primarily devoted to the surviving part of the fourth book of Philodemus' treatise *On Death* (*De mort.*; PHerc. 1050). It also makes brief mention of Philodemus' treatment of superstitious fears concerning death in [*On Choices and Avoidances*]. The chapter is divided into three parts. The first surveys certain distinctive features of the Epicurean treatment of the fear of death and sketches out Philodemus' original contributions to that topic. The second part focuses on Philodemus' discussion of cases in which the thought of death appears particularly hard to bear; while the third deals with the central themes of the peroration of the treatise. Here, more than anywhere else, readers are invited to appreciate the originality and subtlety of Philodemus' analyses, as well as the variety of arguments and literary artifices that Philodemus puts to use for therapeutic purposes.

PART I

1

First Things

> in all circumstances of
> [life], [we have been guided]
> by him as well as possible,
> in accordance with everything
> useful to nature.
>
> Philodemus, *De Epic.*; PHerc. 1232, XVIII. 6–10

> [O]ught we not to feel the greatest gratitude to him who listened to these truths, almost pronounced by the voice of Nature, and grasped their meaning so firmly and fully that he has led all sane-minded men on the road to a joyful, tranquil, quiet, and peaceful life?
>
> Cicero, *De fin.* I. 71

At the outset, I should like to say something about the sources and the nature of my argument in this chapter. Philodemus does not often state the philosophical underpinnings of his analyses, and he defends them even less frequently. There are two exceptions, however: the text [*On Choices and Avoidances*], [Περὶ αἱρέσεων καὶ φυγῶν] (*De elect.*; PHerc. 1251) and the remains of *On Epicurus*, Περὶ Ἐπικούρου (*De Epic.*; PHerc. 1232, 1289b).[1] The former presents the basic tenets of Epicurean hedonism and explains how they are debated among rival Epicurean groups, while the latter eulogizes Epicurus by discussing the cornerstones of his ethical thought. Both reflect Philodemus' own priorities and his close engagement with the canonical texts of his school.[2] Both defend the coherence of

[1] Philodemus is, in all probability, the author of both these texts. Cf. Tepedino Guerra 1994, and Indelli and Tsouna-McKirahan 1995: 61–70.

[2] Also, both conform to the agenda set by Zeno of Sidon. I explore the relations between Philodemus and the school of Athens in Tsouna 2007. The material in this chapter and the next overlaps in part with the contents of Tsouna 2007, but the emphasis is different.

Epicurus' doctrine, fight against heterodoxy, and uphold the cults of communal life. Moreover, both raise larger issues: for instance, whether Philodemus has good reasons for considering heretical the views of certain Epicurean rivals, and also whether his own views are actually consistent with those of Epicurus. There is indirect evidence too about Philodemus' first principles, drawn from his treatment of individual vices and emotions. Moreover, there is external evidence found mainly in the exposition of Torquatus, the Epicurean spokesman in the first and the second books of Cicero's *De finibus*. Torquatus' account derives either from Philodemus' own writings[3] or from some other source of which Philodemus would approve.[4] However, my argument has limitations, and I wish to state what

[3] I have defended the hypothesis that Cicero uses Philodemus as a principal source on Epicurean ethics in Tsouna 2001*a*. In outline, my argument was this. Torquatus' presentation of Epicurean ethics is based not on the writings of Epicurus, but on some later author. For the Epicurean spokesman incorporates in his account divergent views of rival Epicurean factions, grounded in conflicting interpretations of Epicurus' text and undoubtedly postdating it (see Sedley 1996: 316–17). Several additional considerations point towards Philodemus as Cicero's principal Epicurean source. First, there can be little doubt that Cicero was familiar with Philodemus and his work. For he says that his summary of Epicurean ethics is just as accurate as the surveys of current members of the school (*De fin*. I. 13), and hence he must have knowledge of contemporary Epicurean writings. These cannot belong to Latin authors, for Cicero also says that those Epicureans who write in Latin are not genuine philosophers (*Tusc*. II. 7), and he adds that he has never read their books. Therefore, it seems likely that he compares his own summary to Philodemus' writings (sc. a contemporary Epicurean who writes in Greek) or to compendia of Epicurean ethics that would represent Philodemus' own interpretation of the Epicurean doctrine. Second, Cicero identifies as Siro and Philodemus the Epicureans to whom Torquatus volunteers to refer the argument in order to get instructed by them as to how to settle it (II. 119). And he informs us that these philosophers are his principal opponents: unless they are refuted, 'all virtue, honour, and true merit must be abandoned' (II. 44). It follows that, in the dialectical context of the two first books of the *De finibus*, the rival interlocutors take for granted the same version of Epicurean ethics. Third, there is a methodological reason why Cicero might borrow his version of Epicureanism from Philodemus rather than from earlier Epicureans: viz., that he often (though by no means always) relies on contemporary authors in the composition of his philosophical treatises. Fourth, the theses defended by Torquatus, and subsequently interpreted and refuted by Cicero, have close philosophical parallels in Philodemus' own treatises. Fifth, textual parallels as well point in the same direction. Finally, Cicero takes into account, and sometimes integrates, Philodemus' ethical views in his own treatment of moral subjects, e.g., in the *Tusculan Disputations*. For these reasons it has seemed to me probable that he may have used Philodemus' treatises in the *De finibus* as well. However, alternative hypotheses about Cicero's source are also attractive: see next note.

[4] In that case, the most likely source would be the teachings of Zeno of Sidon and his associates. My recent research on Zeno and his school inclines me now to favour this hypothesis. It is worth noting that Torquatus' presentation is of a different character from Philodemus' account of Epicurean ethics in the extant fragments. While Torquatus argues fundamental principles of Epicurean ethics, Philodemus usually states or presupposes them. However, it seems to me that this fact should not influence our speculations concerning Cicero's source. For instance, Cicero and Philodemus may use a common source, but in different ways. Or they may draw on different authors belonging to the same school, i.e., Zeno's school—in which case their sources would contain essentially the same version of the principles of Epicurean philosophy.

they are. In so far as the cardinal principles of Epicurean ethics belong to the doctrinal tradition of the school, they are endorsed by all its members; so, my claim is that Philodemus *too* holds them, not that he *alone* does. On the other hand, I credit him with original interpretations or developments of the canonical doctrine, but these are not always easy to spot. Sometimes he demarcates his own contributions, while in other cases he introduces them without warning.[5] For instance, he sometimes advances his own position as the only correct one and, if necessary, contrasts it with the positions of his rivals. Torquatus makes similar moves in the first book of *De finibus*. He distinguishes among divergent Epicurean views on a certain ethical topic, and then endorses one of them on his own account. I find that in every case of this sort, Torquatus' preference coincides with Philodemus' own. But although arguments to that effect may be convincing, I must warn against taking them as definitive proofs.

I

A good place to start is Philodemus' acknowledgement of his greatest debts to Epicurus. 'Above all, he establishes the principles of philosophy, by which alone it is possible to act rightly and, moreover, the congenital ends yielding the most conspicuous evidence, by which are performed the calculations concerning the things to be chosen or avoided' (*De elect.* XIII. 5–12). Philodemus endorses the core of Epicurus' hedonism, the cardinal tenets which support it and also its central thesis, that pleasure is the moral end. But as we learn from Cicero (*Tusc.* III. 17. 38), pleasure is a vague concept, and by the first century BC, its nature was debated both inside and outside the Epicurean school. One subject of controversy concerns the nature of the moral end and in particular its definition both as pleasure (ἡδονή) and as the absence of pain (ἀπονία). For the idea that the highest pleasure is absence of pain is counterintuitive; and the claim that pleasure has several distinct aspects seems to undermine the unity of the supreme good. While some first-generation Epicureans disputed the thesis that ἀπονία is part of the τέλος, the moral end, Philodemus holds

[5] This is true especially in cases in which he modifies and even corrects Epicurus' teachings. Cf. Indelli and Tsouna-McKirahan 1995: 43–5.

the view that Zeno's school attributes to Epicurus' canon:[6] namely, that ἀπονία, the absence of physical pain, and also ἀταραξία, the absence of mental suffering, are parts of the supreme good.

For example, in Philodemus' diatribe *On Death*, the concept of ἀπονία underlies the arguments for the theses that death implies complete loss of sensation, and that even the moment when the soul leaves the body is relatively painless. The contention that death is painless alleviates suffering by attacking false beliefs about the event. As for the reasonings explaining why we should not fear or grieve about an untimely or violent death, and why we should not agonize about issues of inheritance, burial, and post-mortem glory, they promote ἀταραξία by removing the sources of disturbance about such issues. The treatise *On Property Management* also promotes these twin goals. Following Metrodorus, Philodemus declares that the best life is the one involving the greatest tranquillity, peace, and minimal worry (*De oec.* XII. 45–XIII. 1–3). And he argues that the good administration of our estates allows us to lead a life that is free of both anxiety and physical toil.[7]

Furthermore, the ideal Epicurean is a person who lives in a stable and joyful condition, not in a swirl of kinetic pleasures. Indeed, Philodemus attributes to Epicurus a related belief. On the one hand, our active enjoyment of life depends on our continuing capacity to savour and store memories of bodily pleasures (*De Epic.*; PHerc. 1232, XVIII. 10–17); on the other hand, the sage would not be in a position to do so if his mind were not untroubled in the first place. Arguments to the same effect are rehearsed by Torquatus in his exchange with Cicero in *De finibus* book II (6 ff.).[8] Both the pleasures that stir us with a kind of

[6] Demetrius Laco insists that Epicurus considers the τέλος, pleasure, as the removal of pain (PHerc. 1012, I. 1–8) and corrects Epicurean copies (ἀντίγραφα) which contain equivocal formulations of that thesis (XXXVIII. 1–13).

[7] Philodemus maintains that we should not avoid all toil and effort indiscriminately, but engage in activities whose practice entails fewer worries than our neglect of them (XIII. 3 ff.). He determines the sources of acquisition and preservation of wealth (XXII. 6 ff.) compatible with the goal of living a philosophical life free of pain and disturbance (XXII. 36–48). And he singles out the teaching of true and serene philosophical arguments as the best source of income for the philosopher, for the reason that it secures for him a tranquil and painless life (XXIII. 23–32).

[8] Cicero criticizes Epicurus' definition of the supreme good on the grounds that it violates the principle of semantic monism: it uses the same word, 'pleasure', for two different kinds of experience (*De fin.* II. 6 ff.), disregarding the preconception related to the meaning of 'pleasure' (*De fin.* II. 16) as well as the evidence of the senses. Cicero unpacks the evidence of the senses in terms of our awareness of ourselves. His argument against Epicurus is that, in truth, we are aware of ourselves as being at

smoothness, the kinetic pleasures, and those that we perceive once all pain has been removed, the static ones, qualify as pleasure. Formally, they both accord with our preconception, and empirically, we pursue them both as intrinsic goods. Torquatus reiterates here what he takes to be the orthodox position of his school, which is also Philodemus' own.

Whether the goodness of pleasure is self-evident is another matter of dispute. Epicurus says that it is, and that it requires no proof in order to be established (cf. Dem. Lac.; PHerc. 1012, LI. 4–8). Torquatus confirms that this was indeed Epicurus' view but that, nonetheless, some of his followers attempt to demonstrate it by appealing to preconception rather than sensation (*De fin.* I. 30–1). Yet others observe that, since rival philosophers used elaborate arguments to defend the thesis that pleasure should not be counted as a good nor pain as an evil, the Epicureans too need to use arguments in order to refute their opponents. Torquatus explicitly sides with this last group.[9] He points out that anti-hedonism appears plausible, for the reasons that we often do not correctly interpret our own motives, that we fail to recognize the importance of the hedonic calculus (*De fin.* I. 32),[10] and that we therefore form the mistaken impression that there is such a thing as disinterested conduct (*De fin.* I. 32–6). On the other hand, according to Torquatus, anti-hedonism is refuted and hedonism is confirmed, if we stress the importance of the calculus, and in that manner bring out the rationality inherent in the pursuit of pleasure. Philodemus assumes exactly the same stance. In addition to the fact that he stresses the obvious goodness of the congenital ends, he first refutes the suggestion that pleasure may not be the ultimate good after all. As we saw, he quotes Epicurus' saying to Metrodorus that one cannot wish to preserve life when all pleasure and all hope for pleasure is gone (*De Epic.*; PHerc. 1232,

different times in three different conditions: viz., pleasure, pain, and an intermediate condition in which we feel neither pleasure nor pain. Moreover, Cicero remarks that Epicurus takes none of the options available for removing that inconsistency: he neither equates pleasure with kinetic pleasure, nor defines it exclusively as static pleasure, nor does he posit two supreme goods instead of one.

[9] Given his allegiance to this last group, it is not surprising that Torquatus later *argues* that pleasure is the supreme good and pain the supreme evil by examining hypothetical cases of extreme and sustained pleasure and pain (*De fin.* I. 40–1).

[10] Torquatus observes that people often do not know how to seek pleasures rationally (*ratione*), and therefore bring pain upon themselves. And also, they do not realize that pain is occasionally preferable to pleasure not because pain is intrinsically desirable, but because it is expected to procure greater pleasure in the future (*De fin.* I. 32).

XVIII. 10–17), in the way of an argument for hedonism. Second, he stresses the paramount importance of the calculus in general terms,[11] and also points to specific ways in which vices and passions obstruct it. Examples are the damages caused by arrogance, greed, and anger and, on a more abstract level, the results of anti-philosophical attitudes[12] dictated by anti-rationalism and the fear of death.

Another controversy within the Epicurean school concerns the ways in which it is possible to secure the most important aspect of the supreme good: i.e., tranquillity. A central question is precisely how the understanding of the first principles of Epicureanism affects moral choice and brings about our peace of mind. It seems that different Epicurean groups held different opinions about this matter. In the following passage, Philodemus mentions two rival views, one of which is his own.

> The thesis that [understanding] and memorizing of the cardinal tenets (*τῶν κυρι[ωτ]ά[τ]ων*: *De elect.* XI. 9) contribute greatly to what we actually choose and avoid is not tantamount to claiming that some choices or avoidances are traced back to the states of tranquillity concerning them [sc. the cardinal tenets] as some people have clumsily interpreted it; it rather amounts to the claim that they [sc. our choices or avoidances] are accomplished successfully when we measure them by the ends laid down by nature.
>
> (*De elect.* XI. 7–20)

One group of Epicureans, then, believe that we attain tranquillity (simply) by learning the cardinal tenets of the Epicurean system; moral decisions flow, as it were, quasi-automatically, from tranquillity and can be considered the direct result of that kind of learning. Philodemus objects to this approach.[13] He considers it clumsy and simplistic (cf. *ἀγροίκως*, ll. 13–14), presumably because it diminishes the role of moral deliberation and thus distorts the meaning of Epicurus' original claim. In response, Philodemus advances the view that the basic principles of the doctrine secure tranquillity not directly but indirectly; i.e., they help us to use the natural goals of pleasure or the absence of pain in the calculus concerning particular ethical issues.[14] The basic principles do not yield information and guidance with

[11] Cf. *De elect.* IV. 10–19, V. 1–VI. 21, IX. 13–20, XI. 5–20.

[12] *De elect.* I. 1–III. 21, XVII. 3–20.

[13] His objections exhibit the intellectualism characteristic of Zeno of Sidon and his circle. See Snyder 2000: 45–65.

[14] The two rival views are discussed in detail in Indelli and Tsouna-McKirahan 1995: 160–6.

regard to particulars. Rather, they contain the kind of information which enables one 'to arrive by oneself at the solutions to many of the problems concerning particulars' (cf. D.L. X. 82).[15]

The cardinal tenets (τὰ κυριώτατα) mentioned in the passage quoted above comprise, importantly, the four theses (cf. τῶ[ν] τεττάρω[ν]: *De elect.* XI. 6) which constitute the so-called fourfold medicine (τετραφάρμακος, translit. *tetrapharmakos*), and also some other ethical claims.[16] In its canonical form the *tetrapharmakos* is that 'god presents no fears, death no cause for alarm; it is easy to procure what is good, and also to endure what is evil' (*Ad.* [...]. IV. 9–14).[17] So far as we know, all Epicurean philosophers endorse these maxims and defend them against their critics. As for Philodemus, he establishes each of these maxims separately and all of them together in a number of writings and in ways which are distinctly his own. For example, in [*On Choices and Avoidances*] he mentions the disastrous consequences of superstition (*De elect.* VII. 1–X. 19) and argues for the superiority, both ethical and pragmatic, of the view that we should not fear the gods. Also, he denounces the irrationality of the fear of death and its destructive impact on everyday life (*De elect.* XVI. 1–XX. 21).[18] Moreover, he jointly examines the third and the fourth tenets of the *tetrapharmakos* concerning, respectively, the limits of good and evil. '[We should know both that the good is not only limited in intensity and duration, but is also easy to attain][19] and that the bad not only has limits in magnitude and time, but is also easy to bear. For otherwise it would be of no use (to us) that the good [should be limited] but impossible or difficult for us to achieve, or that the bad should be limited but unbearable because of its long duration' (IV. 1–10). As the sequel of the text suggests,[20] the principles embodied

[15] Note that this is not a Philodemean source.

[16] On the meaning of the expressions τὰ τέτταρα as distinguished from τὰ κυριώτατα, see Indelli and Tsouna-McKirahan 1995: 161.

[17] Again, the canon concerning the *tetrapharmakos* seems to be determined by Zeno of Sidon and his circle. For Zeno incorporates in his description of the happy life the fourth tenet (*Tusc.* III. 17. 38), and Demetrius deals with puzzles (ἀπορίαι) concerning the other three (cf. PHerc. 1055 and also PHerc. 1012, XXXVII. 1 ff., XLI. 1 ff.).

[18] In *On Death* he takes this matter further, analysing the complex morphology of the fear of death and supplying arguments which allay that fear as well as other related emotions, such as anxiety and grief.

[19] The restoration of this phrase is *exempli gratia* but, nonetheless, there are good grounds for it: see Indelli and Tsouna-McKirahan 1995: 87.

[20] 'What results from these points of knowledge is that we pursue nothing which does not naturally remove pain (and such are most matters that people take a serious interest in), and that we do not

in these maxims have an important effect on our choices. Notably, they underlie the analysis of virtues and vices, and also the correct evaluation of practical activities, such as the acquisition and management of wealth. To conclude this point, regarding all four maxims of the *tetrapharmakos*, Philodemus closely follows the tradition, but does not stay with it alone. He offers arguments supporting each tenet and explores its implications and the ways in which it works. Thus, he integrates the *tetrapharmakos* into a context defined by his own philosophical interests and therapeutic objectives.

Epicurus' firm belief that the study of nature is all-important for ethics remained uncontroversial within the Epicurean school. Philodemus asserts that 'one must unfailingly draw the moral arguments regarding both choices and avoidances from the study of nature (ἐκ φυσιολογίας) in order that they should be complete' (*De elect.* XIII. 12–17). His extant remains do not contain any contributions of his own to the physics first developed by the founder of the school. Nevertheless, he takes for granted the soundness of Epicurean atomism as an account of the universe and of its processes. Moreover, he has new things to say about human nature and motivation.

> [Of natural pleasures some are necessary, others not necessary; and of the necessary pleasures themselves], some are necessary for life, others for the health of the body, others for living happily, according to their different causes, but not all of them taken together. Further, [we call] different causes those causes some of which, as it seems, produce terrible storms while others do not, some are formed prematurely because of certain defects and others because of our feelings of joy, some are the result of habit while others come to be even regardless of our habits, yet some originate in ourselves while others arise because of external factors, or because things which became desirable due to the fact that we lacked them inflicted (on us) [something like] a wound by the very thought of them.
>
> (*De elect.* VI. 1–21)[21]

Epicurus' tripartite taxonomy of the desires into natural and necessary, natural and not necessary, and neither natural nor necessary (D.L. X. 127) is modified by Philodemus, probably in order to meet an Academic

avoid what does not stop us from having pleasure and we must [conceive] as such most things related to improvement' (*De elect.* IV. 10–19).

[21] I have slightly modified the translation of these lines proposed by Indelli and Tsouna-McKirahan 1995: 104.

objection reported by Cicero, that Epicurus' distinctions between different kinds of desires do not follow the formal rules of division (*De fin.* II. 9, 26). Reinterpreting earlier teachings with the help of current analytic tools,[22] he classifies natural desires and natural pleasures as the genera of which necessary and non-necessary desires and pleasures are the species.[23] Also, he develops the canonical doctrine of the school about desires and their various causes. On his view (*De elect.* VI. 7–21), the origins or sources of desires differ, and the same holds for the ways in which we experience them. Thus, desires may arise from factors related to our individual nature, such as certain physical defects, feelings of deprivation, and also habits. Alternatively, they may be triggered by external things, like power and wealth. Depending on their causes, we experience our desires as mild or violent (these latter being compared to 'terrible storms') and feel pain of different kinds and degrees.[24] Intense pain typically derives from error,[25] which stems from an incomplete understanding of human nature and, specifically, from the fact that one often misidentifies one's desires and is unable to assess the value of one's choices.

> [Having looked into those matters], one should also consider the differences among the desires, both with regard to the pleasures and with regard to their causes. For it is very much because of [our failure to distinguish between them] that important errors occur through them regarding what we choose and what we avoid. Indeed, men suffer the worst evils on account of the most alien desires, which they take to be most necessary—I mean, desires for sovereignty and a brilliant reputation and great wealth and, in general, luxuries of such kinds and other similar things. And they neglect [in turn] the most necessary appetites as if they were the most alien to nature.
>
> (*De elect.* V. 4–21)

Philodemus' treatises on vices and passions throw additional light on these subjects. For instance, he analyses the kinds of desires which fuel arrogance,

[22] Attempts to transform and even to correct the doctrine of the authorities of the school by using current analytic techniques were made by other Epicureans as well. See Sextus, *Adv. Phys.* II. 219–27.

[23] So his taxonomy is as follows. He distinguishes natural desires and pleasures from unnatural ones, subdivides the natural desires and their corresponding pleasures into necessary and non-necessary (*De elect.* V. 5–7, VI. 2–5), and then differentiates the species further by determining the various things that necessary desires are necessary for (VI. 3–5). Note that Epicurus too differentiates the species in the same manner.

[24] Cf. Philodemus' comparison of our desire for things of which we have been deprived to a kind of wound (*De elect.* VI. 17–19).

[25] Regarding the cognitive aspects of emotions see below, pp. 39–41, 48–51.

flattery, and greed;[26] he brings out the negative value of their causes as well as of their objects, and gives arguments intended to help us modify our desires in ways that lead to happiness.

Pleasures and pains can be either of the mind or of the body, and the relations between these physical and mental experiences cause a number of problems in the Epicurean doctrine. On the one hand, Epicurean rationalism entails that the mind has a dominant role over the flesh in enjoying and understanding pleasure. Epicurus claimed that mental pleasures and pains are far more intense than bodily ones, since the body can experience only present pleasures or pains, whereas the mind can take into account the memory of past experiences and the anticipation of future ones and, therefore, can greatly increase present pleasures or pains (D.L. X. 137). Following suit, Zeno emphasized the importance of past and future pleasures for living a happy life (*Tusc.* III. 38 = fr. 8). On the other hand, Epicurus located the centre of gravity of the doctrine in bodily pleasures and pains, and made the natural desires of the flesh our chief guide in the search for pleasure. Cicero claims that Zeno too urges us to concentrate on bodily pleasures, or 'on such pleasures as on account of the body find their place in memory or expectation' (ibid.). The exact nature of the view remains unclear.[27] But it is relatively clear that for Torquatus (*De fin.* I. 55–6) and for Philodemus the primacy of bodily experiences is consistent with the ideas that mental experiences are more intense than bodily ones and that they are central to our happiness in ways in which bodily affections are not. Several Epicureans must have challenged the consistency of these theses, since Torquatus finds it necessary to assert the primacy of bodily pleasures and pains, adding the following comment: 'Any Epicureans who think otherwise put themselves out of court; and I am aware that many do, though not those who can speak with any authority' (*De fin.* I. 55). As for Philodemus, in the eulogy *On Epicurus* he emphasizes Epicurus' concern with the well-being of the flesh ([ε]ὐσαρκία: PHerc. 1232, XVII. 15), and states that 'we should not cause

[26] e.g., arrogance involves the desire to be perceived as superior to other people, susceptibility to flattery involves desires for fame and greatness, and greed is related both to the desire for ever more wealth and to the desire for protection against death.

[27] The point may be that mental pain is always in the last analysis the fear that one will suffer bodily pain; and mental pleasure is *either* the memory or anticipation of bodily pleasure *or* the memory or anticipation of mental pleasures that themselves result from bodily conditions, e.g., freeing oneself from bodily pain.

harm to the flesh (οὐ πημα[ί]νειν); nor, on the other hand, should we be preoccupied with it (οὐ μελή[σε]ιν)' (PHerc. 1289b, XXVI. 1–3).[28] He endorses Epicurus' claim that, when life has been stripped of physical pleasures as well as of hopes and memories of them, we have no reason to wish to preserve it any longer (*De Epic.*; PHerc. 1232, XVIII. 10–17). And besides, in the text [*On Choices and Avoidances*], he elaborates Epicurus' thesis by urging us not to fear death and disease but, nonetheless, to do what we can in order to remain alive and healthy (XXIII. 3–12).[29] Weak versions of the canonical view underlie Philodemus' analysis of vices and selective emotions. Character traits, such as arrogance or susceptibility to flattery, and feelings, such as intense anger or erotic passion, should be eradicated because they shatter tranquillity: i.e., a stable pleasurable state *of the mind*. But one important reason why they have this effect is that they cause one to undergo a great deal of *bodily* suffering. Hence, Philodemus' assumption is, minimally, that physical and mental pains are interdependent, and maximally, that states such as violent rage are undesirable, first of all, on account of their physical basis and/or their physical consequences.

The tensions between the role of the mind and the role of the body in the pursuit of pleasure, and also the potential resolution of these tensions, are manifest in the Epicurean concept of limit (πέρας). On the one hand, Epicurus speaks of 'the goal and limit of the flesh' (*KD* 20) and claims that 'in the flesh, pleasure is not increased once the pain due to need is removed' (*KD* 18). These statements suggest that the limit of pleasure is built into the body (i.e., in the satisfaction of bodily need), and hence that the body and its natural desires, not the mind, dominate our pursuit of the good. However, the flesh cannot lay the basis for the good life, because it is limited to the awareness of the present. And even if it had

[28] The immediate context is missing, but it seems that Philodemus is alluding here to the following objection which was raised by some rivals. It is inconsistent to hold both that pain in the flesh is the greatest evil and that we should not be excessively disturbed by it (since it can be counterbalanced by mental pleasures). If it is the greatest evil, we should fear it and try to avoid it. But since it can be overpowered by pleasures of the mind, it is not the greatest evil. It would seem to follow that the moral end does not lie in the flesh at all, but belongs squarely to the mind. Like the criticism brushed aside by Torquatus (cf. *De fin.* I. 55–6), this kind of argument is designed to bring out the paradox of locating the moral goal in the body and, simultaneously, of endowing the mind with the capacity to transcend it.

[29] Moreover, Philodemus contends that this attitude belongs to a well-reasoning mind, as opposed to minds clouded by superstition (*De elect.* XVIII. 9–16).

a grasp of time, it could conceive of the good life only in terms of an infinite sequence of pleasures which would require infinite time.[30] On the other hand, therefore, Epicurus contends that the mind alone is equipped to plan for an optimal balance of pleasure and pain. For it has a grasp of time (D.L. X. 137), comprehends the limits of pain and of pleasure (*KD* 4) as these are defined by the two last principles of the *tetrapharmakos*, and delineates a broader perspective in which the goal of nature should be pursued.

> The flesh receives the limits of pleasure as unlimited, which (only) unlimited time provides. But the mind, appraising the goal and limit of the flesh and banishing fears about the future, brings about the complete life (παντελὴς βίος) and needs unlimited time no longer. It neither avoids pleasure nor, when circumstances prepare us to depart from life, does it approach the end as if it fell short in any way of the best life.
>
> (*KD* 20)

Philodemus' emphasis on the limit of pleasures and pains, and also on the hedonic boundaries of a complete life, echoes the belief that there is a limit to pain, and that reflection on it would make one feel content. Following Epicurus, he determines the magnitude of pleasure or pain within the bounds of the natural needs of the body (*De elect.* IV. 1–10). He appeals to the finite nature of the good and the bad in order to support the theses that (natural) pleasure is easily attainable and pain is easily endurable (*De elect.* IV. 1–4; cf. *KD* 21). He develops his concept of a complete life by reference to the limits of pleasure set by the flesh (τὸ σάρκινον: *De mort.* III. 37).[31] And he argues on that basis that death is not to be feared.[32] In all these instances, Philodemus drives home the point first made by Epicurus, that the mind alone can place the limits of the body in a proper moral perspective. Moreover, he implicitly acknowledges the

[30] Epicurus' claim in *KD* 20 cannot be that the flesh actually perceives pleasure as unlimited or wants it to be unlimited, for that would imply assimilating the perspective of the flesh to that of empty belief. Therefore, it is preferable to read the argument in counterfactual terms.

[31] 'The flesh achieves very quickly the [exact same] magnitude of pleasure that infinite time itself has ever contained' (*De mort.* III. 37–9).

[32] Death cannot really deprive us of the good, even if it is sudden or premature (*De mort.* XII. 2–XIV. 10). Once the man of sense comes to realize that he can readily 'attain that which is sufficient for a happy life, from that point on he walks about as if he were laid out in his shroud ready for burial [Armstrong's elegant translation of ἐντεταφιασμένος: XXXVIII. 17–18], and enjoys every single day as if it were an age' (XXXVIII. 14–19). See pp. 305–6.

predominance of the mind by ascribing a special role to the virtues and to friendship.

II

Epicurus held, controversially, that the rational pursuit of pleasure can be conducted only with the aid of the virtues. On the other hand, it is obstructed by the vices, and also by certain emotions or passions (πάθος, pl. πάθη, translit. *pathē*) which, like the vices, are disturbing and often destructive. His account of the virtues is quite complex, and it determines both certain psychological elements of morality and the place and function of the virtues in Epicurean hedonism. However, my argument does not require me to discuss its intricacies, but only to point to some relatively uncontroversial features.

Epicurus conceives of the virtues as inner states, and he usually explains them by reference to their cognitive components. Although he does not clearly state the thesis that virtue is a unitary state of the soul, he appears to assume that the virtues form a sort of unity; i.e., they grow together in one's soul, and none of them can be found in the soul without the others.[33] He defends the claims that the virtues are the only reliable means to happiness and that, therefore, they are worth cultivating. But although he ascribes to the virtues a clearly instrumental status, he conceives of them as indispensable and inseparable traits of the rational search for pleasure.[34] Torquatus' account of the virtues in the first book of *De finibus* and Philodemus' extensive treatment of virtues and vices both exhibit the canonical traits of the virtues mentioned above, albeit in places they differ from each other in emphasis or in content.

Torquatus' exposition chiefly aims to refute opponents who hold that the virtues, rather than pleasure, are the dominant claimants to the position

[33] Epicurus' mild cognitivism—viz., the position that the virtues importantly (but not solely) consist of beliefs—lends plausibility to the suggestion that, in his view, the virtues form some kind of unity. Cf., e.g., Epicurus' claim that from prudence spring all the other virtues (D.L. X. 132; on this point, see Mitsis 1988a: 75 ff.). Someone might object that the mere fact that all virtues spring from prudence does not show that they form a unity, as it is possible to have prudence in one area of life but lack it in another. However, it seems quite plausible that Epicurus is speaking about prudence as applying generally to all areas of life, and not as applying to some areas of life to the exclusion of others.

[34] Cf. Epicurus' assertion that we cannot lead a life of pleasure which is not also a life of virtue, and, conversely, we cannot live a life of virtue which is not also pleasurable (D.L. X. 132).

of the supreme good. Hence he dwells at length on the position that the virtues are not desirable for their own sake, but only for the pleasures resulting from them.[35] Precisely because his goals are mainly polemical, he focuses his argument on the traditional virtues of wisdom, temperance, courage, and justice. He determines their cognitive components in terms of beliefs on which the virtues are crucially dependent,[36] and he also appears to assume that the virtues form some kind of unity.[37] However, he does not specify just how these virtues are related to each other or to pleasure.

Again, Philodemus' treatment of virtue is, in places, parallel and, in places, complementary to that of Torquatus. He too conceives of the virtues as inner states worth cultivating for the benefits that they procure, rather than for their own sake. On the other hand, he is not pressed by the challenge that Torquatus has to face: namely, that virtue has intrinsic value and should take the position of pleasure as the supreme good. So he simply assumes the instrumental goodness of the virtues and shifts his attention to their actual benefits, both psychological and pragmatic. And conversely, he studies in considerable detail the material and moral disadvantages resulting from vice. The main objects of his analysis are not the traditional virtues,[38] but distinctly Epicurean ones. Notably, he examines the nature of such virtues, their causal relations to each other, the manner in which they secure pleasure, and the ways in which they stand in opposition to their corresponding vices. He believes that the virtues, and also the vices, grow together in the soul. But, unlike Torquatus, he argues systematically and at length in order to substantiate that view. In conformity to the tradition of the school, he adopts a moderate cognitivism[39] regarding the nature of the virtues, the conditions under which they develop, and their cultivation.[40] In particular, he suggests that the virtues are dispositions to act for certain reasons and/or to perform certain kinds of actions, and they involve beliefs

[35] See Torquatus' concluding remarks at the end of the discussion of each virtue (*De fin.* I. 46, 48, 49, 53) as well as his overall verdict that only pleasure, not the virtues, is intrinsically desirable (*De fin.* I. 54).

[36] e.g., he defines wisdom as sound reasoning which corrects our ignorance of good and evil, roots out all our errors and prejudices, and, in that manner, quenches the flames of unnatural desire and guides us safely to the attainment of pleasure (*De fin.* I. 42–3).

[37] Torquatus often remarks that it is impossible to sever or sunder wisdom, temperance, courage, and justice from pleasure: see, e.g., *De fin.* I. 50.

[38] The reason is that, unlike Torquatus, he does not have to argue against opponents who propose the traditional virtues as the moral end.

[39] Cf. n. 33 above.

[40] See Tsouna 2001*b*: 236–7.

as well as feelings, attitudes, etc.[41] Also, Philodemus discusses at length the beliefs involved in specific virtues and individuates each virtue, usually by contrasting it with its opposite vice or vices. Besides, he directs our attention to their non-cognitive or affective aspects. As we shall see in detail later, the clearest example occurs in *On Anger*. The natural anger (ὀργή translit. *orgē*) of the virtuous person 'differs in quality' (*De ir.* XLV. 35) from the unnatural rage (θυμός, translit. *thymos*) of the fool; it is felt in a different manner.

Turning now to the relationship between the virtues and pleasure, we surmise that Epicurus' claim that they mutually entail each other was criticized both outside and inside the Epicurean school. This is probably why Philodemus mentions this matter.

> [It is impossible for one to live pleasurably without living prudently and honourably and justly[42]], and also without living courageously and temperately and magnanimously, and without making friends and [without being philanthropic], and in general without having all the other virtues. For the greatest errors in things we choose or avoid occur when some people accomplish individual actions while they hold the opposite view and, because of that, are in the grip of vices.
>
> (*De elect.* XIV. 1–14)

The thesis stated in the above passage differs from Epicurus' own (cf. D.L. X. 132) in two significant respects. Philodemus adds to the list of the four traditional virtues several new items, which take their meaning in the context of the canonical doctrine and play a central role in Philodemus' system.[43] Second, the passage as it stands states only a one-way entailment between the virtues and pleasure and leaves open the question whether a relationship of mutual entailment can obtain between them. Unless this fact is due to the poor condition of the text, it may indicate a tacit modification of Epicurus' doctrine.

Epicurus' doctrine of friendship is notoriously controversial. One central issue is whether Epicurus' claims about friendship—for instance, that the wise man will sometimes die for his friend (D.L. X. 121), that he will love

[41] According to Philodemus, vices and also emotions have a similar structure. However, Philodemus does not make clear just how dispositions, beliefs, feelings, etc. are related to each other. I shall return to this issue in the next chapter, pp. 42–3.

[42] This part of the text is restored *exempli gratia*: see Indelli and Tsouna-McKirahan 1995: 93 and 175–6.

[43] Ibid. 177–9.

his friend as much as himself and exert himself as much for the pleasure of his friend as for his own (*De fin.* I. 67–8), and that every friendship is an inherently virtuous state of the soul (*SV* 23)[44]—are consistent with Epicurus' egoistic and hedonistic ethics. Interpretations differ regarding this problem. However, a very rough distinction can be drawn between, on the one hand, the view of some scholars, that Epicurus held that friendship has elements of altruism and disinterested concern for others[45] even if these elements cause problematic tensions in his doctrine and, on the other hand, the view proposed by others, that Epicurus values friendship or the good of one's friends only instrumentally, for the sake of pleasure.[46] On balance, it seems plausible to infer that Epicurus and some of his immediate followers held that friendship is both self-interested and self-regarding, whereas later Epicureans chose in response to Academic criticism to admit of sources of motivation other than pleasure[47] so as to be able to say, for example, that friendship is intrinsically choiceworthy[48] and that friends are loved for their own sake.[49]

Support for the existence of this difference is found in Cicero. Torquatus outlines three distinct and even rival approaches to friendship, and suggests that they were defended by different Epicurean groups. In all probability the first was not a later innovation[50] but represents Epicurus' own view.[51] Although it contains some of the seemingly most altruistic sayings—for instance, that friendship requires that we love our friends as much as ourselves, share their joys and sorrows as if they were our own, and take pains for their good as we would for ours (*De fin.* I. 67–8)—nonetheless, it also emphasizes that friendship is useful for security and pleasure (I. 66–7) and that friendship is related to pleasure as the virtues are (I. 68). Moreover, when Torquatus describes the second Epicurean position on friendship,

[44] This is the point of *SV* 23 if we keep the manuscript reading *δι' ἑαυτὴν ἀρετή*. Powerful defences of that reading are offered by Bollack (1975: 450 ff.), Long (1986: 305 ff.), and, more recently, E. Brown (2002). Alternatively, if we accept the emended clause *δι' ἑαυτὴν αἱρετή*, the claim would be that every friendship is choiceworthy in itself.

[45] See, e.g., the accounts of Mitsis (1988*a*: ch. 3) and Annas (1993: esp. ch. 11).

[46] Cf., most recently, O'Keefe 2001; E. Brown 2002.

[47] Cf. O'Keefe 2001: 287–8; E. Brown 2002: 78–9.

[48] Cf. the emended reading of *SV* 23, *δι' ἑαυτὴν αἱρετή*.

[49] On the distinction between friendship broadly understood as fellow feeling (*φιλία*) and friends (*φίλοι*), see Konstan 1996*a* and 1996*b*.

[50] *Pace* O'Connor (1989: 184 f.); cf. the criticism of his views by O'Keefe (2001: 289–90 n. 44).

[51] Cf. *De fin.* I. 68, II. 82.

he suggests that its basic difference from the first is that the first values friendship entirely on instrumental grounds; i.e., it holds that friendship is desirable 'only for the pleasure that it affords to ourselves' (I. 69). If the altruistic elements of Epicurus' position are interpreted egoistically in some satisfactory manner,[52] we may conclude that, in fact, the original Epicurean account of friendship excludes disinterested concern and care for others apart from whatever instrumental value they may have for us.

The third position mentioned by Torquatus will not concern us here. Suffice it to mention that, according to it, friendship is a kind of contract or agreement between sages to the effect that they will love their friends no less than themselves (*De fin.* I. 70). Most interesting for present purposes, however, is the second position. Torquatus assigns it to certain Epicureans who are more timid (*timidiores*) in the face of the sharp criticisms of the Academics and who fear that 'if we hold friendship to be desirable for the sake of our pleasure, all friendship would seem to be as it were lame' (I. 69). Cicero explicitly distances them from Epicurus (II. 82), and says that they are 'more modern', and their doctrine is 'more humane' than his thoroughgoing utilitarianism (ibid.). According to Cicero's text, then, these Epicureans become willing to accept sources of motivation other than pleasure in order to allow friendship to have independent value (I. 69). So they propose a kind of emergence theory, maintaining that while our original motivation for seeking friends lies in the egoistic desire for pleasure, our subsequent intimacy (cf. *familiaritatem*) makes the relationship blossom (*efflorescere*) into selfless love (ibid.).[53] Their position is made to appear more plausible with the help of an analogy. As we become fond of locations, pets, activities, and the like by becoming familiar with them, much more so we become fond of our friends through the familiarity (cf. *consuetudine*) that derives from spending time with them (ibid.). In both cases our feelings of affection develop even if we gain no advantage from

[52] Cf. O'Keefe 2001: 292–7, which argues that we should interpret talk about 'loving one's friends as much as oneself', etc., in behavioural terms; it prescribes a strategy of action rather than describing what one ultimately values. One problem with his interpretation is that the Epicureans usually appear to treat love as a dispositional attitude and not as a pattern of behaviour.

[53] As O'Keefe (2001: 287–8) and E. Brown (2002: 78–9) point out, it makes very good sense to attribute the emended version of *SV* 23 to the 'more timid' Epicureans mentioned by Cicero. We originally enter into friendship for self-interested reasons, but we later come to love our friends for their own sake; so it would seem that friendship becomes worth choosing for its own sake, as *SV* 23 affirms. However, neither O'Keefe nor Brown speculate as to who these 'more timid' Epicureans might be.

the relevant associations. Neither Torquatus nor his interlocutor reveals the identity of the emergence theorists. All the same, they make reasonably clear the fact that the emergence theory constitutes a later modification of the canonical doctrine (cf. also D.L. II. 82). However, it seems to me that there is a good chance that its proponents are Philodemus and his disciples.[54] Let me argue this point.

Torquatus prefaces his exposition of the dispute about friendship by marvelling at the master's capacity to maintain a whole company of friends in one single house. And he adds, 'This still goes on in the Epicurean school. But let us return to the matter at hand; for there is no need to talk about particular persons' (*De fin.* I. 65). The philosophers who in all probability lived in Piso's villa[55] come readily to mind. Coming to the defenders of the emergence theory, Torquatus notes that they are 'fairly insightful' but 'somewhat more intimidated by your criticism' (*De fin.* I. 69); i.e., the Academic contention that if friendship is desirable only for the sake of egoistic pleasure, it is not really friendship. Notice the personal tone of the passage: the compliment paid to the intelligence of these philosophers; the adjective *timidiores*, which invokes the effect of a face-to-face confrontation and reflects Cicero's view of Philodemus (cf. *De nat. deor.* I. 21. 59, I. 33. 93; *Tusc.* III. 17. 38); and the address to Cicero as the spokesman of the Academy on this issue (*vestra convicia*: ibid.). As mentioned, Cicero characterizes the emergence theory of friendship as 'more humane' than Epicurus' theory (*De fin.* II. 82), and again, one is inclined to think of Philodemus in this connection. For Cicero says that Phaedrus was 'the most elegant and humane old gentleman' (*De nat. deor.* I. 33. 93), and he describes Philodemus in similar terms. He is learned and decent, and so are many of his philosophical stances (*De fin.* II. 119). However, Cicero's subtle and ambiguous sketch of Philodemus in his invective against Philodemus' patron Piso (cf. *ad Pis.* 68–72)[56] suggests that 'the little Greek' is also a bit of a weakling in his intellectual and moral life.

Whether or not Philodemus was the originator of the emergence theory, do we have any evidence from his writings supporting the hypothesis that he endorsed it? As suggested, the emergence theory of friendship makes room for elements of disinterested affection and care for others in

[54] Cicero may have in mind Zeno and his circle as well.

[55] Cf. Gigante 1995: *passim*.

[56] See Gigante 1983: 35–53.

ways in which Epicurus' utilitarianism does not. In my view (which I hope to substantiate in subsequent chapters), these elements are present in Philodemus' ethics. Notably, disinterested concern for others determines to a large extent the kinds of attitudes that Philodemus urges us to adopt with regard to social relationships, worldly activities, and external goods. Also, affection for others regardless of whatever advantage they may bring to us appears to mark Philodemus' conception of Epicurean pedagogy, his description of the Epicurean teacher as a doctor of the soul, and the practice of *parrhēsia*, frank speech.

In this chapter I have attempted to offer a survey of the theoretical basis of Philodemus' ethics. Although sketchy and selective, I hope it sheds light on Philodemus' own interpretation of Epicurus' doctrine and on the ways in which Philodemus' interpretation compares with the views of his Epicurean rivals. On several controversial points, Philodemus' stance appears philosophically more substantial and more sophisticated than those of his opponents. Moreover, he introduces a number of clarifications, elaborations, and even emendations of the original doctrine of the school, which appear to reflect in many cases Zeno's version of what constitutes Epicurean orthodoxy.[57] However, he may be considered to have made a serious break with the founder in at least one important matter. If Epicurus held a thoroughly egoistic and hedonistic conception of friendship, and if Philodemus abandoned it in favour of a softened theory allowing for disinterested affection and concern for others, it is arguable that Philodemus' theory of friendship is actually inconsistent with that of Epicurus. If so, this invites us to raise questions concerning Philodemus' relationship with Epicurus and, generally, the relationships between earlier and later members of the Epicurean school.

[57] On Philodemus and the Epicurean tradition as it was determined by the school of Athens, see Tsouna 2007.

2

Vices, Emotions, and 'Bites'

I

Philodemus' account of the vices (κακίαι) and of harmful emotions or passions (πάθη, sing. πάθος; translit. *pathē*, sing. *pathos*) has characteristics corresponding to his account of the virtues, but it is much more elaborate. For it is the vices and the passions, not the virtues, that are the primary objects of analysis and treatment. In fact, the extant remains of Philodemus' ethical works focus primarily on these. They contain some of his most important contributions to the Epicurean doctrine, as well as to our own understanding of topics in ethics and moral psychology. Philodemus' discussions of arrogance, flattery, anger, etc., find parallels in the works of the Peripatetics, Seneca, Plutarch, Lucian, and others. However, those familiar with the relevant literature are likely to conclude that Philodemus' analyses are superior to rival ones to the extent that they have a robust theoretical grounding, consistently apply specific methodological principles, and yield an unusually rich and sophisticated understanding of their subject matters.

Like the virtues, the vices are states that Philodemus describes as stable dispositions to believe certain things and to feel and behave in certain ways, under certain circumstances, for certain reasons.[1] They may be considered content-sensitive states, to the extent that they involve certain types of reactions to situations as they are perceived by the agent. Like the virtues

[1] Typically, the beliefs that, e.g., the arrogant man *tends* to have are more general and more theoretical than the specific reasons for which he acts arrogantly in a specific set of circumstances. He has the disposition to believe that he is superior to others, but he refuses to cooperate with others regarding a particular project because he believes that he can accomplish the task on his own.

and also the emotions, the vices are often illustrated by reference to their individual manifestations. 'Arrogance', 'flattery', 'greed', and their cognates indicate, primarily, the corresponding dispositions and, secondarily, tokens of each of these dispositions. However, Philodemus' analyses focus on the former meaning of such terms.

Thus, the arrogant man has the disposition (*διάθεσιν*: *De superb.* II. 27) to think of himself as superior to others, to feel disdain towards them (VI. 29–30), and hence to express his arrogance in his actions and be generally hubristic (VI. 30–4). The flatterer has the disposition ([*διά*]*θεσιν*: PHerc. 1089, I. 13; cf. also IV. 5) to speak in a pleasing but usually untruthful manner (PHerc. 1457, I. 5–6) for self-interested purposes (PHerc. 222, III. 4–6). His vice manifests itself fully only in the presence of lovers of flattery: namely, people who are disposed to believe good things about themselves regardless of their true deserts, feel pleasure when they hear them, and consequently, surround themselves with adulators. Likewise, Philodemus determines different ways of administering one's property in terms of the disposition of the agent. The traditional manager is inclined to overvalue wealth and property, to develop 'an obsessive zeal concerning the more and the less' (*De oec.* XIV. 26–7), and, as a result, to do everything in order to maximize his revenues, subjecting himself to great labours and risks (cf. XI. 11–14, XXVI. 34–9). Also, he is prone to feel distress over his losses (XIV. 23–5) and elation over his gains. Contrast the disposition of the Epicurean manager, who ascribes little value to his estate, administers it with considerable emotional detachment, regulates his efforts according to the pleasure that they bring, and does not agonize over what he loses (XIV. 23– XV 2).

Moreover, Philodemus occasionally contrasts the inner with the outer aspects of vicious persons. Arrogant persons sometimes behave with thoughtfulness and courtesy (*De superb.* VIII. 21–8), when circumstances force them to do so. Flatterers conceal their true character as best they can. For otherwise they do not gain the trust of their victims and do not achieve their goals (*De adul.*; PHerc. 222, III. 7–10). Whether or not the vice manifests itself in particular instances, however, it has the same firm hold on one's soul. For it is a matter of how one *tends* to react, not of how one always actually does. Also, Philodemus distinguishes the vices from each other as well as from their corresponding virtues on dispositional grounds. The disposition of the inconsiderate person consists of different features from that of the know-all, and the disposition of the dignified person is contrasted with that of the man affecting dignity who, 'starting from the disposition (ἀπὸ τῆς διαθέσεως) mentioned above, looks down upon everybody' (*De superb.* XXI. 21–3). Although the flatterer may say and do the kinds of things that a friend says or does, he is not a real friend because he does not have the relevant dispositional underpinnings; for example, he does not have attitudes of benevolence nor feelings of affection (*De adul.*; PHerc. 1457, fr. 2; PHerc. 222, XII. 1–2). Something similar holds for arrogant men as well.

As indicated above, the vices are cognitive dispositions in the sense that they are dispositions to hold certain beliefs both about how things are or ought to be in general and about the particular situation at hand. Thus, a person believes that he is superior to others as a human being, or that wealth secures happiness, or that flattering the powerful is a good way to earn a living. Accordingly, he makes the *ad hoc* judgement that he should abuse his servant who broke a glass, or that he should risk his all in a high-profit adventure, or that he should tell the king exactly what he wants to hear. Contrary to the true beliefs related to the virtues, those involved in the vices are empty (κεναὶ δόξαι), both false and harmful.[2] They resemble the former kind of beliefs, because they too point to broader views about what people do and why. But while the true beliefs of virtuous persons lead them to acquire a correct understanding of action and motivation, the empty beliefs of the fools preclude this. Arrogant persons cannot understand how people perceive each other as equals, assist each other (*De superb.* VIII. 28 ff.), or work together towards a common goal (XVIII. 19–25, XVIII. 35 ff., XX. 1–3), or why they do so. Greedy managers cannot see the point of giving gifts (*De oec.* XXV. 42–XXVI. 1) or of helping friends with part of one's income (*De oec.* XIV. 37–41, XV. 1–3, XXV. 1 ff.). Flatterers and parasites are unable to explain why others choose not to court kings, and the same lack of understanding is also found in their victims.

The failures of understanding of vicious persons involve, importantly, understanding of themselves. They do not recognize the falsehood of their beliefs, the inappropriateness of their attitudes, and the wrongness of their actions. So long as they are morally blind in this way, they do not feel any need to have their condition treated and to improve themselves.

[2] The same holds for the beliefs involved in the passions: see below, pp. 39–41.

Philodemus holds that all vicious persons are irrational, on account of their false beliefs and judgements and, especially, their lack of self-awareness.[3] Versions of that concept of irrationality occur in other Hellenistic authors as well.[4] According to Philodemus, irrationality does not entail the idea that vicious people are impervious to reason or that they are incapable of performing a means–ends analysis in order to achieve their goals. It entails only that they set their goals improperly, precisely because they determine them on the basis of empty beliefs, and also that they perform the hedonic calculus incorrectly. On that view, vicious people are irrational not in the sense that they cannot explain their moral attitudes, but rather in the sense that they cannot justify them on adequate grounds. For example, the arrogant man cannot possibly justify that 'he does not mistreat whichever animals he happens to be living with, for instance [horses], dogs and other such animals, but he mistreats man, a being so very different (from these animals) and most akin to himself on account of the fact that he has been adorned with [reason[5]]' (*De superb.* XV. 33–40). The flatterer can of course give reasons for his practices, but no valid justification for them. For his apparent needs derive from empty desires (*De adul.*; PHerc. 1457, fr. 15. 10 ff.) and an excessive appetite for material benefits (PHerc. 222, I. 29). As for the avid property manager, perhaps he is the best illustration of the kind of irrationality attached to vice. He would be rational on most accounts, since he engages successfully in means–ends calculations in order to amass as much wealth as possible. However, on Philodemus' view, he is irrational because he cannot justify his goal in terms of the hedonic calculus. He cannot show that the pains involved in the single-minded pursuit of wealth are outweighed by the pleasures secured over a lifetime (cf. *De oec.* XI. 30–40). As we shall see, Philodemus considers the passions irrational for similar reasons. Moreover, he acknowledges that both the vices and the passions can occasionally eliminate reason altogether. Recall Xerxes' command to yoke the Hellespont and cast fetters into the sea (*De superb.* XVI. 15–27).

The vices obstruct the hedonic calculus and, thus, the rational and successful pursuit of pleasure all the more because, like the virtues, they typically appear to coexist in one's soul. For instance, flatterers are

[3] In subsequent chapters I shall supply references to places where Philodemus talks in that way about irrationality and irrational people.

[4] Cf. Nussbaum 1994: 38. [5] XVI. 1 [λόγωι] *Tsouna*.

envious, slanderous, avaricious, and full of mischief (*De adul.*; PHerc. 1457, XII. 21–5); selfish, ungrateful, arrogant, and incredibly vulgar (PHerc. 1457, fr. 21. 29–39). Some of these characteristics also mark the victims of flattery, together with the love of power, the love of glory, intemperance, and even cruelty. The expert property manager suffers not only from his greed and love of money (φιλοχρηματία), but also from arrogance and stupidity (*De oec.* VII. 2), presumption (VII. 21–6), harshness (IX. 32), inhumanity (X. 15–21), imprudence (XI. 11–16), and folly. Philodemus gives no explicit argument for these claims in individual treatises. However, he suggests that the vices often occur together in so far as they share the same cognitive basis.

The vices are also dispositions to have certain feelings, attitudes, etc. Philodemus highlights the affective aspects of vices less than those of the emotions. Nonetheless, he makes clear that there exist such aspects and distinguishes them from beliefs. The 'insurmountable disgust' (*De superb.* VIII. 3–4) of the arrogant man differs from the reasons accounting for it, and the feeling of elation (cf. συναισθάνεται μετεω[ρ]ιζό[μεν]ος: X. 31–2) that one may experience is distinct from the thoughts that cause it or those that cure it (cf. X. 32–5). The flatterer's anxiety, insecurity, and frustration do not seem reducible to the empty beliefs on the grounds of which he is inclined to flatter. And the emotional intensity of the greedy property manager, which also appears in other vicious types, is an experiential rather than a cognitive feature. On this picture, then, beliefs and feelings coexist in a vicious disposition and are essential features of it. Also, cognitive and non-cognitive elements coexist in particular manifestations of a given vice: e.g., in an instance of arrogant behaviour. In such cases, what makes their relationship non-contingent is the fact that they derive from a particular kind of disposition. The arrogant man's belief that he honours his benefactor greatly for deigning to accept something from him (*De superb.* IX. 17–20) and his feelings of disdain and ingratitude on such an occasion (IX. 14–17) are found together regularly or even necessarily, precisely because they result from the man's arrogance, his disposition to believe such things and experience such feelings.

As we saw, vices are typically (though not always) expressed in one's demeanour and behaviour. The arrogant person appears unwilling to seek advice or cooperate (*De superb.* XIV. 2 ff., XIX. 21–2, XX. 27 ff.); the inconsiderate type is rude at the public baths and the slave market

(XVI. 34 ff.); flatterers behave like lap dogs or monkeys (*De adul.*; PHerc. 222, IX. 14–16); parasites cluster around the master's table (PHerc. 222, VII. 18 ff.; PHerc. 223, frs. 1. 1 ff., 3. 1–9, 4. 2, 5b. 1, and 6. 1–20; PHerc. 1089, VI. 2 ff.); and country gentlemen like Ischomachus talk and act in certain ways as they go assiduously about their everyday tasks. According to Philodemus, it is important to study such behavioural manifestations of the vices in order to diagnose and treat them, and also in order to protect oneself from vicious people.

As the virtues shape one's attitudes towards others, so do the vices. Philodemus acknowledges that fact, and thus traces important connections between one's moral dispositions and the ways in which one reacts to other people. He may also make an even stronger claim, that the vices actually determine one's reactions. In any case, he brings out the interpersonal aspects of each vice and explores the ways in which it undermines social relationships. Arrogance is, first of all, a particularly vicious way of assessing and interacting with others: it is directed at those whom the arrogant person considers inferior to himself and for whom he reserves his disdain (*De superb.* IV. 22–6, VI. 30–2, VIII. 11–12, IX. 1–4, 10–11). Flattery requires fertile ground in order to develop: i.e., people susceptible to it and seeking adulation and praise (PHerc. 1457, I. 3; PHerc. 1457, fr. 23). Avarice and greed are also partly other-directed: they obstruct good will and benevolence (*De elect.* XX. 8–10), and corrode friendship (*De oec.* XXIV. 20). Many external consequences of the vices derive, precisely, from their interpersonal aspects. To conclude, if the virtues belong to a rational structure harmonizing distinct components of our lives, the vices pull that structure apart: they involve irrationality and confusion, and they distort our moral attitudes and social behaviour.[6] Philodemus' analyses of individual vices establish that each vice is wrong both pragmatically and psychologically. Not only does it have painful external consequences, but it is a painful psychic condition, and it damages valuable elements of the good life.

[6] Like Epicurus and most other Greek philosophers, Philodemus presupposes, then, that there is such a thing as character, that character is formed by individual character traits, and that these importantly include virtues and vices. These entail characteristic patterns of feeling, desire, and motivation, and also involve the exercise of particular skills in some morally relevant manner. People are ethically different in virtue of the fact that they possess different virtues and vices. In so far as they differ in this way, they hold different beliefs, have different feelings and reactions, make different choices, and regularly behave in different ways.

II

Epicurus holds that the rational pursuit of pleasure is also obstructed by certain emotions or passions (*pathē*) which, like the vices, are disturbing and often destructive. Although in his extant remains he does not really have a theory of emotions and does not examine any particular emotion in detail,[7] nonetheless he holds views concerning the kinds of desires involved in emotions (both benign and malignant), the relationships between desire, emotion, and belief, and the reasons why emotions such as anger and the fear of death ought to be eradicated. There is an extensive literature on these subjects,[8] and also on the topics of erotic love, anger, and the fear of death. Therefore, here I shall point only to features of harmful emotions,[9] which were probably systematized and elucidated by members of Zeno's school.[10] Philodemus takes them on board and expands them in his own way.

Philodemus refers to the emotions primarily as dispositions, and secondarily as individual occurrences deriving from the corresponding dispositions.[11] Thus, when he talks about emotions such as anger, erotic love, and envy, he has primarily in mind stable inclinations to have certain beliefs, feelings, attitudes, etc., and to act in certain ways in certain types of circumstances for certain reasons. Irascible people (ὀργίλοι: cf. *De ir.* XIV. 32, XXVI. 11, XXXVI. 20, 33) tend to become angry on the occasion of what they perceive to be an intentional offence.[12] Passionate persons are liable to fall in love when they meet someone they consider attractive. And envious ones will predictably be bitten by envy when they see their neighbour prosper. Like the vices, emotions are content-sensitive states: they involve one's reactions to certain types of situations in accordance with what one

[7] The point is made carefully by Annas 1989.

[8] In the way of example, I should mention Annas 1989; Cooper 1998*a* and 1998*b*; Nussbaum 1994; and Sorabji 2000.

[9] For the sake of brevity, I shall use 'emotions' interchangeably with 'passions', i.e., in the negative sense of harmful emotions, unless I indicate otherwise.

[10] Cf. Dem. Lac.; PHerc. 1012, XXI. 1 ff.

[11] Although Philodemus usually distinguishes clearly between the disposition to experience a certain emotion and individual occurrences of that emotion (cf. pp. 39 and n. 14), nonetheless, he can sometimes be ambiguous. For instance, he can sometimes use 'anger' where irascibility is meant.

[12] Cf. Philodemus' description of anger as 'that disposition on account of which they [*sc.* enraged people] become distracted and because of which they are afflicted by innumerable evils' (*De ir.* II. 15–18).

perceives to be the case. The fear of death too is a dispositional state of that sort, for it involves a range of reactions to what one perceives as the greatest evil. Denial, morbidity, sybaritism, asceticism, avarice, and superstition count among them (*De elect.* VII. 4–X. 19, XVI. 2–XX. 20).

Concentrating on individual occurrences of an emotion helps determine the characteristic features of all such occurrences. On Philodemus' view, outbursts of rage, crises of envy and malice, and so on, derive from the relevant dispositions and are explained in terms of these dispositions. For instance, an outburst of anger results from irascibility, 'a merciless, savage, and harsh disposition (διαθέσει: XXVII. 21) ... to which the emotion (πάθος) is conjoined' (*De ir.* XXVII. 19–23). Moreover, it is an evil precisely because it results from that wicked disposition (XXXVIII. 1–3). Achilles rages at Agamemnon 'mixing [earth with] heaven' (*De ir.* XVIII. 16–17), because he is prone to excessive anger when he is slighted or even accidentally overlooked (XVIII. 18–23). Nicias was superstitious, and because of it, he followed the omen of a lunar eclipse and delayed the departure of the Athenians from Sicily (cf. *De elect.* VIII. 7–10).[13] Individual occurrences of anger or superstitious fear are causally related to irascibility[14] and the tendency to fear the gods and death. Every occurrence has essentially the same typology as every other occurrence of the same emotion, and all of them spring from the same kind of disposition. As indicated, however, an outburst of anger is not identical with one's irascibility.[15] Achilles was always irascible, but not always angry, and Odysseus' superstitious fear of dying at sea (*De mort.* XXXIII. 9 ff.) was not always made manifest. We might put it this way: one's disposition is the necessary antecedent cause of an emotion, whereas some external event is the auxiliary cause of a particular occurrence of it.

Like the vices, the emotions consist of cognitive and non-cognitive or extra-cognitive elements. This applies to all kinds of emotions, healthy or

[13] Nicias is not named in this passage. However, it is probable that the author alludes to Thucydides' description of Nicias (VII. 50. 4); see Indelli and Tsouna-McKirahan 1995: 146.

[14] As we shall see later, not every outbreak of anger must result from irascibility. A distinction will be made between vicious and non-vicious instances of the emotion. Only the vicious ones come from irascibility, while the non-vicious outbreaks do not.

[15] e.g., Philodemus distinguishes the merciless and harsh διάθεσις of the irascible person from the πάθος itself (XXVII. 19–23). He draws a similar distinction in connection with the claim that the sage pretends to be irascible but, in fact, acts 'without the emotion itself and the disposition to it' (XXXIV. 18–21).

destructive, passionate as well as mild.[16] Assuming that they all comprise desires,[17] and that Epicurus classifies desires into natural and empty according to the kinds of beliefs on which they depend (*KD* 29), we may infer that he would classify emotions in a similar manner.[18] In any event, Philodemus suggests that, e.g., anger and the fear of death belong to the category of unnatural or empty emotions, since both are related to empty (i.e., both false and harmful) beliefs or presumptions[19] about their objects. What kinds of empty beliefs and judgements are involved in harmful emotions? Philodemus' analyses of anger and the fear of death might suggest that he concentrates on the issues of whether there is evil at hand and whether one reacts in an appropriate manner; that is, the kinds of judgements which (rightly or wrongly) have been considered jointly constitutive of Stoic emotions.[20] Moreover, it would seem that he addresses both the descriptive and the evaluative components of such judgements.[21] However, it is difficult to generalize about this matter, since Philodemus' analyses are tailored specifically to each passion, its variations, and individual episodes illustrating the disposition identical with the passion. We shall get a better idea of the cognitive elements of an emotion if we look at a concrete example.

Philodemus says that all emotions, including anger, are 'consequent upon our own entertainment of false opinion' (ψευδοδοξ[ίαν]: *De ir.* VI. 14–15); in other words, upon empty beliefs. In the case of anger, such beliefs chiefly concern the intentions of the offender, the magnitude of the offence, and

[16] Epicurus suggests that the arousal of emotions involves both beliefs and a focusing of the *pathos* at something definite (*De nat.* 25, XXXIV. 18–20); see Annas 1992: 191.

[17] Cf. Philodemus' description of anger as consisting jointly of bodily symptoms and the fierce desire (ἐπιθυμία) and anxiety (ἀγωνία) for revenge: *De ir.* VIII. 21–7.

[18] In short, the canonical view (which Philodemus endorses) is that natural desires can easily be satisfied and cause no anxiety or worry, whereas unnatural desires are limitless, unsatisfiable, and accompanied by a kind of painful intensity peculiar to the pursuit of their objects. These characteristics are causally connected to false or empty beliefs. The thirsty man may be intent upon finding a glass of water as soon as possible, but he is not strained in the same way as the person who desires to become powerful and wealthy. For he simply feels thirst, usually finds water easily, and after he drinks it, is satisfied. By contrast, the ambitious person pursues his objectives in the belief that power and wealth have high value, often finds it difficult to obtain them, and remains anxious and dissatisfied even if he gets what he wants.

[19] Cf. Epicurus' reference to the beliefs underlying religious fears as ὑπολήψεις ψευδεῖς: *ad Men.* 124.

[20] For discussion of the emotions as value judgements in Chrysippus see, recently, Sorabji 2000: 29–47.

[21] Frede (1986) discusses this issue regarding Stoicism.

the value and appropriateness of revenge. The irascible person is disposed to become angry and seek revenge whenever he believes that someone has intentionally slighted or injured him and that the damage is considerable. Achilles' first outburst of anger involved his beliefs that Agamemnon intended to dishonour him, that he succeeded in doing so, and that he must now pay for that damage.[22] Compare cases in which the offence is indeed intentional, the victim's beliefs true, and his anger to an extent justified. Philodemus notoriously argues that the victim's anger in such cases differs in kind from the anger 'consequent upon false opinion', partly on account of their different cognitive bases. Technically speaking, the latter is rage (θυμός, translit. *thymos*), an unnatural and excessive emotion, whereas anger involving true beliefs (ὀργή, translit. *orgē*) is natural[23] and remains within bounds (cf. XXXVII. 20 ff.).[24] As we shall see, Philodemus clarifies in that way the meaning of Epicurus' claim that the wise man is capable of anger.[25]

All emotions involve also extra-cognitive elements, notably feelings and imaginings. As mentioned, Philodemus suggests that emotions belonging to the same or similar kinds differ in the ways in which they are felt. Natural anger (*orgē*) differs from empty anger (*thymos*) in its experiential quality (cf. ποιότητι: XLV. 34–7). It does not feel the same as *thymos* (*De ir.* XLIII. 41–XLIV. 35), and it does not motivate one to seek the offender's punishment in the way in which rage does.[26] Philodemus contrasts the mildness of natural anger with the intensity and obsessive power of *thymos*, and intimates a similar contrast in connection with the fear of death.[27] So

[22] Consequently, the angry person is not willing to accept any explanation or apology that the offender might offer (XXIII. 20–4).

[23] Moreover, *orgē* is usually a mild emotion (cf. μετρίως: XLV. 8). And even though it can be intense in some cases, it is not overpowering, and it does not tend to escalate. Also, in contrast to *thymos*, it lasts only a short time (XLV. 8–12).

[24] By drawing that distinction, Philodemus dispels the vagueness and ambiguity of terms referring to the emotion. This is a primary concern of Zeno of Sidon and his associates. In particular, Demetrius maintains that we must pay close attention to the context in which Epicurus employs a given term in order to interpret his thought correctly (PHerc. 1012, LXVI. 1–5, LXIX. 1–10). It is possible that Philodemus finds the distinction between *orgē* and *thymos* in the literature of Zeno's school.

[25] He argues that people misunderstand the claim that the wise man is capable of *thymos*, because they do not realize that the term carries the commonest sense in that statement, i.e., the sense of *orgē*, natural anger (*De ir.* XLIV. 1–5). See pp. 299–30.

[26] Ideally, the person affected by *orgē* has a practical and merciful attitude towards his offender. Instead of desiring revenge, he wishes to have the wrongdoer punished and rendered unable to cause any more harm (XLI. 3–8). When he achieves this goal, he does not experience *orgē* any more (XLII. 21–32, XLIV. 1–35). See pp. 228–9.

[27] See below, pp. 49–50 and elsewhere.

he points to aspects of emotions which are distinct from if not independent of beliefs. Pictorial thinking, mental images, etc., are also important, both because they accompany violent passions and because they are useful for therapy. On the one hand, the enraged man imagines himself as a god or a hero (*De ir.* XVI. 18–26), and the fearful person who is about to set sail is horrified at the picture of what might happen to his corpse at sea (*De mort.* XXXII. 36–7). On the other hand, such patients can be treated, the former by being made to see himself as a madman (*De ir.* XVI. 28 ff.), the latter by being induced to imagine what might happen to his corpse in a grave or on a pyre (*De mort.* XXX. 1–5, 17–20).[28] Furthermore, Philodemus brings out certain physical and physiological aspects of emotions, especially their bodily manifestations and the inner movements commonly associated with some of them.[29] Anger is composed in part of 'pyrexia and high swelling and itchy irritation' (VIII. 21–3) related to a series of random movements (κεινήσεις: *De ir.* VIII. 33–4) spread about the body. Whether or not the description is drawn from a Stoic source, Philodemus seems to endorse the idea that episodes of violent anger involve physiological movements of some sort.

Philodemus does not make explicit just how the different aspects of individual emotions, notably beliefs and feelings, are related to each other. He suggests that beliefs have a predominant role in the generation of the emotions, and also that they have both causal and temporal priority with regard to the corresponding feelings. The emotions of the soul are consequent upon false opinion (*De ir.* VI. 14–15). The wise man's alienation and hatred towards those who harmed him greatly follows from (cf. ἀκ[όλο]υθον: XLII. 3–4) his correct assessment of the situation. And the fool's feelings of grief about dying childless are caused by (cf. [δ]ιότι: *De mort.* XXIV. 7) his belief that his property will go to heirs more distant than his children would have been, and that this is an evil. One possibility is that such beliefs are necessary conditions of the emotion. However, Philodemus probably thinks that they are more than that. They are essential components of the emotion at least as much as feelings are. Achilles rages *at* someone *about* something, and Odysseus' irrational fear is *about* dying at sea.

[28] Cf. Philodemus' defence of that therapeutic technique (sc. the technique of 'bringing-before-the-eyes') against the criticisms of Timasagoras (*De ir.* VI. 27 ff.). I discuss the technique in some detail in Tsouna 2003.

[29] i.e., expansions and contractions. The latter are typically associated with distress.

On this interpretation, an emotion is a cognitive and also an affective event. The beliefs which are the cause of an emotion also persist and fuel the emotion. In fact, one might say that they persist as the intentional content of the emotion, and in virtue of that fact, they explain the emotion's intentionality—what the emotion is about. Feelings, on the other hand, correspond to its affective content. Furthermore, it would seem that beliefs and feelings do not coexist in the emotion accidentally. When they occur jointly, they both derive from the same pre-existing state: namely, the disposition that the emotional outburst makes manifest. Believing oneself slighted and feeling thirsty for revenge are found together only when one is irascible, and precisely because one is disposed in that way. As we shall see in examining the individual treatises, Philodemus is of the view that empty beliefs are not sufficient conditions for corresponding passions, and are not identical with them.[30]

Philodemus does not explain precisely on what the distinction between vices and harmful emotions or passions rests. For instance, he does not tell us why irascibility is an emotion and not a vice, if irascibility is a disposition and all vices are dispositions as well. However, he strongly suggests that passions and vices are distinct kinds of states. For example, the fear of death is causally connected with a number of vices, but it is not itself a vice. However, as Philodemus also makes clear, there exist intimate connections between passions and vices. First of all, they are found together in the soul. Arrogant students succumb to bouts of rage, and the same holds for people susceptible to flattery who tend to get enraged at their flatterers and abuse them. Avarice, anger, and arrogance accompany the fear of death (*De elect.* XX. 6–18); and so on. Moreover, vicious people experience an intensity of feeling which is also characteristic of the passions. The expert property manager pursues the acquisition of wealth with an anxious determination comparable to that of the enraged man who seeks revenge. Besides, both passions and vices tend to become manifest in one's appearance and conduct, although this is not always the case.[31] Finally,

[30] Compare Chrysippus, for whom false beliefs are identical with passions, and also Posidonius. On Sorabji's interpretation, Posidonius holds that beliefs are neither sufficient nor necessary for the arousal of emotions; see Sorabji 2000: 109–32.

[31] e.g., acting angrily is not the same thing as being angry. Likewise, treating people arrogantly is not the same thing as being arrogant (cf. Philodemus, *De superb.* VIII. 1–2, 21–8). Both anger and arrogance are chiefly a matter of how one *tends* to behave, not of how one actually does.

as indicated above, both passions and vices involve cognitive as well as non-cognitive elements. The same holds for a special category of emotions that Philodemus calls 'bites' or 'pangs', to which I shall now turn.

III

Philodemus is by no means the only Hellenistic philosopher to mention 'bites', or the first. The concept is used by both early and later Stoics, and their views are the relevant background against which we should examine Philodemus' own. The Stoics are generally in agreement that 'bites' constitute one species of movements of the soul or the mind, and that they are independent of judgements and, therefore, different from emotions.[32] Notably, Chrysippus describes them as physical movements of the mind,[33] which are associated with contractions and, further, with distress,[34] and which are felt in the vicinity of the heart.[35] Seneca refers to 'suggestions and shadows of emotion' (*De ir.* 1. 16. 7), natural and unavoidable occurrences which are the result of one's passive confrontation with appearances, and which move the wise man from his usual calm to some slight disturbance. In contrast to full-fledged emotions, an occurrence of this sort is a shock of the mind (*ictus animi*: 2. 2. 2) or a jolt of the body (*pulsus corporis*: 2. 3. 2), a first agitation of the mind (*prima agitatio*

[32] However, it is not entirely clear what Zeno's position is regarding emotions and their relation to physical movements. On one interpretation (cf. Sorabji 2000: 34–5), unlike Chrysippus' purely intellectualist account, Zeno defines emotions as movements of the soul (D.L. VII. 110), i.e., contractions and expansions, perhaps reachings or leanings away, caused by beliefs; e.g., pleasure is irrational expansion resulting from the presence of something believed to be desirable. And pain or distress is an irrational contraction caused by the 'fresh' idea of a present evil (Cicero, *Tusc.* 3. 75). Other interpreters tend to minimize the differences between Zeno's and Chrysippus' accounts (e.g., Inwood 1985). Note, however, that the distinction between genuine distress and a mere 'bite' of distress cannot be drawn if both are considered involuntary movements of the mind.

[33] According to Chrysippus, however, several kinds of movements of the mind are involved in emotions: cf. Galen *PHP*, IV. 2. 4–18, 3. 1–5.

[34] Cf. Galen, *PHP* II. 8. 4, 18; Cicero, *Tusc.* 3. 82–3, 4. 14–15. Note that Cicero refers to the sting of poverty and the prick of disgrace (*si paupertas momordit, si ignominia pupugit*: 3. 82) in the context of the medical analogy. Also, he dissociates the acute distress of mourning (*aegritudo*), which is voluntary and which we can remove by an act of will, from 'the bite and certain little contractions of the mind' (*morsus et contractiunculae quaedam animi*: 3. 83), which are natural and presumably involuntary, and remain in the soul (ibid.). On the association of these passages with Chrysippus, see Sorabji 2000: 38.

[35] Galen, *PHP* III. 5. 43–4.

animi: 2. 3. 5), a first movement (*primus motus*: 2. 4. 1),[36] or a preliminary prelude to the passion distinct from the passion itself (*De ir.* 2. 2. 5). Seneca often speaks of 'bites' in ways strongly suggesting that they are identical with first movements. They precede in time the birth and growth of the corresponding emotion, and do not involve judgement (*iudicium*).[37] Epictetus has a similar view. While he associates 'bites' with disturbance (ταραχή), he identifies neither of these with genuine emotion.[38] Almost two centuries earlier, and in the context of his own moral psychology,[39] Posidonius suggests that 'bites' are a different kind of *pathē* from emotions, since he classifies them in a different category. They are physical *pathē* occurring in the mind, to be distinguished from both purely mental ones, i.e., the emotions, and from purely physical ones, e.g., fevers and chills.[40] Since 'bites' belong to the same class as lethargy and melancholy,[41] and also are physical *pathē*, we may infer that they are natural and involuntary.[42] In

[36] On the distinctions between first, second, and third movements, see Seneca, *De ir.* 2. 4. 1. Particularly interesting is Sorabji's contention (2000: 66–75) that Seneca's distinction of first movements from both second and third movements was used therapeutically as well as polemically: to control emotion, and also to defend Chrysippus from some of the objections raised by Posidonius.

[37] e.g., urging Lucilius to grieve for the death of his friend Flaccus only as much as is fitting, he remarks that even the wise man 'will be stung by an event like this, but it will be only a sting' (sc. *vellicabit*: *Ep.* LXIII. 1). Also, when he addresses Marullus on the occasion of the loss of his little son, he declares: 'yours is not pain (*dolor*); it is a mere bite (*morsus*), and it is yourself who are turning it into pain' (*Ep.* XCIX. 14). Both examples imply that stings differ in kind from true grief (ibid.). However, sometimes Seneca's position is less clear-cut than this: cf. *Ep.* XCIX. 15, 20.

[38] Cf. Epictetus, 4. 6. 10, and, on this passage, Sorabji 2000: 68, 69 n. 24.

[39] The extent to which Posidonius' view of the emotions differs from Chrysippus' view is a controversial matter. Much depends on the weight that various interpreters give to Galen's evidence in *PHP* IV and V, and in particular to Galen's assertion that Posidonius rejected Chrysippus' theory of the *pathē* in favour of Plato's tripartite psychology and of the corresponding explanation of the emotions as independent of reason. Edelstein and Kidd (1972–89), in various places in their commentary, offer valuable comments on the concept of Stoic orthodoxy and on Posidonius' commitment to being faithful to the authorities of his school. Sorabji (2000), while recommending caution regarding Galen's testimony, on the whole emphasizes the differences between Chysippus and Posidonius, and argues that, according to Posidonius, judgements are not sufficient or always necessary for emotions. On the other hand, Cooper (1998*c*), makes a powerful case for the claim that Posidonius' theory of the emotions preserves central insights of both Chrysippus' and Plato's views, in particular Chrysippus' thesis that the emotions are ultimately functions of the rational faculty.

[40] Cf. Pseudo-Plutarch, *De libid. et aegr.* 6 Sandbach (cited and discussed by Sorabji (2000: 104)).

[41] Posidonius probably conceived of them as physical states lacking intentional objects.

[42] This surely holds of appearances and expansions, the last two items in the same category. Appearances arise by nature, from our contact with the world, and we do not choose the ways in which things in the world strike us. As to expansions, they must be the counterpart of contractions, 'bites'. On the other hand, Posidonius locates 'bites' and the other physical *pathē* mentioned in the mind, not in the body. This indicates that they may be related to beliefs or judgements, not in the sense that they are based on judgements (since in that case it would be hard to distinguish them from emotions), but perhaps in the sense that a 'bite' remains in the mind even after an emotion has been

any event, Posidonius he does not make much of them in his psychological or ethical theories.

I shall now turn to Epicurean 'bites'. We do not know whether that concept was initially formed by Zeno or invented by Philodemus, or whether it was used by all Epicurean groups of the first century BC or only by Philodemus and his disciples. In any case, the concept of 'bites' found in Philodemus may have been influenced by earlier Stoic views, and presents many affinities with them. Like the Stoics, Philodemus considers 'bites' natural and to some extent unavoidable even for the sage. But, I suggest, unlike Chrysippus and his followers, he interprets 'bites' in terms of evaluative reactions to events and treats them as genuine emotions.[43] We find evidence for this thesis in *On Anger* and *On Death*. In the former treatise, he draws the distinction between *orgē* and *thymos*, and from then on[44] he regularly associates 'bites' with *orgē*, natural anger (which is pivotal to his contention that the wise man may experience anger of some sort).[45] Conceptually, the association between 'bites' and *orgē* seems a successful choice. For when the wise man or his friends are intentionally harmed, the wise man gets an alien and unavoidable feeling (ἀνέκφευκτον: *De ir.* XL. 20), of mild intensity (XLIV. 9–10), small magnitude and duration (XLII. 39, XLV. 34), detached from the lust for revenge (XLII. 21 ff., XLIV. 7 ff.), compatible with a good disposition (XXXVII. 30), and different in quality from violent rage (XLV. 35). The 'bite' of natural anger looks in these respects like Stoic 'bites'—so much so, that one might think that the

removed. One may feel pangs of distress when thinking of a friend's death, even though one may have stopped grieving about it: Cicero, *Tusc.* 3. 82–3.

[43] I am not concerned here with, e.g., the case of the envious man who, clinging fast to his victim, literally bites him (*De inv.* XII. 12–36).

[44] Before he draws the distinction between *thymos* and *orgē*, he also associates 'bites' with unnatural anger. He remarks that anger makes its victims use inappropriate language and hurl stones 'as it bites at them' (δάκν[ων]: XII. 18), and also that people consider anger an evil if they have experienced its sting (τῶ[ι] δακνηρῶι προσπίπτοντες: XXXVII. 19). This might lead us to think that 'bites' apply indiscriminately to *thymos* and *orgē*. However, so long as these two kinds of anger have not been distinguished from each other, there are no adequate grounds for differentiating the pain of rage from a mere pang. On the other hand, after that distinction has been introduced, Philodemus is in a position to single out the natural kind of anger, which is not an evil in itself but 'only in so far as it is apt to bite' (δηκτικόν: XXXVIII. 7), and contrast it with empty anger deriving from a vicious disposition (XXXVIII. 1–3).

[45] Philodemus does not clarify whether the 'bite' is identical with the emotion, e.g., natural anger, or whether it is caused by the emotion. In any case, the important point is that the 'bite' associated with a natural and acceptable emotion differs from the pain associated with an unnatural one. On this point, see also below, n. 47.

dispute between Philodemus and the Stoics concerning anger is little more than verbal. This might be true only if the 'bite' of natural anger were not an emotion. In fact, one might think that it is not, but that natural anger is almost indistinguishable from Stoic εὐπάθειαι (sing. εὐπάθεια; translit. *eupatheiai*, sing. *eupatheia*)[46]—i.e., good states of feeling.[47] In my opinion, however, Philodemus' 'bites' differ considerably from both Stoic first movements and *eupatheiai*. They are healthy emotions and have the morphology of emotions. I shall try now to defend these claims.

According to *On Anger*, teachers who are not truly angry but feign anger for pedagogical purposes act 'without the emotion itself' (χωρὶς αὐτ[οῦ τοῦ] πάθους: XXXIV. 18–20). But pretending to be angry differs from being truly affected by natural anger. When the sage is affected in that way, he experiences an emotion—namely, an alien or inappropriate one (ἀλλότριον πάθος: cf. *De ir.* XL. 36–9) as opposed to an appropriate emotion (οἰκεῖον πάθος: XL. 39–40). Philodemus concludes that 'it is this kind of emotion[48] that we call (natural) anger' (XLI. 8–9).[49] And although he recognizes that the term 'anger' (*orgē*) is ambiguous,[50] the fact that he uses it to refer to the 'bite' of natural anger is significant in itself: this latter is a kind of *anger* (τισιν ὀργαῖς: XLI. 30), not an altogether different

[46] Some of the *eupatheiai* we might recognize as emotions, but most of them not. However, one must be careful when comparing 'bites' with *eupatheiai*. While Philodemus' 'bites' might bear some resemblance to Stoic *eupatheiai*, Stoic 'bites' are very different from *eupatheiai*. For a Stoic *eupatheia* has the same structure as a Stoic emotion, the crucial difference being that, in the case of the *eupatheia*, the relevant judgements are true. This makes a Stoic *eupatheia* entirely unlike a Stoic 'bite' (but not totally unlike Philodemus' 'bites').

[47] Philodemus does not only take on board the idea of a 'bite' and the Stoic terminology of expansions and contractions (*De superb.* XI. 31–3), but like the Stoics, he also considers several external things almost indifferent (cf. *De inv.*, fr. 18). He contends that the sage, even when affected by natural anger, is not greatly disturbed because no external thing is all that important (*De ir.* XLII. 6–7). And he maintains that, in contrast to the fool, the sage desires the punishment of the offender not as if it were an enjoyable thing (XLII. 21–32), but as something 'most necessary and most unpleasurable' (XLIV. 18–20). However, it runs beyond the theme of my book to pursue this comparison further.

[48] Cf. XLI. 8: τὸ δὲ τοιοῦτο[ν] should be complemented by πάθος. In the lines immediately preceding the passage, Philodemus mentions that this kind of anger goes together with the wise man's knowledge that his offender will be restrained by punishment and will become unable to cause damage in any way in the future (XLI. 2–8).

[49] Cf. also *De ir.* XLI. 9–16.

[50] See XLIII. 1–14. The text is badly damaged, but it seems reasonably clear that Philodemus emphasizes 'the difference that the emotion has' (ll. 8–9: note, however, that π[άθο]ς in l. 9 is largely conjectural), and also the meaning that *orgē* has as it applies, respectively, to the many and to the wise man. While in the former case the meaning of 'anger' is associated with 'things other than the feeling itself' (l. 6), notably the lust for revenge, in the latter case 'anger' refers to the kind of emotion that one naturally has as a result of being subject to intentional harm.

type of psychic event. We may draw the same inference from Philodemus' assertion that the wise man is capable of *thymos* in so far as it is a synonym of *orgē* (XLIII. 41–XLIV. 5), but is not capable of *thymos* in the technical sense of rage, for 'he does not fall into such intense emotions' (XLIV. 5–10). The implication is, clearly, that both *orgē* (or its 'bite') and *thymos* are emotions, and that the wise man exhibits the former, but not the latter, when he suffers some intentional offence. Natural anger is the anger of the wise man, whereas rage is the anger of the fool.

As for the structure of *orgē*, it involves both ways of experiencing and beliefs. When affected by it, the wise man usually is mildly annoyed, but sometimes he may become alienated from the offender and even hate him (XLII. 2–5). Regardless of their intensity, however, his feelings remain self-contained and do not last a long time. This may be true of other extra-cognitive elements too, but there is no evidence about them. In addition, natural anger involves true beliefs: the sage judges correctly that the offender caused or intended to cause great harm, and that it is appropriate to feel very angry towards him (XLI. 40–XLII. 2). He may even hate the offender (XLII. 3–4). Such remarks seem intended to apply to *orgē* of various degrees of intensity: that is, both sharp and light 'bites'. It would seem, then, that the difference between Philodemus and Chrysippus on this matter is not merely verbal. The Epicurean sage feels the 'bite' of a real emotion (which is more or less severe), whereas the Stoic sage senses the 'bite' of some pre-emotional state. Besides, Philodemus' 'bites' are natural and involuntary only up to a point. For, since they involve judgements, they are able to be influenced by reason. By contrast, Stoic first movements or equivalent Stoic 'bites' are non-rational, and one job of reason is, precisely, to preserve the gap between these occurrences and its own assent.

Philodemus' concept of the 'bite' of natural anger does not amount to a Stoic *eupatheia* either. Despite the fact that both are based on true judgements, and both involve acceptable states of feeling, *eupatheiai* are peaceful and, most of the time, constant states (*constantiae*: Cicero, *Tusc.* 4. 12–14), and this holds both for eupathic dispositions and for eupathic events deriving from such dispositions. On the other hand, the Epicurean sage's anger, although natural, is neither peaceful nor constant. It is a disturbance (ταρα[χ]ήν: XLII. 4–5), which involves some pain and is removed as soon as the offender is punished. Moreover, there cannot be a eupathic analogue for rare cases in which the sage 'is profoundly alienated and hates' (XLII. 2–3) those who have damaged him greatly. From the Stoic point of view, that kind of psychic movement cannot be reasonable (εὔλογον),[51] and the strong reaction that it causes can never be appropriate.[52]

Let us pass on to the diatribe *On Death*. A large part of its fourth book discusses cases in which it is particularly hard to face death, our own or that of others, with a peaceful mind. As we shall see in detail in a later chapter, in some of these cases Philodemus dismisses any kind of distress as sheer folly. In others, he acknowledges that it is natural to feel a 'bite' of sorrow.[53] He contrasts 'bites' of distress with deep grief (λύπη), and treats them as distinct but conceptually related kinds of *pathē*. For example, he compares 'the portion of pain' (μέρος ὀδυνῶν: XX. 2) that one feels at the approach of premature death with 'the part about how one's enemies will rejoice' (XX. 4), and he argues that the former is forgivable (συγγνωστόν: XX. 3), whereas the latter is unforgivably vain (XX. 4–5). Any thoughtful and sensitive person would be likely to shed tears and feel 'a truly natural bite' (φυσικώτατον δηγμόν: XXV. 8) at the thought that his beloved ones will face material hardships because of his death (XXV. 2–10). This 'bite' differs in kind from the unnatural distress that people feel, for example, because they leave their property to heirs other than their children (XXIV. 5–10). The prospect of death in a foreign land brings naturally 'pangs' of grief (νύττειν: XXVI. 3), especially if one has family back home. Philodemus contrasts them with 'great grief' (λύπην μεγάλην: XXVI. 4) that makes the difficulties of living and dying in a foreign country even harder. Dying is painful anyway, therefore its pain and distress (πόνους: XXXIII. 34–6) should not become worse by

[51] On the other hand, according to Cicero, they define will (*voluntas*) as rational longing, joy (*gaudium*) as rational and tranquil satisfaction, and caution (*cautio*) as rational aversion to evil (*Tusc.* 4. 12–13).

[52] The following objection can be raised. If 'bites' are a kind of disturbance, isn't the Stoic sage better off than the Epicurean sage, especially if the Epicurean sage can be profoundly alienated and hating (cf. XLII. 2–3)? Philodemus can answer that objection by appealing to the senses in which a 'bite' is natural: it is useful, rests on sound judgement, constitutes an unperverted reaction to certain circumstances, and cannot be avoided altogether (cf. pp. 224–5). Sometimes the sage simply does not have the option not to experience, e.g., the disturbance of natural anger. And he should not wish not to experience it, for this would indicate that there is something wrong with him.

[53] Unlike *On Anger*, *On Death* uses terms such as 'bite' (δηγμός) or 'pang' (νυγμός) and their cognates for natural states of feelings, not for both natural and unnatural ones. However, like *On Anger*, as I maintain, it describes 'bites' concerning natural states of feeling as real emotions.

the prospect of dying at sea. The wise man too may have to confront the pains of an unjust and violent death, whether it concerns himself or another. Although such circumstances can perhaps move him to real grief (λυπεῖσθαι: XXXIV. 1), he usually perceives a death of this sort like a 'bite' of bad fortune (XXXIV. 25). In any case, his distress differs from the anguish (ὀδυνήσεσθαι: XXXV. 9) of those who are responsible for an unjust condemnation and who repent it.

In all these cases, 'bites' consist of both sensings and beliefs, just as 'unforgivable' forms of distress about death do.[54] in Chapter 10. But contrary to unnatural distress, 'bites' of sorrow are natural, and therefore everyone including the wise man is vulnerable to them. Occasionally they can be fairly severe, e.g., in the case mentioned above of a sage's unjust sentence. But even then the sage will make sure that his pains are only moderately troublesome (XXXIV. 11–12), and that they disturb him no more than in sickness (XXXIV. 25–6). In general, natural 'bites' of distress are usually associated with moderate as opposed to intense feelings. Cognitively, they involve true beliefs concerning the kind of death in question and its impact. For instance, it is true that subjecting a sage to torture is an event highly contrary to reason and very rare (XXXIV. 4–6). It may be true that a father's death will be a financial disaster for the family, that one's death abroad will bring great sorrow to one's parents back home, and that dying at sea can be excruciatingly painful. However, none of these beliefs undermines the theses that death implies total lack of sensation and the extinction of personal identity, and also that if there is any pain involved in dying, it cannot be too intense and last for too long. Since Philodemus endorses these canonical theses, he has good reason to maintain that 'bites' of distress, rather than deep grief, are appropriate emotional responses to those circumstances.[55]

Again, 'bites' of distress, like 'bites' of natural anger, should be distinguished from Stoic *eupatheiai*. Whether or not Stoic 'bites' of distress are present in Stoic lists, they are kept distinct from the emotion: namely,

[54] These are unnatural and in our power to avoid. They involve deep and intense grief (λύπη, ὀδύνη), true horror (cf. πεφρικέναι: XXXIX. 7), wailing and sobbing (XXXVII. 6), and also mental pictures of one's corpse becoming food for fish or decaying in the grave. Moreover, emotions of this sort are grounded on false beliefs, and also on the mistaken assumption that some things matter to the dead. Cf. pp. 258–9 *passim* in chapter 10.

[55] e.g., he tries to explain why deep grief about dying away from home is irrational: *De mort.* XXVI. 3–17.

distress itself.[56] On the other hand, on Philodemus' view, 'bites' of sorrow concerning death exhibit the features and structure of genuine emotion, just as the 'bites' of *orgē* do. This fact is important for purposes of therapy. To the extent that 'bites' arise from our human nature, they should be acknowledged and accepted. *Orgē* is an understandable and even appropriate reaction to aggression, and gentle sorrow caused by someone's death, surely, can be forgiven. However, in so far as 'bites' have cognitive elements, they can be weakened and may even disappear: not because of exhaustion of feeling, as Posidonius would have it, but because they can be influenced by argument, as other emotions can.[57]

The concept of 'bites' found in Philodemus is an important addition to Epicurean ethics and moral psychology. Philodemus' use of 'bites' invites instructive comparisons between him and the Stoics. It raises questions concerning the legitimacy of *natural* emotions which might otherwise have been overlooked. And it can be viewed as a successful attempt to make certain aspects of the Epicurean doctrine, in particular the treatment of anger and of the fear of death, palatable to a wider public.

[56] According to Cicero (*Tusc.* 4. 14), grief has no corresponding eupathic state. As Sorabji points out (2000: 51 nn. 109 and 110), Philo of Alexandria takes the liberty of inserting 'bites' of distress in the Stoic lists of *eupatheiai* precisely because, like the Stoics, he distinguishes 'bites' from distress itself.

[57] I wonder whether Philodemus' concept of 'pangs' might not be used in order to interpret Epicurus' alleged claim that the sage is more susceptible to emotions than the rest of us (D.L. X. 117), but his wisdom is not hindered by that fact.

3

Analysis and Treatment: Methodological and Epistemological Prolegomena

I shall now turn to Philodemus' method of analysis and treatment in the ethical treatises. I shall confine my remarks to the ensembles *On the Passions* and *On Vices and the Opposite Virtues*, but to a degree they also concern other writings. Each book belonging to these collections studies a single major character flaw whose explication and treatment require discussion of other related traits as well. Like many philosophers of his era, Philodemus is eclectic in his use of sources, and open-minded in his choice of therapeutic techniques. However, he relies on the epistemological principles first determined by Epicurus, and he endorses the methodological empiricism advanced by Zeno and his associates mainly in opposition to Stoicism. This is neither pedestrian nor philosophical empiricism in the modern sense. Broadly speaking, 'empiricism' here signals an approach that is based on the methodology of Greek empirical sciences, and especially of empirical medicine. It exhibits features plausibly identified as empirical, including certain methods of reasoning, assessment, and appraisal. And it involves an implicit contrast with the doctrines of the so-called rationalist philosophers, who are influenced by mathematical or deductive models, employ specialized techniques of proof and syllogism, and consider reason both the principal source and the principal instrument of knowledge.

I shall comment on some general features of Philodemus' empirical approach to ethics, many of which are developed in his work *On Signs* and are also found in his treatment of various arts and sciences, moral education, and even religion. These features comprise Philodemus' reliance on observation and experience, and his use of methods of reasoning that are focused on experience or directed towards it; the development of the medical analogy in connection with such methods; the kind of definitions intended to describe ethical concepts; and Philodemus' appeal to preconception (πρόληψις, pl. προλήψεις; translit. *prolēpsis*, *prolēpseis*) in order to solve problems in practical ethics. I shall suggest that, on these counts too, Philodemus remains close to the canonical tradition of his school, and expands it in ways appropriate to his own project.

I

First, a word about structure. Perhaps despite appearances, the writings concerning specific vices, such as arrogance and flattery, and emotions, notably anger, are composed with a fair degree of systematicity and completeness. In fact, Philodemus seems to have in mind a model of analysis which varies greatly from one work to another[1] but nonetheless usually has many of the following general features. He gives some kind of definition or outline[2] of, e.g., the vice that constitutes his principal topic.[3] He describes both its distinctive nature and some secondary characteristics. He compares it with other vices which might be related to it in some way, and also contrasts it with one or more virtues that are its opposites. In these ways, he individuates the trait under examination, brings out its complexity, and shows its conceptual and empirical connections with other traits. Moreover, he distinguishes the character trait itself from its behavioural manifestations. He points to its consequences, psychological as well as pragmatic. By that point, he has explained sufficiently why a certain character trait, such as arrogance or flattery, is an evil. Moreover, he proposes strategies for its therapy.[4]

[1] The way in which Philodemus proceeds depends to a significant extent on the particular object and aims of each treatise, as well as on the opponents that he attacks.

[2] This outline is intended to function as a definition. As we shall see, the Epicureans disapprove of definitions in a technical sense.

[3] Recall that vices, rather than virtues, and undesirable emotions, rather than desirable ones, constitute the focus of Philodemus' writings, because these are the traits that he wishes to remove. In the extant remains of the treatises, the outline which functions as a definition of the relevant trait does not necessarily come first in the order of analysis, and the steps outlined above do not always occur in the same sequence.

[4] The clearest illustration of this pattern is found in *On Arrogance*, and it is also evident in the vestiges of *On Flattery*. *On Property Management* exhibits features of the same methodological scheme,

Philodemus does not explicitly lay out, let alone defend, the epistemological basis of his analyses. However, there can be no doubt that, as an Epicurean, he is committed to Epicurus' theses that all sense-impressions are true,[5] and that sense-impressions (αἰσθήσεις, sing. αἴσθησις), as well as preconceptions (προλήψεις) and feelings (πάθη), are the criteria of truth.[6] He assumes that falsehood can arise only at the level of opinions or judgements, not of sense impressions, and that opinions can be verified or falsified by reference to the criteria of truth. Moreover, he complies with Epicurus' requirement that we observe the evidence of αἰσθήσεις taking whatever we perceive, just as we perceive it, as evidence or a sign (σημεῖον) for what is unobserved (cf. *ad Herod.* 38).[7] *On Signs*[8] amply confirms that he is committed to the Epicurean methodology developed and defended against Stoic criticisms by Philodemus' teachers in Athens. Its hallmark is the similarity method (ὁ καθ' ὁμοιότητα τρόπος)—namely, a method of

but deviates from it to some degree. One reason is that the subject is not a single vice and its opposite virtue, but rather the activity of property management (οἰκονομία, translit. *oikonomia*) which involves the exercise of many character traits. So, e.g., Philodemus does not describe virtues as opposed to vices related to *oikonomia*, but rather the good property manager as opposed to one who engages in that activity in an inappropriate manner. Moreover, he does not individuate, e.g., greed (the central vice related to the obsessive pursuit of *oikonomia*) by comparing it with other vices, but studies together the cluster of vices underlying wrong attitudes towards *oikonomia*, and contrasts it with the virtues dictating right attitudes. Turning to the ensemble *On the Passions*, we find that Philodemus' mode of analysis preserves many of its central characteristics, but is refined and enriched with new elements. e.g., *On Anger* clarifies ambiguities in the concept of anger, and defines different kinds of anger in different ways; it sharpens our capacity to distinguish the emotion from other, related emotions by studying its symptoms in detail; and in addition to proposing therapeutic techniques, it contains theoretical discussion of the Epicurean approach to the treatment of rage. The surviving parts of *On Death* also display many of the above features, notably the concern to distinguish different forms of the emotion and to propose different therapies for each. Here too, we are invited to compare undesirable forms of the emotion with each other, and also with acceptable 'pangs'—a procedure of identification and individuation which brings out the complex nature of the fear of death. Here too we are led to realize that the fear of death is an evil by reflecting on its internal and external consequences.

[5] Cf. Dem. Lac.; PHerc. 1012, LVII. 8–LVIII. 14. It is controversial just how Epicurus wanted his thesis to be understood. If he meant that every proposition expressing exactly the content of a given sense-impression is true (see Striker 1996: 77–91), he merits a place in the tradition of empiricist philosophers who try to find in sense perception an infallible foundation for knowledge. On this point, see Striker 1996: 90–1.

[6] See De Lacy and De Lacy 1978: 175 ff.

[7] Asmis (1984: 83 ff.) gives a detailed interpretation of this problematic passage and briefly discusses alternative interpretations.

[8] Philodemus composed this work in the mid-first century BC. It reports the arguments of Zeno's Stoic opponent, Dionysius of Cyrene (a pupil of Diogenes of Babylon and Antipater of Tarsus), against the Epicurean method of sign inference, and Zeno's answers to them, and it also draws information from Demetrius Lacon on the same subject. De Lacy and De Lacy 1978 is the most recent edition of the thirty-eight columns of continuous text and eight fragments. Particularly helpful discussions of its contents are offered by Sedley 1982 and Barnes 1988.

sign inference based on analogy and induction that Zeno of Sidon[9] and his associates oppose to the deductive elimination method (ὁ κατ' ἀνασκευήν τρόπος) upheld by the Stoics. A related procedure is ἐπιλογισμός (translit. *epilogismos*). It was introduced by Epicurus, who intended it to apply to scientific theory as well as ethics (cf. Epicurus, *KD* 22). Philodemus shows himself committed to it in a way reflecting Epicurus' own usage. Let me, then, outline the method briefly, and indicate how it bears on Philodemus' treatment of ethical problems. In doing so, I shall also highlight aspects of the inductive similarity method,[10] of which *epilogismos* is an important step.

Contrary to the view that *epilogismos* and its cognates are themselves names for inductive inference,[11] *epilogismos*, as such, is not inference.[12] At root, it appears to be a kind of survey,[13] assessment, or appraisal[14] of the phenomena (cf. *De sign.* XXII. 38–9, XXVII. 22–3) which allows us to establish a similarity among them and, on that basis, make inferences (cf. σημε[ι]ούμεθα: IX. 3) to what is not or may not be immediately apparent. For example, making an *epilogismos* of all the features that, in our experience, always attend things in motion, we infer that these same features accompany all moving objects in every case; on the basis of the similarity between moving objects in our experience and moving objects anywhere, we infer that void is necessary for motion (VIII. 32–IX. 3). In a comparable manner, angry people are confronted with a complete survey of the sufferings and dangers involved in anger (*De ir.* IV. 4–12, VII. 26–VIII. 8) enabling them to assess (ἐπιλογίσασθαι: VII. 17) the true nature of the evil.[15] And those who have fallen in love are asked to consider, one by one, everything that is hurting them, the very unpleasant

[9] Cf. Zeno's polemic against Posidonius concerning geometrical first principles (Proclus, *In Eucl. Elem.* p. 199, 3–200, 6, and p. 214, 15–218, 11 Friedlein = fr. 27).

[10] As I mentioned, Philodemus' discussion of the similarity method in the treatise *On Signs* is quite technical, and is primarily aimed to refute Stoic objections to that method. Therefore, it is not of particular importance for my subject, although aspects of that method are relevant. In addition to De Lacy and De Lacy 1978, Sedley 1982 and Barnes 1988 explain fully how Philodemus and his teachers conceived of the similarity method.

[11] Cf. De Lacy and De Lacy 1978: 100 n. 34, 202 ff., and *passim*.

[12] However, arguments involving ἐπιλογισμός are called sometimes ἐπιλογισμοί or ἐπιλογιστικοὶ λόγοι: cf. Philodemus, *De ir.* XLVI. 17–18 and XLIV. 38–9.

[13] Cf. Barnes 1988. [14] Cf. Sedley 1973: 31 ff.; Schofield 1996: esp. 232–5.

[15] In this and other instances, one might take *epilogismos* in an ordinary, non-philosophical sense. However, Philodemus refers implicitly to the sort of assessment that is conducted in accordance with Epicurean principles. As Schofield (1996: 224–5) remarks, in Epicurean literature, ἐπιλογίζεσθαι and its cognates may retain their usual sense, but are often pregnant with Epicurean philosophical connotations.

consequences commonly attending that condition (cf. [κοι]νῆ<ι>: VII. 24), and sometimes also evils that have hurt them personally (cf. [ἰδίαι]: VII. 25).[16] The obvious similarity of the symptoms and consequences befalling, e.g., angry persons in our experience (cf. VII. 26–VIII. 8) constitute the grounds for inferring that they hold of every case of anger. Moreover, they serve as signs on the basis of which one can draw inferences about one's disposition.[17] For instance, the physiological symptoms of pyrexia and high swelling reveal that one is actually angry, and, moreover, they point to one's irascibility (the disposition from which a particular crisis of anger derives).

As these examples show, the procedure of *epilogismos* does not require demonstration. It is a matter of careful observation of evident facts, which underpins inductions by similarity to what we do not experience directly. Observation of this sort typically involves calculation and comparison. We must compare all our clear impressions of things in motion to determine what they share in common and what is peculiar to each case. Then we shall be able to infer the features of moving objects that we have not seen and, furthermore, draw conclusions concerning the necessary conditions of motion. Likewise, Epicurus urges us to appraise (ἐπιλογίζεσθαι) the moral end (*KD* 22) by comparing the person who does not fear the gods and death with everyone else and, moreover, by calculating how easy it is to attain good things and to endure bad ones (*ad Men.* 133).[18] Philodemus recommends the same procedure in practical ethics, although he does not always demarcate it by the term *epilogismos*. The good property manager is the kind of person who determines (δ[ιο]ρίζων: *De oec.* XIII. 22) many things by reference to what is profitable and makes choices in accordance with comparative calculations (XIII. 8 ff.). The cure for arrogance requires that arrogant men contrast the evils caused by the vice with the goods deriving from a sense of social equality and restraint. And irascible persons in treatment assess the pains and perils of anger by comparing them with the pleasure and security of a life untainted by that vice. They form comparative judgements of that sort with the aid of several

[16] Note that the text is heavily restored, and its translation uncertain. However, even if we restore the text differently, the main point remains: i.e., sufferers from erotic love are made to appraise the nature and consequences of their passion.

[17] On the nature of these inferences, see below, p. 64 n. 51.

[18] Both texts are discussed by Schofield (1996: 230–1).

devices, intellectual as well as psychological. For instance, the Epicurean teacher lists one by one the consequences of anger (*De ir.* VII. 22–6), depicts them vividly (cf. III. 5–V. 4–24), and makes the patients aware of evils that they were ignorant or had forgotten or had never contemplated as a whole (III. 7–13). In these ways, irascible people can appraise correctly the magnitude of the pain involved in anger and infer that they must seek remedy.

Comparison and analogy are the key features of the three *epilogismoi* (XLVI. 17–18) reported in the final section of *On Anger* (cf. also ἐπιλογιστικοὶ λόγοι: XLIV. 38–9),[19] and also figure prominently in Philodemus' refutation of these arguments.[20] Notably, Philodemus objects to the grounds on which his opponents draw similarities between gratitude and anger, and hence to the validity of the inference that just as the wise man can feel intense gratitude, so he can feel violent anger (XLVIII. 5–32). Also, he rejects his rivals' contention that if the sage gets as drunk as other good men, then he gets as angry as they do. His main reason is that whoever the 'good men' may be, no relevant similarities obtain between them and the sage, and therefore no inferences can be drawn from them to the sage (XLVIII. 33–XLIX. 26). To conclude this point, the comparative judgements involved in Philodemus' *epilogismoi* do not require any particular technical skill,[21] but nevertheless, usually have philosophical connotations. These are drawn from either Epicurean methodology and logic, or Epicurean ethics, or both.

Appraising on the basis of similarities and differences is important for theoretical purposes as well, notably for individuating various vices or passions. The disdain of the arrogant person is shown to be different from that of the sage (*De superb.* VI. 12–13) on account of their different objects (V. 3 ff., VI. 12–14, 30–2) and behavioural differences between these two types of men (e.g., IX. 1 ff.). Arrogance is not magnanimity, since these traits differ in both their external manifestations and their physiological aspects (XV. 29 ff.).[22] The beliefs underlying arrogance, envy, and malicious joy (XII. 12–36) are individuated by observing the behaviour of people afflicted by these vices. On similar grounds, Philodemus draws distinctions between flatterers and their victims, parasites, sycophants, and those who

[19] Ibid. 227. [20] For detailed discussion of these arguments, see pp. 230–8.

[21] On *epilogismos* as a common or garden procedure, see Schofield 1996. [22] See pp. 151–3.

like to please.[23] Flatterers and parasites differ in the manner, frequency, and contents of their speech (PHerc. 1457, fr.1. 5 ff., II. 14–16, I. 10–12); sycophants differ from both in that they engage in mean gossip in order to gain favour for themselves (PHerc. 1457, IV. 7 ff.); contrary to these types, people who like to please may do so even if they do not gain any advantage; and so on. The force of such remarks derives mainly from their evident character and empirical accuracy: we *see* that this is usually how things are. Therefore, we may feel inclined to follow Philodemus' practical recommendations and therapeutic advice.[24]

Again, the methodological basis of theoretical distinctions in ethics lies in the treatise *On Signs*. Philodemus shows himself aware of the importance of selecting the relevant similarities or differences and making inferences from some of them, but not from others. He leaves room for possible variations and peculiarities, and occasionally finds ways of accommodating them in a systematic manner. His refutation of the suggestions that the wise man is arrogant and that he is irascible reflects these concerns.[25] It also exemplifies the principle that everyone who infers well must carefully observe the phenomena, so that there may be no conflicting evidence; only then is one entitled to make a judgement concerning what follows from what is seen (*De sign.* XXXIII. 9–15). Even assuming that the wise man presents some superficial similarities to the arrogant person, those who attribute to him arrogance on such grounds fail to consider evidence to the contrary—for example, the nobility of his appearance and way of life (*De superb.* VI. 9–21), his obvious respect for others, his hospitality and friendliness (IX. 7–10), and his lack of pride at good fortune (IX. 1–7).[26] In sum, allowing for limited deviations within appearances and perhaps for different degrees of inferential probability, Philodemus assumes that we are able to establish regular connections between people's dispositions and their external manifestations. The necessary proviso is that we follow the

[23] Just how these vices are related to each other remains unclear. On this point, see pp. 128–32.

[24] e.g., he recommends that we should avoid parasites, although they are observed to be more passive, more servile, and less dangerous than flatterers (PHerc. 1457, fr. 4. 37 ff.); and he warns strongly against obsequiousness, for pedagogical as much as for moral reasons (PHerc. 1457, X. 17 ff.).

[25] Philodemus refutes these suggestions by selecting and focusing on certain behavioural features of the wise man which might give the appearance of arrogance or of irascibility, and subsequently by showing how these features differ from corresponding features of arrogant or irascible men. Moreover, he suggests that sages can vary in their behaviour because of many factors, and that some of them may be more likely to appear arrogant or irascible than others. On these points, see pp. 150–1 and 219–21.

[26] See pp. 54–7.

rules of proper inductive inference, which amount to an empirical method of enquiry comparable in places to that of the so-called empiricist doctors. Let me elaborate this point.

As indicated, reasoning that involves *epilogismos* and inference on the grounds of similarity is conducted on the basis of empirical data,[27] and is directed towards experience.[28] Moreover, Philodemus emphasizes the *ad hoc* recognition of signs, the importance of second-hand reports (*De lib. dic.* 50. 3–12), and the use of ἱστορίαι (*De lib. dic.* Vb. 8–9; cf. also *De sign.* XX. 31–XXI. 3): namely, records of the treatment of vices and passions effected by the early authorities of the Epicurean school.[29] Similar features also mark the method of the empirical school of medicine, established in the third century BC, which rejects the dogmatic theories of causation underlying the approaches of the so-called rationalist doctors, and advances a pragmatic approach based on observation and inference by means of signs. Here I cannot discuss the method of empiricist physicians in any detail. Suffice it to mention that they adopt the vocabulary of *epilogismos* and its cognates[30] to indicate a kind of reasoning relating to the phenomena and available to all human beings (Galen, *Comp. Med.* 150. 13–14D).[31] Unlike the Epicureans, they apply *epilogismos* primarily to the inference drawn on the grounds of appraising similarities and differences, not to the procedure of appraisal itself, and also proceed from the visible to the visible. However, they observe some of the rules of inference that Philodemus reports in *On Signs*, and they follow the principles of direct observation or autopsy involving the use of signs, the use of medical records (ἱστορία),[32] and the transition from similar to similar.[33] It is plausible to believe that Philodemus kept abreast of recent developments in the empirical tradition of medicine and was strongly influenced by the empirical school.[34] In any event, he

[27] See Sedley 1973: 27 ff.

[28] Perhaps the prefix ἐπ- indicates, precisely, the focus of this sort of reasoning on something given in experience.

[29] Philodemus mentions Metrodorus and possibly Cleanthes in that connection: *De lib. dic.* Vb. 2–4.

[30] See De Lacy and De Lacy 1978: 175 ff.

[31] See Schofield 1996: 236.

[32] Compare with the ἱστορία used by empiricist doctors: Galen, *Sub. emp.* 2–3 (44. 4–49. 29, Deichgraeber). On empiricist methodology see Asmis 1984: 189 f.; De Lacy and De Lacy 1978: 175 ff.; Frede 1987c: 243–60; and von Staden 1975.

[33] This last feature seems to be a late addition to the empiricist doctrine: see Frede 1987*a*: esp. 249–51.

[34] At the end of *On Signs* (*De sign.* XXXVIII. 25–32), Philodemus promises to take note of 'what some of the physicians have said and written about analogical inference' (XXXVIII. 25–8). It seems

shows himself aware of its methods in his development of the so-called medical metaphor.

II

The metaphor of the philosopher as a doctor of the soul has received much attention in the literature. Therefore, I shall limit my comments to Philodemus' own conception of that analogy, especially its methodological features. Much of what I say of Philodemus applies to philosophers of his own school and of the other Hellenistic schools. Following Epicurus, Philodemus assumes that the principal goal of philosophy is to secure one's happiness,[35] and that that result can be achieved only by removing the principal causes of human suffering: namely, the vices and certain emotions or passions. Considered in the light of a normative conception of nature and psychic health,[36] these are diseases of the soul which must be cured. Like Epicurus, then, Philodemus perceives the philosopher as a kind of doctor who removes disturbance and anxiety and restores the soul to its healthy natural state, much as the physician removes the ailments of the body and restores its unimpeded functioning.[37] The philosopher acts in that way motivated by considerations of philanthropy, compassion, and also friendship and other-concern. If he becomes aware of a person's suffering, he is inclined to help, as a physician would. In both cases, the therapist's realization that someone is affected by a particular disease is a first step towards its healing.[38] And in both cases, the therapist views

plausible that he has particularly in mind the empiricist doctors. On this point, see De Lacy and De Lacy 1978: 129 and n. 114.

[35] Cf. Sextus' formulation of the Epicurean definition of philosophy as 'an activity that secures the happy life by means of arguments and reasonings' (*M* XI. 169).

[36] Cf. Nussbaum 1994: 29–32.

[37] Note, however, that Philodemus does not isolate a specifically 'therapeutic' aspect of philosophy or a genre of 'therapeutic' argument, and also that his reliance on the medical model does not exclude the parallel use of other complementary or even competing models. A different interpretation is defended by Nussbaum (1994) regarding Hellenistic philosophers in general: she carves out a category of specifically therapeutic arguments and defines what she takes to be their principal characteristics. Her analysis is challenging and informative, provided that we bear in mind that Hellenistic uses of the medical metaphor do not necessarily entail a consciously medical approach to argument to the exclusion of other approaches. On this point, see David Sedley's review of Nussbaum 1994 (Sedley 1999), and also Diskin Clay's review of that work (Clay 1996: 501).

[38] Nussbaum 1994: 32–4.

his active interference as an important part of his mission. In fact, the medical model suggests that philosophical therapy is an ongoing activity integrated into the context of ethical *praxis*. The important thing is to live the philosophical life, not merely to be engaged in theoretical discourses.[39] This applies both to the doctor of the soul and to his patients. For, ideally, the therapeutic process takes place in alternative communities such as the Garden of Athens and the schools of Rhodes and of Campania, in which the Epicurean teachers exercise *parrhēsia*, frank speech, to erring students in order to remove their faults and lead them to the Epicurean way of life.

On this picture, the doctor of the soul occupies a position which may appear asymmetrical with regard to his patients. Although he takes into account his patients' perception of their own condition, he critically assesses it according to a kind of expertise that his patients do not often fully possess.[40] Likewise, the physician of the body has expertise in matters of health that his patients do not share, and on the grounds of that expertise judges and treats their ailments even if they do not fully understand the nature of their problem or the way the medicines work. Because of the inequality between the therapist and his patients, it is essential that the people treated trust and even obey those who treat them. These features may appear more pronounced in the Epicurean school than in other Hellenistic schools. The medical model in this case may thus seem more vulnerable to the criticism that, in contrast to medicine, the practice of philosophy requires intellectual initiative on the part of the student and reciprocity between the parties.[41] Also, Epicurean therapeutics might be subject to the charges that they numb one's intellect and critical spirit,[42] discourage the fair consideration of competing alternatives,[43] and ascribe to

[39] See Hadot 1995: 49–70.

[40] On the critical distance between the doctor and the patient implied by the medical model, see Nussbaum 1994: 13 ff. Nussbaum contrasts medical philosophy, on the one hand, with Platonism, which she describes as locating values solely at a transcendent level, and, on the other hand, what she calls 'the approach based on ordinary belief' (p. 16). I shall not discuss these contrasts here, but I wish to point out that they may be somewhat forced. Nussbaum's version of Platonism contains several controversial claims (e.g., that any connection between human interests and the true good is purely contingent, and that looking into ourselves is irrelevant to ethical enquiry). And her ordinary belief philosophers who, according to Nussbaum's description, limit themselves to the uncritical acceptance of existing beliefs are hard to identify.

[41] Cf. Nussbaum 1994: 69 ff.

[42] On this point, see ibid. 130–2, 137–9.

[43] Cf. ibid. 45–7 and elsewhere.

arguments merely instrumental value.[44] In addition, like other philosophers wedded to the medical model, the Epicureans face the objection that arguments alone cannot cure the passions, for they are long entrenched in one's habits and character (cf. Aristotle, *Eth. Nic.* X. 9), and that arguments have no effect on people whose rationality is not developed (cf. Aristotle, *Eth. Eud.* I. 3).

There may be truth in these criticisms. However, they are mitigated by the following considerations found in Epicurean writings, especially Philodemus' treatise *On Frank Speech*, which is based on lectures by Zeno of Sidon. While Philodemus emphasizes the wisdom of Epicurean teachers with regard to their students, he also suggests that their relationships with each other are more reciprocal and dynamic than is usually assumed.[45] The therapy often begins with the patient's awareness of his error and his decision to confess it and ask for help. Believing that one has bronchitis could be unrelated to the presence of the disease or to the antibiotics prescribed for its cure. On the other hand, realizing that one's rage at one's neighbour is inappropriate is essential to its subsequent removal. Patients can contribute to their own treatment by maintaining positive thoughts and attitudes. In particular, they must struggle to keep down their own defences and preserve their trust in the teacher's good will. They must learn to bear the discomfort caused by frank criticism and feel grateful for it. In general, they need to make constant mental and psychological efforts in order to benefit from the teacher's candour, develop their self-awareness, and get rid of their faults. On a practical level, they may help the therapist in his

[44] e.g., Nussbaum (ibid. 14–16, 46–7) argues that although therapeutic arguments often exhibit logical rigour and clarity, they are prized only in so far as they succeed in extirpating vice and passion from the human soul. As the medicines administered by the doctor are considered good only if they are effective, so the arguments used by the Hellenistic philosophers are deemed good only if they prove suitable to the specific malady that they are intended to address. While this claim can hold only with qualification for the Stoics, for they show a genuine interest in logical and epistemological matters, it might seem to hold unqualifiedly for the Epicureans. Recall Epicurus' reservations about traditional education, the Garden's practices of repetition and memorization of canonical writings, and the uneven quality of the dialectical arguments by which they 'correct' the views of other schools. Consider also Epicurus' assertion that a philosopher's discourse is empty if it does not cure any disease (Porph. *Ad Marc.* 31).

[45] In general, it can be argued that, unlike medical patients, the student of Epicureanism is meant to be learning the norms according to which his condition is assessed by the teacher. Within the context of an Epicurean community, Epicurean therapy would seem to work only if the student has already been informed of Epicurean norms and is willing to be judged according to them. Of course, Epicurean teachers may use frank speech also towards people outside the school, but this does not bear on the relation between teachers and students in Epicurean groups.

job by reporting the errors of their fellow students. Or they may undertake the role of the therapist by applying *parrhēsia* to their peers. Conversely, the therapist is willing to tolerate a certain amount of aggression from patients whose feelings have been hurt by frank speech. He acknowledges openly his failings and seeks correction. And he occasionally switches roles with his students, if only for educational purposes.[46]

Moreover, it would seem that Epicurean students are not altogether deprived of critical spirit, and become cognizant to some extent of the views of their rivals. Consider the complex dialectical structure of Philodemus' *On Poems I*, *Rhetoric I and II*, *On Music*, and also *On Signs*, *On Anger*, and the writing tentatively identified as [*On Choices and Avoidances*]. Philodemus' dialectical arguments in these works vary in rigour and clarity, and can be unfair or fallacious. However, they can also make high intellectual demands of their readers. For instance, these last must be able to distinguish the positions of different rival factions from each other and from those of their own school—sometimes a formidably difficult task; follow the development of an argument to its conclusion; understand the reasons why a certain position should be rejected, and separate the stronger from the weaker reasons to that effect; and so on. Popular writings too, such as epitomes, require a certain degree of sophistication.[47] I doubt that one could really digest Epicurus' *Letter to Herodotus* or the principles of Epicurean ethics laid out in [*On Choices and Avoidances*] if one were not able to grasp the highly condensed formulations of complex doctrines and arguments found in these works. In short, Epicurean students may well be partial, but this does not mean that they reject alternative views merely on authority or that they endorse their own without reflection. Besides, although the Epicureans set stringent ethical constraints upon therapeutic arguments, it does not follow that they would have been happy to substitute for reasoning a drug that would make one forget all empty beliefs and retain only true ones, assuming that such a drug existed.[48] As

[46] For discussion of these features, see, pp. 91–118 *passim*.

[47] A different view is proposed by Nussbaum (1994: 129–30).

[48] Nussbaum (1994: 128) advances this hypothesis. In my view, however, Epicurus says that if we had never been bothered by fears concerning things in the heavens and death, as well as by our ignorance of the limits of emotion and desire, we would not stand in need of the science of nature (*φυσιολογία*: *KD* XI), but these claims are counterfactual. In truth, we are very disturbed by the fear of the gods and of death, and by worries concerning the evil and the good, pain and pleasure. And we can only be cured by making use of our reason (*λογισμός*) throughout our life (*KD* XVI). Even if

Philodemus remarks, we successfully accomplish our moral choices only when we measure them by the ends laid down by nature (*De elect.* XI. 17–20): namely, when we perform correctly the hedonic calculus. And since our ability to do so is the very stamp of human rationality, no drug can ever take its place.[49]

The above considerations might suggest that the Epicurean philosophers deviate from the medical model when it suits their purposes. Whether or not this is true, Philodemus remains closely bound to that model in so far as he proposes a plurality of therapeutic strategies, many of which he borrows from other schools.[50] He appears to accept that for the philosopher, as for the doctor, the choice of therapy is determined by the symptoms of the disease. Let us then look at some aspects of Philodemus' method of diagnosis and treatment. Like the doctor of the body, the Epicurean physician of the soul treats psychic diseases—for example, anger (*De ir.* II. 6–15)—on the basis of symptoms which are evident to everybody.[51] He uses conjectural or stochastic reasoning (*καταστο[χάσεται*]: II. 7) in order to make the patient recognize the nature and causes of his anger, the falsehood of the beliefs underlying the emotion, and the desirability of having it cured (VII. 5 ff.). He treats the patient by reminding him of the consequences of anger, both those that one has suffered in the past and those that are likely to occur in the future.[52] Every irascible person knows

φυσιολογία were merely a means to tranquillity, it would be a very special one. Precisely because we are rational beings, we find it impossible to enjoy unadulterated pleasures without knowing the nature of the universe (*KD* XII), and, like Epicurus, we reach serenity in our lives 'most of all by engaging constantly in the science of nature' (*ad Herod.* 37).

[49] It is significant that Philodemus tends to attribute to parrhesiastic arguments both instrumental and intrinsic value. When they are employed by the sage, they both serve as means for admonishing and correcting his students' characters and reflect aspects of the sage's own personality. Not only do they represent what the sage says and does as a teacher, but they are also part of the ideal person that he is: i.e., wise, peaceful, and truly happy.

[50] See next chapter, pp. 75–80 and *passim*.

[51] One might object that the method of the Epicurean doctor is unlike that of the empiricist physician in so far as the former speculates about something non-evident—i.e., the disposition of the patient—whereas the latter refuses to speculate about what is in principle non-evident. However, the Epicureans do not treat one's disposition as an unobservable theoretical entity, and, moreover, Philodemus does not draw inferences based on evident symptoms about what is going on in the atomic structure of the soul (which *is* an invisible structure).

[52] Sc. the philosopher should 'number one by one everything [that is hurting them], both the very unpleasant consequences [for the community] and also, sometimes, the evils that harmed them [personally]' (VII. 22–6). For instance, enraged people suffer in body and mind (X. 27–30), behave recklessly (X. 19–24, XIII. 13–17), and hurt or destroy themselves (XXVI. 25–34). In their pursuit of revenge, they consume their life and property (XXIII. 26–35) and are punished by the law

from experience that these are the likely results of his affliction, and that they are painful. And although they are not true or false for oneself until they materialize,[53] the fact that they have regularly been observed in the past carries a lot of weight: one anticipates them[54] and forms the wish to avoid them.[55]

Like other psychic maladies,[56] anger should be treated *ad hoc*, as manifested in an individual patient. Philodemus insists against Timasagoras, a rival (*De ir.* VI. 10–12, 27–9),[57] that treatment should always be corrective rather than preventive. For the Epicurean physician cannot predict in advance the exact nature of one's passion or the ways in which one will respond to a given remedy (VII. 2–4). In addition to personal experience of anger and other maladies, instructors rely on second-hand reports of a student's error (*De lib. dic.* 50. 3–12)[58] as well as on records of therapeutic experience (*De lib. dic.* Vb. 8–9). Typically, they judge from personal and collective experience how to treat individual occurrences of a passion in the past or in the future. Occasional failures in diagnosis or treatment are usually caused by empirical factors and are explained on empirical grounds.[59]

Another important element of Epicurean methodology is the kinds of definition used by Epicurean authors.[60] In particular, the definitions used by Torquatus and Philodemus in ethics show a strong commitment to

(XII. 33–40). They make enemies stronger than themselves (XII. 22–5) and betray their political allies (XXV. 15–21). They abuse their social relationships (XVII. 8–9, XXVI. 1–2, XXIV. 1–4, XXIII. 35–8) and live without friends.

[53] Compare Epicurus' concept of what is expected to occur (τὸ προσμενόμενον) in the context of scientific enquiry (*ad Herod.* 38).

[54] Anticipation may involve visualizing these evils, 'setting-them-before-the-eyes'. Contemplating them induces one to feel horror (*De ir.* II. 14–18), and to become strongly motivated to seek remedy. Cf. pp. 204–6, 208–9.

[55] In addition to mentioning the consequences of anger, the philosopher should convince his patients that avoiding these evils is completely within their power (III. 15–17).

[56] Philodemus mentions erotic love (*De ir.* VII. 18–20), but the claims made about anger apply, with the necessary ramifications, to every undesirable passion and vice.

[57] Regarding Timasagoras, see Longo Auricchio and Tepedino Guerra 1982, and also Indelli 1988: 150. One of his criticisms of Philodemus is that the *ad hoc* corrective application of therapy is ineffective, because enraged persons 'have become unable to reason about their passions' (*De ir.* VII. 7–9). I discuss Timasagoras' criticisms of Philodemus and Philodemus' answer to these criticisms at pp. 204–9.

[58] Epicurean students are encouraged to tell on their friends so long as they act out of disinterested motives. The teacher should interpret one's denunciation in that light, and should be able to distinguish the genuine desire to benefit one's friend from the vicious urge to bad-mouth one's fellow students. Cf. p. 14.

[59] For further discussion of this topic, see Tsouna 2007.

[60] As indicated (n. 2), they are not proper definitions, but rather outlines which function as definitions. I elaborate this point immediately below.

empirical principles and reflect the methodological and logical views of earlier Epicureans, notably Epicurus and Zeno of Sidon. There is very little about definition in Epicurus' extant writings, but later sources attribute to him the theses that words (ὀνόματα) are clearer than definitions (ὅροι: *Anonymus in Theaet.* col. 22. 42–23. 8) and that definitions are redundant and even harmful, since they destroy the clarity peculiar to each term (Erotian, *gloss. Hippocr. praef.* p. 34, 10 Klein).[61] However, his requirement that the subject of every investigation must be clear from the very beginning, and indeed, that we must have acquired primary concepts which can be seen and which do not need demonstration (*ad Herod.* 37–8), might look like a concession to those who insist that definitions are necessary if one is to conduct clear, coherent enquiries. On the other hand, his assertion that 'one must engage in the study of nature not according to empty axioms (ἀξιώματα) and conventional stipulations (νομοθεσίας) but as the phenomena request' (*ad Pyth.* 86) has plausibly been considered a wholesale rejection of definitions and, generally, of a priori assumptions in natural science.[62] Zeno too steers clear of a priori elements in semantic and logical enquiry, but believes that empirical generalizations are possible on the basis of common characteristics of things or generic classes.

In his exposition of Epicurean ethics, Torquatus preserves the concerns both to secure clarity and order in his exposition and to do away with definitions (*De fin.* I. 22). He prefaces his account as follows: 'I shall start in the manner approved by the very author of the doctrine: I shall determine what and of what sort is the object of our enquiry, not because I think that you do not know it, but so that my speech may proceed in a rational and methodical way. We are enquiring, then, what is the final and ultimate good which, in the opinion of all philosophers, is such that everything must be referred to it, whereas it itself is not referred to anything else. This Epicurus finds in pleasure' (I. 29). Here, Torquatus makes a gesture towards giving a definition, but, in fact, he simply demarcates what is empirically known to be a commonly shared conception of the moral end. Moreover, he denies that his formula will capture or reveal anything,[63] and at the same time stresses its procedural usefulness. Cicero is only partly correct,

[61] See Asmis 1984: 39 n. 15. [62] See ibid. 40 ff.

[63] Asmis (ibid. 39–47) draws informative comparisons between Epicurean and Platonic definitions. Cicero claims that although Epicurus approved the rule set by Plato (*Phdr.* 237b), that the parties to each debate should agree what their subject is, nonetheless he failed to realize the implications of that

then, when he remarks that Torquatus does not altogether disapprove of definition and practises it when it suits his purposes (II. 5). For a formula that points to what we already know (I. 29, II. 6) and understand without further assistance (II. 6) does not really define anything. At most, it outlines or explains the object of investigation by reminding us of its prominent characteristics.[64] Torquatus' explanation of the supreme good is such an outline. And his discourse in the first book of *De finibus* has the clarity and systematicity that he promises in his preface.

Likewise, Philodemus' definitions contain no theoretical elements and remind us, rather than reveal, what the thing under examination is. They clarify the primary concepts involved in the investigation and set the agenda for the analyses to follow. They therefore remain faithful to the spirit of earlier positions much in the same manner as Torquatus' definitions do. However, they have a new area of application: namely, practical ethics and, specifically, flaws of character. As to their contents, they are drawn from the stock of characterology, and are best understood as empirically based descriptions of human types. One example is the outline of the arrogant person. 'A man is called ([λέγ]εται) arrogant who ... appears scornful, insults everybody in those cases where he maintains his arrogance even in his actions, and is generally the sort of person that this characterization reveals both with regard to all those for whom he reserves his arrogance and through his actions, and moreover is the kind of person who is generally hubristic' (VI. 27–34). Variations notwithstanding, there are good empirical grounds for conceding that arrogant men are marked by a sense of superiority and contempt for others. Philodemus' summary description does not tell us anything new. But it does bring to the fore the primary concept of the examination as a point of common agreement (cf. [λέγ]εται, VI. 27) between the author and his audience. Another example concerns flattery. Piecing together the evidence, it seems that Philodemus describes the flatterer (κόλαξ) as 'the man who speaks in order to please' (PHerc. 1457, I. 5–6) and who, in that manner, 'procures for himself what is necessary for life' (PHerc. 222, III. 4–6).

rule (*De fin.* II. 4). In Cicero's view, the process of definition is, precisely, 'to disclose latent meanings and to reveal what a particular thing is' (II. 5).

[64] Asmis (1984: 42) suggests that Epicurean definitions are intended as summary descriptions of the initial concept, and that they are technically known as ὑπογραφαί or ὑποτυπώσεις. She discusses evidence from Galen and Sextus on p. 43 n. 26.

Additional characteristics of the vice are that the flatterer exercises his influence principally through speech (ὁμιλία: PHerc. 1089, VII. 5–6); causes pleasure to his victim through implausible and exaggerated praise (PHerc. 1457, fr. 14. 2 ff.); acts regularly in that manner; and aims to bring his victims into the right frame of mind so as to make them cater to his own needs (χρείας: PHerc. 222, III. 2). The poor condition of the papyri does not allow us to speculate about the orderliness of Philodemus' treatment of this vice. However, the remains of his explanation of what a flatterer is achieves, for the most part, the goals of Epicurean definition articulated by Torquatus. So far as we can judge from the surviving texts, the concept of flattery is made clear before the ethical enquiry begins. And the characteristics of the vice stated in Philodemus' outline orient the analysis towards the phenomena and away from theoretical constructs.

III

Assuming that initial or first concepts[65] are identical with preconceptions (προλήψεις; translit. *prolēpseis*), we may take Epicurus' methodological demand, that before we investigate a problem we must grasp what is correlated to the words used to state the problem (*ad Herod.* 37–8), as a demand to have *prolēpseis*, empirically acquired concepts formed from repeated clear views of the same kind of thing[66] and stored or latent in the mind before we begin our enquiry (cf. the prefix προ-). Epicurus' related statement, that we must be able to refer to the first concepts in order to be able to judge (*ad Herod.* 37), points to the role of *prolēpseis* as yardsticks of

[65] There is disagreement about what 'first' means here. Different views are proposed, e.g., by Bailey (1928: 268 ff.), Long (1971: 124–5), and Asmis (1984: 31–4), who also offers a brief bibliographical survey of three leading interpretations of 'first concept': conceptually first, i.e., the primary or basic meaning of a word; pragmatically first, i.e., the obvious common meaning of it; and historically first, i.e., the first meaning associated with a word in the history of man. These interpretations overlap to some extent, but I am inclined to favour the variant defended by Long (1971): viz., that the first thing assigned to each name is the concept first associated with the word in a person's experience. As Long remarks, only that first concept is canonical, because only that concept is causally linked to the sense-impressions from which it derives. The point is relevant to my interpretation of Philodemus, *De oec.* XX. 11–32; see below, pp. 70–3.

[66] The term, which was probably coined by Epicurus (cf. Cicero, *De nat. deor.* I. 44), covers concepts of strictly sensory origin and others such as the *prolēpseis* of the gods.

truth.[67] Their criterial power depends on the fact that 'they can be seen and do not require demonstration' (*ad Herod.* 38): they are evident and clear (ἐναργεῖς: D.L. X. 33), they are naturally rooted in perception and therefore are considered the best starting points for doing philosophy. Among the many applications of *prolēpseis*, one that is particularly important for my purposes is their use in order to clarify ambiguities and correct the errors deriving from them (Epicurus, *De nat.* XXVIII, fr. 4, col. III. 6–12).[68] Whatever the exact origin of such errors, Epicurus probably thinks that the polysemantic nature of language[69] leads us to associate the wrong *prolēpsis* with an ambiguous term. However, he is conservative regarding changes in customary linguistic usage (cf. *De nat.* XXVIII, fr. 1, col. IV. 1–10), and recommends that we maintain the obvious sense of words and leave unchanged names which refer to things evident to the senses. *Prolēpsis* is crucial to correct naming, because it guides us in keeping words correlated with the things that they are intended to designate. But speaking correctly is dependent upon thinking correctly about the facts of nature as well as of morality.

There is very little evidence concerning developments of the concept of *prolēpsis* after the time of Epicurus. However, in determining one of the meanings of the words 'in so far as', 'according as' (καθὸ καὶ παρό: *De sign.* XXXIII. 33–4), Demetrius associates preconceptions with defining properties (although in interpreting this we must allow for the fact that the canonical doctrine rejects definitions as such), whereas he does not mention preconceptions in connection with any of the other three meanings of these words.[70] He also recommends that in conducting a refutation 'we should observe (βλέπειν) the properties of the predicated terms (τὰς ἰδιότητας τῶν ἐπικατηγοριῶν), starting from the difference in the doctrines, since the doctrines are of all kinds' (PHerc. 1012, LXIII. 5–9). And he warns

[67] Striker (1974), shows just how the criterial role of προλήψεις is distinct from that of αἰσθήσεις and πάθη.

[68] See Sedley 1973.

[69] Cf. πολυτρόπους ἐθισμοὺς τῶν λέξεων: *De nat.*, fr. 4, col. III. 11–12. Long (1971: 123) suggests that by that expression Epicurus meant both using the same word in more than one sense and using general terms with multiple reference.

[70] Cf. his point that the second meaning of the words 'in so far as', 'according as', is that 'this is the particular definition (ἴδιος λόγος) of that and this is the preconception, as when we say that body as body has bulk and resistance, and man as man is a rational animal' (*De sign.* XXXIV. 5–11). The first of the four meanings corresponds to essential but non-defining properties: men as men have flesh and are subject to disease and old age (XXXIII. 35–XXXIV. 5). See De Lacy and De Lacy 1978: 162.

against the practice of people (who do a bad job of formulating refutations, because they believe that) refutations ought to be conducted by reference to the preconceptions of the refuted terms but (do not need to have) a basis in the terms themselves (paraphrase of LXIII. 1–3). The relevant text is fragmentary, but on my provisional reading, Demetrius contends that in refutation, as in exegesis,[71] one should be sensitive to varying context: i.e., διδασκαλίαι, the individual teachings in which a given term occurs. Moreover, he brings out the methodological importance of both the proleptic meaning and of other meanings as they occur in particular teachings or doctrines. I wonder whether Demetrius and Zeno extended the concept of *prolēpsis* beyond single words—which is all that Epicurus seems to have envisaged. As we shall see below, Philodemus probably does.

Both Philodemus and Torquatus appear aware of the complex role of *prolēpsis* in settling ethical disputes. As mentioned, Torquatus attests that some members of the Epicurean school defend the goodness of pleasure by appealing to 'a notion naturally implanted in our minds' (*De fin.* I. 31). Moreover, he defends Epicurus' conception of pleasure, which Cicero takes to be ambiguous, on proleptic grounds. He contends that nothing is more pleasant than freedom from pain, and infers that *indolentia* is the same thing as *voluptas* (II. 11). And although he does not use technical terminology, there is little doubt that he relies on the *prolēpsis* of pleasure in order to reiterate without argument that there is no intermediate state between pleasure and pain, but that 'all who are without pain are feeling pleasure and, what is more, the highest form of pleasure' (II. 16).[72] Consistently with Torquatus, and in a way which encompasses both Epicurus' rule of enquiry and Demetrius' methodological advice, Philodemus uses the concept of *prolēpsis* in the treatise *On Property Management* to solve a concrete problem in practical ethics, the problem of judging what the good administrator is like.

We must not [absurdly] violate this [sc. the meaning of the expression 'the good money-maker'] through the ordinary use of language, just as sophists do, especially as we would be showing nothing about the sage's acquisition and use of wealth.

[71] Cf. Demetrius' exegesis of Epicurus' contention that love for one's children does not occur φύσει (PHerc. 1012, LXVI. 5 ff., LXVII. 1–LXVIII. 9).

[72] The fact that Torquatus simply repeats his initial thesis is particularly striking, because it constitutes his response to Cicero's accusation that the Epicurean thesis 'violates the senses and uproots from our minds the meaning of words ingrained there'; i.e., it violates both αἴσθησις and πρόληψις (*De fin.* II. 16).

Rather we must refer to the preconception (πρόληψις) which exists about the good money-maker (ἀγαθὸς χρηματιστής), ask in whom that preconception is (found), i.e., in what manner he makes money, and ascribe the predicate 'good money-maker' to whoever it may be in whom those features are attested. Just for this reason, if we want to claim that, in preconception (ἐν προλήψει), the good money-maker is the one who acquires and takes care of wealth in accordance with the useful, then we must proclaim above all the sage as such a man. But if, on the other hand, in preconception (ἐν προλήψει) we apply the quality of the good money-maker rather to the man who obtains for himself many possessions with ability and expertise, and also not in a dishonourable way but lawfully, however much it may be true that [in this mode of acquisition] he encounters [more sufferings] than pleasures, then we must affirm that it is people other than the sage who belong to that category.

(*De oec.* XX. 1–32)[73]

At the outset, it is worth noting that the text does not make entirely clear what *prolēpsis* is introduced here as a criterion for settling an ethical dispute. It could be a simple one—either the *prolēpsis* of good, which would then be applied to the money-maker, or the *prolēpsis* of the money-maker, which would reveal also what a good money-maker is. Alternatively, it could be the complex *prolēpsis* of the good money-maker. On balance, the last option seems the most straightforward reading and, moreover, is supported by a parallel in Philodemus. In the fifth book of *On Poems*, Philodemus appeals to the preconception (cf. προειλήφαμεν) of the goodness (ἀρετή) of a poem in order to refute the view that what we mean by the goodness of a poem is moral goodness (*De poem.* V, XXX. 32–6 Jensen).[74] Assuming

[73] Philodemus' general aim is to examine whether the philosopher may engage in financial activities concerning the management of his estate (οἰκονομία, translit. *oikonomia*), and also to what extent and in what manner he may do so. Central to his task is the contrast between a traditional conception of *oikonomia* marked by the aggressive and single-minded pursuit of wealth (which, however, must come through legitimate means and from socially acceptable sources) and an Epicurean *oikonomia* based on ethics, and in particular on the hedonistic calculus. The passage cited above comes fairly late in the argument and anticipates an objection that might run as follows. Even conceding that the sage is superior to the traditional property manager (οἰκονόμος, translit. *oikonomos*) in respect of pleasure, he must be inferior regarding administrative efficiency and especially money-making. For the traditional *oikonomos* regulates the activities of acquisition, preservation, and use of wealth solely in accordance with quantitative criteria (sc. 'the more and the less'), whereas the sage acts chiefly according to ethical considerations and downplays the pursuit of economic goals. To settle the matter, Philodemus uses the relevant *prolēpsis* as a standard against which the rival view is to be tested.

[74] Mancini Concolino (1976: 62) suggests that Colotes too speaks about the *prolēpsis* of a good poet and maintains that the phrase 'good poet' should be used according to what is evident (see also De Lacy and De Lacy 1978: 190, 200). However, Mancini Concolino's view is not well supported, and may be

that this reading is the correct one, we should now look at the argument in the passage cited above.

The opening sentence puts us on our guard. The expression 'the good money-maker' is ambiguous.[75] As the conditionals indicate, Philodemus acknowledges that reasonable people can disagree about the content of the relevant preconception.[76] Following Demetrius' advice, Philodemus takes into account the different doctrines in which the expression may occur,[77] and sets out the properties attached to the good money-maker in each context. So he sketches two different ways of developing the preconception. According to the former, the good money-maker is a money-maker who is a good person: namely, someone who acts with a view to what is useful for pleasure; hence, ideally, he is the sage. According to the latter, the good money-maker is a person who is good at money-making: namely, an expert who lawfully procures as many riches as possible.

At this point, we are invited to consider which one of these two options captures the *prolēpsis*, but the issue is left open only in form.[78] For in substance Philodemus guides us to endorse the first option: the good money-maker ideally is the sage. He has argued beforehand that the sage cannot, at any rate, be considered a bad manager.[79] Now, he relies on the clarity of the *prolēpsis*[80] itself in order to advance a stronger claim. His assumption is, I submit, that once we escape the snares of language and consult our *prolēpsis*, it will become obvious to us that the sage is the best

false. If so, it would seem that talk of having a preconception of a good X belongs to Philodemus' own generation, but is so far unattested for early Epicureans.

[75] Compare the simpler cases in which the ordinary use of a term coincides with its proper meaning: e.g., earlier on in the treatise, Philodemus criticizes Xenophon's Socrates for calling poor those who are obviously rich and, conversely, rich those who have very little money, and he contends that Socrates speaks in that manner as a matter of opinion ([δ]οξαστικῶς), not preconception according to ordinary language (προληπτικῶς κατὰ συνήθειαν: V. 1–4).

[76] Philodemus must be aware, e.g., of the different ways in which Epicureans and Stoics unpack the *prolēpsis* of God: Epicurus relies on it to reject the idea of divine providence, whereas Chrysippus uses it to refute Epicurus' rejection of divine providence.

[77] i.e., the context of Epicurean teachings (cf. διδασκαλίαι: Dem. Lac. 1012, LXIII. 6–7) as opposed to Peripatetic or Academic doctrines.

[78] Asmis (1984: 44) advances a different view.

[79] In outline, the argument is this. The philosopher cannot reasonably be called a bad manager in the ordinary sense of the term. For while he does not amass (XIX. 4–5) or watch over great wealth (XVIII. 37–9) because of the intense worry and effort that these activities require (XIX. 10 ff.), nonetheless he is perfectly able to administer and preserve an estate of reasonable size (XVI. 18–39). I discuss Philodemus' position in detail on pp. 191–4.

[80] Ambiguity affects only the term 'good money-maker', not the *prolēpsis* or the kind of thing that corresponds to it.

money-maker. He even gives a reason why people often think otherwise. 'We envy those who acquire many goods and quickly because we believe that these men have the (kind of) money-making which is advantageous for earning a living, by our failure to observe (ὁρᾶν) how those whom (true) advantage [follows] [control] their money' (XX. 38–45). Compare Torquatus' own strategy: Philodemus points to the evident character of the preconception, but supplies argument as well.[81]

Like Epicurus, Philodemus urges us to pay attention to *prolēpsis* without proposing thereby that we change our normal ways of speaking or that we deny the realities underlying them. Not only does he concede that there are assiduous money-makers; he also recognizes that there is an art, a τέχνη (translit. *technē*) of property management, and that there exist experts (τεχνῖται) in that field (XVII. 2–40).[82] What the *prolēpsis* reveals is, simply, that the person who lives the philosophical life cannot be one of them.

[81] As mentioned, Torquatus sides with those Epicureans who adopt this attitude (*De fin.* I. 31). However, he relies mainly on preconception in order to refute Cicero's criticisms concerning the dual nature of pleasure (II. 17).

[82] Philodemus' distinction between the economic expert and the philosopher draws a clear line at which the philosopher's involvement with property management ought to stop: cf. XVII. 2–40, and also pp. 192–4. On the Epicurean concept of *technē* and the distinctions pertaining to it, see Blank 1995.

4

Therapeutic Tactics

As I mentioned, the theoretical analysis of vices and emotions has a practical goal: namely, their detection and removal. So, I should like to offer a rapid survey of Philodemus' methods of treatment and determine the place that they occupy in the therapeutics of the Hellenistic era. There are at least two ways of doing such a survey. I shall call them vertical and horizontal. A vertical treatment could be a matter of going through the treatises one by one and studying the methods employed in each treatise concerning a single trait or a cluster of related traits. What I call horizontal approaches are broader and more conceptual. They cut across long time periods, geographical areas, schools, and objects of treatment. Both ancient and modern scholars have proposed such classifications of therapeutic methods, which vary according to the criteria that they have applied but also overlap significantly with each other. They are flexible regarding what counts as a single method or exercise, whether it is simple or complex, what are its connections to other similar exercises, and so on.

On the ancient side, little survives from writings that codified therapeutic techniques and gave instructions concerning their application.[1] However, two partly overlapping and mutually complementary lists, which belong to the Stoico-Platonic tradition and are preserved by Philo of Alexandria, give us some idea of the variety of therapeutic exercises available. The first list consists of 'all the elements of training (ἄσκησις) [that] are food fit for eating: namely enquiry, investigation, reading, listening, attention, self-mastery, and indifference to indifferents' (Philo, *Who is the Heir of Divine Things*, 252–3). The second list refers to 'the mind in training' (ἀσκητὴς νοῦς) and 'the parts of its training' (μέρη τῆς ἀσκήσεως): that is, 'readings,

[1] One such treatise is Musonius Rufus' compendium *On Exercise* and D.L. VII. 166–7. According to Hadot (1995: 83–4), the techniques cited in compendia of this sort were widely known, since they were parts of daily life and subjects of oral instruction.

meditations, therapeutic acts, remembrances of good things, self-mastery, and the successful accomplishment of duties' (*Allegorical Interpretations*, III. 18).[2] On the modern side, the horizontal categorizations proposed by several authors provide an important frame to which I shall refer in order to outline the kinds of techniques that Philodemus uses[3] and the trait that each of them aims to eradicate.

I

First, I shall make some general claims. Philodemus' exercises sometimes depend on Epicurean doctrine, but other times are not attached to it: they derive from other schools, notably the Stoics and the Peripatetics,[4] or are consistent with their teachings. Many exercises are of this last sort. For Philodemus realizes, as do his rivals, that psychic diseases require a plurality of methods because they can be hard to cure. Also, he wishes to address people of various intellectual orientations, not just Epicureans.[5] Although treatment can be applied in principle before or after the manifestation of the psychic disease, Philodemus rejects preventive therapy. For he believes that the application of treatment must be *ad hoc*, and that the physician of the soul cannot predict in advance just how each patient will respond to a given remedy (*De ir.* VII. 2–4). Exercises, physical as well as mental, have different degrees of difficulty and draw on different resources of the patient. They are harsher or milder, more or less lengthy, more or less strenuous, and so on. Philodemus' exercises cover a considerable part of that scale. Also, they vary, depending on their nature and the psychic powers that they are intended to address. Behavioural and practical exercises

[2] Hadot (1995) discusses the contents of both lists, which are also mentioned by Sorabji (2000).

[3] My main point of reference is the account of Pierre Hadot (1995) and, more recently, that of Richard Sorabji (2000). Sorabji engages with philosophical literature and also offers the most comprehensive account of exercises to date. It will be obvious that my own exposition is greatly indebted to his. An interesting outcome of the procedure that I follow is that most types of exercises used by the Hellenistic schools are also found in Philodemus.

[4] e.g., he takes the description of the enraged man from Stoic sources, and he cites the methods of Aristo of Ceos in order to combat arrogance.

[5] Likewise, Chrysippus often leaves aside the doctrine of indifferents, and Seneca uses some of the same remedies that Philodemus uses for anger; e.g., he too puts-before-the-eyes the appearance and countenance of the enraged man (*De ir.* III. 4. 1–5, 21. 1), contrasts rage with greatness (III. 6. 1–6), relates anger to envy and greed (III. 31. 1 ff.), and recommends sober reflection on the reasons for our anger (III. 43. 1–5).

differ from emotional and intellectual ones. Non-cognitive techniques (such as Posidonius' and Galen's dietary recommendations) are different in kind from cognitive ones, and of cognitive strategies some are strictly intellectualist and focused on judgements, while others engage the mind in a broader sense. Shifts of attention (which may or may not be accompanied by changes of belief), pictorial thinking, imaginings, etc., belong to that last kind. I suggest that virtually all of Philodemus' methods of therapy are cognitive in a broad sense, and many among them are judgemental. So, in this respect at least, I am inclined to consider Philodemus closer to Chrysippus than to Posidonius, Panaetius,[6] or Galen. Lastly, whatever term we choose to designate such strategies,[7] we should insist that for Philodemus as for every other Hellenistic philosopher they are intended to engage one's whole being, and therefore they involve many factors: intellectual as well as moral, self-reflective as well as instinctual, dispositional and also behavioural, drawing on reason and sensibility, imagination and sensitivity.

Classifications of ancient exercises by modern authors are often based on Philo's lists and arranged around less or more concrete objectives or themes. Let me begin with a broad thematic classification into four groups:

[6] It is not clear to what extent Panaetius modifies Chrysippus' intellectualism. There is some evidence that he does (Cicero, *De off.* I. 101, II. 8). If this is right, he might have cast a friendly eye on the non-cognitive strategies of Posidonius.

[7] Different scholars refer to therapeutic strategies using different terms. The most frequently used include therapeutic 'techniques' or 'strategies' or 'exercises' (words which I use interchangeably). We also encounter 'moral' or 'ethical exercises', 'intellectual' or 'thought exercises', and also 'spiritual exercises'. This last expression was proposed by Pierre Hadot, who defends it as follows. '"Spiritual exercises". The expression is a bit disconcerting for the contemporary reader. In the first place, it is no longer fashionable these days to use the word spiritual. It is nevertheless necessary to use this term, I believe, because none of the other adjectives we could use ... covers all the aspects of the reality we want to describe. Since, in these exercises, it is thought which, as it were, takes itself as its own subject-matter, and seeks to modify itself, it would be possible for us to speak in terms of "thought exercises". Yet the word "thought" does not indicate clearly enough that imagination and sensibility play a very important role in these exercises. For the same reason, we cannot be satisfied with "intellectual exercises", although such intellectual factors as definition, division, ratiocination, reading, investigation, and rhetorical amplification play a large role in them. "Ethical exercises" is a rather tempting expression, since, as we shall see, the exercises in question contribute in a powerful way to the therapeutics of the passions, and have to do with the conduct of life. Yet, here again, this would be too limited a view of things ... These exercises in fact correspond to a transformation of our vision of the world, and to a metamorphosis of our personality. The word "spiritual" is quite apt to make us understand that these exercises are the result, not merely of thought, but of the individual's entire psychism' (Hadot 1995: 81–2). Although this passage contains much that I agree with, nonetheless I do not use 'spiritual exercises', because I fear that its associations with early Christian thought might cause some confusion.

namely, learning how to read, how to discuss, how to live, and how to die.[8] Learning to read comprises reading (ἀνάγνωσις) as well as meditation (μελέτη),[9] concerns both the means and the ends of one's intellectual nourishment, and has ultimately a practical purpose: one's self-realization and moral improvement, living according to nature or pleasure, and, for many authors, the rediscovery of one's true self.[10] In Epicureanism, learning to read concerns, among other things, the distinction between natural and unnatural, necessary and not necessary desires,[11] and, more generally, the theoretical aspects of the system.[12] Philodemus emphasizes the importance of understanding and memorizing the cardinal tenets of Epicureanism (*De elect.* XI. 7–20) and debates the issue of precisely how it brings one peace of mind (XI. 7 ff.). Also, he recommends that ungrateful students should be disciplined by being asked to read aloud extracts from canonical writings and compose speeches against ingratitude. They will get rid of their affliction 'if ever they read aloud to some people well-arranged treatises (συντάξεις)[13] or ask by means of writing to be stripped of their hostile nature (φύσις ἐχθρά) in more respects (than they have already been)': (*De grat.* XIV. 14–18).

At first glance, one might say that learning how to engage in dialogue is not an Epicurean objective, since the school puts so much emphasis on authority and trust.[14] Philodemus' account of frank speech, *parrhēsia*, indicates otherwise. Philodemus does not clarify the relationship between the educational method of *parrhēsia* and various forms of strong language with or without another person present. Specifically, he does not explain

[8] Hadot 1995: 81–125. His analysis of these four categories of exercises concerns not only the Hellenistic philosophers, but also Plato.

[9] Cf. the lists of Philo of Alexandria, pp. 74–5 above.

[10] Hadot argues that the (re)discovery of one's authentic self consists primarily in a profound transformation of one's attitudes to oneself and one's acquisition of a cosmic, universal perspective (Hadot 1995: 206–13). Hence, he rejects the aestheticism of Michel Foucault, and in particular his idea that Greek and Roman therapeutics are, ultimately, an ethics of the pleasure that one takes in oneself (cf. Foucault 1984: 83 ff.). A powerful analysis of Foucault's position is found in Nehamas 1998.

[11] See Hadot 1995: 103.

[12] On the other hand, Hadot contends that, in Stoicism, learning to read includes the Stoic technique of distinguishing what is from what is not up to us and, of course, the physics and logic of the doctrine.

[13] The context yields no information regarding the exact form and content of these writings. However, it seems fairly certain that they are composed in parrhesiastic mode, and, furthermore, that they include the arguments in defence of gratitude.

[14] Cf. pp. 91–118 *passim*.

how *parrhēsia* exercised live between members of the school is related to articulate self-scrutiny and self-correction or to the stark language that Philodemus uses in some of his treatises in order to impress a point upon his audience. We may view *parrhēsia* as a generic method of moral correction, of which *parrhēsia* in a narrow technical sense (viz., the method used in the personal interchange between members of Epicurean schools) is a species. The candid submission to self-examination and self-correction (found, e.g., in some therapies for arrogance), the uninhibited presentation of truths concerning the vices and the passions (especially anger and the fear of death), and, generally, strong language used for therapeutic purposes can also be considered species of *parrhēsia* taken generically. Although Philodemus does not identify these as instances of *parrhēsia*, he acknowledges that *parrhēsia* is not practised only in the context of Epicurean schools.[15] Moreover, I think he realizes that, if mankind is ever to be saved, some form of therapy must be available to broader audiences at all times. For his ethical treatises lay out strategies for the treatment of specific maladies, and also illustrate precisely how these strategies are supposed to work. They are books as well as drugs, registers of therapeutic wisdom as well as exemplifications of treatment carrying a therapeutic value of their own.[16] It would seem reasonable to infer that they contain forms of *parrhēsia* that the readers are invited to apply to themselves. At any rate, regarding the educational method of *parrhēsia*, we recall that both Philodemus and Zeno of Sidon delimit it by reference to the relationship between a teacher and a student who has been at fault. In the context of Epicurean education, then, *parrhēsia* consists primarily in the frank admonition and correction of a particular error, and is considered a kind of medicine intended to effect a cure.[17] I shall discuss that method in detail in the next chapter.

Here, I should like to reiterate a point that I made earlier in connection with the medical metaphor: namely, that the *parrhēsia* in question involves elements of equality, reciprocity, and even dialogue.[18] Not only does the process begin at the student's own initiative (*De lib. dic.* 49. 2–5) and

[15] e.g., it seems unreasonable to assume that *parrhēsia* practised towards powerful rulers, and often women and old men as well, takes place within Epicurean communities (cf. *De lib. dic.* XXIIa. 1 ff.).

[16] Compare the function of the monumental stone inscription composed by Diogenes of Oenoanda (an Epicurean philosopher of the second century AD) and raised next to the public road 'to put out in public the drugs bringing salvation' (fr. 3, V. 14–VI. 2).

[17] Cf. the discussion of the medical analogy, pp. 60–5.

[18] Cf. pp. 62–4.

is conducted with the student's active participation in his own healing.[19] But also, it occasionally involves the switching of roles between teachers and students, and it obtains between peers (students, teachers, or even sages).[20] Although such parrhesiastic exchanges do not have the structure of dialogue, nonetheless, in some respects, they come surprisingly close to the paradigm of engaging in dialogue: namely, Plato's Socrates.[21] For *parrhēsia* in such cases can be either a communal or a personal exercise, or both. It is a mental and psychological itinerary that presupposes, crucially, self-examination and self-criticism. When conducted with others, it exhibits not just reasoning but also other means of persuasion and psychagogy. And it aims to cause a profound transformation of one's way of thinking about important issues. Besides, in his short work *On Conversation*, Philodemus recommends exercises that cultivate appropriate ways of speaking (ὁμιλία, συζήτησις) as opposed to inappropriate ones (κακομιλία). These include theoretical talk about nature (θεωρία) and, generally, about the activities 'of sight and intellect' (*De conv.* IV. 8–9). On occasion, silence (σιωπή) must be practised as well, for a variety of reasons.[22]

I have few remarks to make about learning to live and learning to die, for we shall encounter these categories again under different labels. The former prescribes exercises aiming at the therapy of the passions. Suffice it to say that they have both intellectual[23] and practical[24] dimensions,[25] engage reason as well as imagination and affectivity, and, in Epicureanism at least, involve preparing oneself for every turn of fortune. Learning to die is the supreme moral exercise for all Hellenistic authors. Philodemus' strategies aim to make us understand the nature of the phenomenon and acquire a 'training for death'. In outline, this consists in changing one's point of view and ceasing to perceive death as an evil. Like the Stoics and the leaders of his own school, Philodemus believes that a radical conversion of this sort can

[19] In fact, Philodemus makes clear that the teacher bears little or no responsibility for failing to cure morally corrupt people, much as the doctor cannot be blamed for failing to heal an incurable disease (*De lib. dic.* 69. 1–8).

[20] Thus, the members of Epicurean schools take turns in admonishing and correcting each other. Philodemus proposes therapies for arrogance and anger which have precisely that form.

[21] Cf. Hadot 1995: 89–93. [22] See pp. 122–3.

[23] Cf. exercises of reading, studying, listening, etc.

[24] Self-control, indifference to indifferents, the performance of duties, and the creation of virtuous habits belong to the Platonic and Stoic traditions of practical exercises.

[25] On both aspects of ἄσκησις, see Goulet-Cazé 1986. Her study concerns Cynicism, but also throws light on the concept of exercise in the Platonic and Stoic traditions in general.

happen only if we view human affairs from an impartial perspective,[26] realize that they are of small importance, and perceive death as being 'nothing to us'. Just how he drives these points home will be clarified below.[27]

II

I shall now use another kind of classification of exercises arranged according to narrower themes.[28] I shall show how Philodemus' methods fit into the relevant categories, and mark out his contributions.

One strategy is to cultivate what I called above an impartial perspective: i.e., a perspective which is objective and natural, as opposed to one that is subjective and human. That technique is valuable because it enables us to detach ourselves from the things that people ordinarily prize, including life itself.[29] Philodemus presents the therapeutic dimension of the physical overview from a new angle: it is part of the last mental flight of the dying Epicurean, who is able to survey in a brief moment both his personal enjoyment of life and the impersonal nature of death, and to make a good end (*De mort.* XXXIX. 15–25). A related exercise (or an implication of 'the view from above') is to observe in a detached mode men's weaknesses and sufferings and to judge the true dimensions of things.[30] While Lucretius

[26] Lucretius ties this kind of contemplation to atomist *φυσιολογία*: the mind soars in free flight in the infinity of the universe, beyond the walls of the world (*DRN* II. 1044–7), making its own the truths that Epicurus' cosmic flights secured for mankind, and possessing 'lofty sanctuaries serene' (II. 7–8) from which to contemplate in perfect bliss the workings of nature. Cf. also *DRN* III. 963–71, where Nature urges us to view our deaths as part of a cycle of life and death.

[27] At this point, I can substantiate my earlier claim that there is considerable overlap between exercises and the different categories to which they belong: e.g., reading and rehearsing the doctrinal theses of each school are parts of learning how to read, how to live, and how to die. Moreover, learning to live and learning to die belong to the same endeavour. Similar links can also be forged between learning to read and to converse, to converse and to live, etc.

[28] In outline, I shall follow the classification of exercises proposed by Sorabji (2000).

[29] Notice that this exercise cuts across the categories of learning to live and learning to die. The same holds for many other exercises cited below. Also, recall that Stoic and Epicurean writings contrast the human and the 'physical' viewpoints in many ways. The former is subjective, habitual, bent on individual interest, engaged. The latter is objective, natural, disinterested, detached. The message is always the same. To acquire 'the view from above', we must separate ourselves from our daily lives, our usual ways of looking at things, and our personal agenda. Importantly, we must remove the passions, since they are tightly connected with the subjective elements of our existence and hence obstruct the tranquil contemplation of nature and/or the divine.

[30] Seneca uses that strategy in connection with another therapeutic technique: viz., reminders of human fallibility and the evils to which men are prone (*De ir.* II. 10. 1–4). 'What, then, keeps the

focuses on the pleasure that we feel when we perceive what evils we are free from (*DRN* II. 1–4, 9–13), Philodemus concentrates on the healing aspects of such perceptions: behold the pains of those who strive for superiority, personal advantage, great wealth, honour, or some kind of immortality, and you will keep away from arrogance, flattery, greed, anger, and vain efforts to cheat death.[31] Moreover, in order to cure envy and malicious joy, he recommends strategies of detachment based on the claim that external goods are of little or no relevance to happiness, and the same holds for evils provided that they are not very many (*De inv.* fr. 18. 1–9).[32]

Reinforcement too is used for purposes of therapy, and is of several kinds. Philodemus develops that technique in connection with the practices of memorizing and rehearsing the cardinal principles of Epicureanism which fortify the students against error (*De elect.* XI. 7–20), and also in connection with frank speech. The teacher should use the same parrhesiastic admonition many times over, even after a pupil appears to have been cured (*De lib. dic.* 63. 4–13, 16. 1–5). And he should bestow praise and encouragement on those who have done well (14. 5–10, IIb. 2–10). Yet another technique is redescribing familiar things in an unfamiliar light.[33] Versions of it consist in moral reassessments which lead us to revise our previous characterizations of apparent goods or apparent evils, and also in reidentifications of 'things underlying words' (cf. Epicurus, *ad Herod.* 37), especially in matters of ethics.[34] A Stoic example is calling anger a 'jolt of the mind'.[35] An Epicurean example mentioned earlier on[36] is to reidentify according to the relevant preconception (*prolēpsis*) the kind of person that

wise man from anger? The great mass of people at fault. He understands both how unjust and how dangerous it is to grow angry at universal vice' (II. 10. 4; Loeb trans. by J. W. Basore, modified).

[31] The Stoics propose comparable exercises. In his consolation to Marcia, Seneca describes to her the blessed state of her son in heaven, where he gets initiated into nature's secrets and the causes of celestial things, and is bid 'to turn his gaze upon the things of earth below, for it is a pleasure for him to look back upon all that has been left behind' (*ad Marc.* XXV. 3; Loeb trans. by J. W. Basore, modified). Also, both Seneca and Marcus Aurelius contrast the emotional safety of those fortified by philosophy with the insecurity and falsehoods plaguing the rest of humanity.

[32] See pp. 124–5.

[33] This technique may include, but is not restricted to, what Sorabji (2000: 222–3) discusses under the heading of 'relabelling'. His account and mine overlap in part, but they focus on different types of cases.

[34] Discussion of this topic in connection with Epicurus' scientific theory is found in Asmis 1984: 19–34.

[35] Cicero objects to just that kind of relabelling when he insists that 'pain is pain' but can be overcome (*Tusc.* II. 13. 33).

[36] Cf. pp. 70–3.

we call a good money-maker. It is not someone who aggressively pursues great wealth, but rather the sage (*De oec.* XX. 1–32). Relabelling is often driven by theory, as in the above examples. However, in other cases it is simply done for psychological effect. For instance, Philodemus uses it as a kind of shock tactic in connection with the vivid depiction of events (the so-called technique of bringing-before-the-eyes). Soldiers falling gloriously in battle 'are killed like farm animals in the ranks' (*De mort.* XXVIII. 37–XXIX. 2), and the heroes of Plataea became 'bird food and dog food' (XXXIII. 21–2).[37]

Another group of exercises has to do with time, and may also involve conceptions of the self.[38] The passions displace one's happiness away from the present to some uncertain future, and force us to think wrongly, in general, about all temporal modes. One reason is that the desires involved in, e.g., anger and lust, are of a special kind. They do not concern the present and cannot be satisfied in the present; in truth, they cannot be satisfied at all. However, we should not infer that, without any qualifications, for the Epicureans 'only the present is our happiness'.[39] For, on the one hand, they contend that pleasure is complete at every moment, that death cannot affect present happiness, and that the sage's contemplation of nature reveals to him timeless truths.[40] On the other hand, they also believe that the pleasures of the past and those anticipated in the future are relevant to present happiness (cf. D.L. X. 22, 137; *De fin.* I. 18. 60), and that we should think *rightly* about the past and the future rather than think of them not at all.

Philodemus' exercises develop both these strands of thought: i.e., the attention to the present and the importance of viewing the past and the

[37] Compare Lucretius' suggestion that in order to escape the snares of erotic love, one should try to avoid self-delusion and see the objects of one's desire exactly for what they are (*DRN* IV. 1141–54): in other words, relabel 'the sweet disorder' as 'dirty and rank', 'the modest' as 'dumb', 'the slender' as 'too skinny to live', and 'the woman who is all kiss' as 'one with thick lips' (cf. *DRN* IV. 1159–70). On this topic, see Betensky 1980; R. D. Brown 1987; Clay 1983; Fitzgerald 1984; Nussbaum 1994: 140–91; Schrijvers 1970; and Sorabji 2000: 222.

[38] An incisive analysis of exercises concerning time and the self is found in Sorabji 2000: 228–52. Nussbaum (1994) discusses such strategies in several chapters; see esp., pp. 192–238. Hadot (1995) studies them in connection with his controversial thesis that many ancient philosophers found value only in the present; see Hadot, '"Only the Present is our Happiness": The Value of the Present Instant in Goethe and in Ancient Philosophy', trans. in Hadot 1995: 217–37. Individual strategies concerning our attitudes to temporal modes and to personal identity are also discussed by contemporary philosophers. Parfit (1984) has greatly influenced modern interpretations of the Symmetry Argument.

[39] Cf. Hadot 1995.

[40] Cf. Robin 1962: 150–2.

future correctly. He argues, for instance, that one should try not to measure goods by time (*De mort.* XII. 11), since when one has become wise, one's happiness and the goods in which it consists will be the same regardless of time (XIX. 1–6). Time will not make a difference to the fool's happiness anyway, for if he is not happy now, he will never be happy (XII. 28–30, XXXVII. 1–5). As to the sage, time truly does not affect his happiness in so far as he realizes both that pleasure is his at present and that death cannot alter that fact. Moreover, in parallel to his brief gaze over the infinity of nature, the sage at the point of death also sums up in his mind, briefly and clearly, the totality of the pleasure he has experienced and the unconsciousness that is to come (XXXIX. 15–25). In short, Philodemus stresses the universal and atemporal nature of the sage's perspective in connection with the supreme good and with death.[41]

On the other hand, Philodemus dissociates a *carpe diem* attitude from one's true enjoyment of present pleasures (*De elect.* XVII. 3–20). The good Epicurean should deliberately focus his attention on past pleasures in order to round off his mental survey of his life and die content (*De mort.* XXXIX. 15–25). On a different plane, the past is important for the exercise of frank speech, *parrhēsia*, which requires that the students' past errors be brought to the fore in order to be addressed and corrected. Following Epicurus, Philodemus attributes moral relevance to the future as well. First of all, by emphasizing the importance of the hedonic calculus, he shows the role of anticipation and foresight in the rational pursuit of pleasure[42] and the avoidance of pain.[43] Moreover, he maintains that anticipation and hope add to one's happiness so long as they are of the right kind and are directed towards the right objects. Thus, we should nurture good hopes for the future: for instance, that we will remain healthy or recover from disease (*De elect.* XXIII. 7–13), share our goods with others and get benefits in return (XXII. 17–21), retain our friendships and make more (XIV. 5), and conduct philosophical

[41] This seems to be the main reason why Pierre Hadot and others conclude that both Stoics and Epicureans recommend that we should concentrate only on the present.

[42] In this connection, see Cicero, *Tusc.* V. 38. 95.

[43] Epicurus seems to have sharply differentiated the anticipation of future pains in the context of the hedonic calculus from the Cyrenaic exercise of anticipating suffering and misfortune. While the former is part of a rational enterprise, the latter makes us suffer on account of evils that have not yet happened (Cicero, *Tusc.* III. 15. 32).

conversations in tranquillity and leisure (*De oec.* XXIII. 1–20). All the same, we must not disregard present and past pleasures on account of a future that may never be ours. For in that case we would be deprived of every enjoyment (XIX. 12–14)[44] and would cut ourselves off 'from every means to a better life, exactly like men sentenced to death' (*De elect.* XVIII. 9–11).

Death itself is a primary object of future-directed thinking. It is not feasible to predict when or how it will come, and it is altogether impossible to avoid it. Therefore, we need to anticipate it and get accustomed to the thought that some day we shall die, as all humans must. This is no easy task because, as mentioned above, the fear of death is an extremely powerful emotion, with long-range implications and devastating effects. The Epicureans address it by many different exercises, but the most famous one involving temporal modes is the so-called Symmetry Argument,[45] versions of which are found in the extant remains of Philodemus' treatise *On Death*. On the other hand, Philodemus' surviving works do not mention another much discussed Epicurean argument concerning temporal identity, that even if the precise atomic structure of which we are now formed were gathered together again sometime after our death, that future identity would not concern *us*, just as past identities do not concern *us*, because the continuity of memory is interrupted at death (Lucretius, *DRN* III. 847–62). However, Philodemus was probably aware of this last argument in some form or other; at any rate, he says much that is compatible with it and nothing that contradicts it. The same holds for the reasoning that even supposing that the soul retains sensation after its separation from the body, death would still be nothing to *us*, because *we* are a union of soul and body, and that union is dissolved at death (*DRN* III. 843–6).[46]

[44] In these passages, Philodemus refers to people who act irrationally because of the fear of death. The translations are from Indelli and Tsouna-McKirahan 1995, slightly modified.

[45] One interpretation of it is that, since nothing evil affected us in the past, before we were born, nothing evil can happen to us in the future after we are dead (Lucretius, *DRN* III. 832–42). For if an event is to be evil or good for anyone at any time, there must a subject for whom it will be evil or good at that time. But we were not a subject at the time before our birth and shall not be after our death. However, it is controversial whether the Symmetry Argument is directly concerned with our present attitudes towards past and future events, although many modern interpretations claim that it is. On the Symmetry Argument and its critics, see pp. 253–4. On Philodemus' use of Symmetry Arguments, see pp. 250–3.

[46] See Furley 1986: 77.

In order to address the fear of death, Philodemus appeals to concepts of subjecthood in accordance with Epicurean tradition. For instance, he holds that death implies loss of sensation (ἀναισθησία, translit. *anaisthēsia*) and extinction of personal identity (*De mort.*, *passim*), and argues for the conclusion that death is 'nothing to us'.[47] Moreover, he uses a cluster of concepts of the human self that exhibit standard Epicurean features. One's self is determined by reference to the specific aggregate of body atoms and soul atoms constituting an individual person. In this sense it is a complex self, but it also has unity. Treatment addresses the whole person, not some better part of it, nor yet different kinds of forces within oneself.[48] Selves have temporal continuity. So long as the organic union of body atoms and soul atoms persists, we are the selfsame persons who remember their past, live in the present, and hope for a future whose duration remains unknown. Death dissolves that union and disperses the self forever. In advanced stages of therapy, we are expected to draw comfort from that thought.

Philodemus' treatments of individual vices and passions also involve concepts of the self, principally in connection with issues of rationality, self-control, and self-knowledge. *On Frank Speech* points out that people too keen on pleasure or too afraid of pain shrink at *parrhēsia* (*De lib. dic.* 30. 1–11), and those affected by vices do the same because they are irrational and do not know themselves. They do not recognize the falsehood of their beliefs, the inappropriateness of their attitudes, and the wrongness of their actions. On the other hand, seeking correction implies a certain level of awareness of oneself. The student becomes aware of the fact that he has committed an error and that he should submit to correction. *On Arrogance* describes arrogant people as having no knowledge of themselves (*De superb.* fr. 1), for if they did, they would register negative reactions towards them, would grieve about their own condition, and would seek to improve themselves (cf. *De superb.* II. 1–33, V. 5–6, XVIII. 37–8). Those susceptible to flattery may falsely believe that they merit the flatterer's praise, or they may be dimly aware of the fact that they do not (*De adul.*; PHerc.

[47] In my view, Epicurus is the first to develop these two interrelated strands of argument, one emphasizing that death implies the complete absence of sensation (I call that the *anaisthēsia* thesis), the other pointing to the removal of the subject and the extinction of personal identity. Both lines are explored further by Epicurus' followers, especially Lucretius and Philodemus. On this topic, see pp. 248–50.

[48] Compare Posidonius' conception of the self, which consists of rational and irrational forces.

1457, fr. 14. 5–10). In either case, their therapy requires that they get to know their own selves. *On Anger* holds a mirror in front of the enraged man and invites him to look at himself. If he does not like the picture, he will endeavour 'to become himself' again: get cured of the passion and retrieve his rationality and self-control.

Shifting attention is also a strategy related to temporal modes. A distressed person may feel happier by focusing on a pleasant memory, a much anticipated future event, or something that distracts him at present. Such shifts are often prompted or accompanied by belief. Take the case of anger. Often we actively try to distract ourselves, precisely because we have become convinced that nothing terribly bad has happened to us after all. Moreover, consider the unjust death of a sage. He finds peace by concentrating on past pleasures, because he tells himself that he counts the pain as nothing (Cicero, *Tusc.* V. 26. 73).[49] However, Philodemus also discusses examples in which he stresses the shift of attention, not of belief. Melody, which is irrational, cannot directly affect emotions and judgements, which are rational: 'it only distracts people into switching their attention, just like sex and drunkenness' (*De mus.* book IV, col. XV. 1–7, Neubecker).[50]

Lastly, I should like to mention a therapeutic device which cannot readily be classified under some general heading and has not received much attention in the literature. We may call it moral portraiture. In outline, it consists in drawing vivid if elliptical portraits which bring out characteristic features of certain types of persons, good or bad. It is used by many schools, but plays a particularly prominent role in Epicurean authors. It is determined by their conception of the philosophical life and by institutional celebrations of Epicurus and his associates as moral paradigms. Both these factors influence Philodemus and underlie his entire therapeutic enterprise. He depicts sages, but also fools, and represents character traits as well as the manner in which sages and fools, respectively, engage in human relationships, social roles, and activities of daily life. Examples are the

[49] Despite Cicero's accusations (*Tusc.* V. 26. 73–5), and also Plutarch's (*Non posse*... 1089C–D), Epicurus' position may be counterintuitive, but not inconsistent. The sage's pains are confined to the present, whereas his recollected pleasures (which are primarily mental) extend over all of his past, and hence have greater intensity than present pains.

[50] Since this statement can be interpreted as rather negative, it remains unclear whether Philodemus considers melody a valid form of therapy.

elaborate models of the wise man and the superstitious person,[51] as well as the pictures of those suffering from vices and their corresponding virtues: the arrogant man, the flatterer and his victims, the greedy money-maker, the envious and the malicious persons, and, in sharp contrast, the sage. Even subtler are the vignettes of the enraged man and those beset by the fear of death. The compelling portrait of Epicurus, and also the cameos of apt or incompetent teachers, educable or recalcitrant students, ill-wishers, charlatans, and professional rivals, give an idea of the range of subjects of moral portraiture in Philodemus' surviving works.

What is the therapeutic value of these portraits? As I mentioned, they are often organized in an antithetical manner which facilitates their principal purpose: namely, to 'put-before-the-eyes', to compel us to imagine just what it is like to be superstitious, arrogant, irascible, etc., and also what it is like to be the opposite. Imaginings of this sort can be very effective, but the success of the technique depends on the literary qualities of the representation. In particular, we must be induced to assume that a single person can believe and do everything that the portrait represents[52]—that there is a single coherent character who has the dispositional, behavioural, moral, and theoretical features depicted. If the technique works, we feel aversion not only towards isolated elements, such as arrogance or rage, but towards the entire personality of someone arrogant or irascible. We simply do not want to be that sort of person, but just the opposite. For the most part, Philodemus' portraits serve his philosophical agenda nicely. They work apotreptically as much as protreptically, and contribute to the removal of disease and the restoration of moral health. They are also self-referential to a degree. For Philodemus must have endorsed for himself the moral ideal that he represents so well.

[51] These portraits point to theoretical beliefs, the psychological counterparts of such beliefs and their practical implications, and also the different ways in which the sage and the fool handle matters such as the acquisition and disposal of money.

[52] See Nehamas 1998: 3.

PART II

5

Frank Speech

Philodemus' treatise *On Frank Speech*, Περὶ παρρησίας (*De lib. dic.*, PHerc. 1471) is the only book with that title known in antiquity.[1] It discusses frank speech, παρρησία (translit. *parrhēsia*), in a narrow technical sense of the term:[2] namely, as a specific educational method that involves candid criticism, is practised live between the members of Epicurean schools, and aims at moral correction and improvement.[3] Thematically, *On Frank Speech* constitutes part of the larger project *On Characters and Ways of Life*, Περὶ ἠθῶν καὶ βίων.[4] In fact, as we shall see, frank speech is both a method of pedagogy and a way of speaking which forges bonds of benefits and gratitude among the members of Epicurean communities and is essential to the development of genuine friendships.[5] Structurally, *On Frank Speech* is an ἐπιτομή based on the lectures of Zeno of Sidon, which Philodemus attended.[6] As Philodemus points out, this form of writing

[1] I use the edition of the work by Olivieri (1914); Gigante 1983*d*; and the translation by Konstan *et al.* (1998). Unless otherwise indicated, the translations of passages in this chapter are my own. However, I have often relied on the translation by Konstan *et al.* (1998).

[2] I have suggested (p. 78) that the uninhibited presentation of truths concerning the vices and the passions, notably the vivid depiction of the characteristics and consequences of anger and of facts pertaining to death and the disposition of one's remains, can be considered species of *parrhēsia* taken in a broad sense.

[3] The term παρρησία is found in many different contexts, political, social, and cultural, and it has a variety of meanings: e.g., it is one of the words for the right of free speech (the primary term is ἰσηγορία). For information on this topic, see Konstan 1995, 1996*a*, 1996*b*, and 1997; and J. T. Fitzgerald 1996. Generally, we may say that παρρησία refers to the uninhibited expression of one's mind, and also has connotations of equality, integrity, trustworthiness, and friendship. In philosophy, παρρησία is a hallmark of Cynicism, while many schools mention it in connection with standing up to powerful rulers.

[4] It has been suggested that *On Anger* also belongs to *On Characters and Ways of Life* (see Konstan *et al.* 1998: 6). The same holds for PHerc. 1082, whose topic is flattery in opposition to true friendship.

[5] It is important to note in this connection that Philodemus usually contrasts flattery not with frank speech, but with friendship (Gigante 1983*a*: 59 ff., and Konstan *et al.* 1998: 6 and nn. 17, 18).

[6] It is impossible to tell which parts of the work reflect Zeno's teachings and which ones are Philodemus' own comments and developments of those teachings. However, the issue whether Zeno

precludes thorough treatment of details (*De lib. dic.* VIIb. 6–11), but concentrates instead on certain major themes. In fact, at various points the text appears to be structured by a sequence of questions, one of which is characterized once as 'commonplace' (cf. τόπωι: 83N = 81. 5). The answer to each of these questions is given immediately after the question is asked, repeating to a large extent the terms of the question itself.[7]

This chapter is divided into four sections, corresponding to the following topics: first, the nature, scope, kinds, and circumstances of application of *parrhēsia*; second, the characters of the students and their positive or negative reactions to parrhesiastic criticism; third, the dispositions of the teachers and the ways in which these dispositions affect the use of frank speech; and fourth, the confessional and corrective practices applied at every level of hierarchy of the Epicurean school, and especially among the sages. Philodemus' discussion of these topics presents both historical and theoretical interest. Among other things, it gives us a fairly detailed idea of life in an Epicurean school in Zeno's and Philodemus' times, the interchange between teachers and students, and the methods used for the assimilation of the Epicurean values and way of life. Also, as we shall see, *On Frank Speech* advances challenging views about central problems of philosophical psychology and the philosophy of education.

I

Parrhēsia is a conjectural or stochastic (στοχαστική) method[8] embodied in speeches, both admonitory and corrective. Every such speech is composed of two kinds of elements. The first consists in stretches of reasoning, and typically proceeds by means of signs (σημεῖα), points to likelihoods (εὐλογίαι), and establishes its conclusions not in any rigid way (παγίως) but only for the most part (*De lib. dic.* 1. 5–10, 57. 1–10). 'Indeed, reasonable conjectures do not always turn out as expected, even if the reasonable

or Philodemus is the originator of particular views is unimportant for my purposes here, which are exegetical and systematic rather than historical.

[7] One can only tell whether such a structuring question is present by its form and its repetition in the answer. (There are no underlined headings in the papyrus, as Konstan *et al.* (1998) seem to suggest.) However, the presence of a structuring question will not always be apparent, because of the state of preservation of the text.

[8] See Gigante 1975; Asmis 1990: 2393 ff.; Ierodiakonou 1995.

is concluded strictly from what is likely' (57. 5–10). The second type of element consists in certain literary or rhetorical features and techniques. Predominant among them are terms of encouragement and endearment; violent invective; and tirades (καταφοραί) of the sort delivered by the wise man and not by one's father, relatives, elders, etc. (VIIa. 1–8), for whom it is not right to deliver such assaults. I shall say more about these features later on in this chapter. As for the rhetorical strategy of 'setting-before-the-eyes' or 'bringing-before-the-eyes' (cf. τιθένα[ι πρὸ ὀμμάτων]: 42. 1 ff.), which also appears to be part of the method of *parrhēsia*,[9] I shall postpone detailed discussion of it until the chapter on anger and the desire for revenge. In any case, it seems that arguments and rhetorical features are necessary and, jointly, sufficient components of Philodemus' conception of *parrhēsia*. The former address the reason of the patients, the latter stir their emotions, and both elements work together towards the achievement of therapy.

Philodemus determines the kind of therapy in question and the precise way in which it is achieved by drawing a sustained analogy between philosophy and medicine. I have already discussed elements of that analogy and have also mentioned that Philodemus develops the medical model of *parrhēsia* by referring primarily to the relationship between teacher and student, although he acknowledges other kinds of parrhesiastic relations as well, which obtain between members of the Epicurean schools.[10] Here, I shall say more about these topics in connection with *parrhēsia* as a pedagogical method.

Our sources indicate that the senior members of the Epicurean schools pay close attention to the behaviour of the students (11. 1 ff.), and that the students themselves are very aware of each other's comportment. Thus, it is often the case that the teacher approaches a student to admonish and

[9] The extant remains of *On Anger* contain discussion of the strategy of 'setting-before-the-eyes', whereas the surviving text of *On Frank Speech* appears merely to mention it. The phrase τιθένα[ι πρὸ ὀμμάτων] (*De lib. dic.* 42. 1 ff.) is a conjecture. The expression τιθῶμεν πρὸ ὀμμάτων (26. 4–5) is not conjectural, but it is not clear whether it refers specifically to the technique in question. As for the phrase ἔνια τῶν ἔν τισ[ι] τόποις ἐπιδεικνυμ[ένων π]ρὸ ὀ[μ]μάτων (77 = 78N), it probably does refer to the technique of 'setting-before-the-eyes', but it is hard to guess in what context because of the condition of the text. Although this evidence is slim, it suggests that *parrhēsia* understood as a pedagogic method applied to students of Epicurean schools does comprise the technique of 'setting-before-the-eyes'. Moreover, the treatises *On Anger* and *On Death* give us good reason to believe that Philodemus and his teachers consider 'setting-before-the-eyes' an important part of moral admonition, whether that admonition is delivered in the environment of an Epicurean school (sc. *parrhēsia* in a narrow sense) or outside it (sc. *parrhēsia* in the broad sense).

[10] Cf. pp. 78–9.

correct him because he has observed him being at fault or has heard about it. Ideally, however, the teacher offers help, like the doctor, in consequence of the patient's own initiative. The latter feels an 'itching' (*κνίσμα*: 32. 9), a discomfort at something that he has done, which prompts him to seek relief by confessing his action to the teacher. The desire to do so is a natural desire, and the same holds generally for the need to open one's heart to another human being. These desires are supported by reason, in so far as the student realizes that 'the censures for the things that would be revealed are less important than their benefit' (49. 2–5).[11] A necessary presupposition for the student's confession is trust. This is less a matter of the student's beliefs and expectations regarding the teacher's abilities[12] than a matter of feeling secure about the instructor's attitudes and motives.[13] Of course, the student's sense of security is related to his tendency to believe what the teacher says and his reliance on the teacher's competence.[14] Nevertheless, it is not identical with that tendency, but might be best defined as the disposition to have confidence in the teacher and to banish from one's mind sceptical or negative thoughts concerning him.[15] 'If he (sc. the student) has considered this man (sc. the teacher) to be his sole guide both of right speech [and of right action, whom he calls] the only saviour, exclaiming "let him accompany me", (and to whom) he has given [himself] over to be treated, how would he not reveal to him (sc. the teacher) those things in which he needs treatment...?' (40. 5–14). For his own part, the teacher cultivates trust by making his motives entirely transparent to the student and by being open about the parrhesiastic process and its goal.[16]

[11] Heraclides reasoned in this way, and, consequently, he decided to disclose his errors to Epicurus (49. 1 ff.). In general, one's decision to give oneself over to the teacher for therapy is based on just this sort of calculation.

[12] See the so-called cognitive accounts of trust, e.g., Coleman 1990. Notice that contemporary discussions of trust often focus on its social and political dimensions rather than on relationships between individuals.

[13] For accounts emphasizing the non-cognitive dimensions of trust see, e.g., Becker 1996 and Jones 1996. A key criticism levelled against cognitive approaches to trust is that they render it very difficult to distinguish between trust and belief or knowledge.

[14] On the distinctions between credulity, reliance, and sense of security, see Becker 1996: 45–6.

[15] Jones (1996) defines trust, partly, as an affective attitude of optimism.

[16] Similarly, the patient trusts the physician of his choice and gives himself over to be treated. He feels safe in the hands of his physician, reveals to him everything concerning the disease, follows the doctor's instructions without questioning them, and, assuming that he is not in a terminal condition, is optimistic about his cure.

The treatment is *ad hominem*. It begins by observing carefully a specific set of symptoms which are, for the most, behavioural and point to the presence of a particular psychic disease. In my view, the medical analogy implies that the teacher, ultimately, addresses the student's moral disposition precisely through the *ad hoc* correction of individual faults. *On Frank Speech* attests that, in his capacity as a pedagogue, the Epicurean teacher comes across every major vice and irrational emotion afflicting human beings. Flattery, arrogance, irascibility, slander (13. 2), envy and malicious joy,[17] a misplaced sense of dignity and shame, vanity, self-conceit and vainglory constitute primary targets of his plain speaking. Stubbornness and overconfidence, harshness and insolence, egocentrism, insecurity and ingratitude, laziness and procrastination (Va. 2–3) are also added to that list. Moreover, the teacher sometimes has to deal with terribly grave character faults: namely, foolishness, intemperance, impiety, and injustice. When these occur in men who are very wealthy (XXIIb. 10 ff.) or politically powerful (XXIIIb. 12), they motivate serious wrongdoing and, sometimes, actual crimes.[18]

However, not every behavioural error is of interest to the teacher. He does not correct factual mistakes, although he may tackle them incidentally in the course of a parrhesiastic speech. Also, he addresses moral slips only discriminately and with due regard for the particulars pertaining to each case. 'He does not do this continually, nor against everyone, nor does he criticize every error, nor just any chance error, or in front of those who should not be present, or with ridicule, but rather [takes up the errors] sympathetically [and without insult or scorn]' (79 = 81N. 4–12).[19] Both the selectiveness and the *ad hoc* nature of frank speech stem from the Epicurean belief that the teacher must never wage an overall attack against the personality of the student. 'To reproach a student for everything without circumscribing it is an unfriendly thing (ἄφιλον) to [his security] and a foolish harshness' (78–80N. 1–3). Similar considerations underlie the principle that one should not be blamed *simpliciter* for an error committed once. 'Then, if something of this sort has been neglected, we do not

[17] Specifically, the joy that some students derive from denouncing the faults of their classmates to the teachers.

[18] The Epicurean teacher is careful about speaking candidly to kings and tyrants. However, he might feel inclined to do so, and sometimes he might pay for it with his life. See *De mort.* XXXIV. 1 ff.

[19] See also 3. 3–7.

stop someone from blaming it, but we do not think that it is correct for an error committed once to be used to blame someone on the whole' (35. 4–11).[20]

Particular errors of the same person or of different persons vary considerably in kind as well as in magnitude, just as ailments of the same patient or of different patients vary. Hence, the parrhesiastic speeches treating particular faults also differ in their contents and severity, just as medicines differ in their composition and effectiveness.[21] The most fundamental difference concerning parrhesiastic speeches lies in the contrast between the mild kind (*μέτριον εἶδος*) and the harsh (*σκληρόν*) or bitter (*πικρόν*) kind of *parrhēsia.* For instance, 'when Leonteus, because of Pythocles, did not admit [belief] in gods, Epicurus reproached Pythocles in a moderate manner (*μετρίως*), but he wrote to the other one (sc. Leonteus) the so-called famous letter' (6. 4–11), which, presumably, was composed in stronger language. Furthermore, the mildness or harshness of *parrhēsia* admits of degrees. 'The teacher intensifies (*ἐπιτίνει*) his plain speaking towards the stronger ones (*μᾶλλον ἰσχυρούς*) among the tender (*τῶν ἀπαλῶν*) and towards those who are somewhat more in need of treatment, and he will also use the harsh kind of plain speaking towards the strong-minded students (*ἰσχυρούς*) who will hardly change their mind even if they are really shouted at' (7. 1–10). Corresponding to the degree of intensity is the extent to which *parrhēsia* causes pain to its recipient: harsh or bitter criticism may be very painful, whereas more moderate reprimands are relatively painless. However, it seems to me that all parrhesiastic speeches must involve some discomfort, no matter how gentle they may be. For in so far as they are corrective, they frustrate to a degree certain desires and passions (*πάθη*: 65. 8, 66. 7–8) of the student.

A number of additional ramifications should also be taken into account. Corrective *parrhēsia*, both bitter and mild, stands in opposition to *parrhēsia* which occasionally includes a measure of praise and which is exercised by the teacher with pleasure (cf. IIb. 2–10). Terms of blame and praise can be

[20] This passage mainly concerns the sage, but the principle in question probably applies to all the members of an Epicurean school.

[21] Aside from the nature and magnitude of the faults, there are also other factors that the teacher takes into consideration in deciding what kind of *parrhēsia* he will use on a particular occasion: viz., the student's age, character, and disposition, as well as his provenance and rank, and also the teacher's own disposition and training, his pedagogical skills, and his experience. See below in this chapter, *passim*.

blended into the same speech, and in the event, they usually are. 'When he (sc. the teacher) does not give up hope for some students or is not very forcefully making manifest his own annoyance, he will not forget, as he speaks, to use "dearest", "sweetest", and other similar expressions' (14. 5–10). Generally, the mixture of pleasurable and painful elements in the same corrective speech is recommended not on the basis of a naive faith in shock tactics. Rather, it derives from the far more challenging principle that the student should be emotionally supported while he is undergoing therapy, and that it is essential to convey love in teaching virtue.

However, there are cases in which the teacher will refrain from expressing affection altogether: namely, cases in which the student commits a major error, and therefore the teacher gives full expression to his disapproval. On such occasions, the severity of the teacher's criticisms is proportional to the nature and intensity of his emotions, and notably to the quality and magnitude of his anger. Anger-in-combination-with-hatred renders the admonition particularly harsh and painful, whereas anger-together-with-blame is somewhat less hard on the student. Indeed, if the teacher is dealing with a fault 'that is bearable and expected to cease, he will not be angry with an anger that hates (μισοῦσαν ὀργήν) but rather with an anger that blames (μεμφο[μ]έ[νη]ν ὀργήν) acts of foolishness' (87 = 92N. 4–9) and, presumably, the opposite holds if the teacher is addressing a truly severe and deeply rooted failing.[22]

How much anger the teacher puts into his frank criticism also constitutes the basis for deciding whether his *parrhēsia* is artful or artless, simple. 'In most instances, he (sc. the teacher) will act with artistic sophistication (διαφι[λ]οτεχν[ή]σει)[23] in such a way. But at times he will also exercise plain speaking simply (ἁ[πλ]ῶς) in the belief that this risk must be taken if the students do not obey otherwise. And he will criticize with great anger and [blame] ... those who are very strong-headed both because of their nature and because of the progress that they have made' (10. 1–11). Artful

[22] A possible objection is this. Hatred and blame need not be (or are not) separate categories, but might often overlap so that there can be anger-together-with-hatred-and-blame. In response, one may concede that Philodemus is wrong to assume that hatred and blame do not overlap. Alternatively, one may defend Philodemus' assumption on the grounds that hatred and blame here are not emotional attitudes but pedagogical features of *parrhēsia* that fulfil different functions.

[23] On the meaning of the term see Gigante 1983*a*: 73.

parrhēsia is mild in so far as it does not convey to the student the impression that the instructor is greatly upset with him.[24] Rather, it is a mixture of both praise and blame; moreover, it is applied to the erring student cautiously, e.g., in an indirect manner (9. 6–9). On the other hand, criticism exercised ἁπλῶς, simply and artlessly, can be quite harsh and leaves the student in no doubt of the teacher's indignation. This sort of criticism consists chiefly of reprimands, and it addresses the student's fault in an entirely direct manner. Notice that the teacher's choice of a specific way of exercising criticism is not at all influenced by the nature of his feelings concerning the error under correction: e.g., it does not depend on whether he truly feels anger or simply pretends to experience it.[25] Whether his emotions are genuine or faked, they should be viewed as an educational tool, not as an element of self-expression.

Next, the teacher may choose to focus his criticism directly on the student *qua* perpetrator of a particular error, or, alternatively, he may deflect the force of the reprimand by appearing to criticize the same type of error, but committed sometime in the past by himself. 'The wise man will also sometimes transfer (μετάξει) to himself an intemperate error [saying that it occurred] in his youth' (9. 6–9). Presumably, criticism by projection is appropriate only for some kinds of errors, not for all, and it works only for students with a gentle disposition, not for strong, stubborn ones. Indirect reprimands are useful, because they are milder and easier to accept than direct ones, and also because they shift the focus of attention of the student from himself to someone else, thereby allowing him to assess his error in an objective manner. Additional options available to the teacher concern the point of departure of the parrhesiastic speech and its length and style. He might begin by talking about something apparently unrelated to the fault that he wishes to correct, or he might get straight to the point. Besides, he might admonish the student vehemently and/or at length (cf. [κατα]φοράς: VIIa. 5) or speak to him less vehemently and/or more briefly. The specific course of the chosen therapy determines in part the pace of the student's improvement and cure.[26] In sum, *parrhēsia* is a flexible and nuanced technique in ways comparable to the ways in which the methods of medicine are often elastic and varied methods of treatment. In both cases,

[24] See Asmis 1990 and Gigante 1983*a*. [25] See *De ir.* XXXIV. 16–31.

[26] See fr. 32, keeping in mind, however, that the text is very uncertain.

the application of therapy imposes high demands upon the practitioners. However, the doctor's task is perhaps less challenging than the teacher's, in so far as the physical constitution of human beings is more uniform and transparent than their intellectual, psychological, and social make-up.

As mentioned, both kinds of physicians occasionally fail in their tasks, for similar reasons.[27] Like the doctor, the teacher makes mistakes in diagnosis when he misreads the signs and comes to the wrong conclusion. For instance, he may infer falsely that a certain error has occurred for blameworthy reasons (*μεμπτὰς αἰτίας*: IXb. 3), while, in fact, it was committed for non-blameworthy ones (*οὐ μεμπτάς*: IXb. 4), 'because he has not yet grasped the matter, but has been misled by common traits' (IXb. 6–9). Or he may mistakenly conclude that the students have been at fault, precisely because he has not witnessed their deeds at first hand; i.e., he has not 'caught them in love or in the grip of certain vices, but has inferred (their errors) by means of signs' (*σημειωσάμενον*: 57. 1–5). Reasonable conjectures (*εὐλόγιστα στοχαστά*) do not always turn out as expected (57. 5–10), and students are thought guilty of errors that they have not committed (61. 6–12, 62. 7–13). Compare the physician who assumed from reasonable signs that his patient needed a purge and then, having erred in his inferences, never purges this man again when he is afflicted by another illness (63. 3–11).[28]

At the level of treatment, the teacher may fail in his choice of frank speech (8. 4 ff.) because he is ignorant of the specific conditions of perpetration of the error (8. 4–8), or simply because he has wrongly assessed the student's character. For instance, he may treat a student 'more pleasantly and more easily' than he should (8. 4 ff.), or he may criticize harshly where gentle admonition would suffice. Also, the teacher might succeed in correcting one's error at a superficial level but, nevertheless, might leave untouched the dispositional trait that has caused it. In such a case, the student will again commit the same kind of fault, and will again be in need of therapy. Sometimes the teacher does not realize that his admonition has truly transformed the character of the student, who now needs it no more. 'Sometimes, although well-being has been restored, and although often it has even become clear to others, it has escaped the teacher's notice' (61. 6–10). Or *parrhēsia* might prove ineffective not because the teacher

[27] Cf. p. 65 and n. 59.

[28] Psychosomatic symptoms often lead to mistakes of this sort.

has done something wrong, but because the student has reacted badly to his criticisms. 'There are times when he will even shun philosophy, and perhaps on occasion he will also hate the wise man, and sometimes he will submit but will not be benefited, although the teacher has assumed that he will' (59. 1–7). Overall, the student's reactions towards his teachers are signs from which one can infer whether or not treatment has been successful (74. 5–13). Positive attitudes, such as good will and gratitude towards one's teacher, signify that the fault has been corrected and the student's character purged of the relevant flaw. On the other hand, negative attitudes, such as anger, resentment, ingratitude, and hatred, indicate that frank criticism did not work, but should be applied again, perhaps more severely.

Since the teacher is often a sage, the objection might be raised that the sage's occasional failures in matters of therapy indicate that his wisdom is less than perfect.[29] Philodemus' answer is this. 'Now he (sc. the sage) does not appear to us to be going to err, since the preconception of him[30] includes the perfection of his reasoning and practical wisdom. But in not attaining his goal and in overlooking some[31] of the things which cannot always be observed by a human being it seems to us that the sage will indeed slip [in frank speech]' (56. 4–14). According to this passage, the sage does possess perfect reason (*λογισμοῦ τελειότητα*) and practical wisdom (*φρόνησις*), but, nonetheless, he is subject to the factual and epistemic constraints to which all men must be subject. His occasional failures in the practice of *parrhēsia* establish not that he is a fool, but that he too is human. At any rate, the teacher should not be discouraged by failures, although he should be greatly encouraged by success (4. 1 ff.). For if he gave up trying to correct the student at fault, he would act irrationally, like a bad doctor who 'on the basis of reasonable signs assumes that a certain man stands in need of a purge and then, having made a mistake in the interpretation of the signs, never purges this man again even if he is afflicted by another disease' (63. 3–11).

Instead, the teacher should act rationally, like a good doctor (63. 11–13); that is, he should make successive attempts to cure the same or a different

[29] This may be the content of 56. 1–3. However, these lines are heavily restored, and cannot be relied upon. The issue whether the sage can ever be mistaken in the application of *parrhēsia* has probably been a matter of dispute. For, first, it is strikingly similar in structure to the issue whether the sage ever feels anger and, second, Zeno and Philodemus settle it by appealing to preconception just as they do in other cases of debated topics.

[30] 56. 5–6 *προειλημμένο*[ι]s.

[31] I was told that *τι* is legible after *παρελθεῖν* in 56. 10.

patient, of the same disease or of a different one, by means of similar or of different drugs. And he should not stop trying until he can show that the students have been entirely purified (16. 1–5). Even if his *parrhēsia* has accomplished nothing the first time around, and even if the student did not heed the frank criticism, he will speak frankly again. 'For the doctor, although he has achieved nothing through a clyster in the case of the same disease, will [purge the patient] again. For this very reason, i.e., because he has achieved nothing before, the teacher will speak frankly again and, indeed, he will do this again and again [in order to succeed], if not this time then another time' (64. 5–13). Provided that he perseveres, he is very likely to bring the student to the point of becoming reasonable and of being corrected (66. 1–16).[32]

The student's condition, both when he is at the mercy of the passions and after he has been relieved, is rendered in physicalistic terms borrowed from the realm of medicine. Philodemus tells us that the student undergoes a swelling (συνοίδ[η]σι[ν]: 67. 1), but that the swelling gets reduced (67. 5–6) and eventually disappears at the completion of the therapy. At worst, the teacher will manage to hinder the swelling from spreading further, even if he does not eliminate it altogether (91N. 1–6).[33] His rate of success increases with time, as he gains knowledge of the reports that others have given of their observations and experience (ἱστορία: Vb. 8–9).[34] There are limits to Epicurean optimism, however. For, like the doctor, the teacher will sometimes encounter people whose condition is difficult or impossible to cure. Neither of the two practitioners would deny treatment to a sufferer of a terminal sort, because of their philanthropic feelings. The teacher will address 'those who, in so far as reasonable arguments indicate, are not expected to pause (and pay heed to advice), imitating doctors who treat also the patient who is reasonably believed not to recover from his disease' (69. 1–8).[35] However, neither of the two physicians bears full responsibility for the outcome of such cases of therapy. Although the doctor is generally held accountable for the choice and effectiveness of the medicines that he prescribes, nonetheless, he is not considered blameworthy for failure to

[32] Cf. Gigante 1983*a*: 79–80.

[33] My interpretation here is tentative, because the text is extremely lacunose.

[34] Cf. pp. 59–60.

[35] On the practice of using *parrhēsia* towards people who are hopelessly corrupt, cf. *De conv.* X. 9–12.

restore the health of a dying man. In a somewhat comparable manner, the teacher is accountable for the nature and quality of his admonitions, but cannot be held responsible regarding their effect on a totally corrupt man. In fact, as Philodemus makes clear, the complete extirpation of vice is a matter of at least joint responsibility between the teacher and a patient of this kind. To wit, while the teacher consents to criticize individual errors of a truly perverted person, 'he does not at all labour over how that man will fare in life' (21. 4–6). After he has used every parrhesiastic resource at his disposition, including maledictions (*κατάρας*) and insults (*λοιδορίας*: 21. 10–11), he realizes that there is nothing more that he can do and lets the matter rest.

The nature of *parrhēsia* gets clarified further by comparing and contrasting frank speech with other forms of discourse. On the one hand, harsh forms of *parrhēsia* should not be confused with curses and offences, although they may comprise such elements. The main difference lies in the nature and motives of the person who utters the hurtful words. It must be conceded that such distinctions might be hard to draw. In fact, some teachers 'have judged it right to speak frankly ... but [moderately], because bitter [frank speech] bears some similarity to insult, as if they were actually insulting out of ill will' (60. 1–7). On the other hand, Philodemus recommends that the teacher should use harsh words according to his judgement, notwithstanding the risk of being misunderstood. But even the most bitter *parrhēsia* may not contain expressions of derision and contempt. Besides, *parrhēsia* does not include irony. 'Let us set-before-the-eyes also the difference that exists between a caring admonishment and an irony [which is pleasing] but bites virtually everybody' (26. 4–10). It is inappropriate to laugh at the errors of the students and ridicule them (23. 1–4).[36] As a matter of rule, the sage never humiliates his young, headstrong students by putting ironical twists on his words, i.e., by saying the opposite of what he means[37] with the intention of mocking or deceiving them (cf. 87N. 13).[38] Moreover, as mentioned, it is inappropriate for parents, elders, etc., to deliver assaults which are open to the sages. 'Neither an older man nor a teacher nor a

[36] The fragment refers to bad teachers who address their students in that manner. It may contain an implicit criticism of Plato's Socrates.

[37] Irony is a complex phenomenon, and there are many more dimensions to it than the traditional one, which has been summarized here based on Quintilian (*Inst. or.* 9. 22. 44). However, Philodemus speaks about irony in the traditional manner.

[38] The fragment is heavily restored.

father ought to interpose tirades ([κατα]φοράς) available to the wise men' (VIIa. 2–6). Bitter *parrhēsia* coming from ordinary people might harm the student, whereas the frank criticism of a wise man can only be beneficial.

On the other hand, we must not confuse mild forms of *parrhēsia* with general advice, e.g., about what is the right thing to do. For *parrhēsia* is not deliberative (συνβου[λε]υτικόν: XIIIb. 3–4), but corrective. It primarily addresses a specific error, not a kind of error. And it explains what the student should or should not have done on a particular occasion, not what he ought or ought not to do in general. Also, *parrhēsia* stands in opposition to flattery, κολακεία (translit. *kolakeia*). Although this topic rarely rises to the surface of the argument in *On Frank Speech*, nevertheless it underlies much of Philodemus' analysis of the method as well as of the human relationships obtaining within the Epicurean community. The antithesis in question can be traced back to the early post-classical era in which '*parrhēsia*' denotes the candour displayed in conversation between true friends, whereas '*kolakeia*' refers to deceitful and adulatory speech. Philodemus builds further on that theme. The good teacher never makes use of flattering arts (cf. the conjecture [κολ]ακευτ[ι]καῖς [τέχναις]: Ib. 13–14), likes and loves his students, and provides genuine help and support to those who are in distress. By contrast, the bad teacher 'neither likes nor [loves] but flatters' (Tab. I, fr. 2), taking advantage of the emotional fragility of the students and manipulating them for his own ends (60. 8–12).

In sum, the method of *parrhēsia* represents a pragmatic as well as optimistic approach to human fallibility and to the possibility of correction and salvation. It has humanitarian and philanthropic dimensions, involving as it does elements of empathy, compassion, and forgiveness. Equally important are the social and institutional bonds forged by that practice, in particular the friendship and solidarity which glue together the members of each Epicurean school.[39]

II

The school's cohesion gets undermined, however, by the negative reactions of some students to frank criticism. In this section, first, I shall reconstruct

[39] However, Epicurean solidarity is not nourished by frank speech alone, but also by a variety of other factors. See Clay 1998: 55–120.

Philodemus' account of counterproductive attitudes to *parrhēsia*. Second, I shall discuss his thesis that negative reactions to *parrhēsia* are determined by the character, inclinations, values, and status of the individuals who display them. Let me begin, then, by pointing out that the reactions in question vary in nature as well as in intensity. Notably, they may be more or less passive, involve greater or lesser assertiveness, be aggressive or defensive or both, and be manifested in more or less straightforward ways.

First, some students invite frank criticism in the belief that it will do them good, but they do so for the wrong reasons and in the wrong frame of mind. Hence, they are vexed when they are actually subjected to *parrhēsia*, especially if they consider themselves superior to others. 'Earlier they see the benefit deriving from frank speech but at a later time, being confused for many reasons, they do not [see] it, just like some people who make jokes but [do not endure others] making jokes at their expense' (XVIIb. 8–14). We find similar attitudes in students who are internally resistant to *parrhēsia* but who, nevertheless, pretend to pay heed to their teachers. 'They are vexed at those who speak frankly because they do not speak deep from the heart, [but rather] counterfeit the appearance that they are in truth lovers of frank criticism. But when the rebuke comes they have their pretence exposed, just like those who are forced to dine together for the sake of politeness, when they correct something' (XVIb. 1–11).

However, most of the students who dislike frank criticism do not bother to pretend that they accept correction, but oppose it openly, expressing their discontent in various ways. Some simply stick to their guns: they are unwilling to admit that they have erred, remain unmoved by the teacher's rhetoric and arguments, and because of their perverted nature, show ingratitude and behave towards their teachers in a base manner (19. 1 ff.). Other, more aggressive students, 'if they are not satisfied after having obtained every [suitable nourishment] and aid while that was possible, try to slander and abuse the sage who has assisted them [and to mock him by means of ridicule]' (18. 4–10). Yet others refuse to accept what the teacher says, although they might recognize that, in some sense, he is wiser than they are. At first glance, their attitude might be perceived as paradoxical (cf. XXa. 1–5). If you believe that the man rebuking you knows better than you do, and is better than you are, why, one might wonder, would you not pay attention to his criticism?

In order to solve that paradox, Philodemus makes several qualifications. In the first place, although such students may leave the teacher's general wisdom unchallenged, nonetheless they may question the prudence of his admonition by raising specific objections. Depending on the occasion, they may claim that the teacher has attributed to them faults that they have not committed; that he has accused them of errors that no human being could have avoided, including the teacher himself and even the sage; and that the teacher's criticisms derive from less than commendable motives (XXIa. 4–11). Besides, they might interpret the wisdom of the teacher in such a way that it becomes irrelevant to educational purposes. Notably, they might describe the teacher as someone with a type of theoretical knowledge which is useless for practical life. 'They believe that they are surpassed only in answering philosophical questions, but that in disposition and the ability to understand what is preferable, especially the affairs of practical life, they themselves are far better' (XXa. 5–12). Furthermore, they may disregard the admonition of a wise teacher because they are confused by inconsistent beliefs, swayed by intense contradictory emotions, and hence unable to reason correctly about their own good. 'This is how Timocrates[40] said that he both loved and hated his brother as no one else did. For the souls which are unable to calculate what is beneficial suffer and do many things that are opposites' (XXb. 3–10). Their inability to reason correctly may be related either to weakness of the will or to sheer moral blindness.

The types of reactions to *parrhēsia* described above, and also other related attitudes which we shall examine shortly, are found in several types of people. I shall now discuss each of them in turn. At the outset, it should be noted that they are not mutually exclusive, but that there is significant overlap between them. For hostility to frank speech typically does not stem from a single characteristic, but rather from a combination of several features—natural, social, intellectual, and moral.

First, both the lovers of flattery and the flatterers themselves resist frank speech. The former often are wealthy, famous, or powerful persons, admired and praised on a daily basis by adulatory subjects. Therefore, they find it intolerable (ἀφό[ρητ]ον) to be treated themselves as subjects and to have to accept admonition and blame (34. 1–5). On the other hand,

[40] Metrodorus' brother (cf. Konstan *et al.* 1998), who apparently had a difficult character (cf. *De ir.* XII. 26 ff. and Indelli 1988: 167).

adulators presumably oppose frank speech for fear that it might expose their character in the eyes of their victims, and thus frustrate the achievement of their self-serving goals. Even greater hostility to frank speech derives from arrogance and other related characteristics.[41] Arrogant men object to *parrhēsia*, because it shatters their sense of superiority, humiliates them by revealing their shortcomings, and places them at the same level as everyone else. 'They are hurt [because] they believe that none of the things which they suspect are occurring and will occur through the actions of others are happening and will happen through their own actions' (XVa. 1–7). Their reactions to the teacher, which are compared to those of colts to the colt-tamer (87N. 1–8), are prompted in addition by empty beliefs concerning their own abilities, and indicate an excessive amount of self-love. These beliefs underscore both their refusal to submit themselves to frank speech and their eagerness to apply it to others (XIXa. 5–13; XIXb. 1–12). Lack of self-confidence and low self-esteem are also impediments to the successful application of frank speech. Oversensitive and timid students are likely to feel great shame on account of their mistakes, are reluctant to confess them, and are terrified at the prospect of being rebuked. And although the competent teacher does take into consideration their nature and uses gentle rather than bitter forms of *parrhēsia* towards them (7. 1 ff.), nonetheless, they may find even mild admonition hard to take.

Another great impediment to *parrhēsia* is irascibility. It is frequently found together with arrogance and other interrelated traits. Those prone to anger tend to fall prey to the emotion as a result of a perceived slight directed intentionally at themselves by some other person or persons. The higher the opinion they have of themselves, the more likely they are to feel that they do not get what they deserve and to perceive themselves as offended on that account. In the Epicurean school in particular, irascible students perceive the teacher's admonition as an intentional attack on their dignity or intelligence. As a result, they get enraged when he employs frank speech towards them and remain in that condition 'although they have obtained every [suitable nourishment] and help so long as it was possible' (18. 4–6). Those 'clothed in Greek style' (31. 4–5)—i.e., wearing the philosopher's

[41] Such characteristics are stubbornness, self-importance, overconfidence, and a misplaced perception of dignity and pride.

dress and having philosophical pretensions[42]—are also irritated whenever they must submit to criticism. 'They accept with annoyance what is said [in frank speech], and for this reason [some of them who have been through it] cannot possibly [endure listening to the teacher] with good will' (31. 6–12). Stubborn silence, but also mockery, slander, and abuse, are ways in which these students express their anger towards the wise man.

The surviving text leaves unclear the issue 'how the teacher will handle those who have become angry towards him because of his frank speech' (70. 7–9). There seems to be no definite policy on the matter. Rather, the instructor decides *ad hoc* what is the best thing to do: e.g., whether he should further confront the enraged student or interrupt his admonition in order to try again later. Philodemus' physiological analysis of the passions, as huge swellings which force one to disobey but which are eventually reduced to the point of allowing one to listen to reason, indicates that the instructor usually prefers to relent in his criticism and bide his time. Every good instructor is prepared to tolerate a certain amount of frustration and anger in the student. For he is well aware of the fact that, in the course of parrhesiastic correction, the student is subject to pain, and therefore must react in some manner. If the student has a strong character, it is natural for him to show some anger or irritation at the initial stages of the process. The teacher abides him, provided of course that the student's emotions remain moderate and are kept within bounds.

These vices, and other ones besides, are all the more obstructive to frank speech if the agent is too keen on immediate pleasure or has too much of a dispositional aversion to pain. 'He pays less attention to his own injury, both the man who still is very badly in need of external things, and also some person who, in virtue of his disposition, opposes one thing with medicines and obstructs another because pain is present' (30. 1–9). The former's excessive attachment to immediate pleasure drives him to concentrate his efforts on the acquisition of material sources of enjoyment, and thus to neglect his moral and psychological well-being. As for the person who is (exceedingly) sensitive to pain, he shrinks at the pain of his admonition and is unable to pursue the therapy in any systematic manner (30. 6–11).

[42] See Gigante 1983*a*: 98–9.

Now we shall examine three sets of individuals: namely, rulers, women, and old men. Philodemus attributes to each of them a typology of intellectual, psychological, and moral characteristics, which purports to explain why its members vehemently resist frank speech. He determines each set in accordance with social and cultural criteria that reflect the values and prejudices of his own environment. Therefore, this stage of his analysis is of only limited interest to us, although it contains some valuable and thought-provoking elements.

The first category is introduced with the following question: 'Why is it that, other things being equal, those who are illustrious both in wealth and reputation endure frank speech less than others?' (XXIIb. 10–13). Philodemus answers as follows. In the first place, people of this sort believe themselves to be luckier, abler, and wiser than others just on account of the fact that they possess much money or a brilliant reputation or political authority (XXIIb. 13–15). Their sense of superiority constitutes the basis for their assumption that they are envied and hated by everyone else (XXIIb. 15–16),[43] and notably by those who reproach them. On the other hand, 'they are accustomed in a way to being spoken to by everyone so as to curry favour' (XXIIIa. 4–6). Consequently, they form the habit (*συνειθισμένοι*: XXIIIa. 4–5) of listening to flattering speeches and are surprised by frank speech (XXIIIa. 7).[44] Moreover, they suspect that their teachers criticize them for self-serving reasons (XXIIIb. 7–12). And even if they do not perceive the teacher as malicious or self-seeking, they may judge him to be useless (XXIIIb. 3–7). Rulers and kings (*βασιλεῖς*) have yet another reason to resist *parrhēsia*. Especially if they wield absolute power (XXIIIb. 13–14), 'they consider reproach to be insubordination. They wish, and believe that it is advantageous, to rule over everything [and to have everything depend on] and be subject to themselves' (XXIVa. 1–7). Philodemus strikes a Socratic theme here. There cannot be a happy tyrant, because the very characteristics that place him in a position of absolute power also constitute formidable obstacles to moral improvement. The sage who attempts to speak candidly to kings or tyrants does so at his peril. For inexperienced as he is in hard politics, he runs the risk of being persecuted, subjected to torture, and suffering an unjust death.

[43] Note that l. 16 is conjectural.

[44] Several Epicurean authors discuss people's reactions in respect of things familiar or unexpected and surprising (cf. *παράλογον*: XXIIIa. 7).

Philodemus is only too aware of the fact that this is not merely a conceptual possibility, but a misfortune that can afflict one in real life (cf. *De mort.* XXXIV. 1 ff.).

Women too submit to *parrhēsia* with no pleasure at all. 'They [believe] that they are being reviled, and they feel more distressed by the disgrace, and they are more prone to suspect evils concerning those who admonish them, and, generally, they find more upsetting all the things because of which some people feel stung and, besides, they are more rash and more frivolous and [more concerned with their reputation]' (XXIIa. 1–11). So, some reasons why women resist *parrhēsia* lie in their vices. Philodemus does not clarify whether he considers these vices natural or cultural or both. His main point is that the oversensitivity and suspiciousness of women, which is coupled with insolence, vanity, and ambition, constitute obstacles to admonition and improvement. They are all the more formidable in the light of the social expectations that women have. For women view themselves (and are perceived by men) as the weaker sex. '[They demand] that the weakness of their [nature] should be pitied and pardoned and should not be intentionally abused by stronger people. Hence, they quickly end up in tears, because they believe that they are being reproached out of contempt' (XXIIb. 1–9). Although Philodemus' position concerning women is full of prejudices, it invites us to draw an interesting implication: that no woman who genuinely wishes to receive a good education should ask for gentler treatment on grounds related to her sex.

A last category of people recalcitrant to frank speech consists of old men.[45] Like eminent people, and also women, elders may be criticized both outside and inside the school. For in the spirit of Epicurus (*ad Men.* 122), his disciples are eager to help everybody, young or old, to engage in philosophy and live the good life. Old men, however, are not often willing to put up with *parrhēsia* for a variety of reasons, only some of which are peculiar to their age group. 'They think that they are wiser because they have lived a long time, and they believe that some people proceed to frank speech and to great [outrage] out of contempt for their weakness' (XXIVa. 9–15). Like wealthy or eminent individuals, old men believe themselves to be superior to others. Like women, they are very

[45] It is introduced at XXIVa. 7–9 by the question 'Why is it that old men are more annoyed (by frank speech)?'.

prone to misinterpreting the teacher's motives, and attribute his criticism to insolence and contempt. Like powerful rulers, they have acquired the habit of receiving gracious and respectful treatment and set great store by it. Therefore, they are unwilling to have their errors exposed for fear that their authority may be undermined and their reputation tarnished (XXIVb. 1–9). Deep down they feel very vulnerable, precisely because they know that old age is not always perceived in a positive manner. 'The saying "old men are children for a second time"[46] gets under their skin and pricks them' (XXIVb. 10–11). In this case too, Philodemus' analysis is biased by prejudice, but also has useful normative implications. The teacher should apply *parrhēsia* to old men, just as he would apply it to everyone else in need of therapy. However, he should take into account their physical and emotional fragility and treat them with sensitivity and compassion.

In general, people's reactions to frank speech reveal a great deal about their character, and also about their social and cultural identity. '[By observing their words and deeds], the teacher gets to know more thoroughly regarding each of these two [what kinds] of common features they will exhibit even after they are perfected. Again, he knows which ones come from rather courtly parents or were brought up in the company of people who exercised frank criticism mildly towards the weaker. Equally, he knows both the origins and the [upbringing] that [the many] had' (IVb. 1–12). One reason why he is in a position to do this lies in the capacity of *parrhēsia* to stir the emotions, and thus to highlight factors that have shaped the student's soul. Another reason is this. The *parrhēsia* applied to a young person—e.g., by his parents and teachers—both reflects the moral characteristics of his educators and eventually instils them in the youth himself. It determines who one is and reveals where one comes from.

III

No one can contribute more than the teachers to the solidarity and cohesion of each Epicurean school; but also, no one can harm it more than they can. Of course, it is not the same instructors who cause benefit and harm,

[46] On the meaning and comic sources of this proverb, see Konstan *et al.* 1998: 129 n. 193.

but different ones. In what follows, I shall examine several criteria which, according to Philodemus, enable us to distinguish the bad teachers from the good ones, and especially from the wise men. Moreover, I shall explain why, in Philodemus' view, criticism issued by bad teachers undermines the well-being of individual students and of the entire school, while the *parrhēsia* of good teachers cultivates positive features in persons as well as groups. I shall use the expression 'bad teachers' in a very broad sense to refer to people who are inexperienced, others who are incompetent, and others who are completely corrupt and therefore, strictly speaking, are not teachers at all. Each one of these categories of bad teachers displays not just one, but many, of the faults discussed immediately below. Indeed, like the wrong kind of student, the wrong kind of teacher has a personality marred by many interconnected traits rather than by a single moral flaw.

The fundamental difference between a bad teacher and a good one lies, predictably, in their respective dispositions. The former exercises frank criticism from a mean and petty disposition (διάθεσις φαύλη: Ia. 3–4), and his badness is determined, precisely, by reference to it (Ia. 4 ff.). Assuming that his moral characteristics stand in opposition to those of the good teacher (IIa. 7–9), we may infer that he neither loves nor cares for his students, but bears ill will towards them; is small and petty in character, minds too much about his reputation, and behaves like a demagogue; is versed in the arts of flattery, and also often expresses contempt, insolence, and rage (37. 1–9); he is full of envy, considers himself perfect and infallible (46. 5 ff.), and lacks self-control; says lots of irrelevant things in his criticisms, looks for faults in his students, and has a very harsh tongue (Ib. 1–IIa. 7).[47] In addition, the two kinds of teachers are distinguished from one another on the basis of their affective attitudes towards praise and blame. In the first place, the bad teacher loves the sound of his own voice and, especially, loves to speak in favour of passion 'as some men do when they are in love' (48. 4–5). Besides, contrary to the sage, he feels little or no pleasure in praising students, but is delighted to rebuke them for their faults. However, although the bad teacher does not actually feel pleasure in praising, he often makes illegitimate and excessive use of flattery and inflames the faults of his students in that manner (44. 1 ff.).

[47] The text describes moral characteristics of the good teacher, and asserts that the frankness of anyone displaying the opposite characteristics 'derives from baseness' (IIa. 7–9).

His abuse is all the more violent because it is motivated by very strong passions related to the traits mentioned above. In particular, while the good teacher may occasionally express anger for educational purposes (cf. 10. 10–11, 87. 4–9), the bad teacher is irritable, gets enraged about small things, and loses control of his tongue (IIa. 1–7; cf. also 74. 2). Harsh and bitter *parrhēsia* dictated by rage (cf. IIa. 5–7) can be related to the practice of reproaching the student for everything without circumscribing a particular error (78 = 80N. 1–2). Philodemus calls that practice a most unloving and unfriendly thing (ἄφιλον: 78 = 80N. 2), which injures the student deeply by stripping him of his dignity and self-respect (cf. 78 = 80N. 8–11).

Although vicious teachers, as well as vicious students exercising *parrhēsia* towards their peers, are eager to criticize others, nonetheless, they refuse to be criticized by others in their turn. 'Their obduracy (τὸ δυσκίνητον) too gives them trouble, and also the fact that they are not aware of [their own] errors and that, although they reproach others, they believe that for the most part they have not [erred] themselves' (XVb. 8–15). Thus, they block the path to self-improvement and undermine the relations of equality which should obtain between friends. Even when they seem willing to submit to *parrhēsia*, they do so only for the sake of appearances, since they are convinced that there is really no occasion for it.[48] Their behaviour entails deep inconsistencies between words and deeds, between professed commitment to frank speech and *de facto* disavowal of its principles.

In sharp contrast, the good teacher '[is frank] from a polite disposition' (διάθεσις ἀστεία: Ia. 1–3) and is identified as such on account of that disposition (Ia. 4–8). Namely, he 'bears good will, practises philosophy intelligently [and continually], is great in character, indifferent to fame, least of all a demagogue, clean of envy, says only what is relevant, does not get carried away so as to insult or [strut] or humiliate or harm (others)' (Ib. 2–12); ... 'he is not loose-tongued—[for he is not silly] so as to be enraged if [someone] harms him even [slightly]—nor irritable, nor harsh, nor bitter' (IIa. 2–7). He is pure (cf. καθαρεύοντι: 44. 6–7), loves his students (cf. στέργοντι: 44. 7), is superior to them in wisdom and skill (cf. κρείττονι: 44. 7–8), and therefore knows how to cure them (44. 8–9). He addresses them with no complacency, and has no motive other than their own good. Furthermore, he has the right feelings and attitudes towards praise

[48] Cf. also XVIIb. 7–XVIIIb. 14.

and blame. 'If one should enquire which thing he does more pleasurably, one is seeking something obvious. For it is obvious that he performs the one thing (i.e., praising) with very great pleasure, whereas he endures the other (i.e., blaming) with displeasure and as though he were drinking wormwood' (IIb. 2–8). However, he determines how much and what sort of *parrhēsia* he uses not according to his inclination towards praise or blame, but according to his considered judgement about a given situation (IIb. 8–13).

Similar remarks apply to the good teachers' expression of anger in parrhesiastic speech. Depending on their individual dispositions and upbringing, they may feel a greater or smaller quantity of natural anger, and also, on some occasions, they may simply pretend to experience anger when in fact they do not. However, regardless of the intensity of their emotions, they never indulge in long and abusive speeches, but rather use anger judiciously to admonish their students. They take pains 'never to say anything [contemptuous] at all nor in a tone at all strained' (38. 1–4),[49] and support the student's self-esteem, thus enabling him in the future to make right decisions for himself.[50] Throughout the therapeutic process, each good instructor remains alert to his own shortcomings as much as to the students' needs, and he strives for improvement. An important aspect of his progress consists in realizing that all human beings are susceptible to error. 'How is he going to hate the one who errs, though not in desperately serious matters, when he knows that he himself is not perfect?' (46. 5–9). In sum, his attitude to *parrhēsia* is entirely consistent with his avowed beliefs about the method. He persuades 'through [deeds] too and not just [through speaking]' (16. 5–7).

IV

The characteristics of competent practitioners of frank speech described in the previous section are found, albeit in varying degrees, in promising beginners as well as in advanced students, experienced instructors, and,

[49] This remark primarily concerns the application of *parrhēsia* to students while they are enraged. However, as is confirmed by other fragments, it also reveals the good teacher's general policy: i.e., the use of angry and bitter *parrhēsia* only *ad hoc* and only intermittently.

[50] Perceived in that way, *parrhēsia* does not involve shock tactics or practices of brainwashing.

notably, wise men.[51] Let us start with the students. As mentioned, they are regularly exposed to *parrhēsia*, submitting themselves to it and also applying it to others. I do not need to say anything more about the passive aspect of their training, but I wish to add a few remarks regarding its active aspect. First, when they assume the role of the critic, good students should try to emulate their teachers, adopting comparable attitudes to the best of their own ability. However, there will be cases in which they will become aware of a fellow student's error and will judge, correctly, that admonition ought to come from the teacher rather than from themselves. In such cases they should report the error to the teacher, as it were denouncing their friend. Provided that they are prompted by disinterested motives, their action constitutes proof of true friendship, and the teacher should interpret it in that light.

> He (sc. the teacher) will not consider to be a slanderer a person who desires his friend to obtain correction when, in fact, he is not a slanderer, but rather he will consider that person to be someone who loves his friend (φιλόφιλον)—for he understands exactly the difference between these traits; on the other hand, if he (sc. the student) does not report the fault, he (sc. the teacher) will consider him a bad friend (κ[ακό]φιλον) and someone who loves the bad (φιλόκακον). (50. 3–12)

Although we may concede that this practice of telling on one's friends is not malicious, it certainly seems patronizing. For it suggests that virtually every student of the school believes that he knows what is best for you and acts accordingly.

Students should be careful in respect of just what they confess and to whom. Addressing the question 'Whether they will declare weaknesses of their own and of one another to their fellow students as well' (53. 3–6), Philodemus issues the following warning: 'One must, then, be cautious in admitting one's own ignorance to his classmates. For some will not help one, because they are bereft of depth of understanding' (53. 6–12). In truth, parrhesiastic confession presents two different kinds of risks, one for the person who opens his heart to others, another for those who listen to what he has to say. The former becomes vulnerable, precisely because he exposes his own errors and shortcomings to people whom he trusts

[51] Following Zeno, Philodemus distinguishes the competent practice of *parrhēsia* by well-meaning individuals and its application by the wise man. '[Most of all, we shall seek] to admonish, even if not like the wise man and the philosopher' (35. 1–4).

implicitly but who may not be trustworthy. The listeners too may be shocked, offended, corrupted, or, generally, harmed by the confession of a classmate. For example, as Philodemus points out, sometimes they are not wise enough or mature enough to understand certain things and, hence, to help their peers who confess to them.

Turning now to the teachers, we find that their confessional practices are considerably more complex than those of the students. As indicated, they put up with a certain amount of bitterness expressed by students whose feelings have been hurt by *parrhēsia*, and, furthermore, they may acknowledge their own errors in front of their pupils. However, it seems that they receive *parrhēsia* chiefly from their colleagues. In fact, the formal recipient of their confessions is none other than the founder of the school. '[They present] with frankness their own errors in front of the students, so that they are put before Epicurus and for the sake of correction' (55. 1–6). It is difficult to guess just what is the purpose of that practice. Perhaps it is intended to emphasize the unity of the school by casting Epicurus in the role of the supreme confessor and guide to the good life. The best teachers are perfected professors or wise men. These interact both with people unconnected with the school—notably, wealthy and politically powerful men—and with the members of the Epicurean community—i.e., students, teachers, and sages. In virtue of their wisdom, they must give admonition far more frequently than they receive it. All of them are kindly disposed towards those whom they admonish, and assess their errors according to the same criteria and in the same manner. 'For they all in the same way both love their students in accordance with the worth of each and see their faults' (IIIb. 10–13).

On the other hand, each sage preserves certain elements of individuality which are apparent in his style (cf. VIa. 2–8)[52] and in his way of exercising *parrhēsia*. So, when they speak to 'a confused person, [or] a weakened [or] an arrogant one, or one too shy [or another] too intense, the wise men will differ for many reasons both from one another and from themselves at different times' (IVa. 1–8). The same wise man will be harsher or less harsh than other sages, towards the same or a different student, with regard to the same or different types of faults. Also, he may be stricter on some occasions but less strict on other comparable ones. Regarding their behaviour, some

[52] That the people in question are the sages is strongly suggested by the context.

sages are rather remote and forbidding, whereas others are more sociable and affable. The former have the tendency to pontificate and to speak in an apophthegmatic manner, whereas the latter show greater discretion and grace, avoid breaking into the conversation, and deliver their admonitions in less terse and pointed terms. However, the *parrhēsia* of all sages is of equal value regardless of the particulars characterizing each parrhesiastic speech. 'Even if a person is rather sententious, as Metrodorus says Polyaenus was, "often rather forcing himself into the conversation and quite sociable", he will still be quite trustworthy' (VIa. 8–15).

Philodemus elsewhere examines the reasons which may account for these differences. Sages vary in respect of their emotional constitution, and in particular in respect of their proneness to natural anger.[53] Although they often simulate anger (*De ir.* XXXIV. 16–24), they also occasionally do feel a kind of anger (ὀργή):[54] namely, a spontaneous reaction to intentional offence which is both brief and moderate, and which is entirely compatible with moral perfection (cf. XXXVI. 17–31). In addition to each sage's idiosyncrasy, various contingent factors as well may be responsible for giving the impression of irascibility. For instance, sometimes the sages 'are reduced to that state because people drive them crazy, and because there is augmentation of the common characteristics on account of which they appear irascible, even to the point of truly feeling anger' (XXXIV. 24–31).[55]

Besides, the circumstances of each sage's birth and upbringing may cause a tendency to strictness which even the sage's imitation of his teachers cannot fully counteract (*De lib. dic.* Va. 3–10).[56] Moreover, 'if one has needed *parrhēsia* minimally while another has been saved by means of it, the former applies less whereas the latter applies more of that through which[57] he became perfect' (VIb. 8–13). For example, Polyaenus, who did not need much *parrhēsia*, applied it only moderately to his own pupils

[53] Compare what Lucretius says about natural temperaments in *DRN* III. 288 ff.

[54] This thesis is vigorously debated within the Epicurean school. Specifically, Nicasicrates argues to the effect that the sage must not feel any anger at all: see pp. 202–3, 223–30.

[55] Other contingent factors causing anger in the sage are cited in *De ir.* XXXIV. 39–XXXVI. 6.

[56] It seems that Cleanthes and Metrodorus are figures whom professors with a tougher disposition strive to emulate. 'Regarding their teaching both in the present and in the past, they shall not differ [in any way] from Cleanthes and Metrodorus—for it is obvious that the one in authority (ἐφεστηκώς) will use more abundant frankness. Besides, [after some more] time, when they have gained knowledge of more cases than others who haven't, they will use more *parrhēsia* regarding these types of cases than these other teachers' (Vb. 1–12).

[57] Cf. the reading τ[ὸ] δι'[οὗ] instead of τ[ὸ] δι'[ὅ] in VIb. 12–13.

(VIb. 13–15), whereas other early authorities had their character formed by means of much *parrhēsia*, and hence used it themselves in abundance. Moving a step back, one might wonder just what determined the amount and kind of *parrhēsia* necessary for the education of each sage. The answer, I suppose, includes reference to the character traits peculiar to each sage, and especially to his inclinations and feelings. Sages beset by relatively strong passions must have needed a lot of bitter criticism, whereas those with a less passionate disposition were probably educated in a gentler manner.

The sage is likely to be subjected to harsh criticism even after he has become completely wise. On the one hand, insolent and abusive frankness may be directed at him by enraged students. In that case, his reaction is identical with that of other teachers: he will accept expressions of frustration up to a certain point, but not to the point of allowing himself to be abused and put down. On the other hand, he is ready to make considerable allowances for the criticisms issued by other philosophers or men of letters, even if they are sharper than they should be. 'If a philosopher or a scholar, but not one of those trained by him, speaks frankly to him in such measure, he will not be angry like Zeus towards Capaneus but, on the contrary, he will [endure] it because he knows that this is the way of those who are foolish and imperfect' (Xa. 3–12). In fact, it seems that the wise man is prepared to make the best of such criticisms, even in those cases in which he has to listen to them in public (Xb. 1–14).

But even though he has some reservations regarding the frankness of learned men who do not belong to the school, he entertains none regarding criticisms exchanged between himself and other Epicurean sages. This practice is traced back to the early authorities of the school. 'A wise man will use frank speech towards his friends as Epicurus and Metrodorus did' (15. 7–10). Leonteus, Idomeneus, Pythocles, Hermarchus, and Dositheus have also been subjected to respectful criticism, presumably by other sages, whose names, however, are not mentioned (Tab. II, fr. 6. 3–7).[58] Naturally, the sage preserves his wisdom whether or not he is acknowledged to be wise. Also, he speaks frankly whether or not he receives such an acknowledgement. However, ideal conditions for parrhesiastic confessions

[58] Tab. XIV, extrem. fr. 4 ff. suggests that Epicurus talked to Polyaenus, but it is unclear whether the expression 'he spoke words' or 'stories' ([μύ]θ[ους ἔ]φη) refers to frank speech. The meaning of the whole passage is obscure, but the last three lines (ll. 9–11) suggest that Epicurus and Polyaenus differed in their ways of exercising frank speech.

between him and any other sage obtain only if both parties fully recognize each other's wisdom. 'A wise man will also be frank towards a wise man sometimes. And if the wise man is also acknowledged as such, then a perfect person [encounters] a perfect person' (VIIIa. 1–5).

Assuming that these conditions are met, we should turn to the issue 'whether the wise man will communicate his own errors to his friends with frankness' (81 = 83N. 1–4), for it seems to have received considerable attention from members of the school. The evidence suggests that most of them answer the question in the affirmative, but make the following qualifications. Like the confessions of all sincere people, the sage's confession of his own errors to his friends will be prompted by the right motives and justified by the right reasons, including the genuine desire to open his heart to a friend seeking admonition and support. He will not lay out his errors indiscriminately in front of everyone, but only in the presence of some fellow sages or, possibly, of one of them at a time.[59] He will speak elegantly and decently, avoiding vulgarity and ostentation. Finally, he will speak in the knowledge that he is rendering a service to himself, as well as to his listeners and to the Epicurean community as a whole.

Philodemus' treatise *On Frank Speech* establishes, then, that *parrhēsia* is a central feature of the Epicurean education and the Epicurean way of life. As a pedagogical method, it is flexible and nuanced, and has effective ways of engaging the students' entire personality in order to achieve their moral improvement. It is applied according to sound educational principles and incorporates astute psychological insights. More broadly conceived, as a way of speaking, *parrhēsia* determines the nature of the Epicurean communities and the relationships between their members. It accounts to a large extent for the cohesion of these communities, the transmission of Epicureanism from the teachers to the students, and the systematic promotion of Epicurean values and goals.

[59] The former alternative is suggested by the conjecture ἐν[ίοι]ς, whereas the latter is implied by Gigante's conjecture ἐν[ί] in 84N. 4.

Appendix I

On Gratitude, Περὶ χάριτος (*De grat.*; PHerc. 1414) is another work which belongs to the same ensemble as *On Frank Speech*: viz., *On Characters and Ways of Life*.[1] Unfortunately, it is too badly preserved for much to be said about it with confidence. The slender, fragmentary evidence suggests that Philodemus discussed good will (εὔνοια), the disposition to bestow favours (χάρις), and the disposition to be grateful for the disinterested actions of one's benefactors (cf. εὐχαριστία).[2] Moreover, he appears to have contrasted these features with their corresponding negative traits: the absence of good will and benevolence, the unwillingness to perform acts of χάρις, and ingratitude towards those who have performed such acts towards oneself. The expression 'in accordance with virtue' (κατ' ἀρε[τά]s: *De grat.* IV. 6) and the fragmentary context in which it occurs may indicate that a favour is genuine only if one bestows it from a benevolent disposition and feels pleasure in doing so (sc. ἡδυσμένοι: V. 6–7). It is unclear what Philodemus meant to say about those who return a favour as they would return a loan (cf. δ[ά]νειον: IX. 14).[3] In the light of statements that he makes elsewhere (especially in *On Property Management*), his position was probably this. A favour should not be linked too closely to expected benefits, for that would make it like a business transaction; on the other hand, it should not be severed entirely from such benefits, for that would kill off good hope. Thus, strictly speaking, the good Epicurean does not regard the favour as a loan, but nevertheless he does expect some benefit in return, especially if the person to whom he does the favour is a good person, who would naturally wish to reciprocate (cf. V. 14, VIII. 1–2, XVI. 11–12).

As Philodemus suggests in many treatises, relations of reciprocal benevolence lie at the basis of genuine friendships, whether inside or outside the Epicurean schools. It is possible that he expresses that idea in *On Gratitude* as well, for in the same column there is mention of bestowing a favour (χάρις: V. 8) and of legitimate friendship ([φιλ]ίας … νομίμης: V. 9–10). A proof of genuine friendship is one's eagerness to provide for the needs of one's friends (περὶ φίλων [προνοεῖ]ν:

[1] I use the edition by Tepedino Guerra 1977.

[2] The topics of benevolence, beneficence, and gratitude are central to modern moral philosophy. The literature concerning them examines them in connection with utilitarianism and also with Kantian ethics, and it emphasizes both their social and their personal aspects.

[3] Cf. Tepedino Guerra 1977: 107, who compares Aristotle, *Eth. Nic.* 1164^{b}33 ff.

X. 10–11),[4] as opposed to one's habit of blaming unfortunate circumstances in order not to do so (X. 6–8; cf. also X. 16–18). Moreover, Philodemus appears to refer to the gratitude due to sages (XI. 16–19), who are pure (cf. *καθ[αρούς]*: XI. 18) and free (cf. *ἐλε[υθέ]ραν ἀναπνοήν*: XI. 7–8), abstain from politics (X. 9–12), and never grab the property of those who are their friends (IX. 2–6). Since the sages are not in need of anything except (some) external goods (XIII. 5–7), Philodemus' idea may be that the sages ought to receive external goods as tokens of gratitude from those who listen to their teachings.[5]

In any case, Philodemus argues elsewhere (cf. *De oec.* XXIII. 23–36) that the many nice things given to the sage should not be considered payment, properly speaking. They are gifts offered by thankful students in return for the privilege of associating with him. In truth, good will, benevolence, and gratitude are at the heart of the relationship between the sage and his students, and they alone explain the inclination of the students to give the sage many of their possessions procuring pleasure. These same traits also explain why the members of Epicurean communities including sages invite outsiders who have benevolent feelings towards the school to participate in the school's festivals and rites (*De Epic.*; PHerc. 1232, XXVIII. 12–21). It is a natural thing to think of friends bound to the school by good will and benevolence, and to reciprocate by including them in the school's celebrations.[6] What about people who are ungrateful (*ἀχάριστοι*) for the favours rendered to them? Presumably, they do not return the favours that they have received; they make no provisions for the needs of their friends, and, as the extant remains of *On Gratitude* indicate, they amass money for no good purpose (*De grat.* X. 5–6). Also, they probably refuse to acknowledge the tremendous benefits that they have received from the sage's teachings. What according to Philodemus is 'an impious thing' (*[ἀ]νόσιον*: XII. 6–7) may well refer to the attitude of such people towards the sage or, for that matter, towards any other teacher.

How can ingratitude be cured? Philodemus suggests that ungrateful people, and in particular ungrateful students, should be made aware of the inappropriateness of their behaviour (XVII. 6) and should be disciplined (cf. *[πειθα]ρχίας*: XVII. 13) in accordance with the judgement of their instructor (XVII. 17–21). We do not have any specific information about what sorts of discipline the Epicurean communities used. In this case, perhaps it merely consists in treating the patients by means of two strategies. The one is to read aloud extracts from certain

[4] Note that [*προνοεῖ*] is a conjecture; hence the interpretation of this passage is tentative.

[5] Cf. Philodemus' claim that the teaching of philosophy is the first and noblest source of income in *De oec.* XXIII. 22–36.

[6] On Epicurean recruitment practices, cf. Frischer 1982: *passim*.

writings—an exercise which might be classified under the heading of reading in Philo's lists.[7] The other requires that patients should compose speeches against ingratitude.[8] The context yields no information regarding the exact form and content of these writings. However, it seems fairly certain that they are composed in parrhesiastic mode, and that they include the arguments in defence of gratitude mentioned above.

[7] Cf. *Who is the Heir of Divine Things*, 252–3; *Allegorical Interpretations*, III. 18. See also pp. 74–5.

[8] The text does not explicitly say that this is a cure, but it seems likely that it is.

Appendix II

We now turn to Philodemus' work *On Conversation*, Περὶ ὁμιλίας (*De conv.*; PHerc. 873).[1] This too probably belongs to the group *On Characters and Ways of Life*. Its few surviving parts indicate that Philodemus determines what constitutes appropriate speech (ὁμιλία, λαλιά), and that he contrasts it with inappropriate speech (καχο[μι]λία: *De conv.* I. 2). The former is found primarily among friends in the Epicurean community and promotes the ideals of the school, whereas the latter occurs in bad society and cultivates vice.

Epicurean conversation includes several elements in addition to frank speech. The theoretical study of nature (cf. ἀποθεωρεῖν: VII. 4)[2] and, in general, the activities 'of sight and intellect' (IV. 8–9) constitute part of daily talk between the disciples of the school and contribute to the enrichment of their lives. For they share their ideas and experiences with their friends and find in this kind of communication a genuine source of pleasure. Consequently, Philodemus urges them to 'practise', first and foremost, 'how to speak well, speaking sometimes and not always being silent; he (sc. the student) can take over fully formed what we have taught about silence and speaking, rather than learning by trial and error' (VIII. 3–12). As to the sage, his pleasant conversations with friends reflect his tranquil state of mind and his love for others. In the light of these remarks, the fact that Philodemus praises silence (σιωπή: VI. 2, VIII. 8) might come as something of a surprise. For silence might seem to undermine the significance that he attributes to good conversation. Moreover, it might appear to stall the intellectual, moral, and aesthetic development of the students and their acculturation to the Epicurean community.

Philodemus points out, however, that silence is not recommended in all circumstances and without qualification (IV. 5–6). For whoever does not talk also does not share his perceptions and thoughts (IV. 7–11) with others. On the other hand, there is 'a limit to conversation' (ὁμιλίας πέ[ρας]: V. 2), and there are circumstances in which silence is a tactic preferable to speech. According to this analysis, Epicurean teachers and, specifically, sages may choose to be silent for a variety of reasons and in pursuit of various goals. Hence, we might say that they employ different sorts of silence, one of which can be regarded as therapeutic.

[1] The text is edited by Amoroso (1975).

[2] Cf. also the term ἀποθεω[ρ]ητής and the implication that such a person is fortunate (εὐτυχής: VII. 2–3).

First, by keeping quiet on certain occasions, wise men are not so vulnerable to slander. Of course, there is always the possibility that vilifiers might attribute to them views that they have never held. Nevertheless, common experience suggests that persons who speak little do not attract gossip as much as those who speak a lot. '[Having become] suspicious and then silent [in order] not to be slandered by foolish people [in a very foolish manner], [we are loved] for good reason by good people' (V. 8–13). Moreover, the sage is silent selectively: i.e., in some circumstances, towards certain people, and about certain things. Although the relevant text (sc. IX. 3–11) is terribly damaged and its restoration problematic,[3] nonetheless, the main point appears to be that the sage does not speak at all if he is not in a position to address the right people and to do so in an informed and coherent manner. His silence in such cases can be interpreted as a mark of his intellectual honesty and consideration for his audience. On the other hand, the sage may choose to speak in certain cases in spite of his supposition that his speech is not likely to bring any results. 'I do not mention (*σιωπ[ῶ]*) that the wise (*φρόνιμοι*) often speak even when they think that they won't for the most part be successful' (X. 9–12).

Finally, Philodemus mentions a use of silence that can be considered therapeutic. 'The power of silence lies in its capability to repress one's wife and children and slaves, and to confront[4] them with the presence of their neighbour' (VI. 2–6). The general point is that sometimes talk does not accomplish anything (VI. 1–2), but silence can. The text leaves unclear how silence can repress one's wife, children, etc., in what respect it represses them, and in what way confronting them with the presence of the neighbour achieves this result. Perhaps Philodemus has in mind circumstances in which, e.g., a child gets very angry and we ask him to stop shouting, pointing out to him that he is disturbing the neighbours. In such cases silence may be perceived as therapeutic in the sense that it serves as a means of controlling and eventually eliminating anger. Of course, Philodemus would be wrong to restrict this use of silence to the categories of people mentioned above. In fact, husbands can benefit from it as much as wives, adults as much as children, and bosses as much as their employees. However, his earlier observation that the instruction 'Do not speak' should not be approved without reservation (IV. 5–6) seems correct. Sometimes it is better to have it out with one's spouse than to repress one's anger. And it may be preferable to let a child get the frustration out of his system than to impose silence and confine him to his room.

3 Cf. the reconstruction and translation of these lines by Amoroso (1975).

4 The infinitive *ἀντεκφέρειν* (VI. 6) is unmotivated, but I do not have anything better to propose.

Appendix III

Let us now turn to the extant remains of a treatise whose author is probably Philodemus and whose title does not survive. It may have been titled *On Envy*, [Περὶ φθόνου] (*De inv.*; PHerc. 1678) or, conceivably, *On Malicious Joy*, [Περὶ ἐπιχαιρεκακίας], and belongs either to the ensemble *On the Passions* or to the work *On Vices and the Opposite Virtues*—in which case it might serve as an introduction to the three subsequent chapters devoted to that work.[1] In any case, the surviving parts of the treatise mention both envy (*φθόνος*) and malicious joy (*ἐπιχαιρεκακία*), but give very meagre information concerning Philodemus' views on these subjects.

He denounces both envy and malicious joy in the strongest terms, as conditions of utter bestiality and savagery (*De inv.*, fr. 3. 1). Like other vices and passions, they involve empty beliefs and violent feelings, and are considered irrational evils (cf. *ἄλογον κακόν*: 16. 2–3) in ways in which avarice is (cf. *φιλαργυρία*: 16. 1). They compel people tainted by them to commit particularly hideous deeds (*μοχθηρὰ πράτ[τ]ειν*: 6. 4–5). Indeed, it would seem that they provide unusually powerful motivation for evil actions. An envious person, who is burning with desire for what belongs to another, is likely to do everything in his power in order to obtain it. And the malicious man is not disposed to remain a passive observer, but actively seeks to harm his victims in order to feel joy at their misfortunes. Philodemus perceives envy and malicious joy as deep character flaws, and appears to believe that their removal is imperative from a personal as well as from a social point of view.

What can be done about such patients? Philodemus' recommendations and methods of therapy focus on the fact that both envy and malicious joy derive in part from the excessive value that people afflicted by them ascribe to external goods and evils. The envious person feels envy of the wealth, power, beauty, etc., of his neighbour and, on account of these goods, considers his neighbour more fortunate than himself. The person affected by *ἐπιχαιρεκακία* observes the misfortunes of

[1] I use the edition by Tepedino Guerra (1985). She argues, convincingly in my view, that the author of the text is Philodemus and that, since the text treats malicious joy (*ἐπιχαιρεκακία*) together with envy (*φθόνος*), and since Philodemus is attested as the author of a treatise *On Envy* (Περὶ φθόνου), it is reasonable to consider PHerc. 1678 part of that treatise. However, Croenert 1906 airs the hypothesis that the lost title of the papyrus is [Φιλοδήμου Περὶ Ἐπιχαιρεκακίας], and that the text may, in fact, belong to the work *On Vices and the Opposite Virtues*.

others, believes that they are utterly miserable, and feels a perverse kind of joy for that reason. Thus, both kinds of patients presuppose that external goods make us happy, whereas external evils often deriving from accidents of fortune render us supremely unhappy. Therefore, Philodemus proposes remedies which aim to reform the beliefs and values of these patients, and also their feelings and attitudes. The reasoning involved is '[of necessity] conjectural' (cf. *στοχαστικόν*: 17. 1), given the nature of the subject matter.

First of all, patients should assimilate and remember the principles of Epicurean philosophy. '[After we have gained understanding about this way of life] and after we have memorized (its principles), we would not fall prey to the passion called malicious joy' (14. 1–6). Especially, patients should internalize the principles concerning the relatively small value of external goods. 'We should always have ready to hand the causes on account of which people feel malicious joy and, as it happens, they are almost the same as the reasons for which people feel envy' (17. 2–7). As mentioned above, the causes in question are external goods coveted by envious or malicious people, and also external evils which may affect envious or malicious men themselves or may afflict their neighbours. If patients are made to realize that externals do not matter very much to one's happiness, they will be able to face bad luck with equanimity and endure the deprivation of goods without complaining or begrudging others.

Probably in the way of complementary treatment, patients should be encouraged to strengthen their feelings of altruism and philanthropy, as well as their commitment to civic ideals. 'We consider it [an indifferent thing] to fall into some evils, provided that they are not many and continuous. And it is necessary to remember that many goods, even if one is deprived of them, constitute a benefit for many people or, generally, for the city [in which we too] are included' (18. 1–9). A third remedy may help as well. In contrast to those who concede that the good person may experience pleasure at the pain afflicting evildoers (10. 1–5),[2] Philodemus insists that if one is to be entirely cured of *ἐπιχαιρεκακία*, one should repress joy even in those cases in which it appears justified. '[If we shall refrain] from feelings of malicious joy when we are confronted with some cases, it will be possible to remove (malicious joy), even if we may want to deal with all the other issues related to it' (19. 1–6). The best strategy for extirpating malicious joy is simply to school oneself never to indulge in it.[3] Philanthropy and compassion should extend to all human beings, not only to the deserving few.

[2] Tepedino Guerra (1985: 114) attributes this view to Aristotle, *Eth. Eud.* 1233^{b}20 ff. Frs. 11–13 may also refer to the same subject, but the text is uncertain.

[3] Compare the Cynic belief that virtue requires both knowledge and exercise (*ἄσκησις*).

6

Flattery and the Desire to Please

On Flattery, Περὶ κολακείας (*De adul.*; PHerc. 222, 223, 1082, 1089, 1457, 1643, and 1675)[1] is, in all probability, the opening treatise[2] of Philodemus' composition *On Vices and the Opposite Virtues and the People in whom they occur and the Situations in which they are found*, Περὶ κακιῶν καὶ τῶν ἀντικειμένων ἀρετῶν καὶ τῶν ἐν οἷς εἰσι καὶ περὶ ἅ.[3] Its subject is developed in two books,[4] passages of which are found in several papyri.[5] Although the state of the evidence poses formidable problems of textual reconstruction, the extant remains indicate that Philodemus covers the following topics.[6] He outlines what kind of trait flattery, κολακεία (translit. *kolakeia*), is and describes its essential characteristics. He analyses the character, motives, and behaviour of the flatterer, and he distinguishes him from other human 'types' that instantiate vices which belong, as it were, to the same family. He examines the interpersonal relationships which flattery brings about, concentrating on the character of the flatterer's victims. He highlights the ways in which flattery is interconnected with other vices, and points out its consequences. He contrasts the flatterer with the sage. And he suggests

[1] I use the following editions and commentaries: Caini 1939 (PHerc. 222, 223, 1082); De Falco 1926 (PHerc. 1675); Gargiulo 1981 (PHerc. 222); Gigante and Indelli 1978 (PHerc. 223); Kondo 1974 (PHerc. 1457); Longo Auricchio 1986; Acosta Méndez 1983 (PHerc. 1089).

[2] See Angeli 1994.

[3] Monet (2001: 200) maintains that the overall title of the work was probably simply *On Vices*, (Περὶ κακιῶν).

[4] Monet (2001) argues that the first book of *On Flattery* mainly treats the vice itself, while the second book focuses on the vices related to flattery.

[5] There is disagreement as to which papyri should be attached to each book of *On Flattery*. It seems that PHerc. 222, of which twelve columns are edited by Gargiulo (1981), is the beginning of Book I of *On Flattery*. PHerc. 1675 constitutes the end of the same scroll. PHerc. 1643, 1089, and 1082 also belong to the first book of the treatise (cf. Angeli 1994; Capasso 2001). It is difficult to decide to which book PHerc. 223, edited by Gigante and Indelli (1978), should be attached. Capasso's readings of two subscriptions of PHerc. 1457 (cf. Capasso 1995, 2001) suggest that that papyrus alone constitutes the second book of *On Flattery*.

[6] Concerning his pattern of analysis, see p. 53.

ways in which flattery and the vices related to it can be cured or altogether avoided.[7]

From what we can tell, Philodemus' treatment of flattery is incisive and in places original, and emphasizes aspects of flattery not always found in the relevant literature. These include, for instance, the conceptual relations between flattery and cognate traits, the interactions between flatterers and their victims, and the reinterpretation of literary figures in the light of the hypothesis that they act as flatterers or as people susceptible to the flatterers' arts.

I

According to Philodemus, flattery, or adulation (κολακεία), is a character trait which amounts chiefly to a disposition (διαθέσεως: PHerc. 1089, IV. 5; cf. also I. 9, I. 13) to react in a certain manner in response to certain situations as they are perceived by the agent. So flattery is what we might call a content-sensitive inner state which has intentionality in a limited sense, and which is typically manifested in one's feelings, attitudes, and comportment. The specific nature of that state is rendered by the description of the flatterer (κόλαξ) as 'the man who speaks in order to please' (PHerc. 1457, IV. 7–8) and who does not try to procure the necessities of life through friendship but rather through flattery (cf. PHerc. 222, III. 6–7).

It is obvious that flattery is exercised primarily through speech. The flatterer gives pleasure to his victim mainly by expressing approval, admiration, and praise. Of course, not all comments of these sorts are instances of flattery. They qualify as such only if they are frequent and regular, if they are partly or wholly unjustified, and are uttered mainly for the purpose of advancing the flatterer's self-interest. The flatterer invents or exaggerates his victim's virtues and deeds (PHerc. 1457, II. 14. 5 ff.),[8] and his aim is to bring his victims into the right frame of mind so as to make them cater to his own needs (χρείας: PHerc. 222, III. 2, 7). Flattering speech is not exclusively laudatory. Depending on the circumstances and the audience, the flatterer

[7] I make no claim about the particular order in which Philodemus examines these topics.

[8] Kondo (1974: 48–9) discusses in that connection Philodemus, *Rhet.* IV I 214. 10 ff., Sudhaus.

may also 'lament about his poverty and tell lies' (PHerc. 1089, VII. 6). He may offend or attack those people whom he perceives as obstacles to his goals (PHerc. 222, VII. 1 ff.). At times, he denounces what other people say or do with nastiness and disparagement (PHerc. 1457, IV. 7 ff.). Or he keeps silent (PHerc. 1457, II. 14–16, fr. 1. 5–6). Flattery is practised also by means of body language and physical demeanour. An admiring eye, a fixed smile, a nod of approval, or a posture of intense attention can bring about the desired effect. In sum, there is a rhetoric pertaining to flattery. It mainly, but not wholly, consists of adulatory speech. And, in contrast to philosophical discourse (PHerc. 223, fr. 2. 9–10),[9] it works with a view to one's own needs and not with a view to what is just (PHerc. 1457, fr. 15. 10–14).

Closer examination brings out additional characteristics of the flatterer's ways and disposition. He must conceal his true character, for 'he will be rather unsuccessful in obtaining a living for himself if he is even suspected to be a flatterer, let alone if he is demonstrated to be one' (PHerc. 222, III. 7–10). This kind of concealment is important for the flatterer for reasons comparable to those for which it is crucial for every orator. The orator influences his audience only if he appears to be creditable and fair-minded and to say simply what he believes to be the case.[10] The more artful he is, the more natural he seems to be, regarding both the delivery and the contents of his speech. Likewise, the flatterer manipulates his victims only if he convinces them, at least superficially, that his praise is sincere, disinterested, and also true.[11] This implies hiding his own personality and motives, appearing to be what he is not.

Moreover, the flatterer makes deliberate efforts to isolate his victims, chasing away everyone who loves them and also every other flatterer who competes for their favours. 'Generally speaking, the flatterer hates all persons who are devoted to the flattered man, but most of all his parents and other relatives, his [wife] and his friends, against whom he fights most vigorously [during meals]. As to [the other] flatterers, he keeps them [at a distance and uncared for], (so that he is the) only one to eat. On the other hand, [he uses soft words] towards the flattered man [especially when he is

[9] The text mentions flattery and philosophy, and I infer that it contrasts them to each other.

[10] See Aristotle, *Rhet.* I. 4.

[11] As we shall see, the viciousness and self-interested motivation of the flatterer can be in some way transparent to his victim.

not] sober—something [not difficult to imagine]' (PHerc. 222, VII. 1–12). The end of that passage indicates that lack of decency, self-respect, and a proper sense of pride are also characteristics of the flatterer's behaviour. He develops, as it were, a thick skin, which allows him to become the willing subject of offence and abuse by those whom he flatters. One might wonder how he reacts to their insults and blows. Perhaps the answer is that he does not react to them at all, or, worse, that he gives signs of appreciating them. In any case, he tolerates these offences in the knowledge that they please the persons he intends to flatter and, therefore, are conducive to his own ends. Again, we get the picture of a man for whom the only thing that matters is the satisfaction of his needs, not the niceties of good demeanour and morality. The same impression is conveyed by Philodemus' comments that the flatterer behaves like 'a little dog [———] or a little monkey or some other tame animal [of that kind]' (PHerc. 222, IX. 14–16).

Banquets, public or private, constitute the paradigmatic context in which the features of the flatterer become especially manifest. For Philodemus seems to think that at table, more than anywhere else, the flatterer gets opportunities to exercise his vicious skills and to pursue his objectives. The extant remains of *On Flattery* are sprinkled with references to the eating, drinking, and dancing taking place during a feast (e.g., PHerc. 223, frs. 4. 2, 5b. 1, and 6. 1–20; PHerc. 1089, VI. 2 ff.), and to the inappropriate behaviour of the participants (e.g., PHerc. 223, fr. 6. 1–20; PHerc. 222, VII. 1–17). Furthermore, Philodemus situates his examples in the courts and tables of rulers. Flatterers and parasites surround Alexander the Great (PHerc. 223, fr. 1. 1 ff.), whose reactions are not recorded, however, in the remnants of the text.[12] Odysseus, who, somewhat surprisingly, is depicted as a parasite, freely uses the table and bed of Aeolus, fills his belly as well as his pouch with the food of Alcinoos, king of the Phaeacians, and even partakes of the bloody meals of the dead in Hades (PHerc. 223, fr. 3. 1–9).

[12] This fragment mentions two persons by name: Alexander (fr. 1. 1) and Timagoras (fr. 1. 6, 11). It has been suggested that Timagoras is an Athenian flatterer of Alexander the Great; but this thesis is implausible for chronological reasons (see Gigante and Indelli 1978: 127). In fact, it seems that the text traces no relation between those two personages. Fr. 1. 1–6 talks about the flatterers surrounding Alexander, and perhaps also his attitude towards them, whereas fr. 1. 7 ff. moves on to another subject which involves Timagoras. As to the identity of Timagoras, Gigante and Indelli (1978: 127–8) maintain that he is probably a heretic Epicurean contemporary of Philodemus, and that he should be kept distinct from Timasagoras, another Epicurean heretic who, together with Nicasicrates, is attacked by Philodemus in the treatise *On Anger* (cf. pp. 203–9).

Meanwhile, back in Ithaca, the suitors help themselves to Odysseus' own goods as they wait for the queen to take one of them as her husband (PHerc. 222, VII. 18 ff.).

In these examples, as well as in other passages, Philodemus suggests that there are certain vices which are distinct from flattery but related to it. He sorts out the essential features of these vices and explains how flattery can be distinguished further from each of them. In contrast to Zeno of Sidon,[13] he does not leave out the vices akin to flattery, but compares and contrasts the flatterer (κόλαξ), successively, with the parasite (παράσιτος), the sycophant (προστροχαστής), and the obsequious man (ἄρεσκος).[14] His view regarding the logical relations among these vices remains unclear. One possibility is that he defines them in terms of a focal vice, flattery, and other peripheral characteristics which distinguish these vices from flattery as well as from each other.[15] Another interpretation might be that the flatterer, the parasite, the sycophant, and the obsequious man illustrate distinct vices which are species of the one genus, speaking in order to please (πρὸς χάριν λέγειν).

As regards parasites (cf. παράσι[τος]: PHerc. 1457, IV. 8), they resemble the flatterer (PHerc. 1457, I. 5–7) in so far as they too aim to please in order to cater to their own needs.[16] However, flatterers rarely keep their mouths shut, whereas parasites do not speak all the time but often choose to please by keeping quiet (PHerc. 1457, fr. 1. 5 ff.). 'They withhold [speech] because they yield to everybody' (PHerc. 1457, II. 14–16), and are very much of one mind with those who behave in a base manner (cf. PHerc. 1457, I. 10–12). In certain circumstances, the parasite 'promptly pretends to feel compassion for those who have met with misfortune and to offer them help at once' (PHerc. 1457, fr. 2. 36 ff.). His hypocrisy is more blatant than the flatterer's, and so is his shamelessness (PHerc. 1457, fr. 4. 36–7). Neither 'type' can make any true judgements, but there are certain differences in their respective dispositions and moral folly (PHerc. 1457, I. 16–18).[17] To summarize, the parasite cuts a more passive, more servile, and less dangerous figure than the flatterer. But although such

[13] See PHerc. 1457, fr. 24. 28–33.

[14] My discussion of these vices is heavily indebted to Kondo 1974.

[15] This seems to be his model for the analysis of vices related to arrogance.

[16] Cf. the discussion of Kondo (1974: 50).

[17] I advance this claim only tentatively, for the text that I cite in support of it is incomplete.

people 'involve us in lesser misfortunes than the flatterers, nevertheless they should not be avoided less than the flatterers should be' (PHerc. 1457, fr. 4. 37 ff.).

Moving on to the sycophant (προστροχαστής: PHerc. 1457, IV. 18), Philodemus observes that the common feature that he has with the flatterer, and also with the parasite, is that he too often speaks with the purpose of causing pleasure to his victim. But, unlike them, he sometimes also tells tales on others, denouncing their words and actions and gossiping about them with meanness in order to gain favour for himself (cf. PHerc. 1457, IV. 17 ff.).[18] In this last regard, the sycophant looks similar to two interrelated types whose respective vices belong to the same family as arrogance: the disparager (εὐτελιστής) or utter disparager (ἐξευτελιστής) and the vilifier (οὐδενωτής) or utter vilifier (ἐξουδενωτής).[19] These 'types' are very similar in nature, but differ slightly in degree, i.e., in the intensity and extent to which each of them slanders his victims (*De superb.* XXIV. 1–10). Their affinity to the sycophant consists in the practice of discussing someone behind his back in a distorting and slanderous manner. However, they differ from the sycophant in two important respects. The latter's slander aims to cause pleasure to the listener, whereas theirs does not;[20] and it is intended to work to the sycophant's own advantage, whereas the denunciations of the arrogant 'types' are usually gratuitous. Perhaps these differences explain why Philodemus does not point out the relationship of sycophancy to arrogance, but classifies sycophancy as a vice related to flattery rather than arrogance. At any rate, he makes clear that the sycophant is a meaner person than the flatterer or the parasite. He can be particularly dangerous, and should be kept away at all costs.

Like the parasite, and unlike the sycophant, the obsequious man (cf. ἀρέσκ[οις]: PHerc. 1457, fr. 21. 39)[21] is, in some ways, a better person than the flatterer. Philodemus describes him as someone who 'wants to please everybody, but perhaps more the eminent people by telling each of them that he is handsome, rich, [magnanimous], beneficent' (PHerc.

[18] Regarding the differences between sycophancy and the practice of reporting the errors of one's friends to the Epicurean teachers, see *De lib. dic.*, fr. 51. 6–12.

[19] Cf. p. 159.

[20] The listener may be pleased, all the same, to hear his fellow men disparaged or vilified.

[21] Philodemus also uses the term ἀρεσκευόμενος (cf. PHerc. 1457, X. 19–20) to designate the person who wishes to please. This term may refer to those who flatter or, alternatively, to people who like being flattered.

1457, V. 19–24),[22] and who attends many people from whom there is no benefit to be acquired (PHerc. 1457, VIII. 15–18).[23] So, while flatterers cause pleasure for the sole purpose of obtaining advantages, obsequious persons have the disposition to please others even when there is no obvious advantage for themselves. It would seem that flattery is found in cold, calculating people who are usually very efficient in the pursuit of their own good. On the other hand, obsequiousness 'is an inseparable feature of dandies and of arrogant men and, furthermore, of people who are shallow and busy with foolish trifles but who are in want' (PHerc. 1457, fr. 21. 33–7). Such people are pathetic rather than dangerous. They often draw upon themselves the contempt and abuse of others (PHerc. 1457, IX. 4 ff.), and are unable to protect themselves because of their weakness (PHerc. 1457, VIII. 19–23). However, Philodemus warns strongly against obsequiousness, for pedagogical as much as for moral reasons (PHerc. 1457, X. 17 ff.).

II

So far, Philodemus' discussion might seem to suggest that flattery and other related vices are personal vices: they are confined to their possessors whose victims, however, are good and innocent people. If we leave aside Alexander,[24] we might be inclined to think of Alcinoos and of Penelope in the way in which the epic tradition suggests: the one as an honourable and generous king, the other as a faithful wife harassed by the suitors and unable to drive them away.[25] However, Philodemus invites us to revisit these examples. Since adulators wish to extract gains from their victims (PHerc. 222, V. 5–8), they naturally swarm around persons who are in a position to yield them: i.e., people exceedingly rich (*μεγαλοπλούτοις*: PHerc. 222, V. 3), holders of tyrannical power (*δυν[α]στευτικοῖς*: PHerc.

[22] Compare Theophrastus, who maintains that flattery enters on the goal of the flatterer to procure some sordid advantage for himself (*Char.* A. 1), whereas obsequiousness (*ἀρέσκεια*) focuses on producing pleasure by all feasible means (*Char.* E. 1).

[23] Regarding the structure of Philodemus' argument, see Kondo 1974: 51.

[24] We are not in a position to tell whether or not Philodemus approves of Alexander's attitude towards flatterers and parasites, because of the poor condition of the text.

[25] This is a perfectly defensible reading of the Homeric texts, although there are also other ways of interpreting them.

222, V. 3–4), or demagogues (δημοκό[ποις]: PHerc. 222, V. 4).[26] People of these kinds are much more numerous than flatterers (PHerc. 1457, fr. 15. 2 ff.). And, as Philodemus' terminology indicates, they are far from being good, presumably because they are greedy for money, power, political influence, fame, etc.

All lovers of flattery (*φιλοκόλακες*) take pleasure in hearing themselves praised, whether they believe that they merit the flatterer's eulogies or they are somehow aware that they do not deserve them. If they do not realize that they have faults, then they both enjoy and believe flattery. But if they are somehow aware of their flaws, they enjoy flattery because of their excessive self-love, even though they do not entirely believe it. In this last case, the lovers of flattery, 'although they are aware that they do not possess the qualities attributed to them but that they have some faults, nonetheless feel joy at the praises; <for in truth>,[27] they do not have any detailed knowledge of themselves' (PHerc. 1457, fr. 14. 5–10). Conversely, people who are not lovers of flattery may not rationally know that they have faults, but do not listen to flattery, either because they do not love money, power, etc., or because they do not love themselves too much, or both. 'Because they do not rationally see the persuasiveness of the praise, they are not actually misled by it' (PHerc. 1457, fr. 14. 2–5). It would seem that, according to Philodemus, self-knowledge of an inadequate sort (e.g., superficial or incomplete) does not influence one's attitude to flattery in any decisive manner. On the other hand, a thorough knowledge of oneself is probably necessary as well as sufficient in order to cure one's susceptibility to flattery and to drive adulators away.[28]

The lovers of flattery behave towards adulators in an inconsistent manner, especially when they know at some level that they do not possess the qualities for which they are being praised (PHerc. 1457, fr. 14. 5–10), or when they recognize that they are surrounded by self-seeking people (cf. PHerc. 1457, fr. 14. 2 ff.). Alongside their willingness to cater to the flatterer's needs, Philodemus registers their open contempt towards him and the fact that they abuse him. 'He is known to be [willing] to let himself be maltreated, and

[26] According to Aristotle, both flatterers and demagogues have great power—the flatterer with the tyrant, the demagogue with democracies in which the decrees of the multitude supersede the law (*Pol.* IV, 1292^{a}1 ff.). Kondo (1974: 47) compares and contrasts the positions of Aristotle and Philodemus on this matter.

[27] 14.10 <δέ> Tsouna.

[28] See Kondo 1974: 48.

he accepts very [many] acts of drunken behaviour and abuses [even to the point of taking many wounds] and blows' (PHerc. 222, VII. 12–17). One plausible explanation for the behaviour of the lovers of flattery is that they correctly grasp the moral quality of the flatterer but cannot deprive themselves of his presence. Much of the frustration and anger at their own selves, then, is turned instead against the flatterer. Even more so if, in addition, they sense that they are being manipulated by him for his own ends.

We may conclude that flattery is an essentially reciprocal vice. For the flatterer's disposition to speak in a pleasing but, usually, untruthful manner for self-interested purposes manifests itself fully only when he comes into contact with lovers of flattery. Philodemus' reference to 'erotic passions' (ἐρωτικὰ πά[θη]: PHerc. 222, I. 6) may suggest a comparison between those passions and the feelings encouraged by flattery. Both are fuelled by empty beliefs, and both can be considered irrational in the sense that they cannot be accounted for in terms of true beliefs about the good.[29] I shall elaborate briefly. Clearly, the flatterer can give reasons why he praises his victim, and also the lover of flattery can tell us why he enjoys listening to the praise, whether or not he deserves it. However, the former has an inaccurate understanding of his true needs and self-interest, while the latter excessively values certain external goods (wealth, power, etc.) and loves being flattered as someone who possesses them. Both may engage in sound means–ends reasoning in order to get what they want, but neither has rationally examined the relevant factors in order to want the right things.

Flattery does not occur alone, but is interconnected with other vices. Flatterers, as well as obsequious people (ἄρεσκοι),[30] 'are afflicted by these passions' (PHerc. 1457, XII. 17–19); that is, 'they are envious, slanderous, avaricious and wantonly destructive and are affected by many other vices' (PHerc. 1457, XII. 21–5). Selfishness and ingratitude can be added to the list. Furthermore, the desire to please at all costs is found 'in vulgar people ... and the love of glory occurs in many men and even in friends, so that all kinds of evils happen to them. Besides, the vice is an inseparable

[29] On this sense of 'irrational', see p. 35. There is no surviving text that actually asserts that flattery and the love of flattery are irrational conditions. I surmise that Philodemus considers these vices irrational, because he says that they involve false beliefs and values and also diminished self-knowledge, and because he proclaims arrogance irrational on precisely these grounds.

[30] On the distinctions between κολακεία and ἀρέσκεια, the κόλαξ and the ἄρεσκος, and also the φιλοκόλαξ and the ἀρεσκευτικός, see Kondo 1974: 51 ff.

feature of dandies and of arrogant men, and further of people who are shallow and busy with foolish trifles but who are inferior. These and other vices follow for [obsequious men], while nothing useful or good does' (PHerc. 1457, fr. 21. 29–39). Similarly, the lovers of flattery have several interrelated moral faults, notably self-love, and also greed, love of power, love of glory,[31] arrogance, intemperance, and even cruelty, which is manifested in their abusive behaviour towards the flatterer. The same holds for people affected by vices belonging to the same family as the love of flattery: that is, people moved by the efforts of those who try to please them (cf. ἀρ[εσ]κεύεσθαι: PHerc. 1457, X. 18) and lovers of praise (φιλέπαινοι: cf. PHerc. 1457, fr. 23).

Philodemus' analysis implies that anyone affected by flattery is bound to suffer serious damage, both internal and external. Flattery and its cognates, in their active as well as their passive form, shatter one's tranquillity and cause anxiety and pain.[32] Moreover, they have bad results in practical life. Predominant among them are the social isolation of the flattered man and the lack of protection that ensues, the fact that he wastes his property catering to the flatterers' needs, and the loss of his respectability and reputation. In fact, according to Philodemus, there is a kind of reputation which is not an evil, but which is appropriate both for the layman and for the philosopher, and is pursued for the sake of security and in accordance with nature; on the other hand, the reputation gained by flattery brings one infamy, not honour (PHerc. 222, IV. 4–12). In short, comments Philodemus citing Homer, '"there is Strife, Tumult, and Death in these assemblies"' (PHerc. 222, XII. 13–14), i.e., 'the habitual gatherings' (cf. συνηθείας (gen. sing.): PHerc. 222, XII. 10), 'social intercourse' ([συν]αν[ασ]τροφῆς: PHerc. 222, XII. 11) and 'conversation' (ὁμιλί[α]: PHerc. 222, XII. 21) between the flatterers and those whom they flatter.[33]

[31] The term φιλοδοξία used by Plutarch to designate the lust for fame and glory typically found in politicians (*De se ipsum* ... 539E–540A; cf. also *Adul.* ... 55E) corresponds to Philodemus' use of the term (PHerc. 1089, IV. 13) and also to his use of δοξοκοπία: see Kondo 1974: 53.

[32] Recall the flatterer's insecurity, as well as the frustration, anger, and shameful dependence of his victims. Besides, think of the friendlessness and loneliness of the lovers of flattery, and also of their bitterness and disappointment when they are abandoned in their hour of need by those who flatter them.

[33] Notice that these terms also describe the Epicurean gatherings of friends. The occasions on which flatterers pay court to the great and powerful are, as it were, a mirror image of encounters within the context of the Epicurean society of friends.

Adulators too have bad consequences to bear. If their insincerity and ulterior motives are detected, they may be dragged to court and fined (PHerc. 222, VI. 19 ff.). Their speech and demeanour renders them utterly ridiculous.[34] Precisely because they encourage vice in their victims, they expose themselves to psychological and even physical pain (PHerc. 222, VII. 12–17; PHerc. 1457, IX. 4 ff.). Besides, 'being obsequious (ἄρεσκος) is the bad luck and misfortune similar to that of enslaved servants or women' (PHerc. 1457, VIII. 19–22). The obsequious man meets the 'contempt and ingratitude of most people towards whom he behaved with courtesy; and he bears the censure even of the most dishonourable men, whereas (he is treated in a hurtful way) by virtuous people who [want] to show in their turn their complete derision, disparagement and sarcasm' (PHerc. 1457, IX. 4 ff.). The moral to draw is that both flattery and one's susceptibility to it cause considerable suffering to everybody concerned.

III

Philodemus maintains that flattery and cognate vices impoverish one's life in so far as they are incompatible with friendship. The flatterer associates with his supposed friends if he can get benefits from them, but he is ready to abandon them and search for new victims as soon as he perceives that they fall upon hard times.[35] By contrast, the true friend is always prepared to lend protection and support. 'The [friend] [comes] readily to one's aid in cases of need and he alone remains in the direst [poverty]' (PHerc. 1089, II. 1–3). Also, the flatterer says the kinds of things that he knows will please his audience regardless of their truth, whereas the genuine friend is truth-telling (cf. παρρη[σιαζό]μενον: PHerc. 222, III. 27–8).[36] Again, the difference between the rhetoric of the flatterer and the *parrhēsia* of the true friend can be put in ethical wording: the former aims at pleasure and material self-interest, whereas the latter aims at truth and the good.

Generally speaking, genuine friendship entails that there is an intimate connection between one's behaviour and one's disposition towards one's friends, whereas flattery implies no relation of that kind. Philodemus marks

[34] See, e.g., the comparison with little dogs, monkeys, and other tame animals in PHerc. 222, IX. 12–16.

[35] On this point, see Acosta Méndez 1983: 130–3.

[36] Cf. *De lib. dic.* fr. 1. 2.

that difference between the outward trappings of friendship, as it were, and its reality in the agent's soul in the following manner. First, in the context of a dispute with the Peripatetic philosopher Aristo of Ceos (cf. 'Ἀρίστ[ω]ν: PHerc. 222, X. 5),[37] he draws distinctions between imitating and emulating a friend: '[for someone] to imitate (*μιμεῖσθαι*) [is one thing], whereas to emulate (*ζηλοῦν*) [is another]' (PHerc. 222, X. 8–10). Also, Philodemus suggests that while the flatterer says and does the kinds of things that a friend might be expected to say or do,[38] nevertheless he accomplishes them in an entirely superficial and quasi-mechanical way. He pretends to be a friend (*προσπο[ι]εῖσθαι*: PHerc. 1457, fr. 2) without actually being one. He makes 'an outward show ([*ὑπό*]*κρισιν*) of affection [leading to the greatest profit]' (PHerc. 222, XII. 1–2),[39] but in fact he does not feel affection. His seeming manifestations of it do not reflect his disposition, and, in that sense, they have no depth.[40] However, they do create a mirage, the impression that the flatterer truly cares for his victim. This sort of imitation is comparable to the image of an object reflected in a mirror:[41] it is an appearance without any reality attached to it, form without a substance. Compare now the person who strives zealously to become a true friend. He too practises imitation, but of an entirely different sort. He endorses the goals that a true friend has, and then sets himself to become the kind of person who would achieve them. Thus, his behaviour is not a pretence or a play-act, but has the relevant dispositional underpinnings. It has depth, in the sense that it is actually anchored precisely in those feelings, attitudes, and actions which characterize genuine friendship.

The truest friend is, naturally, the sage (*σοφός*). For he has both the wisdom or soundness of mind (cf. *φρενήρεις*: PHerc. 1457, fr. 12. 5–6) to reject wealth and the love to guide others towards the good. However, ill-intentioned people often accuse the sage of being a flatterer, and Philodemus takes that charge seriously.[42] He refutes it by explaining why the sage might

[37] Cf. p. 143 n. 3, 143–62 *passim*.

[38] e.g., he expresses approval and support, looks compassionate and understanding, takes one's side against one's enemies, and so on.

[39] Cf. also PHerc. 1457, III. 13 ff.

[40] So flatterers do not really love their friends; they are not *φιλόφιλοι* (PHerc. 1089, I. 4) in the manner in which good men are.

[41] See Plutarch, *Adul.* 53a, and Gargiulo 1981: 123.

[42] In his ethical treatises, Philodemus regularly sets the feelings, attitudes, and behaviour of the vicious man in contraposition to those of the sage. He does so in considerable length and detail,

appear afflicted by the vice and, subsequently, by arguing that the alleged affinities between the sage and the vicious man are only superficial or, in most cases, non-existent.[43] 'While the sage will never behave in a way similar to the flatterer, nonetheless he is bound to create in some people the suspicion that he is such, because [he charms the mind] in a manner that not even the mythical Sirens do' (PHerc. 222, II. 2–7). 'When the relatives and the acquaintances of some students realize that they (sc. these students) prefer him to themselves, they [characterize] him as a flatterer. The sophists too do [the same thing]' (PHerc. 222, II. 18–23). Moreover, the honour and gifts given to the sage often cause the students' relatives to call him a flatterer, and the same holds for the sage's strategy of giving praise and encouragement to deserving students, which they interpret as an attempt to please the students and thus dispose them favourably towards the school (cf. PHerc. 222, II. 9–16). Besides, the extant remains of *On Epicurus* mention that ill-wishers attribute flattery to the sage on account of certain institutional features of the Epicurean school, notably the festivals in commemoration of the dead. They describe as 'demagogy' (*De Epic.*; PHerc. 1232, XXVIII. 15) the long-established practice of inviting to Epicurean banquets 'the disciples themselves and all the other people who are around the house without omitting any non-member of the school who has benevolent feelings towards themselves and their friends' (*De Epic.*; PHerc. 1232, XXVIII. 6–12).[44] Although the surviving part of *On Epicurus* does not clarify the relationship between demagogy and flattery, it suggests that the demagogue and the flatterer manipulate their victims in similar ways, by speaking and acting with the purpose of causing pleasure and promoting their own ends.

One way to refute these charges is to introduce a distinction between gratifying one's companions (cf. *τὸ τοῖς πέλας ἀνδάνειν*: PHerc. 1457,

especially regarding those faults of character which might be attributed to the sage with some degree of verisimilitude, should some ill-wisher be inclined to do so. One reason why he does so is certainly apologetic: to argue that, despite superficial similarities, there is in truth a world of difference between the good and the bad man in the relevant respects. Another related reason, and a more important one for present purposes, is conceptual: to sharpen the focus of each character trait under discussion, highlight its features, and, in that manner, distinguish it from other traits.

[43] Compare the way in which Philodemus handles the accusations that the sage is arrogant, and that he is irascible: see pp. 150–1, 219–21 respectively.

[44] This practice is traced back to Epicurus' *Symposium*: *De Epic.*; PHerc. 1232, XXVII. 12–13 (= fr. 47, Tepedino). On the precise nature of the Epicurean festivals or banquets, see Clay 1998: 75–102, esp. the testimonia for the Epicurean cults, pp. 88 ff.

X. 10–11)[45] and being obsequious to them (cf. ἀρέσκεια: PHerc. 1457, X. 12).[46] That distinction was drawn by the Peripatetics and problematized by Nicasicrates (probably an Epicurean philosopher whose interpretation of Epicurus' views differs from that of Zeno and Philodemus).[47] Following Democritus, Nicasicrates appears to have held that pleasing one's companions is a harmful form of obsequiousness (cf. PHerc. 1457, X. 10 ff.), and thus to have suggested that there is no real difference between these two ways of speaking and behaving to one's friends. But Philodemus rejects that view. He contends that Nicasicrates' wholesale rejection of our speaking in a pleasing manner to our friends is incompatible with Epicurean philosophy, to which, nonetheless, he lays claim. 'I do not see how Nicasicrates can be in agreement with the Epicureans, and in particular with Colotes... when he praises Democritus for censuring the practice of gratifying one's companions[48] on the grounds that obsequiousness [causes harm]' (PHerc. 1457, X. 6–12). More generally, Nicasicrates is not in a position to produce a correct classification and taxonomy. His examination of types who fall victim to erotic love shows that 'he is entirely ignorant about the things [that belong to the same species] and those that belong to different ones' (PHerc. 1457, XII. 14–16).

As we learn from the treatise *On Frank Speech*, the sage feels pleasure when he is able to gratify his students and companions by rightly praising them. That pleasure is not an end in itself, but a natural result of Epicurean education and the Epicurean way of life. Specifically, the enchantment that the sage exercises on his students' minds, far from being harmful, contributes to the edification of their characters and the removal of vice (PHerc. 222, II. 7–9). The same holds for their daily association with the sage, often at the price of temporary alienation from their families and social environment. For in that manner the sage can observe them daily and complete their education without external obstacles. To conclude: although it is true that the sage often praises his students and likes to

[45] The expression οἱ πέλας (PHerc. 1457, X. 11) probably refers to one's fellow disciples and friends in Epicurean schools. See Kondo 1974: 56.

[46] Concerning this distinction, see ibid. 55–6.

[47] Regarding the identity and philosophical orientation of Nicasicrates, see ibid. 55. I agree with Kondo that Philippson's identification of Nicasicrates with the philosopher mentioned in *De ir.* XXXVII. 5 ff. is plausible. PHerc. 1457 refers to him by name three times in all: at X. 10 ff., IV. 7 ff., and XX. 7. More on Nicasicrates is found at pp. 202–3, 223–30.

[48] Cf. X. 11: οἱ πέλας.

cause pleasure in his disciples and friends, he is not obsequious, because he never speaks in a pleasing manner without consideration for the good. He is neither a flatterer nor a sycophant, as his enemies claim. In fact, he shows great skill in detecting flatterers of all sorts: 'he chases them away more than [any other man] and he [never stops] attacking their disposition' (PHerc. 222, II. 13–16). Concerning the accusation that the sage receives many nice things from his students and is being paid in that way for his flattery (cf. *De grat.* VIII. 14), we may infer Philodemus' answer from views that he develops in several treatises. He would categorically deny that the reason why the sage's students are inclined to offer him various goods is that he flatters them. For although the sage sometimes praises his students, more often he admonishes and corrects them (*De lib. dic.*, *passim*). Besides, properly speaking, the sage does not sell his ideas for a fee, but rather receives grateful gifts from his students in return for the privilege of associating with him (*De oec.* XXIII. 23–36).

The behaviour of the sages towards individual students is of a piece with their attitude towards great numbers of people. As Epicurus was first to declare, they will never flatter the crowd (cf. Seneca, *Ep.* 29. 10). Nor will they attract people to festivals for demagogical purposes. The treatise *On Epicurus* tells us that 'by doing this (sc. by issuing such invitations), they (sc. the sages) will not attempt to win popularity through empty and unnatural demagogy but, instead, acting in the realm of things that are in accordance with nature, they will remember all those who have benevolent feelings towards our school in order to perform together the rites in commemoration of the dead, which contribute to their own happiness' (*De Epic.*; PHerc. 1232, XXVIII. 12–21). The invitations issued by 'insiders' of Epicurean groups to well-meaning 'outsiders'[49] to join their private rites do not constitute attempts to curry favour with the masses, but rather express essential features of the Epicurean communities.

The theoretical aims of Philodemus' analysis of flattery having been discussed, it remains to say something about its practical aim: namely, the therapy for the vice or, if that proves impossible, strategies by which we can detect the flatterer and keep him at bay. Philodemus' surviving remarks on this subject are few, and are scattered in different papyrus texts. Although

[49] On the distinction between the inner radius of Epicurean communities, constituted by the teachers and their disciples, and well-meaning outsiders, see Clay's commentary on PHerc. 1232, fr. 8, in Clay 1998: 80 ff., esp. p. 85.

he disagrees with certain aspects of the treatment of flattery proposed by Aristo,[50] he appears to take on board Aristo's distinctions between different types of flatterers,[51] presumably because he finds them useful in identifying the precise nature of the disease and curing the flatterer or protecting his victims. Also, Philodemus selectively employs the techniques of Bion of Borysthenes, pupil of Aristo, whose writings he considers useful for certain purposes, albeit not sufficiently rigorous.[52] Their therapeutic significance probably lies in the accessibility of Bion's exposition and in its persuasive force.[53]

However, it seems that the principal tool by which Philodemus proposes to treat flatterers as well as lovers of flattery is *parrhēsia*, frank speech.[54] The surviving parts of *On Flattery* yield both arguments and rhetorical techniques by which one may treat flattery and related vices. The former can be drawn, for instance, from Philodemus' analysis of flattery, the character and goals of the flatterer, the inaccuracy of his praise, the inappropriateness of his behaviour, and the damage that he may cause. Rhetorical techniques include 'bringing-before-the-eyes' of the patient (κ[α]τάδηλα ποιοῦντες: PHerc. 1457, X. 17) the catastrophic consequences of flattery. In addition, Philodemus issues prohibitions spiced with literary forms of speech, such as personification and metaphor. In our capacity as Epicurean doctors, he says, 'we prevent people from being susceptible to flattery and we shall correct those who are by making obvious to them the things that result from it. Moreover, more could be said in this book, and also in many others, on the subject of not giving up anything that is in accordance with nature in exchange for these evils, and of remaining tolerably remote from this

[50] The text is corrupt and leaves unclear the precise target of Philodemus' criticism, which is either that Aristo is wrong to recommend that we should be mild towards the flatterer (cf. PHerc. 222, X. 1–5), or that Aristo is confused regarding the distinction between the imitation and the emulation of friendship (cf. PHerc. 222, X. 6–10).

[51] See Vogt 2006. Philodemus' use of material derived from Aristo's writings on flattery is parallel to his use of Aristo's letters regarding arrogance: see *De superb.* X. 10 ff., XVI. 34 ff., and also pp. 143–62 *passim*.

[52] See PHerc. 223, frs. 7 and 8, and the commentary by Gigante and Indelli (1978: 130 f.).

[53] See Dem. Lac., PHerc. 1055, XVIII. 1–13.

[54] I mentioned earlier (pp. 77–8) that Philodemus does not explain how *parrhēsia* exercised live between members of the school is related to the language that Philodemus uses in particular treatises in order to influence his audience. Also, I called the former (i.e., the educational method of frank speech practised in the context of Epicurean schools) *parrhēsia* in a narrow, technical sense, and the latter *parrhēsia* in a broader sense, and I suggested that both can be considered species of a generic method of moral correction. Regarding the cure of flattery, Philodemus' language can be identified as *parrhēsia*, whether in the narrow or in the broad sense of the term, or both. The same holds for the language that Philodemus uses to treat arrogance, greed, anger, and the fear of death.

seductive prostitute' (PHerc. 1457, X. 17 ff.). Eventually, or so Philodemus may hope, the students will realize the folly of their ways (*ἀποπληξ[ί]αν*: PHerc. 1457, fr. 13. 9)[55] and will be induced to attend to what is reasonable ([*εὔλο*]*γον*: fr. 13. 10). On the other hand, the above-mentioned remedies are not always effective against active forms of flattery and cognate vices. They may purge us of obsequiousness (PHerc. 1457, fr. 16. 3 ff.) and parasitism, but it would seem that they are relatively powerless with regard to sycophancy and flattery proper.

As mentioned, Philodemus' treatment of flattery survives only in part and in a very fragmentary form. Nonetheless, it allows us to gain a better understanding of the nature of flattery, the reasons why we rightly consider it a vice, and the relations between flattery, candid criticism, and friendship. Moreover, Philodemus' refutation of the charge that the sage exercises flattery for self-interested purposes sheds light on certain important features of Epicurean religion and society, in particular the feasts organized in Epicurean schools to commemorate Epicurus and his early associates and the friendly spirit in which the Epicureans invited well-meaning outsiders to participate in these occasions.

[55] Cf. also *De lib. dic.*, fr. 1. 2.

7

Arrogance and Related Vices

On Arrogance, Περὶ ὑπερηφανείας (*De superb.*, PHerc. 1008) is probably the full title of the tenth book of Philodemus' *On Vices*.[1] A fragment and twenty-four columns of text remain, of which several are reasonably well preserved.[2] Philodemus' treatment of arrogance resembles that of flattery, but has several new elements as well. One distinctive feature that we should bear in mind is that the extant remains of Philodemus' treatise contain a lengthy summary of a work by the Peripatetic philosopher Aristo of Ceos,[3] possibly entitled *On the Removal of Arrogance*, Περὶ τοῦ

[1] Cf. Capasso 1979; Ranocchia 2001.

[2] My discussion is based mainly on Jensen 1911 and, for cols. X and XXI–XXIII, also on Acosta-Méndez and Angeli 1992 and Ranocchia 2001. Moreover, I take into account Jensen's reconstruction of fr. 1 and cols. I–X (Jensen 1933). However, I am sceptical about Jensen's supposition that these columns contain a letter of Epicurus addressed to Idomeneus and relating a dialogue between Epicurus and the god Asclepius. Compelling reasons for rejecting that hypothesis are given by Indelli (2001: 696–7). I have also consulted the text and translation of cols. X. 10–XXIV. 21 by Stork *et al.* (2006), when still in unpublished form—a privilege for which I thank the authors.

[3] Philodemus mentions Aristo twice (*De superb.* X. 10 ff., XVI. 34) by name and, although he does not identify him further, it seems pretty clear that the philosopher in question is the Peripatetic Aristo from Ceos, not the Stoic Aristo from Chios. An argument to the contrary is made by Ioppolo (1996). The chief considerations on the grounds of which she shifted from her earlier position, defended in Ioppolo 1980, to the one maintained in her later publication are the following. First, the treatment of the εἴρων (translit. *eirōn*) attributed to Aristo in the treatise *On Arrogance* differs from the analyses of the *eirōn* offered by Aristotle and Theophrastus. While the former constitutes a negative characterization, the latter are by and large positive, setting the εἴρων in contrast to the ἀλαζών. Besides, while the Aristo of the book *On Arrogance* presents Socrates as the embodiment of the *eirōn*, Theophrastus does not allude to him. Nor does any other Peripatetic treat Socrates in the negative way in which the Aristo of *On Arrogance* discusses him. In general, Ioppolo contends, the characterology of the arrogant types in *On Arrogance* contains moral evaluations, whereas Peripatetic characterology mostly does not, but rather aims at inducing laughter. On the other hand, the Stoic treatment of human characters does have moral dimensions, very much so when it comes to the patron saint of the Stoic school, Socrates. Aristo of Chios in particular has great admiration for Socrates, with the qualification that this is not the *eirōn* Socrates of the Platonic dialogues, but the Socrates of Xenophon, whose portrait is transmitted to the Stoics via Antisthenes. In presenting Socrates as the embodiment of the *eirōn*, Aristo aims to stigmatize as vicious not the historical Socrates, but Plato's interpretation of an aporetic Socrates endorsed also by Arcesilaus. Ioppolo's thesis has some plausibility, but is, I think, incorrect. For not all

κουφίζειν ὑπερηφανίας,[4] and written in epistolary form.[5] The first part of that summary (*De superb.* X. 30–XVI. 27) is a series of injunctions[6] to the vicious man who has become aware that he is arrogant, to help him rid himself of his vice. The second part of the summary (XVI. 28 to the end of the treatise, XXIV. 27) consists of a series of character portraits followed by explanations of the consequences which befall men of the characters depicted in those portraits. Philodemus' use of Aristo raises a number of interesting questions: for instance, what are the merits of Aristo's account, and why Philodemus chose to integrate Aristo's typology into his own treatise. In any case, *On Arrogance* is an important addition to the philosophical literature on that subject. Among other things, it clarifies the sense of superiority involved in arrogance; it highlights the ways in which arrogance undermines human relationships; and it can be interpreted as a largely successful attempt to explain why arrogance is a vice which substantially diminishes our chances of achieving the good life.

Section I of this chapter presents Philodemus' outline of arrogance (ὑπερηφανία), as well as the principal characteristics of that vice, the ways in which it influences one's attitudes and relationships to others, and its consequences. It also discusses the contrast between the sage and the arrogant man whom the sage is sometimes accused of being.[7] Section II concerns Aristo's treatment of people who are arrogant on account of their good luck and Aristo's therapies for arrogance. Section III shows

the Peripatetics have a positive image of Socrates. Nor do all Stoics object to Plato's interpretation of Socrates. In fact, they often appeal to it in order to defend their Socratic pedigree. In particular, it is not clear to me that Aristotle's analysis of the *eirōn* (*Eth. Nic.* IV. 7) excludes a relatively bad characterization of Socrates. True, Aristotle does say that ironical people who, like Socrates, understate things seem more attractive than boasters. But he refrains from praising them (including Socrates) as much as the truthful man. Furthermore, Aristotle's analysis of the role of good fortune in the development of pride (*Eth. Nic.* IV. 3) closely resembles Aristo's analysis in *On Arrogance*. And Theophrastus' description of the proud man has features encountered also in Aristo's descriptions of arrogant types. Another interpretation, according to which the *eirōn* depicted in *On Arrogance* comes from Epicurean sources, also appears implausible: see Kleve 1983, refuted by Ioppolo 1996: 729 n. 44.

[4] Ranocchia (2001: 216) questions whether this was actually the title of the work, given its epistolary character.

[5] Cf. n. 25 below.

[6] As we shall see, many of these injunctions are supported with historical or quasi-historical examples.

[7] Given the nature of my argument in this chapter, it has not been possible to keep Aristo's and Philodemus' views entirely separate from each other: e.g., I have often drawn support from Aristo's summary to substantiate further a point that I have raised in respect of Philodemus, as well as conversely. However, it is probably accurate to say that Sect. I principally concerns Philodemus, whereas Sects. II, III, and IV concentrate mainly on Philodemus' summary of Aristo.

how arrogance is further individuated by being compared and contrasted with other traits. Section IV focuses on Aristo's account of the characters of which arrogance is an important constituent. In particular, I analyse Aristo's conception of complex vices containing arrogance, I speculate on their nature, and I give reasons why Aristo's typology can be considered an appropriate end for Philodemus' treatise.

I

Like flattery, arrogance is chiefly a disposition (διάθεσιν: *De superb.* II. 27)[8] to feel, behave, etc., in a certain manner in reaction to certain situations as they are perceived by the agent. Philodemus assumes that treating people arrogantly is not the same thing as being arrogant,[9] and he also remarks that sometimes people 'place the old mask around their faces' (VIII. 1–2), trying in vain 'to preserve both thoughtfulness and courtesy in their conversations with others' (VIII. 25–8). The most important characteristics of arrogance are a sense of superiority accompanied by scorn, disdain, or contempt for others. These traits are prominent in Philodemus' outline of the arrogant man. 'A man is called arrogant (ὑπερήφανος) ... who appears scornful (καταφρονητ[ι]κός), insults everybody in those cases where he maintains his arrogance even in his actions, and is generally the sort of person that this characterization reveals both in relation to all those for whom he reserves his arrogance and through his actions, and moreover is the kind of person who is generally hubristic (ὑβρισ[τή]ς)' (VI. 27–34).

In so far as these dispositional tendencies are expressed in behaviour, they point to beliefs that the arrogant man entertains about himself and others and that concern his own status, abilities, and talents. For instance, he may believe that he is more important than other people if he performs some major deed (IV. 27–30), or if he happens to render some small service (V. 11–12); or he may convince himself that his talent is such as to ensure future success (cf. XIV. 24–36). Such beliefs are empty in so far as they reflect a false assignment of value to some trait of the arrogant

[8] Cf. also ἀπὸ τῆς εἰρημένης διαθέσεως: *De superb.* XXI. 20–2.

[9] He may be employing this distinction in reporting the anti-Epicurean charge that 'the wise man treats people arrogantly ([ὑ]περηφανεῖ[ν]) and is arrogant (ὑπε[ρ]ήφανος [ε]ἶναι)' (*De superb.* VII. 2–3). Also, in this instance, Philodemus may be citing some other author.

person, or an inflated estimate of the degree to which he possesses it, or both. However, as contemporary philosophers point out,[10] arrogance is a matter not merely of having too high an opinion of one's abilities, but also of forming an excessively high opinion of oneself: that is, of one's superiority as a human being in comparison with other human beings. This so-called virtue-theoretic sense of superiority[11] implies, specifically, that one perceives oneself as best meeting the standards of goodness and, therefore, surpassing others in all respects relevant to the good life.

Philodemus brings out this dimension of arrogance by emphasizing its interpersonal aspects. He first of all presents it as a particularly vicious way of assessing and interacting with other people on the basis of relational judgements that one makes about them in comparison with oneself. For instance, the arrogant person's sense of superiority comes, precisely, from his perception of others as inferior to himself. His convictions that he is better in abilities, skills, wisdom, and virtue entail the corresponding beliefs that all or most other people are worse in the same matters. His disdain towards philosophers, which is dictated by the conviction that they deserve to be despised (IV. 22–6), is connected with his utter confidence in his own wisdom and with the belief that philosophers can teach him nothing. His disgust at others (VIII. 3–4) derives from an excessive appreciation of his own nobility (VIII. 11–12). And his tendency to disparage them is related to his admiration of himself (IX. 1–4, 10–11). Moreover, Philodemus argues that, by treating others in a hierarchical and non-reciprocal manner, the arrogant person both harms his personal relationships and corrodes the social fabric of the community in which he lives. He treats his wife shamefully and his slaves even more so (II. 4–6), considers not even free men worthy of their freedom (II. 6–7), proves unequal to his friendships (VIII. 28–30), and seldom behaves with thoughtfulness and civility (VIII. 21–8). Besides, he is inhospitable and uncommunicative (IX. 7–10), hubristic towards the victims of misfortune (IX. 1–5), suspicious (X. 3–4), and unwilling to acknowledge his faults and to ask for forgiveness (X. 5–8). Moreover, he is unable to desire genuinely the welfare of other people and to act in ways that might promote it. He is equally incapable of feeling gratitude towards those who benefit him, and does not thank them, since he believes that 'he honours them greatly because he has accepted something from them' (IX. 17–20).

[10] e.g., see Tiberius and Walker 1998: esp. 379–81.

[11] See ibid. 380.

Aristo, probably followed by Philodemus, suggests that such attitudes show a lack of good manners, but also undermine more important things than social etiquette: namely, the relationships of mutual respect and trust woven into the social fabric. In particular, they affect areas of human activity which require collaboration and cooperation. 'The arrogant man is not capable of asking other people for advice, partly because of self-conceit, partly because he feels contempt towards the others. And if he does call on others, he finds it difficult to heed their advice, both because of the other reasons for his disgust and because he wants [to make the actions exclusively his own] and then is left unassisted' (XIV. 7–15). The absence of cooperative qualities is most obvious in Aristo's characters of the self-willed man and the know-it-all (cf. XVII. 19–25, XVIII. 12–18, XVIII. 35–7). Perhaps more than the arrogant man, these characters resist the mutual enrichment deriving from reciprocal help and cooperation because they believe that they have no need of other men like themselves (XX. 1–3).

Like flattery and every other major vice, arrogance has two additional interrelated features: ignorance of oneself and irrationality. Arrogant people are not aware of themselves as vicious; 'they have [no] knowledge [of themselves]' (fr. 1).[12] Philodemus suggests that if they did, they would register people's negative reactions towards them, would grieve about their own condition, and would come to revise their attitudes and reform their characters. In fact, the absence of self-awareness constitutes a buffer which keeps at a safe distance whatever might undermine their self-importance and sense of superiority, and which leaves considerable room for self-deception and pretence. Both the absence of self-knowledge and the corrosion of interpersonal relationships are reasons why Philodemus appears to view arrogance as irrational. As in the case of flattery, so in this case the vice is not considered irrational in the sense that the person possessing it is unable to explain his attitudes, beliefs, and actions, but rather in the sense that his explanations are bound to be incorrect, since they are grounded on empty beliefs and involve distorted moral values. The arrogant person's irrationality lies especially in his refusal to acknowledge the value of others as human beings and to treat them as his equals. 'He (sc. the arrogant man)

[12] Compare one's vulnerability to flattery, which may occur even in those having self-knowledge of a mitigated sort.

should reason (λογίζεσθαι)[13] that he does not mistreat whatever animals he happens to be living with, for instance [horses], dogs and other such animals, but (only) man, a being so very different (from these animals) and most akin to himself on account of the fact that he has been adorned with [reason]'[14] (XV. 33–40). In fact, arrogance can eliminate completely the operations of reason. 'Sometimes one worsens one's ailment into stupidity or madness, if indeed Xerxes' deeds do not depend upon both rather than one of these qualities—I mean the yoking of the Hellespont and casting fetters into the sea and the other deeds that people tell of him. The same holds of the acts of people who think that they themselves have turned from men into gods, and all the other features of those who behave with unrestrained arrogance' (XVI. 15–27).

As for the consequences of arrogance, some of them are implied by Philodemus' analysis of the characteristics of the vice, while others are discussed separately in several passages of the treatise including Aristo's summary. Psychologically, arrogance causes trouble to whomever it affects. On the one hand, arrogant people feel pleasure on account of thinking and feeling that they are better than others in all important respects. On the other hand, their disdain of others is surely a source of pain. For they experience emotional strain in many circumstances of ordinary life: for instance, when they need to show courtesy while their tendency is to behave rudely (VIII. 21–8). They feel alienation and loneliness, which derive from their perception of their closest relatives and friends as unworthy of respect and incapable of offering assistance or advice. Moreover, arrogant persons live a friendless life (X. 8–10). Although Philodemus does not argue explicitly for this last claim, he supplies materials for defending it. While friendship presupposes respecting others and viewing them as equal to oneself, arrogance entails the opposite presuppositions. Therefore, it obstructs the development of affection and disinterested care for others, which are essential to friendship. Even when arrogant people are compelled to behave

[13] The injunction that the arrogant person should reason that does not mistreat animals but only men can be interpreted as a strong indication that he is failing to use his rationality. Although one might object that this injunction belongs to Aristo, and not to Philodemus, nonetheless, Philodemus does cite it and thus supports further his own idea that the arrogant person is irrational. As I suggested in earlier chapters, it is important for Philodemus to make the move of generally attributing to the vicious irrationality, not merely vice. For one of his principal aims is to show how the vices and the passions obstruct the rational calculation of pains and pleasures and damage one's natural flourishing.

[14] XV. 40 [λόγωι] Tsouna.

in a friendly manner, they are not true friends. For their comportment lacks the relevant dispositional underpinnings, just like that of flatterers. Besides, Philodemus' analysis strongly suggests that arrogance, like flattery, is bad because it makes the persons it afflicts morally worse than they would be otherwise. Notably, by obstructing the development of friendships and other human relationships, it deprives them of valuable constituents of the good life.

The external consequences of arrogance are painful as well. Many of them derive from the reactions of others to one's arrogant behaviour, as evidenced by both Aristo and Philodemus. People get enraged by the fact that the arrogant person considers them inferior to himself (XIX. 8), and they respond to his haughtiness and offensive behaviour by frustrating his desires, or by positively harming him. They ridicule him (III. end, XVIII. 37–8), suspect his character and therefore undermine him when he occupies positions of power (V. 8–12), grasp any opportunity to slander, offend, and deprive him of goods (VII. 28–34), abuse and attack him (XIX. 36–7), observe and obstruct his solitary tasks (XIV. 15–20), and refuse to have any kind of dealings with him (XIX. 10–12), often dismissing him as a madman (XIX. 13–15). Moreover, the arrogant person frequently acts in a manner which, regardless of other people's responses, leads him to his own ruin. Because of his reluctance to ask for cooperation and advice, he alone bears the burden of his tasks and projects, and so fails to execute them (XIV. 2 ff., XIX. 21–2, XX. 27 ff.). Also, if he is excessively afflicted by the vice, he loses his mind, with the result that he runs considerable risks and undertakes great toils and expenses (XVI. 15 ff.). In fact, it might seem as if the *hubris* involved in arrogance invites dramatic reversals of fortune: good luck changes abruptly into bad luck, shattering the arrogant man's pride and bringing him to his knees (VII. 15–17).[15] 'Fortune may some day force one [to take refuge with those very people] that one looks down upon—something that has happened many times both to cities and to men' (XVI. 6–10).

Concrete incidents of arrogant behaviour are used to illustrate the features and consequences of the vice.[16] An example is this: 'As he was entering

[15] However, one should resist the temptation to attribute such reversals of fortune to the intervention of the gods. Philodemus suggests that they are accidental or caused by the arrogant man's attitude and behaviour.

[16] Another purpose of these examples is to illustrate ways in which arrogance is cured.

the stage, Timocreon of Seriphos, who was arrogant, told a man who asked him where he was born, "in a moment, you will hear the herald". When his retort spread around, it caused such opposition among the spectators that the [arbiter], stretching out the staff to him [while he was singing a hymn to Castor], made him stop. When he withdrew from the stage beaten and the same man asked him where he came from, he replied "I am from Seriphos"' (XIV. 24–36). This example brings out the sense of superiority characterizing every arrogant person, his lack of courtesy and his disrespect of others, his overconfidence verging on *hubris*, the adverse effects of his behaviour on others, the harm that it is likely to cause himself, and the temporary removal of the vice through the reversal of the arrogant person's fortunes.

In the light of the above analysis, it might appear very surprising that the Epicurean wise man was sometimes accused of being arrogant. In fact, Philodemus tells us that critics motivated by ill will and envy (VI. 6–7) sometimes maintain that there are similarities between the arrogant man and the sage (VI. 3–6), using as their starting point 'the disdain (καταφρόν[η]σιν) that he (sc. the sage) has in himself about everything vulgar' (VI. 12–14). Such critics misunderstand the manner in which sages relate to other people, and also 'the nobility both of their appearance and of their [whole] life' (VI. 19–21). The charge seems to be that the sage is arrogant because he is disposed to show disdain, and because he behaves in a proud and haughty manner. On the other hand, Philodemus' answer suggests that the disdain of the sage has different objects and causes different reactions from those involved in the disdain of the arrogant man. First of all, although the sage feels contempt for whatever he sees as vulgar (VI. 12–14), nevertheless he is not generally hubristic like the arrogant man (cf. VI. 32–3). Emulating the sage, any sensible person should not be 'disparaging [of other people], nor an admirer of himself, especially on account of the advantages that come to him from good fortune. Nor should he appear utterly changed in any respect' (IX. 1–7). 'It is not decent to pride oneself on these things (sc. power and the like), but on bearing them in an elegant and intelligent way' (V. 3–6). Compare the arrogant person's disparagement of others, his contempt towards the victims of fortune, and his repulsive manner of showing off his own advantages.

Moreover, the sage is civil, hospitable, and mindful of other people. 'Nor should one be reluctant to welcome people to one's [home], to converse or to have dealings of all kinds with them (IX. 7–10). ... One should keep an eye on one's house-slaves and on one's servants, freemen, and others who live in one's house. For sometimes these people are responsible for an impression (of arrogance), when they are unwilling to bring messages, or [tell people to go to hell], or [put on][17] some such behaviour' (IX. 24–34). The sage's conduct reflects his belief that other people are his equals as human beings, and as such have the right to be treated in a decent, if not overfamiliar, manner. Contrast now the arrogant man's incivility, inhospitability, and disregard of others (IX. 1–10). As was suggested above, such features derive from his sense of superiority, and are intended to make clear just how important he is, how much he knows, and how much more he can achieve than others.

One way to interpret Philodemus' argument is this. Philodemus appears to distinguish between two notions of disdain: one which entails a sense of superiority to others in respect of one's humanity and another which does not. He suggests that the disdain felt and expressed by the sage is of the second sort, while the disdain essential to arrogance belongs to the first sort. And he concludes that the sage is not arrogant, since he is not disdainful in the relevant sense. However, one might object that a truly good man ought to find ways of expressing, e.g., his disapproval of vulgarity which do not involve contempt of any kind at all. Further, one might point out that austerity and remoteness are indications, if not of arrogance, at least of pretentiousness; and that if this is correct, then the Epicurean sage is wrong to believe that such elements should characterize the demeanour of sensible people, let alone of sages. Both objections imply that while Philodemus does establish that the sage is not vicious by virtue of being arrogant, he does not justify why the sage should be disdainful in any sense at all.

II

The nature of arrogance becomes clearer when it is compared with magnanimity or greatness of soul, with which arrogance is sometimes confused.

One must distinguish magnanimity from arrogance and must not confuse them as if they were one and the same thing. For it (sc. magnanimity) differs as much

[17] IX. 32–3 ἐ[πιτιθέν]τες Delattre.

as, on the physical level, a healthy figure differs from a swelling of the body. It is characteristic of the magnanimous man to feel contempt towards people favoured by fortune because he is superior to them with regard to the loftiness of his soul, whereas it is characteristic of the arrogant man to look down upon others because, on account of the levity of his soul, he is inflated by his possessions.

(XV. 22–33)

This passage draws a distinction between arrogance and magnanimity, and gives an explanation of how these traits, and the characters substantiating them, differ. The difference is quasi-physiological, and has to do with the condition of one's soul: the arrogant person's soul is inflated and empty (cf. *κουφότητα*: XV. 30), whereas the soul of the magnanimous person is great and lofty (cf. *ὑπερέχοντι τῶι τῆς ψυχῆς ὄγκωι*: XV. 29). The relation between the two is expressed by means of an analogy, which may be interpreted as follows. Arrogance stands with regard to magnanimity as a swollen body stands with regard to a healthy one: it is a diseased psychic state, an inflammation, produced through an inflated sense of self-worth for the wrong reasons and towards the wrong objects. If compared to greatness of soul, it would look like the mirror image of that virtue, albeit a deformed one. In fact, one might say that magnanimity is the virtue opposite to the vice of arrogance.

Why do we sometimes take arrogance for magnanimity, or magnanimity for arrogance? The passage cited above does not address that question explicitly, but it provides materials for attempting to answer it and also to sharpen the distinction between magnanimity and arrogance. Both magnanimous and arrogant men tend to feel contempt, and both of them are disposed to do so because of a kind of disdain involving the belief that they are better than others. Moreover, magnanimity, as the word suggests, is standardly defined in terms of greatness or loftiness of the soul, and a sort of loftiness also characterizes arrogance. On the other hand, as the physiological metaphor indicates, the disdain pertaining to greatness of soul and that associated with arrogance are different from one another. Assuming that the magnanimous person is someone who 'claims much and deserves much',[18] and hence is especially concerned with honour as the greatest external good,[19] his contempt is naturally directed at people who demand a lot although they deserve very little, and who reap external

[18] Aristotle, *Eth. Nic.* IV. 3, 1123^{b}1 ff. [19] Ibid. 1123^{b}16 ff.

benefits merely because of their good luck.[20] Arrogant persons do precisely these things. They therefore constitute legitimate objects of contempt for those who are great-souled, especially in view of their foolish conviction that they deserve the gifts of fortune. According to this analysis, the sense of superiority involved in magnanimity stems from the very nature of that virtue: namely, the loftiness of one's soul, which induces one to claim greater honours than others in the knowledge that one is fully worthy of them. By contrast, the sense of superiority that characterizes arrogance expresses the arrogant person's inflated opinion of himself in relation to others, and it motivates him to demand for himself more than other people do, whereas, in fact, he usually deserves less.

Moving on to another matter, we should now examine Aristo's injunctions that arrogance often incites the envy of others (XII. 12 ff.), and also their malicious joy when the arrogant person encounters misfortunes (XII. 30 ff.). Consider the following passage:

> [One should recall incidentally] the envy that usually meets arrogant men, which is a kind of eye inflammation of the soul, so that, just as the splendid cloak of those who encounter us does bother our eyes (if we have an eye inflammation), but less sharply than if someone passing by and holding up his cloak shakes it, in a similar way other men's goods do pain the envious man, but not as much as when he realizes that someone is spreading his wings because of these goods and rising up high. That is when envy really clamps on and bites (him, i.e., the envious man). As a matter of fact, all the losses that occur because of envy are obvious to everybody. Moreover, we should consider malicious joy in cases when someone falls from good luck into bad luck. For this is a source of sorrow inasmuch as, when most people join forces with a stumble of fortune to make an attack against acknowledged enemies... .
>
> (XII. 12–36)[21]

This passage talks about one's arrogance exciting envy (*φθόνος*) and malicious joy (*ἐπιχαιρεκακία*) in others. Concerning envy, Aristo's point seems to be that an envious man is generally envious, but much more so in the face of an arrogant person, just as inflamed eyes are generally sensitive to brightness, but much more so when a bright object is waved

[20] Cf. ibid. III. 3, 1124ᵃ25 ff.

[21] The text is interrupted here, but the next column continues on the same topic, offering the example of Euripides, who was considered arrogant, met with bad luck, and went to the court of Archelaus grieving for the fact that almost everyone felt joy at his misfortunes (*De superb.* XIII. 3–8).

right in front of them. Arrogance does not always draw envy,[22] but it has that effect sufficiently often (cf. [εἰ]ωθότος φθόνου: XII. 13–14) to deter people from behaving arrogantly. In any case, it should be evident to them that they are likely to suffer painful consequences if they keep provoking the envy of others. Similar remarks apply to malicious joy, an exceptionally detestable vice that Philodemus characterizes elsewhere as a condition of utter bestiality (*De inv.*, fr. 3. 1). Those who are arrogant will awaken more malicious joy than will other men. It will become manifest on occasions on which an arrogant person is most vulnerable: namely, when he meets with bad luck and undergoes substantial losses.

So far as we know, neither Aristo nor Philodemus asks whether there can be a relationship between arrogance, envy, and malicious joy, and whether these three vices tend to be found in the same person. It should be mentioned, however, that all three traits are based on comparative beliefs concerning what one deserves and what one gets in relation to what others deserve and get. In particular, all three traits appear to involve one's belief that one is superior to others. Like arrogant people, envious people tend to believe themselves better or abler than others, and for this reason covet for themselves what someone else has. Likewise, malicious persons feel joy at the misfortunes of their neighbour in the belief that he deserved his bad luck, whereas they would have done better in his place. Furthermore, all three vices rely on false judgements concerning the value of external goods. As we saw, the disdain of the arrogant man often derives from the worldly possessions and advantages secured for him through good luck. We may infer, then, that he values such things excessively. And he feels entitled to look down upon others, precisely because he considers these things terribly important and has them, whereas others have not. The envious person's feelings towards prosperous people derives from his conviction that they have something very much worth having that he wants for himself. Similarly, one's malicious joy at the misfortunes of others entails the assumption that they have undergone a truly great loss.[23] And so on.

On the other hand, however, it would seem that the sense of superiority involved in arrogance has a broader scope than that entailed by envy or

[22] E.g., a decent person would presumably not feel envy or malicious joy at another's misfortunes, even if that other person were arrogant.

[23] Recall that the therapy for the last two vices consists in part in reassessing the value of externals (*De inv.* 17. 2–7); see pp. 124–5.

malicious joy. For it is not restricted to one's abilities and skills, but (as was suggested earlier) extends to one's value as a human being. By contrast, comparable beliefs held by envious and malicious people appear to be based on a narrower, capacity-oriented sense of superiority. For instance, if you are arrogant, you will treat your colleague with contempt at all times: e.g., before he receives a promotion, after he receives it, and after he loses his job because he fails to fulfil his new obligations. You may or may not have been envious of his ascent, and may or may not have rejoiced at the fact that he got fired. But assuming that you suffer from arrogance, you have perceived yourself as superior to him all along, regardless of whether or not he has been successful.

III

There is an external factor relevant to arrogance: luck.[24] Philodemus mentions that in his book on the removal of arrogance (which was composed, as mentioned, in epistolary form[25]), Aristo of Ceos treats people who are arrogant on account of their good fortune. Aristo may have dealt only with the subject of luck, or he may also have discussed other issues: e.g., being arrogant because of philosophy (cf. X. 18–25).[26] In any case, Philodemus acknowledges the usefulness of Aristo's book (X. 26–30) and summarizes its contents.[27] Arrogant people tend to show contempt towards every victim of bad fortune and, on the other hand, take great pride at the advantages that come to them because of good fortune (XIII. 34–8, XV.

[24] Good luck is considered a major source of arrogance, probably because of the conceptual connections between arrogance and *hubris*.

[25] Cf. the conjecture ἐπι[στ]ολ[ικά] (*De superb.* X. 12–13) proposed by Gigante (1997) and confirmed by Ranocchia (2001: 244), who gives the reading ἐπιστολικά.

[26] Jensen's reconstruction of *De superb.* X. 13–25 (Jensen 1911) suggests that Aristo discussed only the case of people who are arrogant on account of their good luck, and that Philodemus blames him for having left out other cases, in particular those who are arrogant because they are philosophers. However, Ranocchia (2001: 259–60) establishes that Jensen was wrong and that, in fact, Aristo discussed several different kinds of cases.

[27] However, the text of Ranocchia 2001 (X. 10–30) suggests that Philodemus may be distancing himself from Aristo here. For he says that Aristo's treatment is limited, and that Aristo himself suffers the fate of those fools who are arrogant because of good fortune; nonetheless, just in case Aristo will persuade someone, as it is not unlikely, he (sc. Philodemus) will summarize the substance of Aristo's views. On the other hand, as will become clear later, I do not think that Philodemus distances himself from Aristo's account of complex vices, with which *On Arrogance* ends.

26–33; cf. also V. 1 ff., IX. 4–5). In fact, they often boast aloud about such goods in order to make them look even greater than they really are (XI. 24–7). Their disdain for the person who has run out of luck derives from their belief that the unfortunate man got just what he deserved. By contrast, their admiration for themselves on account of their good fortune stems from their conviction that they fully deserve it.[28] In short, they implicitly deny that luck is blind, and they perceive their own blessings in relation to the afflictions of others as the confirmation of their own superiority over others. Consequently, they are terribly pleased with themselves, but feel no pity or compassion on behalf of others.[29] Philodemus considers their attitude hubristic (VI. 32–3) and also indecent, and suggests that such people offend equally against philanthropy and good taste (V. 3–8).

The radical therapy of arrogance is a difficult matter. As Philodemus points out, one reason is that the patient's realization of the fact that arrogance is a bad thing depends in part on luck. 'I am afraid that the arrogant man, [far from setting himself right] so as to become actually wise, may not even (see the) [need] to change his frame of mind. For lack of wisdom occurs in those people [who are arrogant] on account of their luck' (V. 19–26). So long as he remains fortunate, then, he has no occasion to reflect on his ways and improve them. However, arrogance can be cured despite these obstacles. Aristo proposes the following therapies by which the vice can be removed.[30] First, one must remind oneself of the precariousness and unpredictability of luck. 'Dionysius ordered someone—indeed, it was not a bad idea—to exclaim twice a day "do you see tyrants [prospering for a long time]?"' (XI. 9–13).[31] The point is that 'when (the arrogant man) [is stripped] of glorious good fortune, he will pull down his presumption and will appear in the humblest situation' (XIV. 36–40).[32] This remark brings out the inconsistency that marks the attitudes and behaviour of every arrogant person.[33] In so far as they are

[28] Cf. also *De elect.* VII. 15–20 and XVII. 10–19.

[29] In fact, to the extent that arrogance is interconnected with envy and malicious joy, arrogant people feel pleasure at other people's misfortunes.

[30] We do not know whether Philodemus also proposed additional therapeutic strategies on his own account in the lost part of the treatise.

[31] Cf. also *De superb.* XI. 19–24.

[32] Philodemus makes a similar point in *De superb.* VII. 15–25.

[33] Compare the inconsistency marking superstitious people: they are ἀσύνθετοι, emotionally inconsistent and unbalanced (*De elect.* XIX. 19). On the meaning of that term, see Gigante 1983*d*: 266 ff., and Indelli and Tsouna-McKirahan 1995: 207–8.

determined by contingent factors, they are bound to reflect changes in his circumstances, and are therefore likely to conflict with each other. Bearing in mind the turns of fortune, we should also learn to humble ourselves when we have reason to feel proud and, conversely, to encourage ourselves at times when we feel demoralized (XI. 24–33). A related technique is to compare ourselves not with our inferiors but with our superiors. 'One should [measure] oneself [not against those] poorer than oneself, [but] against those who surpass one in each particular [respect], because the former exalts, whereas the latter humbles with regard both to [the possession of lands] and to the government [and kingship] of cities and nations' (XII. 4–12).

Yet another device is 'to collect examples of how very prominent men behave when they show themselves as equals and as restrained in their conversation and as standing, so to speak, in the opposite position to where the weight of fortune lies: for example, Alexander, who seated a shivering Macedonian on his own throne because there was a fire next to it, and Dionysius, who to the man who said "you will be sorry, Dionysius" answered "*you* will, if you will not repeat half of your [warning]";[34] and the others who dealt [gently with people] through words or deeds' (XIII. 8–30). The moral is that such men appear that much greater just because they have not been arrogant, but have behaved with simplicity, humanity, and compassion. On the other hand, 'we should also cite as examples those who dealt with people in the opposite way bringing difficulties upon themselves because of one single harsh word' (XIII. 25–7). Moreover, we should recollect that arrogance is a base thing, and 'as such it shows that the person suffering from it is gross' (XIII. 30–8). Also, we should try to remember that arrogance, if taken to extremes, 'pushes one into foolishness or madness' (XVI. 15–17). Xerxes' behaviour is an excellent illustration of that fact (XVI. 17–27). Yet another therapeutic strategy consists in contemplating the reactions that one's arrogance triggers in other people, whether they are motivated by vices such as envy and malicious joy or by fairly natural feelings. For instance, Euripides, who was considered arrogant,

[34] I provisionally follow Jensen's text, but I am not sure what the point of the story is. One possibility is this. Dionysius is telling the man who threatened him that he must have the courage to repeat the threat along with the name of the person threatened. Another possibility, proposed by David Sedley (in conversation with me), is to supplement [ἐν]θήκη (XIII. 21–2) and translate 'if you don't invest half of your capital'. In any case, the story is supposed to show Dionysius' restraint.

was 'grieved by the fact that almost everybody felt joy at his misfortunes and, therefore, went away to Archelaus' (XIII. 4–8).

These strategies are used for self-scrutiny and self-correction in the following way. 'One should ask oneself many times over "What is it that makes me haughty and arrogant? Is it that I have acquired more pennies? Or that [I am counted] among the nobility or those who serve as generals and who are honoured every year by wearing a general's cloak?" For one will find each one of these things trivial and the boasting about them ill-bred' (XV. 12–22). If language fails to cure the vice, reality may succeed. 'Having gathered together many people who observe him and are ready to trip him up, he naturally goes wrong and, as a result, is rid of his arrogance by means of his failures, since he does not want to be rid of it by means of words' (XIV. 15–22).

IV

As mentioned, the second part of Philodemus' summary of Aristo (XVI. 28 to the end of the treatise, XXIV. 27) presents recognizable human 'types' or 'characters' instantiating essential features of complex vices,[35] at least some of which can also be called 'blends'.[36] In the first place, all types are described, and in the second place, the consequences of being each type are enumerated. All types contain arrogance in different portions and in varying forms, and each of them also contains a number of additional vices related to arrogance. The relationships obtaining between these traits are unclear. We are told that 'the man called inconsiderate (*αὐθάδης*) is a blend (*μεικτός*) of conceit, arrogance, and scorn, and also has a generous share of thoughtlessness' (XVI. 29–33). Also, 'the self-willed (*αὐθέκαστος*) man [is] not so very [rash] or irrational as the inconsiderate man is, but rather, since he has the conceit that he alone has any sense, he follows his own opinion and is convinced that he will be successful in everything (if he relies on himself), but that he will go wrong if he relies on the judgement of someone else; and he also has a share (*μετέχων*) of arrogance' (XVII. 19–25). The concept of 'blending' appears one more time, in connection

[35] Rannochia (2001) maintains that Aristo's writing on arrogance was probably not so much a literary exercise modelled on Theophrastus' *Characters* as an ethical and protreptic work.

[36] Cf. Tsouna 2006*a* and below.

with the self-willed man: 'he is beset both by the (difficulties) that arise from the absurd characteristics of which he is a blend (μέμεικται) and also by the fact that he alone is foolish, since he alone believes that he is sensible about everything' (XIX. 17–21).

However, Aristo does not explicitly say that all his characters are 'blends' or that they 'share in' arrogance. The know-it-all (παντειδήμων) 'has convinced himself that he knows everything, some things because he has learned them from the greatest experts, others because he merely has observed (the experts) making them, others because he has invented them on his own' (XVIII. 12–18); 'he is the kind of man who disgraces himself by laying claim [to all] disciplines and who [calls] ignorant those who laugh at him' (XVIII. 35–8). The man who affects dignity (σεμνοκόπος) pretends to be a truly dignified person in both his way of speaking and his bearing and demeanour (XXI. 3–13). The person who bears himself and behaves in a haughty manner (βρενθυόμενος) 'looks down upon everybody, stares at them with disapproval, shakes his head, and he belittles with ridicule and with barely even a brief retort—a retort which expresses his own superiority and which is dismissive of everybody else—those whom he encounters or those mentioned in his presence, even if they count among those considered important' (XXI. 23–34). The ironic character (εἴρων) is the kind of man who does not say what he means but rather the opposite. 'He praises the man he blames, but whenever he wants, he humiliates and blames himself and those with whom he can be familiar, indirectly making clear what he wants to say. He is aided both by cleverness at inventing things and by persuasiveness' (XXII. 1–10).[37] Two further 'types', each with two names, are the disparager (εὐτελιστής) or utter disparager (ἐξευτελιστής) and the vilifier (οὐδενωτής) or utter vilifier (ἐξουδενωτής). They differ 'in the lesser or greater intensity of the slander that they cast upon their neighbour. The utter disparager describes a person currently absent so as to make him seem relatively unimportant, whereas the utter vilifier (makes him seem) totally worthless' (XXIV. 4–10).

Each 'type' is individuated further by describing in detail the behaviour associated with it, as well as the practical consequences of having that particular disposition. For example, the inconsiderate man is depicted as 'the kind of man who demands hot or cold water in the bath without first

[37] Cf. the text established by Ranocchia (2001).

asking his fellow bather whether [this is agreeable] to him too ... When he buys a slave, he does not even ask for his name or give him one himself, but calls him "slave" and nothing else. The man who rubbed him with oil he does not rub with oil in return. And although he has been offered hospitality, he does not return it' (XVI. 34–XVII. 6). As a consequence, he must confront the difficulties caused by his vice, 'and in particular the difficulties due to thoughtlessness and those due to the anger of those to whom he behaves in this manner; also that he happens upon people who are like him or that he has difficulties because they do not even want to have any kind of dealings with him. In addition, (he must confront the difficulty) that, when dealing with a madman, everybody runs around and performs purifications, because they suspect that he is possessed by evil' (XIX. 7–17). Compare and contrast now the portrait of the self-willed man, as 'the kind of man who, without asking anyone's advice, goes on a trip, buys or sells, runs for office, or carries out any other thing. And if someone asks him what he intends to do, he answers "I know what I am doing". If someone blames him, he retorts "you blame me?". If he is invited to a meeting for the sake of a man who seeks advice, he does not want to say what he thinks unless the man is definitely going to do it' (XVII. 25–35). As a result of believing that he alone is knowledgeable about everything, 'he fails in most things and becomes everybody's target for malicious joy and nasty laughter and gets no help' (XIX. 21–5); 'he inevitably fares badly' (XIX. 30), and is bound to regret many things and to reap lots of abuse (XIX. 34–7).

As mentioned, some of these 'types' are explicitly identified as 'mixtures' or 'blends' of certain characteristics, but others are not. It may seem reasonable to assume that, in fact, all of the vices under discussion are considered 'mixed' in a similar sense. However, the text is disappointingly silent concerning the relationships between different 'blends', the ways in which arrogance is related to the other constituents of each 'blend', and the psychological mechanisms behind each 'character'. I should like to offer the following speculations.

Arrogance figures prominently in all the 'blends' mentioned above. For the sense of superiority essential to arrogance is found in all of them, although it varies in its scope, objects, and expressions. These variations are determined by the specific cluster of vices which occur together with arrogance in each 'blend'. So, while the inconsiderate person acts as superior regarding who he *is*, the superiority of the self-willed man is focused on what he alone can *achieve*, and that of the know-it-all enters on what he *knows*. People who affect dignity, as well as those tainted by haughtiness, attach their sense of superiority to their *appearance* and to the impressions created by their bearing and demeanour. The superiority of the ironic man concerns his *wit*, and also his command of language and of bodily expressions for ironical purposes. As to the disparager and the vilifier, their arrogance is focused *on the objects of their slander*, whom they describe in their absence as relatively unimportant (XXIV. 7–8) or totally worthless (XXIV. 9–10), sometimes displaying their sense of superiority as well.[38] One possibility, then, might be that the 'blends' really are the same disposition directed at different objects. Another possibility might be that they should be understood in terms of a genus and species relation. Arrogance might be considered the genus of which being inconsiderate, self-willed, a know-it-all, etc., would be species. However, different aspects of arrogance are highlighted in different 'blends'. Besides, the ironic man is described as 'for the most part a species (εἶδος: XXI. 38) of the fraudulent man (ἀλαζόνος: ibid.)', not of the arrogant man. Another possibility, which I favour, is that the 'blends' are related to each other through family resemblances. In addition to arrogance, which they have in common, both the inconsiderate man and the self-willed man are scornful and conceited; both the self-willed man and the know-it-all are stubborn; both the disparager and the vilifier slander their neighbour; and so on.

Looking closer at each 'blend', we may interpret arrogance as a focal vice, accompanied by other vices which are peripheral and even secondary to arrogance. Concerning the nature of the 'blending', sometimes it seems that the peripheral traits are largely behavioural, as opposed to the disposition of arrogance (cf. XXI. 21 ff.). At other times, however, Aristo suggests that traits such as conceit, thoughtlessness, overconfidence, haughtiness, and slander have both behavioural and dispositional aspects, just as arrogance does. An alternative interpretation is this. Peripheral vices too are connected through family resemblances to each other as well as to arrogance. In addition to being a peripheral vice, the conceit of the inconsiderate man is presupposed by his scorn and also characterizes arrogance. Likewise, the conceit of the self-willed man is the cause of

[38] Other times, however, these people simply bad-mouth their victims (cf. XXIV. 12 ff.).

his stubbornness, and also a mark of his arrogance.[39] Moreover, Aristo's description of these 'blends' points to the idea that arrogance is prior to the other traits that constitute each 'blend', both in the sense of being the most important constituent and in the sense of being a necessary condition that makes possible the development of peripheral vicious traits. This idea has intuitive force. It seems difficult to find or even to think of a person who would be inconsiderate, self-willed, a know-it-all, affecting dignity, behaving haughtily, ironic, disparaging or vilifying others, without also being arrogant. Furthermore, one's perception of oneself as someone better than others in respect of one's humanity seems to be precisely what enables one to treat other people thoughtlessly, to consider them ignorant and inept, and to offend them through haughtiness, irony, and slander.

Arrogance is a major vice with painful consequences, internal as well as external. It is a fundamental distortion of character and, as Aristo's typology shows, is typically accompanied by other such distortions of character: namely, the 'blends'. They too bring pain, and, like arrogance, they ought to be eradicated from the patients' souls. Considered in that light, Philodemus' choice to end his treatise by citing Aristo's account of complex vices is a fortunate one. Philodemus does not make it merely on account of the paraenetic character of Aristo's writing and its persuasive force,[40] but also for philosophical reasons related to Philodemus' hedonism and the therapeutic aspects of his ethics.

[39] Both conceit and contempt for others are characteristics of arrogance: cf. *De superb.* XIV. 7–15.

[40] These features of Aristo's work are emphasized by Ioppolo 1996.

8

Wealth and Property Management

The treatise *On Property Management*, Περὶ οἰκονομίας (*De oec.*, PHerc. 1424),[1] constitutes the ninth, unusually well-preserved book of Philodemus' *On Vices*. Its subject is οἰκονομία (translit. *oikonomia*) the management or administration of property[2] by those who wish to live the philosophical life. Thematically, it is complemented by Philodemus' treatise *On Wealth*, Περὶ πλούτου (*De div.*, PHerc. 163), of which only a few fragments survive.[3] Relevant material is also found in PHerc. 1570, a papyrus in very poor condition which is currently being edited for the first time.[4] *On Property Management* can be seen as part of a long tradition of literature on that topic flourishing from the fourth century BC onwards. Both Xenophon and Theophrastus, the authors whose views Philodemus refutes in approximately the first half of the extant remains of his treatise (*De oec.* frs. 1 and 2, and cols. A, B, and I. 1–XII. 2), contribute to that tradition, as do several other members of the major philosophical schools. From their writings, *oikonomia* emerges as a complex field which preserves an

[1] I use the edition by Jensen (1907) unless I indicate otherwise. Laurenti 1973 contains an Italian translation and commentary on the treatise. Natali 1995 gives a survey of ancient philosophical approaches to *oikonomia* during the fourth century BC and the Hellenistic era.

[2] Depending on the context, I usually render *oikonomia* as the management or administration of property, of one's estate, of wealth and property, of wealth and possessions, or of some combination of the above. Occasionally, I use 'economics', 'economic', or 'financial' for *oikonomia* and its cognates. These terms take their meaning from the ancient theories that I discuss. They bear no relation to modern conceptions of economics as a theoretical field which involves the study of, e.g., value, exchange, money, the organizational management of state revenues, etc. Natali 1995 remarks that most ancient Greek uses of *oikonomia* preserve the core meaning of the good organization and management of a complex structure.

[3] The extant remains of the first book of *On Wealth* are edited by Tepedino Guerra (1978).

[4] The editor of PHerc. 1570 is J. Ponczoch, who has managed to read the papyrus with the help of multispectral images. I am very grateful to him for sending me a translation, commentary, and index of the text.

intimate connection with the οἶκος (translit. *oikos*), the household and its contents, both animate and inanimate. It concerns practical matters related to the administration of the *oikos*, but the discussion is conducted primarily from an ethical rather than a pragmatic perspective.[5] The authors dealing with *oikonomia* assume that the activities involved in the administration of property make manifest one's qualities and virtues or, alternatively, reveal one's shortcomings and vices. Philodemus shares that assumption, and also the idea that unless *oikonomia* becomes subordinated to ethics, it must be perceived as its competitor on the same ground.[6]

Section I of this chapter gives an account of certain views which were advanced by Xenophon in the *Oeconomicus* (abbreviated *Oec.*) and probably by Theophrastus in the first book of the pseudo-Aristotelian work *Oikonomika* (abbreviated *Oik.*) from the perspective of Philodemus' critique of these authors. Section II articulates Philodemus' criticisms. Section III begins the examination of Philodemus' own position (*De oec.* XII. 2–XXVIII. 10): the nature and scope of his approach to *oikonomia*, and the position that he takes on the subject of an earlier debate between Metrodorus and the Cynics about the value of wealth and the desirability of administering it. Section IV analyses the feelings, beliefs, attitudes, and practices of the Epicurean property manager (οἰκονόμος, translit. *oikonomos*) and of the traditional *oikonomos* respectively, as they emerge from the contrast that Philodemus draws between these two kinds of managers. Section V discusses Philodemus' evaluation of traditional sources of income and his preference for certain ones as being most appropriate for the philosopher. In Section VI I consider a possible objection to Philodemus' account: that the Epicurean property manager is unable, or less able than the traditional manager, to achieve his aims. Subsequently, I explain how Philodemus responds to that charge.

The overall aim of this chapter is to make readers aware of the subtlety, complexity, and importance of Philodemus' book *On Property Management*. Philodemus' treatment is the most extensive treatment of the subject found in any Epicurean author, and, as will be revealed, it is more systematic and philosophical than rival approaches. It contains a compelling critique

[5] Ancient philosophers typically assume that all the principal aspects of *oikonomia* have ethical, or at least pragmatic, value. A general outline of the main subject areas covered by ancient *oikonomia* is found in Natali 1995: 100.

[6] Meikle (1995) argues this point with regard to Aristotle.

of the views of Xenophon and Theophrastus, and gives us a better understanding of the moral issues generally pertaining to the acquisition and preservation of property and wealth. Philodemus asks and gives a plausible answer to a cluster of questions which ought to claim our attention: notably, whether the acquisition and maintenance of possessions are essential to our happiness, and to what extent our pursuit of these activities is ethically justified and compatible with the aspiration to live the good life.

I

Some preliminary remarks might be useful. Like the majority of ancient authors of treatises on *oikonomia*, Xenophon and Theophrastus both believe that property management is an art (τέχνη, translit. *technē*) or a science (ἐπιστήμη, translit. epistēmē) with ethical and practical dimensions. In so far as it qualifies as such, it is organized according to regulative principles, circumscribes a precise field of activity, and entails that the truly competent property manager (*oikonomos*) is an expert in that field. Moreover, in virtue of its technical character, *oikonomia* is considered teachable. The expert property manager is in a position to transmit the general principles of the art, and also to give detailed instructions concerning the application of these principles to specific matters of economic practice. Teachings of this kind have a theoretical basis (θεωρία), in virtue of which they are put forward as pieces of advice about how to administer one's estate.

The theory as well as the practice of property management are typically divided into four distinct domains, which are parts of the art of *oikonomia* and correspond to four separate capacities of the *oikonomos*: the acquisition (κτῆσις), conservation (φυλακή), orderly arrangement (τάξις or διακόσμησις) of possessions, and the use of them (χρῆσις). Particular emphasis is placed on the first of these, the acquisition and increase of wealth, and therefore on money-making (χρηματισμός). In fact, it would seem that Xenophon and Theophrastus do not put any limit on the amount of wealth relevant to the good life. They seem to think that the more riches one procures, the better it is, provided that the riches come through legitimate means and from socially acceptable sources. And while they count *oikonomia* among the occupations constituting a well-rounded life, they do not acknowledge that there can be potential conflicts between the priorities set by *oikonomia* and other priorities.

Overall, the picture emerging from Xenophon and Theophrastus, and generally from traditional treatises on property management, is an ambiguous one. On the one hand, they import ethical categories into the discussion of *oikonomia*. On the other hand, by attributing to property management a considerable level of autonomy and by endorsing its goals and values as an art, they frequently seem to lose sight of its ethical relevance. The ambiguity is all the more problematic because *oikonomia* is perceived not only as an objective discipline, a τέχνη or ἐπιστήμη, but also as a stable state of mind (ἕξις) and even a virtue, specifically a form of practical wisdom (φρόνησις).[7] However, it is difficult to see how *oikonomia* can coincide with a virtuous disposition, when the property manager gives preponderance to financial objectives above all others.[8] This tension constitutes the main focus of Philodemus' criticisms of both Xenophon and Theophrastus.

Xenophon's *Oeconomicus* contains two different approaches to the topic of the administration of property, one philosophical, the other mundane. Socrates converses with Critoboulos, a wealthy Athenian who lives beyond his income and who seeks advice in order to remedy his situation. Socrates asks Critoboulos some questions. These help Critoboulos become clearer about the nature of his problem, but they also afford a glimpse into Socrates' own attitude towards *oikonomia*, in particular the use and value of wealth. Subsequently, Socrates, who asserts that he is ignorant about the art of *oikonomia* (*Oec.* II. 12–13), narrates the views of Ischomachus, a virtuous gentleman and an expert in that art. It is mainly from him that Critoboulos will learn what he wishes in a single lecture. The features of Xenophon's exposition which constitute the main targets of Philodemus' criticisms are the following. In the first phase of the conversation, Socrates induces his interlocutor to concede that the good property manager (ἀγαθὸς οἰκονόμος) should pursue what is useful or profitable (I. 15). Whatever is profitable (ὠφέλιμον) qualifies as wealth and possessions, whereas whatever is harmful is not wealth but loss. Hence the same things are wealth to those

[7] On *oikonomia* as a τέχνη and a ἕξις, see Natali 1995: 103.

[8] The Stoics solve this problem by claiming that only the wise man is an expert in property management, and only he possesses the relevant theoretical and practical disposition.

who understand how to use them but not wealth to those who do not (I. 10). Money, but also friends, enemies, and possessions, are moral indifferents in that sense (I. 12–15). Socrates calls slaves of their passions those people who have the required knowledge of *oikonomia*, but are unwilling or unable to apply it to the administration of their own estates (I. 19–20, 22–3). Although he does not consider Critoboulos one of them, he leads him to realize that he must strike a balance between his income and his needs (II. 10). As for Socrates himself, he has found that balance (II. 10). He calls himself rich because his small property of five minae is sufficient for his needs (II. 2–3), while he calls Critoboulos poor for the opposite reason (II. 2–8).

In the second phase of the conversation, Critoboulos learns from Ischomachus' account how to increase and administer his estate. Salient elements include the detailed instructions that Ischomachus gives to his wife about everything related to the household: how to distribute the income and regulate the expenses per month and per year; how to treat the servants; how to arrange things in the house so as to find them at a glance; how to choose a housekeeper and instil in her loyalty and justice; how to oblige her husband and her children 'by the daily practice of the virtues' (VII. 43); and how to preserve her own natural beauty by going cheerfully about her many tasks. Husband and wife are equal partners in the pursuit of a common goal: 'to act in such a manner that their possessions shall be in the best condition possible, and that as much as possible shall be added to them by fair and honourable means' (VII. 15). Similar instructions apply to the master of the estate. He personally chooses and trains the supervisors (cf. ἐπίτροπος), teaching them justice; develops his ability to rule men (τὸ ἀρχικόν), in particular his servants and slaves, whom he observes closely; is an expert on all aspects of the agricultural art; and so on. Again, Ischomachus claims that that kind of *oikonomia* is easy to learn and pleasant (VI. 9), gives beauty and health to the body, and removes most concerns of the mind (VI. 9–13). It also goes hand in hand with the possession of the virtues.[9]

As Philodemus remarks (*De oec.* VII. 37–45), Theophrastus' account is heavily indebted to Xenophon's, but makes additional claims as well.

[9] Agriculture in particular, Ischomachus tells us, provides the surest test of good and bad men (*Oec.* XX. 14).

Theophrastus too treats *oikonomia* as an art and, moreover, compares it to the art of politics (cf. *Oik*. 1343ᵃ1 ff.).[10] He cites Hesiod's phrase 'Homestead first, and a woman; a plough-ox hardy to furrow'[11] to lend support to his own claim that the main components of the household are human beings and possessions, because the latter are essential to nourishment, whereas human beings are the first necessity for a free man (1343ᵃ18–23). Regarding the human part of the household, he argues that the relationship between a man and his wife is both natural and beneficial and contributes greatly to one's happiness (1343ᵇ8 ff.). He advises about the functions of the wife, the husband's treatment of her, the wife's virginity and habits of sexual intercourse, and her physical adornment. Also, he gives instructions as to how to procure and train both the supervisors of the property and the labourers (1344ᵃ23 ff.); he regulates the correct apportionment of rewards or punishments; and he suggests ways in which slaves can be encouraged to be efficient.[12]

Like Xenophon, Theophrastus believes that another principal task of property management is to study the activities and arts by which one preserves and augments one's possessions (1343ᵃ23–6). The good property manager should be skilful in all four traditional domains of *oikonomia*: acquisition, as much as preservation, arrangement, and use of goods (1344ᵇ22–8). He should make sure that the quantity of fruitful possessions exceeds that of unfruitful ones; avoid risking all his possessions at once (1344ᵇ28–31); determine beforehand the monthly and yearly expenditures; and generally, get personally involved in every aspect of the administration of his

[10] According to Theophrastus, *oikonomia* and politics differ in so far as they apply to different communities, the one to the *oikos*, the other to the city-state (πόλις, translit. *polis*), and also in so far as the government of the *oikos* is in the hands of one person, whereas that of the *polis* is entrusted to many people (*Oik*. 1343ᵃ1–4). On the other hand, the two arts are similar to the extent that both of them are concerned with the making (ποίησις) or the constitution (σύστασις) of their objects, as well as with the use of them (χρῆσις: 1343ᵃ5–10). Theophrastus defines the *polis* in terms of 'an assemblage of households, lands and possessions sufficient for living well' (1343ᵃ10–11) and infers from this that the household (*oikos*) was formed before the *polis* and that, therefore, the art of household management is older than that of politics (1343ᵃ15–16).

[11] Apparently, the second half of the citation was not in the copy used by Philodemus. On this, see G. C. Armstrong's introduction to the Loeb edition of Aristotle, *Oeconomica*: 323–5.

[12] For the purpose of understanding Philodemus' criticisms, note Theophrastus' recommendations that the master must not allow his slaves to be insolent; nor, however, should he treat them with cruelty (*Oik*. 1344ᵃ29–30); that he should give manual labourers abundant food, but no wine at all; that he should hold festivals and give them treats; that he should avoid buying slaves who are either too cowardly or too spirited or who belong to the same nationality; and that he should encourage them to breed so as to keep their children and families as hostages for the slaves' fidelity.

estate.[13] For present purposes, it is important to note that the master of the estate should periodically inspect all implements and stores and the orderly arrangement of utensils. Both he and his wife should rise before the servants and retire after them. Both should closely supervise in person their special department of household work. They should never leave their home unguarded, which might mean getting up in the middle of the night in order to watch over it. And they should not postpone any of their tasks (1345ᵃ12–18). Like Xenophon, Theophrastus maintains that these habits preserve one's health and are also conducive to virtue (1345ᵃ13–14). The same holds for the principal and noblest sources of income: namely, agriculture and farming. However, mining, trade, and the art of war are suitable sources of income as well (1343ᵃ26 ff.).

II

Philodemus levels two sets of criticisms against Xenophon: one concerning Socrates, the other Ischomachus. In addition to their philosophical merits, they are worth studying for a historical reason: they illustrate how Philodemus and other Epicureans thought about Socrates and how they reacted to the so-called Socratic discourses. The former set of objections includes the following: Socrates distorts the ordinary meaning of *oikonomia*-related terms; his conversation with Critoboulos is undercut by ambiguity; he is naive, and even irrational.

According to Philodemus, the primary function of property management, as it is ordinarily understood, is to govern well ([ε]ὖ οἰκεῖν: *De oec.* I. 6) one's own home and the homes of others, 'where "well" is understood as "vastly beneficially and happily"' (I. 8–10). The person who knows the art of governing well will secure such benefits, live happily in his own home, and teach others how to do the same. 'Even if we say that the [good] property manager is a [provider] of possessions and money, these benefits too will [abound] in the possessions and money which he manages, and his job is to govern the house happily and teach [another person] more pleasant

[13] Like Xenophon, Theophrastus is an admirer of the Persian and Spartan methods of property management which require one's personal involvement in most aspects of the administration of one's estate (see below, pp. 173–6). He also commends the Athenian method of selling and buying at the same time (*Oik.* 1344ᵇ32–5, 1345ᵃ18–19).

things, such as [another person] would not have discovered if he looked for them' (IIIa. 6–16). Philodemus probably thinks that ordinary terms related to property administration, such as 'wealth', 'profit', or 'benefit',[14] 'possessions', 'poor' and 'rich', 'masters and slaves',[15] and other related words, capture the usual and also the proleptic[16] conception of *oikonomia* and its functions. Moreover, he seems to assume that so long as enquiry into these matters remains close to the relevant preconceptions, it will proceed smoothly and methodically, and will lead to the truth.[17] On the other hand, if one deviates from the familiar use of words, one is bound to ignore the corresponding preconceptions, conduct the investigation at random, and infer falsehoods.

Socrates is guilty of precisely these errors.

> [Although] ordinary language never uses [these names in this] way, this man counterfeited it (sc. ordinary language) and tries to reason from these names. Also, [forcing] the ordinary meaning, he characterizes as masters, and as extremely wicked ones at that, the vices which act like hindrances, that is idleness of the soul, carelessness, gambling, and bad companionship. Besides, he turns those people who work and make [profits] for themselves but who [squander their household goods] into (the slaves) of [very hard] masters—gluttony and drunkenness and ambition—things against which one must fight more than against [one's enemies].
>
> (*De oec.* IV. 1–16)

'Slaves' and 'masters' refer to people in the household who have these respective positions and roles. By calling 'slaves' the masters of an estate, and 'masters' the vices that afflict them, Socrates extends the ordinary meaning of the terms to a metaphorical meaning causing confusion.[18] A similar objection applies to Socrates' use of 'possessions'. On the basis of the definition of an estate as everything that a person possesses, Socrates infers that, therefore, the enemies that one possesses are also part of one's estate.[19] On the other hand, in a fragmentary passage, Philodemus remarks

[14] Cf. τοῦ συμφέροντος: *De oec.* I. 9–10; τὰς ὠφελίας: IIIa. 5.

[15] Recall that traditional treatises on household management discuss these topics, and that both Xenophon and Theophrastus explore the roles of and relationships between masters and slaves.

[16] Cf. pp. 171–2. [17] Cf. pp. 171–2 and 68–73.

[18] Philodemus does not object to metaphors as such. His point is probably that Socrates' metaphor is confusing, given the particular context in which it is used.

[19] Critoboulos defines the meaning of *oikos*, estate or property, in terms of everything that a man possesses (Xenophon, *Oec.* I. 5). Socrates infers that, therefore, one's estate also includes the enemies

that, if 'to possess' is understood in the principal sense, it refers to both the house and what one possesses outside the house; but the verb does not have its principal sense in the phrase 'certain people possess enemies' (fr. 1. 19–21).[20] The meaning that Socrates lends to 'poor' and 'rich' is subject to similar criticisms. '[How it is possible] for people who have a hundred times more to be poor? [How could it be] that some will have [enough] to live on, whereas others will not? [And how] could we, in accordance with ordinary usage, call the one [of them] poor but the other rich?' (IV. 29–34). Calling rich a man whose entire estate is worth a small sum, but poor someone whose property is worth a hundred times more, entails speaking 'in a manner involving opinion ([δ]οξαστικῶς), not preconception (οὐ προληπτικῶς) in accordance with ordinary usage' (V. 2–4). Hence it is likely to obstruct the proper order of investigation, cause confusion, and lead to mistakes.

In general, the discussion between Socrates and Critoboulos is vitiated by ambiguity.[21] 'They never yet [seem to assume] the same concept, because of [failure] to distinguish between different meanings' (*De oec.* VI. 16–18). For instance, when Socrates says that he will talk about property management (cf. ο[ἰ]κο[νο]μήσειν: VI. 18–19) he means the balance between his needs and his income, whereas Critoboulos has in mind the optimal preservation and increase of his property. In fact, Socrates appears naive to the point of being illogical. He gives instructions about *oikonomia*, although he has said that he has not been taught that subject by anyone (cf. VI. 18–20). 'Socrates himself [affects] to teach Critoboulos the discipline of property management as if he were going to learn such a vast discipline from a single lecture' (VI. 11–16). At any rate, Socrates was always out of touch with practical life (cf. οὐ πραγματικόν: V. 4–6). 'Besides, as regards his statement that five minae seem to him sufficient for the necessary and natural needs of men, that prosperity in life [is something empty], and that

that one possesses, with the result that his friend narrows down the definition of *oikos* to cover only the goods that one possesses (I. 7).

[20] There is some indication that Philodemus had similar objections to Socrates' use of 'wealth', 'money', and 'profit': cf. the reference to the preceding lost lines in *De oec.* IV. 1–4. Philodemus' criticism is also applicable to Socrates' claims that only what is profitable counts as wealth, whereas what is harmful is not wealth (Xenophon, *Oec.* I. 5 ff.), and therefore, possessions such as money (ἀργύριον) should not count as wealth, if one does not know how to use them in a profitable manner (Xenophon, *Oec.* I. 14).

[21] However, it remains unclear whether Philodemus accuses Socrates of using ambiguity out of intellectual dishonesty, or merely out of confusion.

he does not need anything more in addition to those (five minae), it is ridiculous[22] and in conflict with reason' (V. 6–14).

Philodemus scores several points against Ischomachus, some of which apply to Theophrastus as well (*De oec.* VII. 37–45). In both cases, his strategy is to argue (in ways which often overlap) for the following conclusions. Several instructions issued by Xenophon and Theophrastus are trivial, whereas others have no theoretical justification at all, and yet others are not applicable in practice. Besides, many of their doctrines are in fact irrelevant to the subject matter of *oikonomia*. Moreover, Xenophon and Theophrastus hold views which belong to traditional *oikonomia* but, nonetheless, are irrelevant or incompatible with the philosopher's own activities and values. By means of these arguments, Philodemus aims to restrict the scope of *oikonomia*, redefine its focus, and invite us to assess traditional features of property management in the light of the philosophical life.

Thus, the theoretical pretensions of Xenophon and Theophrastus are punctured in several instances. 'It is easy to learn the age [of horses and men, even if no deeper underlying theory is available]. Indeed, Critoboulos was aware of the fact, mentioned in the middle of his exposition, that some men have wives who act in a cooperative manner with the goal of increasing the property, whereas others have wives who act in a very damaging way' (*De oec.* II. 1–8). Nor did Critoboulos need the aid of philosophy to learn things about farming. For that art 'happens to derive from one's own experience, not from philosophy' (VII. 31–3). In fact, one wonders 'who has been educated by the doctrines mentioned above, other than the person who has already approved of them' (VII. 2–5). Theophrastus too makes trivial claims, e.g., about the treatment of servants. 'The instructions concerning their [tasks], nourishment, and punishment are commonplace, observed even by rather ordinary persons, and they are not within the province of the philosopher. As to the precept that one should not use brutal methods of punishment, this does equally concern both theory and practice, but it should not have been taken up here in connection with the treatment of servants. Otherwise, why should only this point be raised?' (IX. 44–X. 7).

Besides, both Xenophon and Theophrastus advance positions that are arbitrary and lack theoretical support. For instance, there is no good reason

[22] I tentatively translate the conjecture [ἄπ]ορον (V. 13), which was recently suggested to me. In general, there may be problems with Jensen's supplementation of V. 13–14.

to suppose that agriculture is in accordance with nature, or that it constitutes the first and best source of income, or that mining and other similar activities are suitable for the good person (VIII. 40–5).[23] Nor should one accept without argument Theophrastus' assertions that the house is the principal element of nourishment and the woman is the principal element of free men (VIII. 32–40). Equally unjustified are Theophrastus' instructions about the way to approach one's wife (IX. 4–5), about marrying a virgin (IX. 8–9), about the paramount importance of slaves (IX. 9–13), and about the recruitment, training, and distribution of tasks in the household to different kinds of servants (IX. 13–26). Furthermore, Philodemus questions the practical applicability of Ischomachus' doctrines, in particular with regard to moral matters. Ischomachus does not make clear how one can teach the servants 'to keep their hands off the master's property and not to steal, even if he exaggerates in a manner befitting tragedy when he speaks of deriving these principles from the laws of both Dracon and Solon and from royal decrees. But if, further, he thought it possible to teach the property manager the capacity to make people just, then I consider him to be saying things similar to the visions that we have in our dreams' (*De oec.* VII. 16–26). Ischomachus' idea that the good estate manager knows enough to be completely self-sufficient and does not need any advice is also unsound. 'That there is no benefit coming from other people is, I believe, the conviction of a stupid person' (VII. 1–2).

Many of these features do not belong to *oikonomia*, but fall outside its proper scope. Notably, this holds for the analogy that Theophrastus draws between *oikonomia* and politics, which, according to Philodemus, is both irrelevant and untenable (VII. 45–VIII. 24).[24] On the other hand, elements which do belong to traditional *oikonomia* are indifferent or harmful to the person who wishes to live the philosophical life. Both Xenophon and Theophrastus prescribe the activities pertaining to property management according to the Persian, Spartan, Libyan, and Attic methods (*De oec.* A. 11–27, B. 11 ff.), and in particular according to the fourfold division of the activities of the *oikonomos* mentioned above. In sharp contrast, Philodemus contends that of the four traditional domains of *oikonomia*, the one that

[23] Concerning Philodemus' own evaluation of these sources of income, see below, pp. 188–91.

[24] Philodemus seems to concede that *oikonomia* and politics are both arts. The Epicurean will not practice either of them as art, and while, as we shall see, he will practice *oikonomia* non-technically, he will not practice politics at all.

is truly useful to the philosopher's goals is φυλακή, the preservation of possessions. Also, while Theophrastus recommends that the tasks of *oikonomia* should be distributed in such a way as to avoid endangering all of the property at once, Philodemus replies as follows: 'This, of course, is good advice for the ordinary person; but the philosopher does not work properly speaking, nor, if he ever works, does he seem to put everything at risk so as to need exhortation not to do it' (XI. 11–21). The meticulous arrangement of possessions is central to the Persian method (A. 18–20) and strongly recommended by Ischomachus and Theophrastus, but Philodemus views it as a waste of time. Moreover, he objects to the importance that his rivals attribute to the wife. While they maintain that it is natural and useful to take a wife, Philodemus denies that she is important to the philosopher's happiness. Even if she contributes as much as her husband to the material prosperity of the estate, she is not necessary for one's happiness, if one is a philosophically inclined man (*De oec.* II. 8–36).[25]

Concerning the care of servants and slaves, Philodemus rejects many of his rivals' views because he finds them harsh and even inhumane.

[25] Philodemus raises a related objection on logical grounds. He concedes that Theophrastus' analytic examination of the two parts of the household belongs, on the face of it, to the subject of *oikonomia*. Nonetheless, he objects to Theophrastus' interpretation of Hesiod's division of the household into two parts, humans and possessions, mainly because of inconsistencies related to the theses that the wife is necessary to the free man and that she is an equal partner in the household. 'It is worth inquiring further how he (sc. Theophrastus) adds to these precepts that "consequently", according to Hesiod, it would be necessary that "first and foremost there is a house and a woman, because the one is the principal element of nourishment, the other of free men", unless the wife and partner in the management of the household is a possession just like food' (VIII. 24–32). It seems, then, that Hesiod's phrase cannot be used to support the distinction of the primary parts of the household into human beings and possessions, or Theophrastus' justification of it. I am unclear as to just what Philodemus' argument is here, but I think that it runs along the following lines. Theophrastus maintains that the wife is necessary to the free man in a sense analogous to that in which the possession of an estate is necessary to nourishment. This entails that the wife is a possession of some sort, while Hesiod's twofold division of the household into a house (or estate, more broadly) and a woman implies that the wife is something different from mere possessions. Besides, Theophrastus seems to contradict himself. For, on the one hand, in the analogy mentioned above, he treats the wife, a human being, in terms of something that the free man needs and gets, i.e., a possession. On the other hand, however, he claims also that the household consists of human beings and possessions, and thus he classifies the wife as a human being, not a possession. Further tension is caused by Theophrastus' view of the wife as an equal partner in the administration of the household. For if she is a possession, just like victuals are, she cannot be her husband's equal. So, it would seem that, in order to be consistent, Theophrastus would have to drop either the belief in the equality of the spouses or the distinction between two parts of the household, as well as the reasons that he gives in defence of it. In fact, we saw that Philodemus calls arbitrary the contention that the woman (γυνή) is the principal element of free men (VIII. 34–5). Subsequently, he argues that this claim is simply not true. '(It is worth asking) why, of the preoccupations of the household which concern men, the wife (γαμετή) is considered first and foremost, since there can be a happy life even without her' (VIII. 46–IX. 3).

The claims (sc. of Theophrastus) that one should not allow the slaves to run riot and one should not press them and should give responsibility to the more trustworthy among them, but more food to the industrious, are more or less correct. However, it is a hard thing to maintain that a drink of wine in general, not just in larger quantities, makes even free men insolent (and that this is why many nations abstain from it), and that for these very reasons it is obvious to propose that one should distribute wine to the slaves either not at all or very seldom, whereas the obvious thing is rather that a certain quantity of wine gives strength by making one cheerful and is to be allowed to those who work most.

(*De oec.* IX. 26–44)

As to Theophrastus' advice to bind slaves to one's service by having their wives and children as hostages, it is even harsher than Xenophon's instruction to raise the children of the good servants but not of the bad ones (X. 15–21). In fact, many such instructions seem inconsistent with moral considerations. An example is Theophrastus' advice that the master should cater to the pleasure and entertainment of the slaves, going to considerable trouble and expense for that purpose. 'At the same time, "to make auspicious sacrifices and to provide enjoyments for the sake of servants rather than for the sake of free men" does more violence to our convictions, "for they have more possibilities of enjoyment, for the sake of which such things have been instituted"' (*De oec.* X. 21–8). Philodemus does not state why he finds these practices objectionable, but a probable reason is that they entail more toils than benefits for the property manager, and they promote the servants' well-being rather than his own.

In general, the assiduous personal involvement of the property manager in every aspect of the administration of the estate (which is the hallmark of the Spartan and Persian methods, and perhaps also of the Attic method of purchasing at the same time as one sells) involves practices 'hard and unfitting for the philosopher' (XI. 30–1).[26] In particular, Philodemus points out that the practice of getting up in the course of the night is toilsome, and he questions whether it is conducive to one's health and one's pursuit of philosophy to follow that practice even when the nights are short.[27] 'I wonder if this habit (sc. getting up in the course of the night), (when

[26] These include waking up before the servants and going to bed after them, and getting up in the middle of the night to make sure that the house is always guarded (XI. 30–8).

[27] Philodemus rejects such habits on the grounds of a general strategy which will become clear later, and which crucially involves the correct performance of the calculus of pleasures and pains. His idea

practised) in the shortest night of the year, is good for health and for the study of philosophy' (XI. 38–41).[28]

Some further points deserve mention. Philodemus accuses Xenophon of introducing Ischomachus not only as a good property manager but also as a man of practical wisdom and virtue (VI. 3–8), whereas he says or does things unworthy of such a man. The immediate context does not reveal just what these things are (cf. VI. 1–3), but it seems likely that they are dictated by the goals of *oikonomia*, the art in which Ischomachus is an expert. Not only are they unphilosophical, but they may derive from vice. Moreover, Philodemus complains that the 'cosmetic' (κοσμητικόν) does not take its place beside acquisition ([κ]τητικόν) and preservation (φυλακτ[ι]κόν) in the art of *oikonomia*, if arranging things in the proper way and place is understood under 'cosmetic'; but he does allow Xenophon to prescribe the kind of arrangement that adds pleasure to the useful part of the province of the manager (X. 39–XI. 3). Subsequently, he makes the point that it belongs to the greedy man to recommend fruitful possessions over unfruitful ones, if Xenophon used those expressions to mean 'productive' and 'unproductive'; but if he meant 'useful' and 'useless', he should have recommended that one should have all useful things and nothing useless (XI. 3–11).

The dialectical part of the treatise *On Property Management* ends towards the beginning of column 12 (XII. 2). Philodemus announces that enough has been said about the doctrines of his rivals, and that he will now present a brief outline of the position of his own school (XII. 2–5).

appears to be that practices such as getting up in the course of the night involve pain that outweighs the pleasure, and they therefore hinder our attainment of the moral end.

[28] The pattern of Ischomachus' life is intended to lend support to the suggestion that hard work is conducive to health and one's well-being. He trains his wife and supervises her doings; thinks a great deal about the building and furnishings of his house and the layout of its contents; selects and constantly checks his servants, housekeeper, and supervisors; rises early, walks to his farm, superintends all the details of farm work, runs back home, has lunch, and returns to work right afterwards; puts an enormous amount of care and toil into the cultivation of his fields; and so on. The duties that he prescribes for his wife are no less cumbersome. She must receive the income, distribute as much of it as must be spent, and save the rest; she must regulate the expenses of the household per month and per year; make sure that the goods are properly stored or used; supervise, instruct, correct, reward or punish, and care for the servants, thus increasing their market value; and oblige her husband and her children 'by the daily practice of the virtues' (*Oec.* VII. 43). Furthermore, she should arrange things in the house so that 'a glance will reveal anything that wants attention and the knowledge of where each thing is will quickly bring it to hand so that we can easily use it' (VIII. 10). She must choose the housekeeper and instil in her the virtues, notably loyalty and justice. She must attend to the possessions herself, if she wishes to have optimal results. If Ischomachus is to be believed, all this labour will help her preserve her physical beauty better than any cosmetics might.

III

At the outset, Philodemus narrows down the scope of his treatment of *oikonomia* and its practitioners. He will not discuss *oikonomia* in terms of a general ethical subject pertaining, as it were, to the private aspects of the good life.[29] He will concentrate on the acquisition and preservation of possessions[30] and our moral attitudes towards them, not on various possible ways of redefining *oikonomia* and other related concepts. His addressee will be the philosopher, not the gentleman or the layman. And his analysis will apply to the administration of possessions in a way suited to the philosopher rather than anyone else. 'We shall discuss, then, not how one can live well at home, but what attitude one must take up both with regard to the acquisition and the preservation of wealth, concerning which property management and the property-management expert are in fact conceived specifically, (and we shall do so) without contending at all with those who prefer to make other meanings underlie the terms, and moreover discussing the acquisition (of property) which is appropriate for the philosopher, [not] for just anybody' (*De oec.* XII. 5–17).

In this way Philodemus places his discussion of *oikonomia* on the right philosophical footing. It does not bear on the pragmatics of the household, or on ways and means of becoming and remaining rich. It aims principally to determine the extent and the ways in which people who desire to live the philosophical life can engage in property management without compromising their ethical principles and without endangering their happiness. The last restriction in particular bears on the objection that the philosopher should not have any property to administer, but should provide for his rudimentary needs on a day-to-day basis. Philodemus addresses that objection by drawing on an older debate between Metrodorus and the Cynics, who had proposed that the philosopher should live in utter poverty in order to be carefree (cf. *De oec.* XII. 29–43). In the passage cited below, Philodemus rehearses Metrodorus' arguments, and also takes a position himself regarding the claim of the Cynics.[31]

[29] The implied contrast is that between the good life at home and the good life in the *polis*, not that between private and public life in any modern sense.

[30] In my view, περὶ ἅ in XII. 9 refers to both κτῆσις and φυλακή (ll. 8–9), not to χρήματα (l. 8).

[31] I shall not discuss here the controversial issue as to whether Philodemus' *De oec.* XII–XXII is, in fact, copied from Metrodorus or chiefly contains Philodemus' own views. I have argued elsewhere

He (sc. Metrodorus) writes—for he [likes saying] this—that the [best] life is the one which is [accompanied by tranquillity], peace, and cares which cause minimal trouble. But it does not seem that this goal is achieved at least in this way, namely if we avoid all those things which, if they were present, may sometimes cause difficulties and distress. For in truth many things do cause some pain when they are present, but they disturb us more when they are absent. Thus, to be in good bodily health does involve some care and effort, but the suffering is infinitely more grievous when health is gone. And in a similar way the faithful friend also, who perhaps causes some [pains when he exists], distresses us more when he does not exist. In fact, it is clear that the good person is the kind of person who, [defining] many things by reference to what is profitable and what is not profitable, [chooses some things rather than others] and who, if he does not do this, cannot live [in the right manner], although he can live virtuously and, moreover, who both needs many things without the possession of which he will lead a more [perturbed] life and is distressed [when he is deprived] of certain things. So, as we have said above, one must not avoid all things which, if they are present, may cause all kinds of troubles, concerns, and worries. On the contrary, [one must accept] some things, among which is in fact wealth, which are less of a burden when they are present, much more so for one's entire life and not only for a time. Moreover, to use as an absolute rule the principle that we should [abstain] from toils is not an unfailing practise. For in fact the person who [provides for himself] day by day [is subject to toils] and the person who is prosperous is sometimes subject to certain troubles. And similarly, it is also not right for the person who has acquired a [moderate] amount of possessions to reject them on account of a change of fortune of this kind, but instead one should consider the thing which contributes for the most part to the most perfect way of life. Wealth does not seem to bring useless difficulties through itself, but through the wickedness of those who use it. For the diligence and vigilance which are fitting for the person who manages it in the proper manner sometimes do give some trouble, but certainly not greater than the manner of providing what is necessary day by day. But even if it is greater than that, it is not greater than the [other] difficulties which it removes, provided that one does not manage to show that natural wealth does not secure profits much greater than the toils of the frugal life—something that [it would take a lot to prove].

(XII. 43– XIV. 23)

According to this passage, Cynics and Epicureans agree that the best life is free from toil and worry, but disagree as to how it can be achieved, in

that Philodemus examines *oikonomia* and other related concepts from a different angle and in a more systematic way than Metrodorus does: see Tsouna-McKirahan 1996. An extensive study of the Epicurean polemic against the Cynics is offered by Gigante 1992.

particular regarding the possession and administration of wealth. On the one hand, the Cynics advocate a beggarly lifestyle for the reason that wealth is troublesome and, therefore, harmful to one's peace of mind. On the other hand, Metrodorus contends that a peaceful and happy life is obtained not by avoiding whatever causes pain or effort without qualification, but by opting for things which may involve a certain amount of trouble at present but relieve us of much greater concerns in the future. Wealth is such a thing, as are health and friendship. Although its possession and administration doubtless require thought and labour, it is better to have it than not. For its presence allows the virtuous man to live pleasantly, whereas its absence is responsible for deprivation and distress. The only way in which the Cynics might be able to establish that the possession of natural wealth (φυσικὸς πλοῦτος: *De oec.* XIV. 19) is less preferable to the day-to-day provision of goods would be to prove that, in fact, the former entails more pains and toils than the latter. However, following Metrodorus' lead, Philodemus suggests that it is highly unlikely that such a proof would be forthcoming. One practical implication of the Epicurean position is that the good person should not reject as useless the wealth that may come his way. The entire argument is based on the rational calculation of pleasures and pains, and also makes use of the concept of natural wealth, which is related to the concept of the measure of wealth (πλούτου μέτρον). Philodemus' presentation of Epicurean *oikonomia* involves both these notions; therefore I shall explain them briefly.

Roughly speaking, natural wealth is one of the many objects which we naturally seek in order to satisfy natural desires and thus feel pleasure. In so far as this kind of desire has a limit, natural wealth also has a limit, and besides, it is easy to obtain (Epicurus, *KD* 15) precisely because it is natural (Epicurus, *ad Men.* 130).[32] Correspondingly, the measure of wealth which is appropriate for the philosopher, as this is determined by Metrodorus and then by Philodemus in their writings *On Wealth*, covers the range of the philosopher's natural needs.[33] 'There is for the

[32] According to certain interpretations (cf. Cicero, *Tusc.* 5. 93), natural wealth is associated not with all natural desires, but only with natural and necessary desires and mainly with the desire for food, drink, and shelter. Even if this is true of Epicurus, it will become clear that Philodemus' concepts of natural wealth and the measure of wealth apply to all natural desires, not merely to necessary ones.

[33] PHerc. 1570 seems to draw a distinction between natural and empty wealth (cf. XVIII. 26–7). Also, the author seems to refer to the thesis that natural goods are easy to procure (XIX. 27–8).

philosopher a measure of wealth (πλούτου μέ[τρ]ον: *De oec.* XII. 18–19) which, [following] the founders of the school, we have passed down in [the treatise] *On Wealth* so that an account can be given of the capacity to administer its [acquisition] and preservation' (XII. 17–25). And in so far as the measure of wealth satisfies the philosopher's natural needs, it is slightly superior (*De div.* LI. 27–30) or, from another perspective (cf. *De oec.* XIV. 9–23), clearly preferable to poverty. In particular, Philodemus brings out the instrumental importance of wealth and its administration for the good life. At the same time, following the authorities of the school, he tries to hold on to the view that the difference between possessing and lacking wealth, and between preserving it and not preserving it, is but small (XVIII. 25–31), and he suggests that the superiority of wealth is mainly practical rather than moral.[34] Although he appears flexible as to just how rich the philosopher can be, he makes clear that very great wealth is not desirable and should not be the object of *oikonomia* for the philosopher. In outline, the position for which he will argue seems to be this: 'more' wealth may be better than 'less', because of the mental freedom and the material comforts that it affords when it is correctly used. Also, 'more' wealth can be interpreted in many ways, since Philodemus does not fix precisely how much money and possessions are optimal for the philosophical life. On the other hand, 'more' corresponds somehow to 'the measure of wealth', but never amounts to the open-ended goal of traditional *oikonomia*: namely, to amass as many riches as possible through socially acceptable and legitimate means.

[34] The position of PHerc. 1570 on the status of poverty and wealth is compatible with Philodemus' attitude to these matters in *On Property Management*. We should bear in mind that the reconstruction of the extant remains of PHerc. 1570 is highly conjectural and tentative. It seems that, on the one hand, PHerc. 1570 defends poverty against a number of allegations. Poverty makes us stingy, deprives us of pleasures, forces us to live in unbearable conditions, and makes us incapable of entertaining guests (XII. 7–10, 16–18). Poverty produces confusion and shame (XII. 3–4). It obstructs the exercise of frank speech (XII. 10). And it deprives us of a decent funeral (XII. 12–15). The author of PHerc. 1570 announces that he intends to answer every one of these charges, but the only answer that survives in part is that virtue, not poverty, is the essential condition of frank speech (XII. 8–12). So, it might seem that the author of PHerc. 1570 considers poverty valuable in its own right. On the other hand, PHerc. 1570 contrasts the difficulty of preserving abundant riches (cf. VIII. 13) with the ease of procuring natural goods (XIX. 28–31). The author probably emphasizes the importance of paying friendly visits, and perhaps of visiting an impoverished friend (XI. 4 ff.). Ponczoch (cf. n. 4) points to a correlation between the author's description of a poor man's breakfast and his use of the terminology of being helpful. If there is such a correlation, the author may be advising us to alleviate a friend's poverty. And if this is right, it would seem that PHerc. 1570 treats poverty as a condition less preferable than the possession of natural goods.

IV

After ruling out the suggestion that wealth does no good at all, Philodemus tries to explain in just what way the possession of wealth and the administration of property are compatible with the principles of the philosophical life. Elements of his pattern of analysis are found in other surviving treatises of *On Vices* as well. They include examination of the disposition of the philosophically minded administrator, his feelings and beliefs, his interests and activities, and his virtues.

Philodemus describes the right approach to *oikonomia* in terms of a certain easy attitude required of the philosopher towards the acquisition and preservation of possessions, and specifies that attitude by referring to the elements deriving from the philosopher's disposition. Notably, the philosopher should not care too much about the goal of traditional *oikonomia*, the more and the less, but should cultivate some kind of emotional detachment with regard to his gains and losses.

I think that the right administration of wealth lies in this, i.e., in not feeling distressed about what one loses and in not [trapping oneself on treadmills] because of an obsessive [zeal] concerning the more and the less. For the labour involved in the [acquisition] of wealth consists both in dragging oneself [by force] and in agonizing over one's losses on the grounds that they might bring one directly into pain, whether present or expected. But if one has removed from oneself such difficulties and does not eagerly desire to amass and make one's property as great as possible and, moreover, does not procure for oneself those resources that wealth offers by oneself watching painfully over one's possessions or [by collecting] them in rich abundance, [for these reasons][35] a readiness for acquisition would become indistinguishable from one's readiness to share things on one's own initiative too.

(*De oec.* XIV. 23–XV. 3)

Also, the philosopher has true beliefs (or knowledge), first of all, about the nature of our desires and inclinations. He correctly believes that 'there are within us natural [desires] for more goods' (XVI. 30–1), on account of which we should choose to preserve our wealth in so far as no unseemly

[35] XV. 1 διὰ [ταῦτα] Sedley. However, it has been suggested to me that Sedley's reading is too short for the space, so that one should probably add [τις]. Jensen proposes δία[ιτα καί], and on that construction, the text has an entirely different meaning: 'one's [life] would acquire stability as would the ready availability of one's property for the life which shares through him as well' (XV. 1–3).

labour is involved (XVI. 25–8). But he is also convinced that wealth has no intrinsic value, and that he can live happily without it.

> The wise man will never be bound by wealth in such a way as to endure, in order to preserve it, toils which are great and are not such as to be exchanged for any quantity of wealth. For what makes its use painless and the enjoyment deriving from it pure must be this, the fact that for the sages no heavy care about how it will be possible to preserve it is attached to the possession of wealth, not even when [circumstances] become most critical. Nor does the moderate person, [full of good courage] towards the future in virtue of his humble and modest way of living, become distressed, since he knows that what is natural is actually provided by that mode of life, but he feels more inclined by his will towards a more affluent way of living. For he is not lazy in getting for himself what is sufficient for him, he whose way of life is moderate and communal and whose doctrine is healthy and true, even if it does not easily attract just anybody. On account of what, then, would he stress himself beyond measure in order to preserve his possessions, since he has such resources for living well in great ease even if he should lose his wealth?
>
> (XV. 31–XVI. 18)

What makes it possible for the philosopher to feel and act in such a way is, indeed, his confidence that Epicurus was right in saying that natural and necessary desires are easy to satisfy, and their fulfilment is all that the philosopher needs in order to pursue his way of life. At the same time, as mentioned, he has a correct appreciation of the instrumental value of wealth, which motivates his efforts as a property manager and is related to his natural inclination towards 'more goods' (cf. XVI. 30–1). In fact, if the philosopher acquires more possessions than he had before, he should accept them, provided that they come to him in a blameless and effortless manner (XVI. 44–6).[36] Generally speaking, he holds true beliefs about what is and is not profitable, and makes choices accordingly (*De oec.* XIII. 20–3).[37]

Dispositional elements underlie the philosopher's *oikonomia* also, in so far as he provides for the needs of his fellow Epicureans and makes some of his wealth available to his friends. In particular, Philodemus mentions in many places the philosopher's attitudes of good will, benevolence, and gratitude;

[36] In this respect, Philodemus' approach to *oikonomia* accommodates his audience, which is partly constituted by Roman patricians, including Philodemus' patron Piso.

[37] Cf. the following remark: 'It is easy for anyone to discern the things which, according to this criterion, are useful and lie within reach for people who do not heap up wealth, but who administer the very [property] that they have' (*De oec.* XVI. 39–44).

his generosity and philanthropy; and his thorough appreciation of the value of friendship. I am not sure whether the text contains specific references either to donations that the philosophical property manager makes to the Epicurean school or to communal administration or to both. For example, the philosopher's 'readiness to share things on his own initiative' (*De oec.* XV. 2–3) may or may not allude to regular contributions to the Epicurean community. Also, Philodemus' statement that the Epicurean manager is capable of exhorting men 'to share freely all their wealth inspired by his confidence in the adequacy of few possessions and assisted by the discourses of the sage' (XVIII. 4–7) can be taken to imply a reference to communal administration, but does not need to be read in that way. In any case, Philodemus' thesis is not merely that the easy attitude of the sage towards the administration of wealth is compatible with having friends, but that it is in part shaped by their presence or absence. 'That the wise man administers these goods in such a manner is a consequence of the fact that he has acquired friends and continues to acquire them' (XV. 3–6). Their needs and pleasures figure prominently in his calculations concerning his monthly and yearly expenses, the distribution of his income, and the manner in which he provides for the future.

Thus, the Epicurean *oikonomos* spends money carefully and in proportion to his income (XXV. 23–4) without, however, acting like a miser. He keeps flexible the amounts that he spends per month and per year, and also the ways in which he allocates his income to different things (XXV. 31–42), because occasionally he wishes to spend much more than usual on his friends, or because the circumstances and his sense of decorum sometimes guide him to offer gifts rather than to buy furnishings for his house or store up his belongings (XXV. 42, XXVI. 1). When he needs to retrench in his expenses, he makes sure that the cuts are not excessive or undignified, and that they primarily affect him rather than his friends. 'As one ought to indulge oneself and one's friends in those desires which are harmless when a larger quantity of goods has happened to come to hand, so one ought to compensate for the losses with retrenchments which are not illiberal, and which are applied more towards oneself than towards one's friends when there is a serious shortage of cash' (XXVI. 1–9). Moreover, the claims of friendship determine the extent to which he needs to save and make provisions for the future. 'If one has friends, one must save more in order that they may have [means of maintaining themselves] even after one's death, and one must regard them as one's children. On the other hand, if one does not have friends, [one must relax] not only the practice of saving money, but also the more parsimonious administration of property' (XXVII. 5–12). Generally speaking, the philosopher acts in these matters 'like those who sow seeds in the earth' (XXV. 17–18). What he spends on his friends represents a more profitable acquisition than lands (XXV. 2–3), and enables him to reap many times more fruits in the future (XXV. 16–23). In that sense, caring for one's friends entails also providing for one's own future (XXV. 11–12). 'This both gives one good hopes right now and, when it has been realized, makes one happy' (XXV. 12–14). As Hermarchus said, it is the treasure that is most secure against the turns of fortune (XXV. 3–4).

As mentioned, Philodemus shares the assumption made by his rivals as well, that one's activities as a property manager involve the exercise of one's virtues or vices. According to his account, the Epicurean property manager is free of greed, the principal vice related to wealth, but possesses the virtue standing opposite to greed, which, however, is not identified in the treatise. We could determine it in negative terms, as the absence of greed or of the love of money (ἀφιλοχρηματία).[38] Alternatively, we might identify it as *oikonomia*, since Philodemus opposes the good οἰκονόμος to the φιλοχρήματος, the lover of money (XVII. 2–14).[39] In any case, that virtue is found together with social virtues: namely, liberality, good will, gratitude, and the willingness to return favours, and also coexists with one's disposition to make and keep friends. Additional virtues are manifested in the relationships of the Epicurean manager to his subordinates, especially servants and slaves: mildness of character, sensitivity, humanity, philanthropy, and decency (cf. IX. 32, X. 15–21, XXIII. 4–5, 20–2). We shall see below that he expresses his gratitude to the sages who have instructed him by offering them gifts (XXIII. 27–9); and if he himself is a teacher, he graciously accepts the gifts of his students (XXIII. 30–2). His inclination to ask other people for practical advice indicates that he is not afflicted by arrogance or presumption (XXVI. 24–8). And his manner

[38] The word does exist in the Greek language, although authors rarely use it.

[39] Also, in the dialectical part of *On Property Management*, Philodemus concedes for the sake of the argument that the arrangement of possessions belongs to the property manager (cf. ὑπὸ τὸν οἰκο[νο]μικόν: *De oec.* XI. 1–2) and, subsequently, opposes the property manager to the φιλοχρήματος (X. 41–XI. 8).

of regulating expenditures shows generosity, as well as moderation and prudence. Finally, the philosopher does not suffer from the vices that obstruct the orderly classification (τάξις) of desires and fears, but rather possesses precisely the virtues that contribute to the successful preservation of his property (XXIII. 36–XXIV. 19).[40] He has moderation in his lifestyle, temperance in respect of physical pleasure, modesty and unaffected manners, fortitude with regard to pain, and justice. He does not fear the gods or death, and does not suffer from the vices connected with such fears.[41] In short, he cultivates all major virtues in practising *oikonomia*, in the belief that to do so is both morally good and financially expedient.

In sharp contrast, the traditional property manager, whom Philodemus describes as an expert,[42] sets as his goal to have as many gains and as few losses as possible, and to increase his property to the greatest extent possible by honourable means. The writings of Xenophon and Theophrastus highlight the fact that the expert manager is intensely involved in all four types of activities related to his art (acquisition, preservation, arrangement, and use), but attributes the greatest importance to the acquisition of money and possessions. By analogy with the case of the Epicurean property manager, Philodemus describes the expert's approach to *oikonomia* mainly in terms of a certain disposition and of the feelings, attitudes, beliefs, and character traits characteristic of that disposition. In addition, he mentions specific practices dictated by the expert's single-minded pursuit of wealth and indicates how they are harmful.

Unlike the philosopher, the traditional *oikonomos* is not easy-going concerning matters of *oikonomia*. He develops 'an obsessive [zeal] concerning the more and the less' (*De oec.* XIV. 26–7), in virtue of which he is willing to subject himself to grave troubles and the heaviest labours. Because of his zeal, he is very much distressed about his losses and is elated about his gains (cf. XIV. 23–5). Trying to maximize his revenues, he often puts 'all of his eggs in one basket', either by distributing financial tasks in certain ways (XI. 11–14) or by investing in possessions belonging only to one kind (XXVI. 34–9). These practices lead him to endanger all of his property at once, sometimes reducing himself 'to utter poverty' (XXVI. 38–9). More generally, his excessive attachment to the goal of 'the more and the

[40] See below, p. 187.

[41] Cf. also *De elect.* XXI. 2–XXIII. 13.

[42] See below, pp. 186–7.

less' is responsible for the practical and emotional instability of his life. He makes himself vulnerable to extreme changes of fortune, and is also racked by violent emotions, including anxiety and fear about the future. These drawbacks are increased by the fact that the traditional manager has no true friends. And he could not have, since, according to Philodemus, he perceives friends as obstacles to his primary goal, the maximal growth and efficient administration of his estate. 'To speak more precisely, acts of imparting money to one's friends and, among one's acquaintances, to those who are not wicked [seem] to some people to amount to [subtractions] from and diminutions of one's property' (XXIV. 41–6). Also, the expert manager is indifferent to the calls of society and to the sufferings of other human beings. He resists paying visits to people (XXVI. 9) and does not mind making money from 'his slaves' forced labour in mines' (cf. XXIII. 4–5).

The feelings, attitudes, and priorities of the expert manager involve empty beliefs and the endorsement of worldly values. Unlike the Epicurean manager, he confuses the natural desire for more goods with non-natural desires whose satisfaction requires great wealth. He sees that kind of wealth as fundamental to his well-being. He considers profitable only what contributes to 'the more and the less', and unprofitable the opposite. As we shall see, he ranks highly the sources of income that bring glory or spectacular gains without calculating how much toil and trouble they may involve for himself or for others. And so on. Philodemus suggests that such beliefs lead the expert manager to make mistakes in the performance of hedonistic calculations: for example, to judge that the absence of friends is more profitable than their presence. In sum, he lives a life full of concerns, hard work, tension and fear, sudden changes, and personal and social loneliness.

Unlike the philosophical manager, the traditional *oikonomos* exhibits major vices in pursuing his tasks. The central one is probably the love of money (φιλοχρηματία), or greed. In addition, Philodemus' criticisms of Xenophon and Theophrastus indicate that the traditional manager is affected by arrogance and stupidity (*De oec.* VII. 2), presumption (VII. 21–6), harshness (IX. 32) and inhumanity (X. 15–21), possibly imprudence (XI. 11–16), and certainly folly. Philodemus mentions these vices in the second part of his treatise, and adds to the list several other faults of character. Greed is often accompanied by avarice, insensitivity, ingratitude, and by a lack of generosity and good will. These traits are responsible for the fact that the traditional manager tends to live a friendless life (ἀφιλία: XXIV. 20). Moreover, deriving one's income from a military career betrays vainglory and a lack of wisdom (XXII. 24); deciding to practice the art of horsemanship is dictated by similar traits; and getting revenues from the work of slaves in mines (XXIII. 4–5) would show in most circumstances lack of humanity and callousness.[43]

Besides, Philodemus maintains that certain vices hinder the orderly arrangement of things (τάξις), and he extends the concept of τάξις so as to include the order of one's desires and fears.

Of the activities leading to the profits and the maintenance both of these (sc. the profits) and of the possessions that one had beforehand, one must keep in mind that the principal one consists in managing one's desires and fears. For, [usually], nothing drains and ruins the most illustrious and [richest houses] so much as [extravagance in lifestyle], lechery, ostentatious actions, [effeminate behaviour], and similar things and, again, the chilling fear of the gods, of death, of pains and of the things that are believed to produce them. Consequently, if one removes from oneself, to the extent that it is possible, the envy of things that are not to be envied and the fear of things that are not to be feared, one will be able both to procure and to preserve (his property) in the appropriate manner. Injustice too is thought to bring about each one of these things (sc. the acquisition and preservation of property) but, in fact, afterwards it takes away the greatest part not just of what one has gained, but also of what one has had beforehand. It follows that, if one actually practises justice, one will both obtain and safeguard the gain acquired in conformity with it.

(*De oec.* XXIII. 36–XXIV. 19)

Philodemus rounds off the argument by claiming that every major fault of character is bound to affect one's attitudes towards property management, and by emphasizing in that manner the close relationship between *oikonomia* and ethics.[44] 'Indeed, I believe that absolutely every vice raises obstacles to the pleasant collection and to the maintenance of one's possessions, whereas their opposite virtues contribute considerably (to the achievement of these goals)' (XXIV. 35–40).

[43] On these sources of income, see below, pp. 188–90.

[44] In particular, Philodemus emphasizes the connection between superstition and the fear of death, on the one hand, and greed and avarice, on the other (cf. *De elect.* XVII. 10–15, XVIII. 12–15, XIX. 12–18, XX. 6–12).

V

Philodemus assesses the traditional sources of income according to criteria drawn from Epicurean ethics. The kind of reasoning that Metrodorus uses against the Cynics constitutes the basis of his argument. 'His (sc. Metrodorus') continuous effort has been to establish that occasional disturbances, cares, and labours are more useful in the long run for the best way of life than the opposite choice (sc. the utter poverty advocated by the Cynics)' (*De oec.* XXII. 9–18). Following him (cf. ἀκολουθοῦντες: XXII. 17–18), Philodemus considers different ways of earning a living in the light of the hedonistic calculus, and on that basis determines which ones are appropriate for the philosopher.

In the first place, it is a mistake to believe that the best way of maintaining oneself is to practice the military art, to win goods by the spear. In fact, only unwise and vainglorious men make that choice (*De oec.* XXII. 17–28), presumably because they do not weigh the toils and dangers of military life against the relatively few advantages that it might offer. Therefore, Philodemus undertakes to refute those who praise the achievements of men of action and who consider philosophers inferior to such men.

> Indeed, they seem generally to attribute these [achievements] to the politicians and the men of action, so that one could often ask what in the world is left for those who [devote themselves] to the search for truth and who consider all these issues. For at least according to them, the people who do as many good deeds as contribute to the tranquillity which derives from the most important things (sc. politicians and military men) and those who contemplate the truth are not the same people, but they will evidently claim either that the ones who are wonderfully gifted regarding the search for truth [do not have] the excellence that achieves this aim (sc. tranquillity), or that nothing remarkable is accomplished because of it, [or that some day one shall be acquainted with] rulers of a city or of an army who are remarkably wise.
>
> (XXII. 28–XXIII. 1)

It is unclear which opponents Philodemus has in mind here. Whatever their identity may be, their accusations against the philosophers imply a complete dissociation of the practical life from the contemplative life. They maintain that tranquillity 'which derives from the most important things' (*De oec.* XXIII. 39–40) results from the actions of politicians and military men, not from the theoretical contemplation of philosophers. Here, 'the most important things' are probably things such as the independence of one's country, personal freedom, material prosperity, and so on.[45] And the main assumption underlying the charge is that peace of mind crucially depends on external rather than internal, psychological factors. As Philodemus indicates, there are different ways in which this charge can be pressed. One may contend that although philosophers have intellectual virtues, they do not possess the kinds of virtues through which tranquillity is achieved, whereas men of action do. Alternatively, one may concede that tranquillity is the achievement of the philosopher, but question its value. Perhaps another suggestion is that only some ideal ruler in the future, who would unite the virtues of the contemplative and of practical men, could secure tranquillity for himself and the city.[46] Philodemus reacts to these arguments by pointing to facts. The *Lives* of notorious men of action—for instance, Gellias of Sicily, Scopas of Thessaly, and the Athenians Kimon and Nicias—testify that these men had neither practical nor contemplative wisdom; they were driven by their love of glory and led miserable lives (XXII. 20–8).

Other traditional sources of income are evaluated on similar grounds.

> It is [extremely] ridiculous to believe that it is a good thing to earn an income from practising the art of horsemanship. Earning an income 'from the art of mining with slaves doing the labour' is unfortunate, and as to securing income 'from both these sources by means of one's own labour', it is a mad thing to do. 'Cultivating the land oneself in a manner involving work with one's own hands' is also hard, while (cultivating it) 'using other workers if one is a landowner' is appropriate for the good man. For it brings the least possible involvement with men from whom many disagreeable things follow, and a pleasant life, a leisurely retreat with one's friends, and a most dignified income to the [wise]. Nor is it disgraceful to earn an income both from accepting tenants into one's house and from slaves who have knacks or even arts which are in no way indecent.
>
> (*De oec.* XXIII. 1–22)

As this passage indicates, Philodemus thinks that the 'craziness' of the philosopher making his living by his own efforts at mining is worse than

[45] Contrast the Epicurean meaning of 'τὰ κυριώτατα', viz., the cardinal tenets of Epicurean philosophy, in *De elect.* XI. 9.

[46] The text is uncertain in *De oec.* XXII. 46–XXIII. 1.

doing so by the efforts of his servants.[47] Philodemus may then be telling us something important about the limits of his humanitarian and philanthropic commitments: in the end, the concern for one's own happiness carries in his view greater weight than the concern for others.[48] His attitude towards agriculture seems to point in the same direction. Working the land in person is a hard thing (*ταλαίπωρον*: XXIII. 7), and, as established in the first part of the treatise, it cannot be justified in hedonistic terms. On the other hand, obtaining revenues as a landowner through the agricultural labour of one's servants is highly recommended as 'a most dignified' (*εὐσχημονεστάτην*: XXIII. 17–18) source of income. The very occupation that the philosopher should not accept for himself, he should tolerate and even desire for his farmers. Ultimately, the reason might be egoistic: the farmers' manual labour secures a pleasant life for the philosopher.

Two further sources of earning a living also appear legitimate in the light of the hedonistic calculus: rentals (probably of houses or other buildings, not of land) and the skilful work of slaves. In so far as neither of these sources involves excessive toil, and assuming that the slaves' occupations are not indecent,[49] the philosopher may get revenues from both (*De oec.* XXIII. 18–22). 'However, these sources of income come second and third. The first and noblest thing is to receive back thankful gifts with all reverence in return for philosophical discourses shared with men capable of understanding them, as happened to Epicurus. And moreover, discourses which are truthful and free of strife and, in short, serene, since in fact the acquisition of an income through sophistical and contentious speeches is in no way better than its acquisition through demagogical and slandering ones' (XXIII. 22–36). There is a long tradition in Greek literature according to which the occupation of the philosopher is ranked first in order. However, the passage cited above contains the first instance in which the teaching of philosophy is identified as the first and best source of money-making: it perfectly suits the philosopher's lifestyle, and in addition it is not really payment, but gifts that the sage receives from thankful students in return for the privilege of conversing with him. This last point is brought out by the contrast between the sage's discourses and the speeches of sophists

[47] He uses a stronger term of disapproval (*μανικόν*, crazy: XXIII. 7) in the former case than in the latter (*οὐκ εὔκληρον*, unlucky: XXIII. 5).

[48] Perhaps this point may be extended to Philodemus' doctrine of friendship (see pp. 29–31).

[49] As would be, e.g., prostitution.

and demagogues (XXIII. 32–6)—whom I take to be mainly teachers or practitioners of forensic or political rhetoric. Unlike them, the sage does not sell his ideas; nor does he use them to get power. He imparts his wisdom in conversation and accepts tokens of gratitude from people who understand and appreciate him.[50] As to the landowner, we may think of him in terms of a gracious host who offers his country property as a peaceful retreat where philosophy flourishes and true enjoyment is achieved.[51]

VI

At this point, however, one might raise the following objection. Even conceding that the Epicurean *oikonomos* is a better person than the traditional property manager, he is worse as an *oikonomos*. Whereas the traditional manager is entirely successful in all four domains of the art of *oikonomia*, because he applies criteria internal to that art and tenaciously pursues 'the more and the less', the Epicurean manager is less efficient. For he gets sidetracked by ethical considerations, and does not aim at the maximal growth of his estate. Moreover, virtues such as generosity, philanthropy, and the disposition to have friends are morally desirable, but they obstruct the optimal administration of one's property in ways in which their corresponding vices do not.

Philodemus has clearly entertained some such objection, and suggests a complex and ingenious response. In the first place, the philosopher cannot reasonably be called a bad manager in the ordinary sense of the term. On the one hand, regarding the acquisition and preservation of great sums of money, the philosopher falls short of being an efficient manager in the ordinary sense. 'He will not be able to acquire a very large quantity of money in a very short time' (*De oec.* XIX. 4–5), and even if he does, it will not be easy for him to keep it (XVIII. 37–9). 'Nor will he be able to examine closely in what manner the greatest part of his possessions could increase as much as possible' (XIX. 4–7), since he does not measure them according to financial criteria (XIX. 7 ff.). Nor yet will he always be able to watch with eagerness over the possessions that he already has, because

[50] On the notion of gratitude and its role in contexts concerning payment for teaching, see Blank 1985.

[51] Recall Epicurus' claim that the wise man 'will love the country' (φιλαγρήσειν: D.L. X. 120).

this would require a level of worry and effort that he does not deem worth his while (XIX. 10 ff.). On the other hand, at least in so far as estates of reasonable size are concerned, the philosopher cannot be called a bad manager (XVI. 21 ff.). For such a person wastes his wealth rather than keeps it, whereas the philosopher administers and preserves it. Moreover, a bad manager is not well equipped for his tasks, while the Epicurean *oikonomos* is. He will not fail 'if he administers his estate with ease by aid of [reason] itself and of the [common] experience which is adequate for the management of one's possessions, though not for excessive money-making' (XVI. 32–9).

In the second place, the preconception (πρόληψις, translit. *prolēpsis*) of the good money-maker (ἀγαθὸς χρηματιστής) guides us to identify the sage as the ideal money-maker (*De oec.* XX. 1–32).[52] Philodemus acknowledges that the expression 'the good money-maker' is ambiguous, and that the relevant preconception can be developed in two different ways, one attaching the property of the good money-maker to a good person, the other attaching it to a person who is good at making a maximal amount of money by lawful means. However, Philodemus relies on the clarity and the criterial power of the preconception in order to unpack the *prolēpsis* of the good money-maker in the right way: it is instantiated in the philosopher, not in the expert, as many people think. In the third place, Philodemus defends the distinction between the economic expert and the philosopher, drawing a clear line where the philosopher's involvement with property management ought to stop.

Perhaps the wise man cannot be called in equal measure an expert (τεχνίτης, translit. *technitēs*) and a producer of possessions (ἐργάτης, translit. *ergatēs*) collected in great quantity and in a short time. For in fact there is an empirical practice (ἐμπειρία) and an ability (δύναμις) specially related to money-making, of which the good man will not have a share, nor will he watch the opportunities in combination with which this kind of ability could be useful too. For all these things characterize the person who loves money. Nevertheless, (what holds in this case) at any rate appears to be exactly like what holds in the case of several other practices in which, although there exist capable professional workmen (ἀγαθοὶ δημιουργοί), each one of us could accomplish quite well, as it were, at least what is sufficient for our needs. We observe this, for example, in the production of bread or in the preparation of food. For everybody is able to make such things

[52] The argument in this passage and, generally, Philodemus' use of *prolēpsis* in order to settle ethical disputes has been discussed at pp. 70–3.

for himself to the point of meeting sufficient needs, although there is an empirical practice involving expertise (cf. ἐμπειρίας ἐν[τέ]χνου) [about] them as well. Now, it seems that something similar holds also regarding the acquisition and preservation of property. For even if we are not, like certain people, experts in amassing and preserving wealth nor earnest ([σ]ύντονοι) and persevering (ἐνδελεχεῖς) managers of property, [nonetheless] there seem to be many persons who are quite able, at least to the point of finding what they need and not [totally] failing in this matter by acting randomly. The good man too must be counted among these people.

(XVII. 2–40)

Philodemus concedes, once again, that there is such a thing as a *technē* of *oikonomia*, and that there exist experts in that field. On the other hand, he asserts that the philosopher does not possess the *technē* in question; nor does he qualify as an expert in that sense. The main criterion, then, according to which he distinguishes the ordinary manager from the philosopher seems to be cognitive: the former possesses a form of knowledge, a *technē*, which the latter does not possess. It seems reasonably clear that here, *technē* is not a strictly rationalistic concept, but involves experience as well as theory. In fact, Philodemus generally uses *technē* as equivalent to ἐμπειρία or ἔντεχνος ἐμπειρία, i.e., an empirical activity involving expertise or artful practice.[53] And he describes the expert (*technitēs*) as a man who has the practical ability to achieve certain results in a regular and knowledgeable manner, rather than conjecturally and at random.[54] In the case at hand, the *technitēs* in money-making has the ability to gain and preserve money in a certain, predictable way, comparable to that of craftsmen in practical knacks such as bread making. On that conception, a *technē* has theoretical dimensions as well. These mainly consist in the systematization of a body of knowledge according to certain principles or rules, and in the attainment of the goal of the *technē* through their regular application. The contents of Xenophon's and Theophrastus' works give us a glimpse into the regulative principles of *oikonomia*. And we find in Ischomachus an excellent instantiation of an expert, a *technitēs* in that art.

On the other hand, Ischomachus can equally well be taken to represent what the philosopher, most emphatically, will not be. The philosopher will

[53] See Tsouna-McKirahan 1996: esp. 710. On the Epicurean concept of *technē* and the distinctions pertaining to it, see Blank 1995.

[54] See Philodemus' definition of *technē* in *Rhet.* II; PHerc. 1674, XXXVIII. 5–19, p. 123 Longo Auricchio. The text is translated and discussed by Blank 1995: 179.

not conduct the administration of his property in a technical manner, but instead will rely on common experience (cf. [κοι]ν[ῆ]ς ἐμπειρίας: *De oec.* XVI. 35) accompanied by reason (cf. λόγου: XVI. 34). For these suffice to secure the financial means to a stable and tranquil life (XIV. 46–XV. 1). The reason why the philosopher will always resist becoming an expert in the administration of property is found in the following passage: 'It is not, then, disagreeable that there should sometimes be another person of this kind, in the role of a servant, just like the expert in the production of bread. But that he himself (sc. the philosopher) should be a producer of such things is inappropriate. For this kind of acquisition, when measured against toil, is no longer profitable' (XIX. 23–32). Ultimately, the expertise of the ordinary manager and the common experience of the philosopher are not merely a matter of what each one does or does not know, but also of what kind of person each one is. To dedicate the time, thought, and effort that it takes to become an expert in *oikonomia*, one must endorse the values and objectives set by that art, much as a servant must make his own the values and goals of his master. This the philosopher refuses to do. He knows enough about *oikonomia* to cater adequately to his needs and those of his friends. More than that would entail abandoning the priorities set by Epicurus, together with all hope of attaining the good life.

9

Anger and the Desire for Revenge

Philodemus' work *On Anger*, Περὶ ὀργῆς (*De ir.*; PHerc. 182) is probably the centrepiece of the ensemble *On the Passions*, Περὶ παθῶν,[1] and the earliest classical monograph on that subject that survives in part to our day.[2] The papyrus originally contained about 120 columns, but roughly the first half of the text has disappeared. The second half consists of fifty well-preserved columns, a number of fragments some of which are quite substantial, and roughly fifteen columns that are almost illegible. From a broad cultural point of view, *On Anger* reflects a widespread ancient preoccupation with the nature, use, and control of anger, from Homer onwards.[3] From a narrower, philosophical perspective, it is a major contribution to the relevant Epicurean literature, and occupies an important place in the ongoing debate about the emotions. Concerning its structure, much of the extant remains of the work (VIII. 16–XXXI. 23) is taken up with a diatribe,[4] or sermon, against anger which 'sets-before-the-eyes',

[1] I have looked at the earlier editions of *On Anger* by Gomperz (1864) and Wilke (1914), but have mainly used the edition of Indelli (1988) as well as the edition and translation of *On Anger* by David Armstrong which, with characteristic generosity, he made available to me. As of present date, it is unpublished, but will appear soon in the series 'Writings from the Greco-Roman World' of the Society of Biblical Literature. The translations are my own, but they are heavily indebted to Armstrong's elegant translation of the text. For cols. XLVII. 18–L. 8 I have also consulted unpublished work by Kirk Sanders, whom I wish to thank. Annas (1992), Erler (1992), Fillion-Lahille (1984), Fish (2004), Harris (2001), Nussbaum (1994), Procopé (1993), Sorabji (2000), and many others shed light on different aspects and implications of Philodemus' treatment of anger.

[2] Two intact monographs on anger survive as well, by the younger Seneca and by Plutarch.

[3] Harris (2001) explains the rise and persistence of the concern to control or eliminate intense anger by drawing on a vast number of ancient texts, from Homer to early Christianity.

[4] The term 'diatribe' is a nineteenth-century term often used to designate Cynic and Stoic writings on moral subjects. e.g., Chrysippus' Θεραπευτικός can be called a diatribe in that sense, and the same holds for the moral sermons of Bion of Borysthenes. I have extended that use to Philodemus' treatises *On Anger* and *On Death*. Like Chrysippus' Θεραπευτικός, Philodemus' *On Anger* contains elements of vituperation or strong censure of anger which involve the use of the technique of 'setting-before-the-eyes' (cf. *De ir.* I. 12–27 and below, pp. 204–9).

vividly depicts, the intrinsic hatefulness of the emotion and its terrible consequences. The remainder is a dialectical treatment of the positions of various opponents both outside and inside the Epicurean school and, at the same time, a defence of Philodemus' own view, which appears to have been held also by Zeno of Sidon and his associates.[5] Stylistic features, such as cluttered and unclear references and infelicities of syntax, indicate that *On Anger* was written quickly and quite carelessly, and was intended for an inner circle rather than the entire school.[6] However, Philodemus also gives advice, indirectly, as to how to deal with one's own anger[7] and may have proposed specific strategies for the therapy of anger in the lost part of the work.

The treatise *On Anger* is densely populated territory. Philodemus argues against many opponents, and it is not always easy to identify either who they are or what positions they hold. Section I of this chapter tries to sort out these matters, and at the outset supplies some semantic and historical context for Philodemus' discussion. Turning to the actual argument, Section II presents the methodological objections raised by Timasagoras, one of Philodemus' professional rivals, and shows how Philodemus responds to them. Section III discusses how Philodemus accounts for the nature and symptoms of anger, the beliefs and feelings that it involves, and its consequences. Section IV is devoted to Philodemus' refutation of certain Peripatetics whom, rightly or wrongly, he takes to encourage one to lose one's temper. In addition, this section discusses the case of people who give the appearance of irascibility without really being irascible. Section V deals with the issue of whether anger is a good or a bad thing. It elaborates Philodemus' distinction between two kinds of anger, which he calls, respectively, ὀργή (translit. *orgē*) and θυμός (translit. *thymos*), as well as his contention that the Epicurean sage experiences the former kind of anger (*orgē*) but not the latter. Philodemus defends his thesis against another professional rival,

[5] Wilke (1914: p. vii) suggests that the contents of *On Anger* belong to the same epitome of Zeno's work as *On Frank Speech* and considers *De lib. dic.* 36. 24–5 evidence supporting that suggestion. Croenert (1906: 91) states essentially the same view. I (Tsouna 2007) suggest that Philodemus may have borrowed the distinction between acceptable and unacceptable, natural and empty, anger from Zeno of Sidon or Demetrius of Laconia.

[6] Cf. Procopé 1993: 174–5. According to Procopé, weaknesses of style and language could be corrected on the spot by the teacher himself.

[7] Contrast ibid. 175, which suggests that *On Anger* is not at all a book of therapy; it is not for people worried about their irascibility so much as for Epicureans who want to become therapists or be knowledgeable about anger.

Nicasicrates, who maintains that even natural anger is an evil. I assess the arguments of both sides, and also Philodemus' answer to the question whether the sage ever feels great anger and, if so, in what sense. Section VI examines a related question: namely, whether the sage experiences *no less* anger than the common man (not just *orgē* anger but also *thymos* anger). I discuss three arguments in the form of ἐπιλογισμός (translit. *epilogismos*, pl. *epilogismoi*)[8] to the effect that the sage feels *as much anger as* the common man, and then another three arguments whereby Philodemus rebuts the *epilogismoi* of his opponents.

I

First a word about the semantics of anger. Already in the Archaic period, literary texts adumbrate a distinction between irresistible and usually long-lasting rage (μῆνις), paradigmatically the wrath of Achilles, and other varieties of anger (indicated, for instance, by the nouns χόλος and κότος and verbs such as ὀχθεῖν and μενεαίνειν).[9] By the fifth century BC, however, these terms are mostly replaced by *orgē*, which in earlier times meant disposition or temperament[10] but in the Classical era usually denotes intense anger, and by *thymos*, a word which is used also in the broad sense of 'emotion' or 'passion' and the faculty responsible for such things.[11] Both Plato and Aristotle call *thymos* the spirited part or faculty of the soul, which does other things in addition to getting angry. In the *Nicomachean Ethics*, Aristotle seems inclined to draw a systematic distinction between *thymos* anger, which operates in the brave and is less irrational, and *orgē* anger, which occurs in people who are only apparently brave and is more

[8] Cf. pp. 55–60.

[9] Cf. Harris 2001: 51–2. As Harris remarks, there is a lot of disagreement on the exact nuances of these terms; moreover, there is no constant meaning always attached to each of them. Homer usually refers to Achilles' anger by μῆνις, but also sometimes by χόλος, and ὀχθήσας can mean 'distressed' and not as often 'angered'. However, it is reasonably clear that μῆνις is uninhibited anger dreadful in its effects and to be feared by its object. On anger and the vocabulary of aggression during the Archaic period, see also Adkins 1969; Considine 1966; and Scully 1984.

[10] Cf. Harris 2001: n. 11.

[11] Cf. ibid. 52; Sullivan 1993. Other words are used as well, often preserving their earlier meanings. They include χόλος, νέμεσις (which typically refers to righteous indignation), χαλεπότης, and the verbs χαλεπαίνειν and ἀγανακτεῖν. Harris (2001: 53) suggests that the last three terms are milder than ὀργή but, nonetheless, refer to emotions which give rise to violence.

irrational than *thymos* anger.[12] *Thymos* and *orgē* are the principal terms for anger in Hellenistic Greek as well, and this includes of course the Hellenistic philosophers. In particular, the Stoics attempt to pursue the distinction between *thymos* and *orgē*, describing the former as *orgē* just beginning (*SVF* II. 886–7, III. 395–7).[13] As we shall see, Philodemus and probably his teachers endeavour to draw a similar distinction, but they reverse the quasi-technical meanings of *thymos* and *orgē*. For Philodemus, as for his teachers, *thymos* denotes anger blown out of all proportion, whereas *orgē* refers to a natural and usually milder species of the emotion.

Aristotle provides the necessary philosophical background for Hellenistic and Roman analyses of anger, including Philodemus' own. In the treatise *On the Soul*, in the context of an argument for the thesis that the affections of the soul involve the body and are λόγοι ἔνυλοι, formulas in matter, Aristotle gives two different definitions of *orgē*, the one physical and pertaining to the domain of the natural philosopher, the other intentional and appropriate for the dialectician. While for the natural philosopher *orgē* is 'a surging of the blood [or heat] around the heart',[14] the dialectician will call it 'a desire for revenge (ὄρεξιν ἀντιλυπήσεως) or something like that' (*De an.* I. 1, 403ª16–32). Perhaps not inconsistently,[15] in the *Rhetoric* Aristotle elaborates this second approach, defining *orgē* as 'the desire accompanied by pain or distress (λύπη) for what is seen as retaliation (cf. τιμωρίας) for some perceived slight (cf. ὀλιγωρίαν) directed towards oneself or one's own, the slight not having been deserved' (*Rhet.* II.2, 1378ª31 ff.). There are

[12] Cf. Harris 2001: 54. Aristotle contrasts courageous men who are also high-spirited (θυμοειδεῖς) with those who merely appear courageous because they rush upon danger like wild animals, spurred by pain and anger (θυμός) (*Eth. Nic.* III. 8, 1116ᵇ23 ff.). Although here there may be traces of a systematic distinction between two kinds of anger, nonetheless, Aristotle's main point is that the truly brave men fight for honour (διὰ τὸ καλόν) and are guided by reason or principle (λόγος), whereas the latter group fight because of passion (διὰ πάθος), viz., because they are angry (ὀργιζόμενοι), feel pain, and look forward to the pleasure of revenge. In any case, Aristotle suggests that *thymos* accompanies at least some acts of courage, but he makes no such claim about *orgē*. And he does not count as instances of genuine courage military deeds motivated, and not merely aided, by *thymos*.

[13] The references are discussed by Harris (2001: 54), who remarks that although it may seem slightly more natural to associate *orgē* rather than *thymos* with long-lasting anger and to think that when it started out it was *orgē* or *thymos* indiscriminately, this distinction is hard to find in the texts.

[14] Renehan (1963) makes a convincing case that the phrase 'ἢ θερμοῦ', 'or heat', is an interpolation and should be deleted from the text. In the direct tradition, i.e., the Aristotelian commentators, the physiological definition of anger in *De anima* Book I becomes standard in a form which contains 'αἵματος', 'of the blood', but not the words 'ἢ θερμοῦ'. In the indirect tradition, 'θερμοῦ' appears often instead of 'αἵματος', but Renehan (1963) maintains that the authors of that tradition do not use the *De anima* as their source in the relevant passages.

[15] See Nehamas 1992.

enormous complexities related to these passages, but for present purposes it suffices to note that, according to Aristotle, anger admits of physicalistic as well as non-physicalistic approaches; in the second case, we should think of anger as being *about* something (a perceived slight) and as including an open desire *to act* seeking retaliation. Most later writers follow Aristotle on these points, although with modifications.

Later writers follow Aristotle also in so far as they attribute to anger many or all the characteristics found in Aristotle's classic treatment of the emotion in the *Rhetoric* (II. 2–4). Anger (*orgē*) involves both pain and pleasure: pain because of the perceived offence, pleasure because one hopes for revenge or dwells on it in one's thoughts. Typically, the offence is some kind of slight directed at something to which one attaches value. Disdain, spite, and insult all imply that the offender inflicted or intended to inflict harm of that sort. Depending on the magnitude of the harm and also on other factors (e.g., the offender's social status and his relation to the victim, the victim's expectations, and who else witnessed the slight), one can be more or less angry and express one's anger in more or less uninhibited ways. In fact, Aristotle seems to make the assumption spelled out by both earlier and later writers that, barring exceptional cases, anger cannot be hidden but must find an outlet in behaviour.[16] Moreover, Aristotle maintains that anger usually has an individual person as its target, and also that the angry person 'wishes to see what happens'; i.e., he wants to witness (or at least to make sure) that the offender feels the full measure of the revenge and knows why he is being punished and by whom. When the slighted man is satisfied that the offender has suffered in his turn, his anger is appeased and eventually disappears. On this interpretation, then, Aristotle considers revenge the best cure for rightful anger. Indeed, anger and the desire for retaliation would seem to be the natural and honourable reaction to intentional offence against oneself or those whom one holds dear. The magnitude of one's revenge should be proportional to that of the harm to which one has been subject. This is important, if one is to redress fully one's injuries and regain peace of mind.

However, it would be a mistake to think that Aristotle approves of anger without qualification. For, on the one hand, he can be read as

[16] Harris (2001: 57 ff.) argues convincingly to that effect.

reinterpreting the Platonic legacy according to which anger belongs to the spirited part of the soul, secures victories on behalf of reason (cf. *Rep.* IV, 440a ff.), and provides necessary protection against wrongdoing (cf. *Leg.* V, 731b). On the other hand, he also elaborates Plato's intuition that anger ought to be restrained and controlled (cf. *Rep.* IX, 572a; X, 606d). Irascibility is a vice, an excess of anger that should be avoided. The same holds for its opposite extreme, the habitual or complete absence of the emotion (*Eth. Nic.* II. 7, $1108^{a}4$–9). The virtue that stands in between these two extremes (let us call it even temper) implies that the person who possesses it will be angry, but only with the right people, for the right reasons, in the right way, at the right moment, and for the appropriate length of time. Thus, the virtuous person can get very angry and desire maximal retaliation when circumstances warrant it. Nonetheless, his natural inclination is towards deficiency of the emotion, and he is not vengeful (*Eth. Nic.* IV. 5, $1125^{b}28$–$1126^{a}3$).

We should turn now to Philodemus' opponents. First, Philodemus distinguishes between two different groups of Aristotle's followers[17] who appear to hold essentially the same position: namely, that anger is necessary in order to fight bravely and, in general, is useful for purposes of self-defence. Moreover, at least one of these groups seems to have emphasized the justice achieved by revenge and the pleasure to be derived from it (XXXII. 26–9). If Philodemus accurately reports their views, they have misinterpreted or overinterpreted Aristotle's own. We do not know anything about the identity of these Aristotelian philosophers. Philodemus says that he has named them in the lost part of his treatise (cf. XXXI. 25–7), and he refutes them in the extant remains.

The Stoics are another target for Philodemus. On the one hand, in the surviving part of *On Anger*, he does not attack them directly but, in fact, defends the therapeutic value of Chrysippus' Θεραπευτικός, the fourth book of his work *On the Emotions*.[18] Indeed, Philodemus probably uses material from Chrysippus' Θεραπευτικός in the long diatribe section of *On Anger* (VIII. 16–XXXI. 23) which 'sets-before-the-eyes' the horrors of

[17] Cf. *De ir.* XXXI. 24–5, XXXII. 3–4.

[18] As we shall see, Philodemus also defends the genuine though limited value of the lecture *On Anger* by the eclectic philosopher Bion of Borysthenes—the first ancient monograph known to be specifically about anger (*De ir.* I. 7–27).

anger and revenge.[19] On the other hand, it would seem that the diatribe section of the treatise is a parody of Stoic writings.[20] Most importantly, Chrysippus' take on disturbing emotions such as anger differs substantially from the Epicurean approach advocated by Philodemus. As indicated in earlier chapters, Chrysippus' position is, very roughly, that the proper development of our rationality requires that we eliminate excessive and irrational impulses which we develop as ordinary emotional responses and which are, in fact, false judgements about value. Chrysippus' position does not entail that a perfected human life will be almost emotionless, but rather that the relevant impulses should be compatible with normative reason, and should never disobey or exceed it. Ordinary, familiar emotions are aberrations of the commanding faculty in precisely that sense and, therefore, should be eradicated. Both earlier and later Stoics claim that anger in particular arises because one misjudges factors relevant to a given situation, notably the intentions of the offender, the magnitude of one's injury, and the desirability of revenge. It is an excessive impulse to pursue the objectives set by that passion, an urge far beyond the limits of normative reasoning which has a momentum of its own and triggers violent psychosomatic movements. As such, it must be eliminated. The Stoics offer two additional reasons why we should wish to remove anger. The false beliefs involved in the emotion also constitute the basis of many other passions; therefore, if anger persists even in moderation, other faults of character remain as well. Furthermore, the nature of anger is such that the emotion cannot be checked, but must escalate into the utmost cruelty and murderousness (Seneca, *De ir.* I. 7. 4, II. 5. 3).[21] In short, there is no room for *orgē* or *ira* (the main Latin equivalent of *orgē*) in the ideal life.

Philodemus' main opponents in the surviving part of *On Anger* are Epicureans, however. Each of them claims, like Philodemus, that he and his followers expound the canonical Epicurean position held by the early authorities of the school. In truth, 'the Great Men' said little on

[19] The point has been argued first by Wilke (1914), but, as Fillion-Lahille (1984) points out, it has not been proved beyond reasonable doubt. Armstrong discusses this matter in a most enlightening manner in his introduction to his edition and translation of *On Anger* (cf. n. 1 above). Part of the diatribe section of *On Anger*, however, dwells specifically on the effects of anger in a school resembling Philodemus' own (XVIII. 35–XXI. 6: it is not entirely clear where that section ends). Procopé (1993: 186) claims that, in fact, the diatribe section of *On Anger* is distinctly Epicurean in tone.

[20] Armstrong ingeniously defends this suggestion.

[21] Both points are discussed in Nussbaum 1994: 396–8.

the subject of anger. Epicurus makes the puzzling remark that the wise man is more susceptible than other men to some passions without this impeding his wisdom (D.L. X. 117), and he asserts that the gods feel neither anger nor gratitude (*KD* 1)—which might imply that lesser beings feel both. According to Philodemus, Epicurus also claims that the wise man will experience *thymos*; similar statements are found in the writings of Metrodorus and Hermarchus as well (*De ir.* XLV. 5–15). In general, 'the Great Men' appear to have held that some sort of anger is unavoidable, and that some sages are more prone to it than others. However, they evidently did not clarify just what kind of anger is ineradicable or whether the wise man is susceptible to every form of anger. Later Epicureans debate these issues, each group giving a different interpretation of the canonical texts and citing scripture to defend it. The position that Philodemus advocates in *On Anger* (probably also held by Zeno of Sidon and his school) is one such view: the sage never experiences an unnatural kind of anger, but is liable to feeling a natural kind of anger compatible with moral perfection. Thus, Philodemus can be perceived as striking a wise compromise between the Peripatetics and the Stoics, and also as holding a middle ground between competing Epicurean factions.[22] To these I shall now turn.

Philodemus refutes two rivals whom he mentions by name, Timasagoras and Nicasicrates. They have been thought to be Peripatetics, because the names of both appear in the columns preceding Philodemus' refutation of the Peripatetics (cf. Νικασικ[ρατ______]: fr. 7. 15; Τιμασαγόρας: VII. 7), and also because both of them have been believed to have, like the Peripatetics, permissive or even positive attitudes towards anger.[23] Alternatively, Nicasicrates has been considered a Stoic or, more likely, an Academic who conceded the existence of natural anger for dialectical purposes; as for Timasagoras, he has been classified as a Peripatetic philosopher roughly contemporary with the Epicureans Thespis and Basilides (both active in the second century BC).[24] In fact, the evidence strongly suggests that Nicasicrates and Timasagoras were Epicureans.[25] Although their names are regularly linked, they hold different views about anger, each advancing his

[22] See Procopé 1993. [23] So Croenert 1906: 89 ff.; Wilke 1914: pp. xxi ff.

[24] Asmis 1990: 2396–8.

[25] See Longo Auricchio and Tepedino Guerra 1982, followed by Indelli 1988: 153–5, 223–4.

own as the authentic view of Epicurus and his associates.[26] Nicasicrates probably headed his own school in Rhodes (cf. PHerc. 1746, fr. IIb. 3–4), with which Philodemus' school had doctrinal disputes.[27] He appears to have taken a hard line on a number of issues,[28] including whether the sage should ever attempt to please anyone[29] and whether he should allow himself to feel any kind of anger. Concerning this last issue, he is a minimalist: one ought to try to feel as little anger as possible and, ideally, no anger at all.

I find it harder to work out Timasagoras' position. He may have had his own school in Athens,[30] and is probably one of the philosophers who challenge the therapeutic value of diatribes and whom Philodemus refutes in a manner verging on abuse (*De ir.* I. 7–27).[31] He has been thought to be a maximalist about anger, i.e., to maintain that the sage may feel intense and prolonged anger as well as moderate and brief forms of the emotion.[32] Indeed, if Timasagoras is associated with 'those who want to be faithful to the books' (cf. *βυβλιακοῖς*: XLV. 16–17) and who attribute to 'the Great Men' the belief that any kind of anger is compatible with sagehood, then he may be a maximalist just as they are. However, we should bear in mind that there is no decisive evidence associating Timasagoras with these thinkers. Also, Timasagoras believes that '[anger] is entirely an evil' (VI. 28–9) and,

[26] Philodemus does not treat them as a pair: cf. Asmis 1990; Procopé 1993. The clearest and most complete presentation of Philodemus' opponents is in Armstrong's introduction to *On Anger* (cf. n. 1 above).

[27] See Longo Auricchio and Tepedino Guerra 1982; Sedley 1989: 103–17; and Procopé 1993: 186. 'Nicasicrates' seems to be a Rhodian name.

[28] See Procopé 1993: 186.

[29] He seems to have praised Democritus for condemning every attempt to please those around one, including one's friends: cf. *De adul.*; PHerc. 1457, X. 10 ff.

[30] See Indelli 1988: 154.

[31] Ringeltaube 1913; Procopé 1993; Armstrong's introduction to *On Anger*.

[32] There are two main arguments in support of that suggestion. First, Timasagoras denies the usefulness of Chrysippus' and Zeno's diatribes, because he believes that to quote from such writings promotes the Stoic goal of eradicating almost all familiar emotions, including anger: Ringeltaube (1913) argues this point. Second, Philodemus may imply that Timasagoras is pro anger when he makes the following gibe at his expense: 'He himself (sc. Timasagoras: the name is not mentioned but is almost certainly implied) was not clear about the misfortunes that were to follow from his anger against Basilides and Thespis, although he had set limits, as he thought, upon its sharpness' (*De ir.* V. 18–25). However, in my view, these reasons are not conclusive. For no connection is attested between Timasagoras' rejection of the diatribes (which is well documented by Philodemus in *On Anger*) and his views concerning anger (which are not explicitly reported anywhere). Moreover, Philodemus' joke does not necessarily show that Timasagoras was pro anger, but can be interpreted in a different way: the fact that Timasagoras was not able to appraise the consequences of his anger against Basilides and Thespis and control it indicates that he would have benefited from the very writings that he rejects (the diatribes). On this point, see below, pp. 207–8 and n. 44.

in this respect, he appears to approach the position of Nicasicrates, who is a minimalist. Again, we do not know who the *βυβλιακοί*[33] are or whether they are the same as the authors of the three arguments in the form of *epilogismoi* towards the end of *On Anger*. Perhaps these authors do not belong to the same group, but represent two different factions of Epicurean maximalists: the *βυβλιακοί* maintain the weaker position that the sage will experience rage as well as milder forms of anger, whereas the authors of the *epilogismoi*[34] claim also 'that the wise man will feel rage [no less than] the common man' (XLVI. 13–16). One may wonder, however, whether the *epilogismoi* are intended to support a maximalist position rather than reduce to absurdity the idea that the sage will feel any kind of anger at all. In the latter case, their authors would not be maximalists, but, on the contrary, they would be minimalists with Stoic leanings (cf. Seneca, *De ir.* II. 6. 3).

II

Let us move on to matters of method. Anger is a moral disease and, in order to treat it, the Epicurean therapist must diagnose it. Part of his method is to appraise the symptoms and consequences that, in our experience, accompany anger; establish relevant similarities; and on that basis identify correctly both the outbursts of the emotion and the irascibility in the patient's soul.[35] But the successful treatment of anger also requires the active participation of the patient. He must be brought to realize that anger is an evil and wish to get rid of it. How are patients truly confronted with the evil nature of their passion? Philodemus, as well as the authors of diatribes on anger, such as Chrysippus and Bion of Borysthenes,[36] believe that reasoning alone does not suffice to achieve the desired result.[37] It should be complemented by the so-called technique of setting-before-the-eyes,

[33] Cf. the translation of *βυβλιακοί* (XLV. 16) by Procopé (1993: 183).

[34] Cf. *τινὲς δέ*: XLVI. 13.

[35] Cf. pp. 64–5.

[36] As mentioned, Chrysippus' *Θεραπευτικός* may well be Philodemus' source for the diatribe section of *On Anger*. Chrysippus' use of vituperation, involving the vivid depiction of evils caused by the passions, suggests that he considers it peculiarly suited to correct the aberrant judgements that constitute a given passion and, in this case, anger. However, there is no reason to believe that Chrysippus belongs to those who '*only* censure but do little or nothing else about it (sc. the disease)' (I. 13–16), as Philodemus seems to suggest.

[37] Cf. the opening columns of the extant remains of *On Anger* (I. 1–VIII. 9 or thereabouts; only some letters of VIII. 9–20 are legible).

vividly depicting the sufferings and dangers of the passion. If that technique is not used, the patient will probably fail to pay attention to these evils and realize how great they are. '[While some] of the doctors [reason or talk about] the magnitude of the disease and the passionate feelings that occur because of it, and its other inconveniences, and sometimes also the dangers, (these things) escape the patients' notice, some entirely ([κα]θόλου), others as they are appraised (ἐπιλογιστικῶς), whence they become more careless about avoiding them as if moderate (evils) were happening to them; but when they are put-before-the-eyes, they make patients eager to be treated' (IV. 4–19).

Just how does the technique in question prompt one to seek therapy? Which particular element or aspect of it operates in ways in which arguments cannot operate? Philodemus does not address this issue explicitly. But since 'setting-before-the-eyes' essentially involves vivid descriptions, it seems reasonable to infer that the technique works by inducing the creation of pictures or images in the patient's mind[38] and engages some form of imagination[39] which has mental pictures and related items as its proper medium.[40] An enraged person *sees* the evils deriving from anger,[41] feels

[38] The technique of setting-before-the-eyes was used in Epicurean schools for purposes of moral education and improvement. Its relation to frank speech is mentioned at p. 93 and n. 9.

[39] If the text has been restored correctly, the conjecture [ἀναγράφ]ων (*De ir.* III. 6) may point to imagination, but does not need to. In fact, the infinitive form of the verb usually means to list or to register. However, it is clear that Philodemus views the mental images induced by means of the technique of 'setting-before-the-eyes' neither as the product of reason nor as the product of emotion.

[40] Dauer (1993: 266–8) compares and contrasts a kind of imagination which involves mental pictures, on the one hand, with belief and, on the other hand, with free imagination. He claims that imagination involving mental pictures is like belief in so far as, contrary to free imagination, it is subject to external constraints. On the other hand, it is like free imagination or daydreaming to the extent that it can coexist with both belief and knowledge to the contrary. Dauer invites us to consider examples such as the following: 'she still imagines him to be the young man she met at the prom'. If she still does imagine him in that way, even though he is a middle-aged man, there must be something youthful about him, at least in her eyes. Also, she can imagine him that way, although she knows perfectly well that he is in his fifties. Dauer's discussion may be relevant to Philodemus' use of the technique of 'setting-before-the-eyes', but only to a point. For although it seems reasonable to infer that 'setting-before-the-eyes' works by creating mental pictures in the patient, nonetheless, it is not clear that Philodemus would distinguish mental pictures from beliefs and daydreaming in the way in which Dauer does. In particular, Philodemus' text suggests that he considers mental pictures distinct from beliefs, but not wholly unrelated to them: e.g., 'setting-before-the-eyes' the evils of rage somehow leads us to form the belief that rage is irrational. We *imagine* ourselves enraged and attacking a stronger person, but we do not *imagine* that this is irrational—we come to be *convinced* that it is irrational.

[41] Philodemus does not make clear whether the patient simply sees the evils of anger, or whether he sees them *as being in the present rather than in the future*. The therapeutic efficiency of 'setting-before-the-eyes' would seem to suggest the latter, but there is no firm indication in the text.

aversion towards the passion, and forms the desire to remove it.[42] What are the contents of such images? Philodemus describes them as 'things that the patient is totally ignorant of, others that he has come to forget, others that he has not calculated at least in respect of their magnitude if not in respect of anything else, yet others that he has never contemplated all together as a whole' (III. 7–13). The really good philosophers depict all these evils even if with moderation (III. 18–21), emphasize that it is within the patient's power to avoid them (III. 15–17), 'and sketch (*ὑπογράφουσιν*: III. 24–5) the ways in which we might least experience angry feelings' (III. 21–5).

Enter Timasagoras. It is virtually certain that Philodemus criticizes him rather than some other philosopher in a passage emphasizing that vituperation including the vivid depiction of evils cannot by itself eradicate anger. 'If he (sc. Timasagoras) had rebuked those that only censure and do little or nothing else about it (sc. anger), like Bion in his *On Anger* and Chrysippus in the Θεραπευτικός of his work *On the Passions*, his stance would have been moderate. But as it is, by taking (the strategy of) setting-before-the-eyes the consequent evils to be generally ridiculous and silly, [he is himself silly and ridiculous]' (I. 12–27). So, contrary to both Philodemus and the writers of diatribes, Timasagoras claims that vituperation involving the vivid depiction of evils is silly, and also that the technique of 'setting-before-the-eyes' has no therapeutic value at all. Moreover, he contends that it is useless to 'set-before-the-eyes' the things which make anger an evil, because 'it is so obvious to all that [anger] is entirely an evil—and for this reason those who rebuke (sc. the diatribists) are acting [irrationally]—...' (VI. 27–31).[43] An even more important criticism is that treatment should be conducted by means of rational persuasion alone: '...for it is not impossible [to escape diseases], but one very much needs those (doctors or remedies) that assist one only in a reasonable manner' ([εὐλ]όγως: VI. 9–12). It seems, then, that according to Timasagoras, moral therapists should use arguments, not vivid descriptions. They should

[42] If the purpose of visualization is indeed to present the evils of anger as being present rather than future, one might ask why the presentation of evils as present would trigger greater aversion from anger than their presentation as future evils. One answer could be that we simply have different attitudes towards present as opposed to future suffering. On this, see Parfit 1984: 149–86.

[43] Here my reconstruction of the argument is tentative. For it is very difficult to tell whose view is being presented—the view of Timasagoras or Philodemus' reply.

engage reason, not whatever faculty is related to the formation of images in the patient's mind. Also, Timasagoras maintains that angry people 'become incapable of appraising (ἀνεπιλογίστους: VII. 7–8) their passions' (VII. 7–9), and for this reason he suggests that the therapy of the passions must be preventive, not corrective (cf. VII. 5–6). Recall that Philodemus' method is precisely the opposite. In sum, Timasagoras' objections against the method used by Philodemus concern important features of that method and represent a real challenge. Philodemus meets it in the following manner.

First, he denounces Timasagoras' 'idle manner' (ἀδολέσχως: I. 10–11) of arguing that vituperation involving the use of 'setting-before-the-eyes' is silly, and he abuses Timasagoras in fairly strong terms (I. 12–27). Fortunately, he does better than that. In the extant remains he actually addresses every issue raised by his rival. Timasagoras' contention that depicting the evils of anger is useless, for they are entirely evident, Philodemus calls 'the most shameless of all' (VI. 26–7). His gibe at Timasagoras' expense drives home this very point. 'He himself (sc. Timasagoras) was not clear about the misfortunes that were to follow from his anger against Basilides and Thespis, although he had set limits, as he thought, upon its sharpness' (*De ir.* V. 18–25). The evils of anger cannot be *that* obvious, since Timasagoras himself made a mistake on that count: he did not appraise correctly what would result from his anger against his fellow Epicureans (who were probably in favour of the technique of 'setting-before-the-eyes'), and he thought that he was in control of his anger when in fact he was not.[44] Also, Timasagoras should have noted that, although the diatribists say that they pay close attention to the therapy and do not pass over it lightly, they do not really explain why the vivid depiction of evils is useful or what are the evils accompanying moral disease (V. 7–17).[45]

[44] As mentioned above (n. 32), an alternative interpretation is this. Timasagoras himself gives grounds for rejecting his own thesis that a lot of anger is permissible, for he offers himself as an example of the fact that intense anger cannot be controlled. My own interpretation of the passage does not exclude that Timasagoras may have been a maximalist. I merely suggest that the point of Philodemus' sarcasm here concerns Timasagoras' claim that the misfortunes of anger are apparent to all, not the thesis that any kind of anger is permissible—which Timasagoras may or may not have held. However, one might ask why Timasagoras would wish (but fail) to set limits to the intensity of his anger, if he were a maximalist.

[45] However, different interpretations of this passage are also possible. In what survives, it is not made clear who are the οἱ δέ (V. 7): they could be Timasagoras and his followers or, alternatively, the diatribists.

Now consider the following passage. 'But as for the passions in our soul that are consequent upon our own entertainment of false opinion (ψευδοδοξ[ία]ν: VI. 14–15), some (of which are bad for us) in kind, others by their intensity, [the chief cause of their removal] lies in contemplating their intensity and the great number of evils that they contain and bring along with them' (VI. 13–22). If this passage contains Philodemus' own view, it may be read as a reply to Timasagoras' charge that therapy should be conducted through rational means and not through vituperation, 'setting-before-the-eyes', and other such forms of persuasion. Philodemus elaborates a point that he has already made: namely, that the passions deriving from false beliefs are bad for a number of different reasons, one of which is the falsehood of these beliefs. Arguing against them is useful, but does not suffice to remove one's affliction.[46] The cure will hopefully be secured only if one contemplates, beholds in the mind's eye (cf. θεωρῆσ[αι]: VI. 19–20), the magnitude and consequences of the passions. The technique of 'setting-before-the-eyes' involves just this kind of *θεωρία*, and is therefore well suited to treat the passions and in particular anger.

Moreover, Philodemus argues that anger should be treated after it occurs: 'there is no need to use these (therapies) before one actually gets angry' (VII. 5–6). When people do get enraged, we should depict to them all the unreasonable things about anger (VII. 13–16) 'and appraise in this way the purity of this evil, just as we are used to doing also in the case of erotic desire' (VII. 16–20).[47] In this passage Philodemus draws an interesting parallel between the treatments of anger and erotic love. It is difficult to capture all the details of that parallel, because the text is corrupt in crucial places. However, it is clear that in both cases the treatment involves comparative assessments (cf. ἐπιλογίσασθαι: VII. 17) highlighting the unmitigated nature of the evils caused by these passions. In the case of anger, as in the case of love, the Epicurean doctor depicts to his patients the

[46] The passage suggests that in addition to 'the chief cause' of removal of the passions, which I take it to mean the technique that holds fast together or secures the therapy (cf. [τὸ] συν[έ]χον: VI. 18), there are other ways of attacking the passions as well.

[47] Philodemus' ethical writings suggest that there are, in fact, several different reasons why the therapy of the passions must be corrective, not preventive. Some are methodological (cf. the debate between Philodemus and Timasagoras concerning the therapy of anger), whereas others derive from the *ad hoc* nature of the therapy, and others from the pedagogical concern of correcting individual errors without attacking the patient's personality as a whole (cf. *De lib. dic.* 78–80N. 1–3).

nature of their passion and shows to them what is evil and irrational about it. Another aspect of the parallel emphasizes the common way in which anger affects and threatens all people alike (VII. 26–VIII. 8), although perhaps the quantity and intensity of anger experienced may differ from person to person. Philodemus contrasts[48] the commonalities in the treatment of anger with some feature of the treatment of love (VII. 21–6), but it is not clear to me just what the contrast may be. According to one interpretation,[49] in the case of love the physician will tailor his vivid depiction of evils according to factors which vary from one person to another (for instance, age), whereas in the case of anger he does not need to mention such details because the symptoms of the emotion are common to young and old alike (cf. VIII. 5–8). However, the passage on love does not mention age or individual habits. Moreover, I wonder whether Philodemus would say that the nature of one's erotic desire depends considerably on one's individual disposition. For the Epicurean treatment of love, for instance in Lucretius, is not particularly focused on individual variations of the passion.

To conclude, in defending his method against the objections of Timasagoras, Philodemus shows himself aware of the pictorial use of language and its power to create images in the mind. He treats these images differently from concepts and arguments, and he also distinguishes them from emotions and desires. He seems to have some intimation that mental images, pictorial thinking, etc., relate to the world in their own peculiar way, veridically or otherwise, and also possess distinct logical properties. He seems to assume that such pictures are representational and sketch an actual personage or a type of person both aptly and accurately. In general, Philodemus shares with the authors of diatribes (especially Chrysippus) the belief that pictures have the power to alter one's attitudes and influence one's actions. I like to think that both Philodemus and Chrysippus realize to some extent that our ability to picture things to ourselves is in part what makes us moral (although there is no evidence that they articulated that view). The next section will illustrate how Philodemus uses material from the diatribes in order to draw portraits of angry men, and how he trades on the depictional possibilities of such images in order to illustrate the nature and consequences of anger.

[48] Cf. *τότε* ... [*ν*]*υνεί* in VII. 21 and VII. 26 respectively.

[49] Indelli 1988: 156.

III

As mentioned in an earlier chapter,[50] Philodemus calls anger both the disposition of irascibility and individual outbursts of anger,[51] and explains each and every one of these episodes by reference to one's disposition.[52] A typical occurrence of anger derives from irascibility, 'a merciless, savage, and harsh disposition (διαθέσει: XXVII. 21)... to which the emotion (πάθος) is conjoined' (XXVII. 19–23). Philodemus specifies it as 'the disposition (τό τε [τῆς δι]αθέσεως: II. 15–16) on account of which they (sc. angry people) [become distracted] and because of which they are afflicted by innumerable evils and, as we know, for the most part create [ever] new evils for themselves' (II. 15–21). Like vices and like other emotions, anger is a content-sensitive intentional state: it has to do with one's reactions to certain types of situation in accordance with what one perceives to be the case. An irascible person (ὀργίλος: cf. XIV. 32, XXVI. 11) tends to become angry and desires to retaliate as a reaction to what he perceives as an intentional offence done to him by someone else. The desire in question is particularly intense and compelling. Philodemus calls it 'unspeakable' (cf. (ἄρρητον: XXIII. 27), 'a desire that buys at any price whatever it lusts for' (XXVII. 28–9) and produces 'a beastly roaring that never rests, like that of the lions' (XXVII. 30–2). In fact, he puts-before-the-eyes both intentional and physical features of anger which, in the terms of the medical analogy, are the symptoms of the disease. 'Anger is a state which consists, as it were, of fever, high swelling, irritation, and indignation, as well as an intense desire for revenge and anxiety as to whether one will be able to obtain it' (VIII. 20–7). It causes random movements spread about the body, rapid shallow breathing, leaps of the heart, tremblings and shakings of the limbs, and even paralysis, like those of epileptics (VIII. 32–IX. 21). Its victims 'are always so liable to black bile that often even their hearts [turn] black' (IX. 37–41). Their eyes are those of a madman (fr. 6. 3–12), their faces

[50] pp. 38–9.

[51] In the first section of *On Anger* (VIII. 16–XXXI. 23) Philodemus does not distinguish different kinds of anger. However, he depicts the characteristics and consequences mainly of what he will later call rage (*thymos*), the unnatural and harmful species of the emotion, not *orgē*, natural and acceptable anger. (However, parts of his analysis are applicable to *orgē* as well as *thymos*.) In this context, the 'bite' of anger is a very painful experience, and should not be confused with the 'bite' that, after drawing the technical distinction between *orgē* and *thymos*, Philodemus will reserve for *orgē* alone.

[52] He may appeal to external factors as well.

red and flushed, their necks tense, their veins swollen, their saliva bitter and salty (fr. 6. 12–20). In addition to 'the [inflammation] and the torn-up condition of the soul' (X. 28–30), anger makes one susceptible to physical, even life-threatening conditions (IX. 29–33, X. 30–2).

Philodemus describes anger both as a cognitive and as an affective event. As in the cases of other emotions, beliefs play an important role in the generation of anger, and appear to have both causal and temporal priority with regard to other elements of the emotion.[53] Leaving aside for the moment the wise man's anger and the true beliefs that it involves, the anger of the irascible person is consequent upon false opinions (ψευδοδοξία: VI. 14–15), which mainly concern what he perceives as the intention of the offender, the magnitude of the offence, and the revenge that would be commensurable with it. Typically, an irascible man believes that the supposed offender has acted with the intention to harm him, that the harm is greater than it really is, and that the offender must suffer considerable harm in turn. When enraged, one is unwilling to accept the offender's explanation or apology, partly because he has false beliefs about the situation (XXIII. 20–4). It is on account of false beliefs that 'not only are some people continually enraged, but sometimes they are caught by bursts of rage which last for several years and are hard to dispel; and even if they are checked, they swell up mightily again and some of them stay with people until death and often are handed down to their children's children' (XXX. 13–24). As will emerge from the contrast between *orgē* and *thymos*, anger based on empty beliefs has a distinct experiential quality (cf. XLIII. 41–XLIV. 35, XLV. 34–7). It is felt as a particularly violent and intense emotion (XLIV. 5–10), persistent and long-lasting, involving an obsessive desire for retaliation and lying outside one's control.[54] As suggested earlier, mental images, pictorial thinking, etc., are also elements of that emotion. The enraged man behaves like the gods and heroes of mythology, whether or not he is fully aware that he imitates them. If he knowingly imitates them, he probably imagines himself as a god awesome in his anger or a hero who

[53] pp. 42–3, offers a suggestion concerning the way in which different aspects of a given emotion may be related to each other: both beliefs and feelings are essential components of the emotion, the beliefs persisting as the intentional content of the emotion, the feelings corresponding to its affective content. Believing oneself slighted and lusting for revenge occur together only when, and precisely because, one is irascible.

[54] These points are elaborated below, pp. 221–30.

seeks revenge for the sake of honour.[55] 'They rave and [are embittered] and [indignant] imitating [out of place] the anger of the gods [of tradition]' (XIV. 1–6).

The anger of the irascible person is interconnected with other faults of character as well.

[The emotion compels you] ... to strive for victory, [give pain], disparage people, and do many other unpleasant things. And when it escalates, it also becomes a cause of misanthropy and [sometimes] even of injustice, since neither juryman nor council member nor member of the assembly nor archon nor, to put it simply, any human being can ever be just if governed by angry feelings. Moreover, for reasons that are easy to see, people who have it must also become despotic, suspicious of evil, liars, illiberal, sneaky, underhanded, ungrateful, and self-centred. There is no need to mention [what everybody can] perceive, that they get no taste of goods throughout their lives, i.e., the goods that derive from taking things easy in acceptable ways, as well as from mildness of manner and deep understanding.

(XXVIII. 5–40)

The interrelations between these flaws probably hold at the level of both beliefs and feelings. The empty beliefs underlying anger are related to those involved in arrogance, vainglory, cruelty, and injustice. Also, one's angry feelings are found together with feelings of superiority, illiberality, ingratitude, suspicion, fear, and so on. On account of these features, Philodemus views anger as a fundamentally irrational condition, which occurs in '[slavish] souls' (XXI. 5–6), blunts the operations of reason, and is comparable to madness (X. 19–26, XII. 20–2, XVI. 34–40). This is apparent both in the symptoms and in the consequences of the emotion. Before turning to them, however, we should take note of the following. Although Philodemus concedes that people in the grip of anger experience a kind of compulsion, he nonetheless emphasizes that 'it is not necessity that creates their [delusions], but rather beliefs, which is just what they experience in the case of compulsion' (fr. 12. 5–10). They are willing to devote major resources to the goal of avenging themselves, and they destroy many things voluntarily (*ἑκουσίως*: XXIII. 25). Philodemus does not explain why he considers voluntary the actions motivated by anger. The contrast between necessity and belief suggests

[55] Among the gods mentioned are Zeus (XVI. 12, XLIII. 3), Apollo and Artemis (XVI. 19–24), and Dionysus (XVI. 24: a safe conjecture), whereas Achilles is the paradigm of heroic anger and revenge.

that, while necessary events are not up to us, it is in one's power to correct one's (false) beliefs, and thus remove one's anger and the desire to retaliate.

So, Philodemus 'sets-before-the-eyes' the irrationality inherent in anger as well as the pain accompanying both the emotion itself and its consequences. First, these are witnessed in the behaviour of enraged persons: 'they leap up, quite often naked, chase people down and grab them as a result of their susceptibility to these intense symptoms' (X. 19–26), and so on; 'borne recklessly onwards, they sometimes through their lack of self-restraint fall upon wood, walls, ditches or some other similar thing' (XIII. 13–17). Irrationality is equally obvious in their choice of targets. They attack not only people, but also animals, inanimate objects, and even shadows (XXVI. 4–7). Blinded by the pursuit of revenge, they cannot correctly assess the consequences of their actions and act against their own good. In particular, they do not realize that they injure their victims much less than themselves (XIII. 4–11). They spend entire fortunes pursuing their offenders; sometimes they lose all their belongings at court (XXIII. 26–35), while other times they suffer the penalties prescribed by the law for engaging in physical violence (XII. 33–40). '[Sometimes] they even attack people far stronger than themselves' (XII. 22–5), who are also irascible. Their anger produces many disasters (XI. 8–9) and 'often even terrible deaths, when they encounter and incautiously associate with kings or tyrants [who have characters like their own] and then, in Plato's words, they reap "the heaviest penalties of their empty and winged words"' (XI. 12–21).

Generally speaking, politics is dangerous ground for irascible individuals, for they cannot be relied upon to keep even those secrets on which their lives and the lives of others depend. 'In their rage they often reveal conspiracies that they have been part of, as well as other secret actions, with the result that for this very reason they fall into great misfortunes' (XXV. 15–21). Great sufferings are also caused by one's fear of being punished for taking revenge, or one's frustration for failing to do so, or the thought of one's many enemies both inside and outside one's house, or feelings of repentance when it is too late to repair the damage done (XIV. 29–33, XXVI. 14–25). Of course, the repentance at issue is not based on a rational assessment of one's error, but is a reaction as irrational as anger itself.

They (sc. enraged men) suddenly sit down pulling their hair out and sobbing over the injuries that they visited on people, sometimes even slaughtering themselves. [Such is the intensity of this feeling] that it makes the enraged man throw away the very things that he most dreadfully desired. There is the greedy Phoenician knave in the comedy, who for the loss of a brass penny chokes himself 'saying "you are walking with your mouth open and pay no attention to yourself"' and whom his anger compels to count all the coins on the ship and, seeking one tetradrachm, to toss the whole pile in the sea.

(XV. 12–30)

Such mental tortures can become literally unendurable, to the point of driving one to fall off a cliff or stab oneself (XVI. 25–34).

Philodemus is one of the first philosophers to criticize the effects of rage in a circle of family and friends, and also to find fault with anger against children.[56] Irascible men, if they marry, accuse their wives of outrageous behaviour (XXII. 32–XXIII. 2), whereas if they do not marry, they suspect their heirs (XXII. 29–31). They take their anger out on their children '[kicking their] children and ripping up their tunics' (XVII. 8–9). They become hateful to parents, brothers, children, and friends (XXIV. 1–4). Although these remarks are few and may retail Epicurean τόποι, they indicate that Philodemus gave some thought to the subject of family anger, and has some concern for the quality of human relationships within that context. Moreover, he condemns extreme expressions of anger against slaves on both moralistic and prudential grounds. Against the background of an unbelievably harsh slave system, Philodemus criticizes the person who tends 'to beat and kick a slave who has said something or got in the way' (fr. 13. 23–6),[57] and in another passage says despondently that he passes over 'the slaves blinded, often murdered, or if they have good luck, running away' (XXIII. 36–40).

Also, in a passage that, oddly, has received little attention, he gives a realistic appraisal of the risks run by irascible slave-owners in such a way as to elicit the reader's understanding if not sympathy for the rebellious slaves.[58] 'How many (bad things) result from these slaves, not only failures in service, but financial difficulties and every kind of misfortune; for because

[56] See Harris 2001: 306–7.

[57] However, we are missing the context in which this remark was made.

[58] Harris (2001: 322) takes the passage to emphasize only the prudential reasons why showing anger towards slaves should be avoided: it makes difficult the control and management of slaves.

of roaring rages, abuse, threats, and undeserved, continual and excessive punishments the slaves are provoked to the limit. If they can kill them (sc. their irascible masters), they would do it with real pleasure; if that is impossible, they would kill their children and spouses; if even that is impossible, they burn their houses or destroy the rest of their property' (XXIV. 17–36).[59] Irascible men are incapable of even superficial relations and ordinary interactions with people.

Some do not have even that involvement and conversation with others without friendship or kinship which is useful, to private individuals in particular, in order to pass the time. For each person avoids approaching such people in order to socialize with them to such an extent that he even runs away when he encounters them at the barber's or in perfume shops or in drinking parties or if he has sat down next to them at the theatre, 'like a bitch that has just given birth'. And similarly, no one dares to embark with them in the same boat or to become their neighbour, much less to share anything with them or to agree to do anything of the sort.

(XXI. 20–40)

Their anti-social behaviour leads to evils such as the theft of their belongings (XXII. 24 ff.), and also condemns them to immense loneliness (cf. ἐρημίας: XXII. 27–8).

Changing his tone and occasionally using quasi-medical language,[60] Philodemus depicts the bad consequences of anger for Epicurean schools like his own (XVIII. 35–XXI. 6). Anger obstructs the students' growth in philosophy for a number of reasons (XVIII. 35–40). Many of them are related to the practice of *parrhēsia*, and are also discussed in the treatise *On Frank Speech*. Irascible students feel too keenly the pain of reproof, lose control of their anger, watch for every opportunity to get even, and are obsessed with repentance as with the desire for revenge (XIX. 1–8). Philodemus suggests that precisely because they have such feelings, they cannot improve their character or concentrate on their studies. Their education may be actively impeded (cf. [κωλύον]ται: XIX. 11)

[59] Posidonius had attributed the Sicilian slave rebellion of the 130s in part to the owners' violent treatment of slaves. As Harris (2001: 321) points out, this must have been a widespread and influential view.

[60] Armstrong (cf. above, n. 1) explains how, in this passage, Philodemus stops being sarcastic about both anger and the Stoic diatribe form itself, but addresses the school in earnest, closely following the medical metaphor as he does in *On Frank Speech*.

by those whom they have made their enemies (XIX. 10–12), although it is not clear how this happens.[61] But a more important reason why they cannot make any progress (cf. ἀπροβάτους: XIX. 12) is that they cannot endure being rebuked and corrected by their teachers or their fellow students, 'just as one's most serious wounds cannot bear the application of the mildest medicines' (XIX. 17–21). Likewise, they are hindered by suspicion: 'even if (the teachers) reprove other students, they most unreasonably suspect that everything is always being said against themselves' (XIX. 21–5). Also, they are unable to participate in the common intellectual and moral life of the members of their school (XIX. 25–XX. 2).

Irascibility makes it impossible to admonish and reprove one's students or peers in the right way. The irascible person does not criticize moral errors selectively (cf. *De lib. dic.* 79 = 81N. 4–12), but 'frowns over trifles' (*De ir.* XX. 18–19). He does not apply bitter *parrhēsia* only when needed, but abuses and slanders others (*De ir.* XX. 20–1; compare *De lib. dic.* Ib. 1–IIa. 7, 79 = 81N. 9–12). He does not correct actual errors, but makes them up (*De ir.* XX. 21–2). 'He discloses confidential words and deeds' (XX. 26–7) and, therefore, cannot be trustworthy.[62] While his anger derives from a vicious disposition, he tries to prove that it is reasonable (εὔλογον ὀργήν: XX. 24–5) by magnifying insignificant faults (XX. 23–6). As Philodemus remarks in the treatise *On Frank Speech*, the reproof of such a person is a most unloving and unfriendly thing (ἄφιλον: *De lib. dic.* 78 = 80N. 2). It disrupts the ambiance of an Epicurean school, undermines the relations among its members, and frustrates its educational objectives.

Why must I add that many people who are well disposed to become friends but have not yet been taken as friends, end up wanting to put an astronomical distance between themselves and the mere approach and sight of such persons? None of those who are related to them in any way whatsoever even wants to give counsel to them, whether spontaneously or by request, since these people [are irritated at

[61] As stated in *On Frank Speech*, good teachers put up with a certain amount of anger and resentment in their students and do not become hostile to them. So, the enemies mentioned here (ἐχθρῶν: XIX. 11) are either fellow students who are themselves irascible or people outside the Epicurean school.

[62] Students need to have trust in their teachers and peers in order to confess their errors frankly: cf. *De lib. dic.* 40. 5–14. But also, they should be very careful in respect of just what they confess and to whom: *De lib. dic.* 53. 3–12.

everyone], or wishes to help them when they are hated, or even [join in work with them] when occasion arises.

(*De ir.* XX. 28–XXI. 4)

To summarize, by portraying the symptoms and consequences of anger, Philodemus shows why that emotion is undesirable, and in what its wrongness consists. Subsequently, towards the end of the diatribe section he begins an attack against all those who provoke or encourage our anger, especially certain Peripatetic philosophers whom Philodemus, fairly or unfairly, takes to be advocates of that passion.

IV

'Quite the opposite:[63] everyone is your opponent, the strangers outside provoking you in every possible manner, your parents and every relative congratulating you most of the time for being manly, and of the philosophers some talking nonsense in their efforts to soothe you (cf. *παραμυθίαις*: XXXI. 19), whereas others strengthening the passion with encouragement (cf. *συνηγορίας*: XXXI. 20)—I dismiss orators and poets and all such rubbish' (XXXI. 11–24). Having demonstrated the limited usefulness of the diatribe, Philodemus now contrasts the Epicurean position concerning anger with both ordinary attitudes and philosophical views. Discourse based on the canonical writings is the only thing that can save one from the evils of anger. On the other hand, almost everything else encourages one to lose one's temper. It is already bad enough that one's closest relations, as well as the orators and the poets, fortify one's anger. But it is even worse that some philosophers inflame it through inept consolations, while others actually recommend it. Philodemus does not identify the authors of such *παραμυθίαι*, but they are probably the Stoics.[64] Philodemus has

[63] Presumably, the text preceding this phrase was something like this: '[they use every conceivable method to help you], except the discourse of canonics' (cf. *πλὴν τ[οῦ] καν[ονικοῦ] λόγου*: XXXI. 10–11)—which is of course the only thing that really helps.

[64] As Armstrong points out (cf. n. 1 above), *παραμυθία* and *συνηγορία* are not exact synonyms. The former usually means soothing or consolation, whereas it also sometimes means the same as *συνηγορία*, i.e., encouragement. (Indelli (1988: 121, 211–12) translates *παραμυθία* in that way.) Consequently, I endorse Armstrong's suggestion that the 'inept soothers' are the Stoics, whereas those who encourage and strengthen the passion are, according to Philodemus, the Peripatetics. The chiastic construction of the phrase brings out precisely that contrast.

already conceded that their diatribes only censure anger and do little else about it (I. 12–20), and he may have dealt more with that subject in the lost part of the treatise.[65] Also, assuming that he has composed the diatribe section of *On Anger* as a parody of Stoic diatribes,[66] he probably reckons that he has said enough to show how silly the Stoic *παραμυθίαι* can be. In the section that follows (XXXI. 24–XXXIV. 6), he turns his attention to certain Aristotelian philosophers whom he takes to encourage anger. One reason why he chooses them as his target may be pre-emptive: to forestall the objection that his own position, that natural anger (*orgē*) is unavoidable and even good (cf. XXXVII. 20 ff.), is essentially the same as their view.

He distinguishes two groups of Peripatetics,[67] one claiming that 'those who remove the anger (*orgē*) and the rage (*thymos*) of the soul cut its sinews,[68] without which there can be neither punishment nor self-defence' (XXXI. 28–32),[69] the other stressing that *orgē* is necessary in order to fight bravely (XXXII. 15–23) and seek revenge (XXXII. 23–6), 'which is a thing proper and just and profitable, in private as well as in public, and in addition is pleasurable' (XXXII. 26–9). Philodemus concludes that 'therefore, they think that both the reasonable excitement of some (philosophers) and a sort of irrational frenzy are the *thymos* of which we are talking' (XXXII. 30–5).[70] On Philodemus' interpretation, then, the claim of the Peripatetics is that anger is an acceptable and useful emotion.

How does Philodemus respond? First, while one can fight bravely and defeat the enemy without anger (χω[ρ]ὶς ὀργῆς: XXXII. 36), one usually suffers damage precisely because one fights with anger (με[τ]'

[65] If the 'soothers' are the Stoics, it is not clear just how their *παραμυθίαι* are related to the censure of anger by means of the technique of 'setting-before-the-eyes'. One possible interpretation is that the Stoic portrayals of the evils of anger are intended to achieve some kind of soothing or relief of the emotion.

[66] Armstrong makes a plausible case for this hypothesis.

[67] Cf. ἔνιοι γοῦν τῶν Περιπατητικῶν (XXXI. 24–5), ἔνιοι [δὲ καὶ α]ὐτο[μ]άτας (XXXII. 3–4). It is not clear how their views about anger differ. Philodemus' account suggests that these two groups hold essentially the same view, although they may have emphasized slightly different aspects of the emotion and the goods resulting from it. In particular, the second group mentioned seems to have highlighted the appropriateness and pleasure of revenge.

[68] Cf. Plato, *Rep.* III, 411b; Plutarch, *De coh. ir.* 457B. It seems likely that Plutarch has in mind the same Peripatetic philosophers as Philodemus.

[69] Philodemus says that he has named them earlier on, in the part of *On Anger* which is now lost (cf. XXXI. 25–7).

[70] Since Philodemus mentions here 'some (philosophers)' who experience a reasonable emotion (cf. εὔλογον: XXXII. 31) as opposed to an irrational one (cf. ἄλογον: XXXII. 32), it seems likely that he has in mind his later distinction between *orgē* and *thymos*.

ὀργῆς: XXXII. 39). For enraged soldiers are uncautious, weakened, and generally worse off than their enemies (XXXII. 39–XXXIII. 7). They disobey their general and do all sorts of damage (XXXIII. 25–8). Rather than giving them endurance in battle (cf. *εὐτον[ί]αν*: XXXIII. 33), the so-called sinews of the soul fall easily apart, leading to violent and reckless acts (XXXIII. 28–34). In fact, anger makes it very difficult to avenge oneself or have the wrongdoer punished (XXXIII. 18–20).[71] Philodemus draws support for these claims from Antipater of Tarsus.[72] According to Antipater, rage is unnecessary and even harmful in fights against wild animals or athletic competitors (XXXIII. 34–40); moreover, it can be dissociated from punishment, since horse-trainers chastise their horses, and grammar teachers punish their pupils without anger (XXXIII. 41 ff.). In sum, anger is not useful for any of the reasons that Aristotelian philosophers give. As to the claim that there is pleasure in revenge, Philodemus refutes it in the course of developing his own view.

What about people who give the appearance of irascibility without really being irascible?[73] Non-irascible persons (cf. *ἀοργήτους*: XXXIV. 16) can be brought to the point of acquiring many of the characteristics of irascible men (*ὀργίλοι*: XXXIV. 31) and even become truly angry (XXXIV. 30–1). But since their anger does not result from an irascible disposition, it is usually brief and not very profound (XXXIV. 32–6). Recall the assumptions that Philodemus makes about the relationship between individual manifestations of a disposition and the disposition itself. Only an irascible character can give a prolonged appearance of irascibility (cf. *φαντασίαν ὀργίλου*: XXXIV. 35), because only his kind of disposition can sustain the beliefs and feelings jointly constituting the passion. A non-irascible person's anger may be triggered by some auxiliary cause, but it does not occur often, and when it does, it cannot be sustained for long. Similar considerations apply to the intensity of one's anger as well. All the same, appearances can be misleading, so that even the wise man, Epicurus for instance, may be perceived as irascible (XXXIV. 39–XXXV. 5). Several factors are responsible for this sort of misunderstanding. Sometimes the commonalities between the irascible man and the sage are of such a kind as

[71] The passage is heavily restored, but this seems to be the basic point.

[72] See Fillion-Lahille 1984: 211–20.

[73] The section treating this question is, roughly speaking, XXXIV. 16–XXXVII. 9. It is not clear precisely where it ends, because several lines after XXXVII. 9 are almost illegible.

to cause confusion (XXXV. 5–7). Although the immediate context does not clarify just what characteristics Philodemus has in mind,[74] they probably concern the sage's methods of instruction and argumentation, and also his relationships with the public and his friends. Precisely because the sage loves his disciples, he rebukes all or most of them frequently and intensely (XXXV. 17–21). He can even be abusive, notably in cases in which he does not fully realize that the error on which he focuses has actually occurred by accident (XXXV. 22–6). He vigorously refutes the faulty arguments of other philosophers in both his writings and his lectures (XXXV. 33–6), criticizes his friends with the result that some of them desert him (XXXV. 36–40) or hate him (cf. [μῖσος]: XXXVI. 1), and generally shows anger when he sees reason for rebuke (cf. ὀργαί: *De ir.* XXXV. 26).[75] His reserved and austere behaviour towards the many (XXXV. 30–2)[76] can also give the impression that he is irascible as well as arrogant (cf. *De superb.* VI. 19–21).[77] And he may even be held responsible for the irascible behaviour of his servants (De *ir.* XXXVI. 3–4).[78]

While earlier in the treatise Philodemus emphasized the commonalities of anger—namely, the ways in which it affects everyone alike (VII. 26–VIII. 8)—here he stresses differences accounting for the fact that some sages give the appearance of irascibility more than others. The former have in them more natural anger (cf. φυσικ[ή]: XXXVI. 20), tend to practise frank speech more harshly or with greater frequency than their peers (XXXVI. 17–23),[79] and may encounter more external provocations than other sages

[74] Only a few characters are legible in the lines immediately following this passage.

[75] Thus, Philodemus rejects the claim of 'some philosophers' that the sage is totally unmoved (XXXV. 28–30). These philosophers could be Nicasicrates and his followers, but more likely they are the Stoics.

[76] Philodemus seems to endorse the view that every philosopher should carry himself in a dignified and somewhat austere manner (*De superb.* XXI. 3–4), which discourages people from taking excessive liberties with him or attempting to tell him what to do (V. 26–33).

[77] However, the sage is accused of arrogance primarily because of 'the disdain that he has in himself about everything vulgar' (*De superb.* VI. 12–14), and also because of his nobility of appearance and life (VI. 19 ff.).

[78] Philodemus makes a similar point concerning arrogance: *De superb.* IX. 24–34.

[79] Philodemus himself connects what he is saying here with his treatise *On Frank Speech*. He points out that the reasons why some wise men are more critical than others are also discussed in *On Frank Speech* (cf. *De ir.* XXXVI. 24–6). According to Zeno and Philodemus, the individualities of each sage become manifest in both his style and his way of exercising *parrhēsia* (cf. *De lib. dic.* VIa. 2–8). When they speak to 'a confused person, [or] a weakened [or] an arrogant one, or one too shy [or another] too intense, wise men will differ for many reasons both with regard to one another and with regard to themselves from one time to another' (IVa. 1–8). The circumstances of each sage's birth and

(XXXVI. 16–18). 'On the other hand, those in whom natural anger is not present, and who do not encounter such things as we are speaking of, will not give the impression of irascible people' (XXXVI. 28–30). At any rate, it is not difficult to distinguish the sage from irascible charlatans by observing the differences between the kinds of criticism that they engage in. While the sage's *parrhēsia*, even at its most bitter, expresses brief and focused anger, the criticisms of charlatans are obviously motivated by persistent and diffused rage (XXXVI. 31–XXXVII. 9). The treatise *On Frank Speech* makes a similar point. Criticism motivated by the passions, and in particular by rage, is continuous and abusive (*De lib. dic.* 79 = 81N. 4–12), intimidates the student and undermines his trust (79 = 81N. 9–10), shatters his self-respect (cf. 78.1 ff.), is an unloving and unfriendly thing (78 = 80N). The contrast between the natural anger of sages and the anger of fools and charlatans prepares the ground for asking whether anger is a good or a bad thing (cf. De *ir.* XXXVII. 17–20). In the next section of *On Anger*, Philodemus addresses that question by introducing a technical distinction between *orgē* and *thymos*, natural anger and empty rage.

V

Since there is false reasoning of some sort induced by the word (sc. *orgē*), we do not make any simple pronouncement (sc. as to whether anger is a fine or an evil thing), but we claim that the emotion itself taken in isolation is an evil because it is painful or close to painful, whereas taken in conjunction with one's disposition it can even be called a good, as we think. For it results from our understanding of the nature of things and from our holding no false beliefs in the matter of measuring the offences and of punishing the offenders. As a result, in the same way in which we called empty anger (cf. κ[ενὴν ὀρ]γήν: XXXVIII. 1) an evil because it arises from a thoroughly corrupt disposition and brings on countless troubles, we must call natural anger (cf. φυσική[ν]: XXXVIII. 6) not an evil—but, in so far as it is something biting,[80] [it lasts a very short time].

(XXXVII. 20–XXXVIII. 9)

upbringing (Va. 3–10), as well as the quantity and intensity of *parrhēsia* that each sage has received from his teachers (VIb. 8–15), account in part for such differences.

[80] On the 'bite' of natural anger and, generally, Philodemus' concept of 'bites' associated with negative emotions naturally and unavoidably affecting people, see pp. 44–51.

In this passage, Philodemus models his own account of two different kinds of anger after Epicurus' distinction between natural and empty desires.[81] First drawing attention to the ambiguity of *orgē*, he distinguishes between anger *per se* and anger in connection with the disposition from which it derives. In the former sense, anger is an evil because it is intrinsically painful or sort of painful. In the latter sense, anger can be a good or an evil depending on whether one's disposition is good or bad.

Philodemus does not clarify here what precisely is the relationship between angry people's disposition and their true or false beliefs, but he probably assumes that one's disposition is, among other things, one's inclination to hold certain beliefs and react in certain ways to certain circumstances on the grounds of those beliefs.[82] The beliefs involved in anger are judgements about how things are and comparative judgements about the magnitude of the perceived offence and the severity of an appropriate punishment (cf. κολάσεσι: XXXVII. 38–9) for the offender.[83] When people have a corrupt (i.e., irascible) disposition, they tend to hold empty beliefs about these matters, and Philodemus consequently classifies their emotion as empty anger and calls it an evil.[84] On the other hand, persons who have a good disposition hold true beliefs about how things are, correctly appraise the nature of the offence and the magnitude of the damage, and on that basis, seek the offender's due punishment. Philodemus calls their anger 'natural anger',[85] and asserts that '[just as when the emotion results] from a good disposition it is not a bad thing but even a good thing, so also we shall call an evil the refusal to accept natural anger' (XXXVIII. 18–22). Feeling the 'bite' of natural anger is bad to the extent that it hurts, but not feeling it is worse. For insensitivity to insult and maltreatment

[81] To my knowledge, Procopé (1993: 173) was the first to point out that the hallmark of Philodemus' account is not the distinction between moderate and excessive anger, but rather that between natural and empty anger. The analysis below gives support to this claim.

[82] Cf. pp. 38–9.

[83] One may think, more generally, that the kinds of empty beliefs involved in anger and other passions have to do with whether there is evil at hand and whether one reacts in an appropriate manner. Cf. p. 40.

[84] I have argued (pp. 42–3) that Philodemus attributes to beliefs a predominant role in the generation of the emotions, and anger in particular. He treats them as necessary conditions of anger (cf., e.g., *De ir.* VI. 14–15, XLII. 3–4), but often suggests that they are, in fact, essential components of anger. The irascible person rages *at* someone *about* something—the relevant empty beliefs both cause the emotion and, so long as they persist, make one's rage persist.

[85] Compare Epicurus' classification of desires into natural and empty according to the kinds of beliefs on which they depend (*KD* 29); cf. also pp. 000–00.

indicates that one has a base character (XXXVIII. 22–7), and also that one is liable to fits of rage about trifles (XXXVIII. 27–33).[86]

Philodemus elaborates the distinction between natural anger and empty anger, *orgē* and *thymos*, as he argues against his professional rival Nicasicrates.[87] Nicasicrates appears to have contended that the consequences of natural anger can and must be bad,[88] although it is unclear whether he genuinely believed that there is such a thing as natural anger or whether he conceded it for the sake of the argument.[89] Philodemus reports Nicasicrates' position as follows. 'In Nicasicrates we read that[90] natural anger is painful not only in its own nature, but also because it darkens one's reasonings so far as it can, generally impedes the tolerance and serenity of one's life [with] friends, and brings with itself many of the evils [enumerated]' (XXXVIII. 34–XXXIX. 7). Nicasicrates maintains, then, that natural anger is an evil both intrinsically and instrumentally. Even the wise man will sometimes harm himself when he experiences the emotion (XXXVII. 4–7) and, therefore, it is best to avoid anger as much as possible. On the other hand, Philodemus objects to Nicasicrates' minimalism about anger for the following reasons.

One is called a wise man partly because one is unaffected by foolish things.[91] Since the wise man feels natural anger, if natural anger were such an evil and foolish thing, he would never have been called wise

[86] Philodemus' point seems to be this. The fact that one does not react with (natural) anger to intentional offence is no proof that one is not prone to any kind of anger. In fact, such a person is likely to be moved to a sudden rage about unimportant things—which, presumably, he considers far more valuable than they are. As Armstrong notes (cf. above, n. 1), the entire passage (XXXVIII. 22–33) is a digression. At the end of it, Philodemus returns abruptly to his main point: viz., that 'at any rate it is a good thing to accept (natural anger)' (XXXVIII. 33–4).

[87] Cf. above, pp. 202–3.

[88] Philodemus briefly mentions Nicasicrates (XXXVII. 5) before his statement that, to avoid false reasoning induced by the word *orgē*, he will distinguish between natural and empty anger (XXXVII. 20 ff.), and starts to discuss Nicasicrates after he has elaborated his own point. This procedure might suggest that Nicasicrates did not use himself the term 'natural anger'. On the other hand, Philodemus explicitly attributes to Nicasicrates (cf. παρὰ δὲ Νικασικράτει λέγετα[ι]: XXXVIII. 34–5) the claim that natural anger (φυσικὴν ὀργήν: XXXVIII. 36) is painful in itself and in its consequences. On balance, I am therefore inclined to think that Nicasicrates did use the term 'natural anger', though perhaps not in the context of exactly the same distinction as Philodemus introduces here.

[89] There is something paradoxical about the position that Philodemus attributes to Nicasicrates: viz., that there is such a thing as natural anger, but that it is bad both in itself and in its consequences. As we shall see, the problem enters on the notion of what counts as 'natural'.

[90] Armstrong's idiomatic translation of XXXVIII. 34–5.

[91] Other reasons why one is called a wise person may have been given in XXXIX. 9–16, but only a few letters survive.

(XXXIX. 17–21). Also, if one endorses Nicasicrates' position, one has no argument left against 'those who would deprive the sage of all anger' (XXXIX. 23–5): i.e., probably, the Stoics.[92] Moreover, since the absence of (any kind of) anger impedes goods such as protection and self-defence and causes many evils, assuming that whatever is natural does not have these results but rather the opposite, total lack of anger cannot be natural. Furthermore, if natural anger is unavoidable, as Nicasicrates seems willing to concede, and if it is called 'natural' in precisely that sense, then either it is a great evil which even the wise man must endure, or there are outbursts of anger which can occur in a good person because they are not followed by evil consequences (XXXIX. 29–38). Philodemus suggests that the first option is absurd, whereas the second implies that the sage occasionally feels natural anger. Also, he bolsters the claim that natural anger is both inescapable for the wise man and compatible with his wisdom by distinguishing the emotion itself from the consequences which both follow and increase violent anger (XL. 2–26). While, generally speaking, anger is inescapable for man (cf. *ἀνέκφευκτον*: XL. 20), the sage avoids altogether the kind of anger that escalates into violence because of what gets added to it (cf. [*ἐ*]*κ τῶν προσθέ*[*σε*]*ων*: XL. 9–10), and especially because of the evils consequent upon that emotion. On the other hand, even Nicasicrates himself must be liable to natural anger in so far as he is human (XL. 22–6).

Concerning this group of arguments, a few remarks are in order. The concept of natural anger involves ambiguities deriving from different senses of the term 'natural'.[93] Philodemus shows himself aware of them and highlights them when he responds to his opponent. In fact, he seems to distinguish at least three[94] or, more likely, four senses in which *orgē* is natural.

[92] In fact, Nicasicrates' thesis may appear to have a Stoic hue: see Indelli 1988: 228.

[93] Zeno of Sidon and his entourage had explored these ambiguities. In particular, Demetrius of Laconia tried to clarify Epicurus' claim that love of one's children is not natural by distinguishing different senses in which something can be said to be 'by nature' (*φύσει*). 'Man is said to be "by nature" a procurer of food, because he does this by unperverted instinct (*ἀδιαστρόφως*: Procopé's felicitous translation (1993: 179 and n. 37)); "by nature" susceptible to pain, because he is so by compulsion (*κατεναγκασμένως*); "by nature" to pursue virtue, because he does it to his own advantage (*συμφερόντως*); moreover, we say that the first utterances of names were "by nature" in so far as …' (PHerc. 1012, LXVII. 1 ff.). According to Demetrius, the expression 'by nature' in Epicurus' statement does not mean without perversion or distortion, but freely, without compulsion or force (PHerc. 1012, LXVII. 1–LXVIII. 10). Semantic clarification resolves the problem (*ἀπορία*) as well as the disturbance that it has caused (cf. [*τα*]*ραχθή*[*σετα*]*ι*: PHerc. 1012, LXVIII. 9–10). On the methods by which the Epicurean canonical texts were studied and used in intra-school arguments, see Blank 2001.

[94] Cf. Procopé 1993: 179–81.

First, *orgē* is advantageous, whereas the total absence of it is harmful and, therefore, unnatural (XXXIX. 26–9; cf. also XXXIX. 29–38). Second, *orgē* derives from and accords with a correct understanding of the nature of things and, in particular, one's accurate appraisal of the factors involved in an anger-provoking situation (XXXVII. 20–XXXVIII. 9). Third, *orgē* is a sound, unperverted reaction to intentional offence. In certain circumstances, one reacts with *orgē* quasi-automatically, as if activating a mechanism of self-defence (cf. Epicurus, *KD* 7). On the other hand, the absence of *orgē* in such circumstances points to serious deficiencies of character (XXXVIII. 22–33). Fourth, *orgē* is unavoidable (XL. 17–22). Even the wise man is bound to experience it, and indeed, he may be considered more prone to it than other people (cf. XLIX. 19–24).

In fact, Philodemus claims that Epicurus calls anger, gratitude, and other such things weaknesses (*KD* 1) in the sense that they are natural drives to which all human beings are subject, not least the wise man.

> [To call anger] a weakness (τὸ ἀσθενές) and then apply it to the wise man, so that we also make him weak, is no great problem to us, as it is to some thinkers. They, writing against the Κύριαι Δόξαι, maintained that it was extraordinary that anyone had dared to claim that anger, gratitude and all these sorts of things occur in weakness, since Alexander, the most powerful human being of all, was subject to frequent outbursts of anger and did favours to countless men. However, it is not the weakness opposite to the strong constitution of athletes and kings that the (Epicurean) argument is talking about. It is rather a natural constitution subject to death and pain, of which Alexander and indeed every other human being have their share, and perhaps most of all those who, like him, are called the most powerful in that other sense of the word.
>
> (XLIII. 14–41)[95]

The naturalness of *orgē* bears on the issue whether *orgē* involves natural and necessary desires or merely natural desires. On the one hand, the inescapability of natural anger would seem to entail that the desire to get even with one's offender is natural and necessary.[96] On the other hand, while we feel pain if our natural and necessary desires are unsatisfied,[97] we

[95] *On Frank Speech* (XXIIb. 10 ff.) may also suggest a similar idea, that anger is found in rulers and kings more than in other groups of people.

[96] See Annas 1989.

[97] Natural and necessary desires are mainly for things that relieve bodily pain.

normally do not suffer if our desire to punish those who have deliberately harmed us remains unfulfilled.[98] If we do, this is a sign that our anger is not natural but empty. Moreover, although the desire for security is a natural desire, and although natural anger does provide a kind of security through self-protection and deterrence, showing *orgē* is not always the easiest or the most expedient way to achieve these goods. But perhaps it would have to be if *orgē* involved desires both natural and necessary.

Philodemus claims that natural anger is self-contained, whereas empty anger has the tendency to escalate because of what is added to it (XL. 6–12). Also, he maintains that the 'bite' of *orgē* is brief (XXXVIII. 8–9), whereas the pain of empty anger appears small at the beginning ([μ]ικρόν: XL. 7) but later on becomes sharp ([ὀξύ]: XL. 10).[99] He elaborates these contrasts in another group of arguments focused specifically on the sage (XL. 26–32), and he addresses the question whether the sage ever feels *great* anger (LXI. 31–LXIII. 41).

> When the wise man has been intentionally harmed by someone or gets the impression that he will be harmed, will he experience a feeling of indifference (ἀδιάφορον: XL. 35–6) as for instance when someone has looked at him, or will he experience an alien or inappropriate one (ἀλλότριον: XL. 36–9), since calling it appropriate (οἰκεῖον: XL. 39–40) would certainly be bizarre? Now, to call it indifferent does violence to our ordinary way of speaking. On the other hand, if it is alien, and he knows that when he (sc. the offender) is punished he will be calmed and will be a deterrent to others, then he would not again come against him in his madness,[100] causing him pain in any way whatsoever. It is this feeling that we are calling anger.
>
> (XL. 32–XLI. 9)

Philodemus maintains, then, that there are three possible ways of interpreting the sage's reaction to intentional offence, two of which should be

[98] On this point, see Procopé 1993: 178.

[99] The text is restored. However, it is certain that Philodemus draws a contrast between the time when anger is first aroused and a later time when the emotion has escalated, and that he opposes the small pain of anger in its early stages ([μ]ικρόν in XL. 7 is a fairly safe conjecture) to the pain of violent anger.

[100] The Greek of this passage is extremely difficult. A conjunction seems needed before the phrase beginning with ἂν ἔλθοι (cf. XLI. 6), which should be taken as an apodosis. Regardless of whether the subject of γιγνώσκει (XLI. 3) is the sage (cf. Armstrong, n. 1 above) or the offender (cf. Indelli 1988: 125), Philodemus' main point is that the anger of the wise man is painful and also directed towards achieving the practical goal of putting an end to the threat and annoyance caused by the offender.

eliminated. The sage's *pathos* cannot be one of indifference, because to characterize it in that way implies that we deviate from ordinary usage and, presumably, from the corresponding preconception as well. 'Indifferent' and cognate terms are ordinarily used for things which are neither good nor bad, but suffering intentional harm is bad, and the sage correctly perceives it as such.[101] Moreover, the sage's *pathos* should not be pronounced friendly or akin to one's nature, much for the same reasons. The one option left is that the sage feels what, according to Philodemus, the Epicureans call anger: to wit, a painful kind of *pathos* accompanied by the natural desire to punish the offender and thus protect oneself. The argument mainly concerns cases in which the sage is personally harmed, but could also easily comprise the sage's angry feelings in response to injuries sustained or inflicted on his friends (XLI. 18–28).

An obvious counterargument is this: 'If the wise man is willing to be angered by intentional injury, and in addition is injured by certain people to the greatest possible extent, how can he fail both to experience great anger and to have a violent desire to avenge himself?' (XLI. 32–XLII. 39). Philodemus' strategy is to concede that the wise man may feel very great anger, but to insist that his anger remains within natural bounds and is different in kind from the anger of the fool.

> We shall tell our opponent that the sage will be profoundly alienated from, and indeed hates, the person who inflicts on him such great [injuries] or will obviously cause him [great] damage in the future—for this is a fitting consequence (ἀκ[όλο]υθον: XLII. 3–4)—but he does not suffer great mental disturbance. [Neither is any] external thing [all that important], since the sage is not even susceptible to great mental disturbance in the presence of great physical pain, let alone in the presence of angry feelings. For [to be in a state of dreadful suffering] derives from folly. So if one is a fool, this suffering can be [inevitable]. Indeed, there are infinite misfortunes both involved in his folly and consequent upon it, into which the wise man, having a completely clear vision of them (θεωρῶν: XLII. 19–20), would never fall.
>
> (XLI. 39–XLII. 20)

Even when the sage gets profoundly angry, his tranquillity remains almost unaffected. For the harm that he suffers concerns external goods, but the

[101] Recall that Philodemus occasionally appeals to preconception (*prolēpsis*) in order to settle aesthetic or ethical disputes (cf. *De oec.* XX. 1–32), and he probably believes that the proleptic, natural meaning of a term is found, in principle, in ordinary language.

sage ascribes little value to them. To put it in this way, the sage's great anger is a natural and automatic response to the hostility coming from the outside. He cannot avoid that feeling; but, on the other hand, he does avoid assenting to the belief that truly great harm was done to him. In this connection, we should consider the sage's attitude towards intense physical suffering. As Epicurus showed on his deathbed, the sage can cope with such pain without losing his serenity and happiness. Surely, it is much easier to safeguard one's peace of mind against the assault of natural anger, no matter how intense it may be.

Natural and empty anger differ radically in respect of the attitudes of the sage and the fool towards punishment. Aristotle counts the prospect of vengeance among the pleasures of anticipation (*Rhet.* $1370^{b}9$–16, 1378^{b} 1–10), and, as mentioned, Philodemus attributes to some Peripatetics the claim that revenge is something fine, just, and profitable, and also pleasant (*De ir.* XXXII. 23–9). However, he contends that the desire to inflict punishment as though it were something enjoyable marks 'great outbursts of anger' (cf. *μεγάλαις ὀργαῖς*: XLII. 24), here equivalent to crises of *thymos*, empty anger. Pursuing revenge as something pleasurable derives from a savage disposition (XLIII. 30–2) and involves empty beliefs, e.g., that perceiving revenge as good and pleasurable is necessary if the offender is to be punished (XLII. 21–30). Only fools seek the punishment of the offender as something desirable in itself, 'even if one sinks oneself in the process' (XLIV. 31–2). In sharp contrast, the sage 'is not impelled towards punishment as towards something [enjoyable]—for it does not offer anything pleasurable—but approaches it as something highly necessary and highly unpleasant, as he would the drinking of wormwood or surgery' (XLIV. 15–22). As he is 'the mildest and most reasonable of men' (XLIV. 26–8), we cannot imagine him enjoying taking vengeance (XLIV. 32–5). Although he is capable of *thymos* in the commonest sense of the term, the sage does not experience persistent rage impelling him to revenge as if to a most pleasurable thing (XLIV. 5–8).

In fact, in addition to magnitude and quality, it seems that one's attitude towards revenge is an important criterion for distinguishing natural from empty anger. For although the sage may feel great anger and even hatred when circumstances warrant it (XLII. 3–4), he never finds pleasure in retaliation. He knows that in the nature of things there is nothing pleasurable about punishment, sees it as something very unpleasant, recognizes that it often has instrumental value for achieving natural goods, and pursues it exclusively in that spirit (cf. XLIV. 15–22). Philodemus compares the irascible man to someone 'who well knows that the greatest vengeance that such a person (sc. an irascible person) takes is on his own self' (XLII. 21–39). On one interpretation, then, the angered sage desires to get even with the offender, but forgoes the pleasure of satisfying his desire because of the greater quantity of pains involved.[102] An alternative interpretation is that the sage who feels *orgē* does not have a desire for retaliation, but only for the goals that would be achieved by punishing the offender.

A related theoretical issue is whether the sage is ever susceptible to true rage, and if so, in what sense. It is fairly certain that the founders used the term '*thymos*', but the exact sense in which they used it appears to be a matter of debate within the Epicurean school. Some Epicureans interpret it as rage, and claim that, according to the founders, the wise man will feel that kind of anger (XLV. 21–3).[103] On the other hand, Philodemus contends that the founders do not use *thymos* in the sense that he denies to the sage (i.e., empty anger), but that '*thymos*' in their writings has rather the sense of *orgē* (i.e., natural anger); hence their position is not that the sage will feel empty anger, but that he will feel natural anger.[104]

Epicurus makes clear in his Ἀναφωνήσεις that the wise man experiences *thymos* and that he will experience it in moderation. And Metrodorus, though he speaks generally of 'the *thymos* of the wise man', also shows that the wise man feels it very briefly. Hermarchus also [does not seem to deny that] the wise man will feel *thymos*, [but only that he will be subject to intense anger]. Thus, I am astounded at those who want to be faithful to the books (cf. βυβλιακοῖς: XLV. 17) and yet, ignoring these quotations and the ones pointed out above, try to demonstrate consistently with the canonical texts that, according to the founders, the wise man will become enraged.

(XLV. 5–23)

In short, Philodemus interprets the canonical writings in a way that lends support to his own view, that the sage will experience natural anger (*orgē*)

[102] Cf. Procopé 1993: 182.

[103] As mentioned, these thinkers may be followers of Timasagoras, and also the authors of the three *epilogismoi* with which Philodemus' treatise ends. Alternatively, there may be two different groups of Epicurean maximalists, the former maintaining the weaker position that the sage will experience both *orgē* and *thymos*, the latter (cf. τινὲς [δέ]: XLVI. 13) claiming that, in fact, 'the wise man will feel *thymos* [no less than] the common man' (XLVI. 13–16).

[104] Cf. *De ir.* XLV. 4–5, XLIII. 41–XLIV. 8.

but not empty anger (*thymos*). His opponents make a similar move: they read into the Great Men's works that '*thymos*' is used in a certain sense, one that upholds their own contention that the sage will feel true rage.

VI

The final five columns of *On Anger* raise a last theoretical issue: namely, whether the sage will feel no less anger than the common man. As we saw, the view that Zeno and Philodemus advance as canonical is that the wise man will never be very angry, because he will never be very hurt. The authors of the three *epilogismoi* (cf. XLVI. 16–XLVIII. 3) deny this, but their own position on anger is uncertain. They are probably Epicureans who defend an extreme maximalist view.[105] There are several textual and interpretative difficulties concerning the study of these arguments and Philodemus' separate replies to each of them. Nonetheless, it is clear that both sides defend their case by relying systematically on comparison and analogy[106] and by pointing to experience. Despite the fact that parts of the text are poorly preserved, it is possible to reconstruct the debate with a fair degree of certainty, at least in general outline.

The first *epilogismos* is this.

If the wise man will feel gratitude towards those who have treated him well, he will also feel anger (ὀργισθήσεται) towards those who have voluntarily harmed him. On the other hand, if he will not feel angry (ὀργισθήσεται) at the latter, he will not feel grateful towards the former either. For the one emotion in each case is the opposite correlative (ἀντίστροφος)[107] of the other, and the element of voluntariness moves us to anger (cf. ὀργήν) just as it moves us to gratitude. For

[105] Less likely, they are followers of Nicasicrates who argue that if the wise man is subject to natural anger, he must also be subject to rage (cf. XLVII. 41–XLVIII. 3) and, therefore, he should try to avoid anger altogether. Procopé (1993: 188) suggests that if the authors of the *epilogismoi* are followers of Nicasicrates (a possibility that Procopé too considers less probable than that they are maximalists), then their aim would be to show that, by approving of natural anger, Zeno and Philodemus become vulnerable to the same objections that they raised against the Peripatetics.

[106] On the substance of the three *epilogismoi*, see Annas 1989; Procopé 1993; Schofield 1996; and, most recently, Sanders (see n. 1 of this chapter). On the meaning of *epilogismos* (cf. XLVI. 17–18) and λόγοι ἐπιλογιστικοί (cf. XLIV. 38–9), see p. 197 and n. 8 above.

[107] Not only can anger and gratitude not be co-present in a person; they are extremes of the same range, and are necessarily correlated: if a person is susceptible to the one, then he will be susceptible to the other as well.

just as we do not feel gratitude towards inanimate objects that produce some good effect, nor towards those animate ones that unintentionally provide us with some good, so we do not feel indignant against them either. But these people claim that we are naturally moved to anger (ὀργήν) just as we are to gratitude by the opposite correlative cause.

(XLVI. 18–35)

The argument contains or alludes to several features which might be considered canonical. Epicurus pairs anger and gratitude, and asserts that neither of these emotions affects the gods (*KD* 1), whereas probably both affect the wise man in so far as he has the vulnerability of a human being (cf. XLIII. 14–41, XLIV. 41–XLV. 15). In fact, Epicurus seems to have held that *only* the wise man is capable of gratitude (D.L. X. 118), presumably because only he will feel it for the right reasons and towards the right persons.[108] Although Philodemus and his opponents have disagreements on the subject of anger, they both accept that the sage will experience gratitude. Moreover, Philodemus would unquestionably agree with his rivals that the voluntary or intentional element (τὸ ἑκούσιον: XLVI. 30) lies at the basis of the analogy between gratitude and anger, and is important in order to understand in what sense these emotions and their causes are ἀντίστροφοι (XLVI. 25–6, 39–40). They are similar to the extent that we are naturally impelled to them by someone's voluntary action, but opposite in so far as the voluntary action in question is beneficial in the one case, harmful in the other.

The argument essentially consists of two conditionals emphasizing the relationship between gratitude and anger, and a suppressed premiss asserting that the sage feels gratitude. Paraphrasing, if the sage feels gratitude towards those whom he perceives as having intentionally benefited him, he also feels anger towards those whom he perceives as having done him intentional harm. Equivalently, if he does not get angry with his offenders, he is not grateful to his benefactors. But he does feel gratitude towards the latter, therefore he also feels anger towards the former. Philodemus has no reason to object to this form of the argument. Assuming that *orgē* and its cognates refer to anger generically, he accepts the premisses as well as the conclusion

[108] This position is not found in the remnants of Philodemus' work *On Gratitude* (*De grat.*; PHerc. 1414). Philodemus focuses on the gratitude that the sage receives from those whom he has taught Epicurean philosophy (cf. *De grat.* I. 5–6), and he describes the way in which persons of good character both bestow and receive favours (cf., e.g., IV. 6, V. 6–14, VIII. 1–2, IX. 14 ff., and XVI. 11–12).

that the sage experiences anger *of some sort*. However, he presents and refutes another version of the same argument, defending the thesis that the sage feels, not some sort of anger, but intense anger. This version too relies on the analogy between anger and gratitude, and, despite the facts that the text is heavily supplemented and that there is a lacuna of about six lines (*c*.XLVIII. 13–18), the reasoning is quite clear. 'If we are naturally impelled to feel intense gratitude (cf. *συντόνως εὐχ[αρισ]τεῖν*: XLVIII. 6–7) towards those who have voluntarily [benefited us], then we are also naturally provoked to intense anger (cf. *συ[ν]τόνω[ς ὀρ]γίζεσθαι*: XLVIII. 10) against those who [by choice] have harmed us' (XLVIII. 5–12). It is very likely that Philodemus' fictional interlocutor (cf. XLVIII. 3–5)[109] affirms the antecedent, whereas, in the missing part of the text, Philodemus denies it. The wise man is not intensely grateful, because he does not attribute great value to externals, whether goods or evils, but the benefits bestowed upon him are such goods: 'since he considers also external favours to be unimportant; for he posits that nothing external is important not only with regard to evils, but also to goods' (XLVIII. 18–24). Towards those who provide him with pleasurable things, the wise man will of course be grateful. But in so far as these things are externals, he will not feel *intense* gratitude, as in the converse case he will not feel *intense* anger.

Unlike external goods, however, wisdom and certain other things (e.g., the goods of friendship and of a proper relationship with the gods)[110] are of the greatest value. It would seem to follow that the wise man will be intensely grateful for such gifts and, by analogy, intensely angry for evils of a corresponding magnitude. Again, Philodemus presents this counterexample as an interjection by an imaginary interlocutor who argues on behalf of his opponents. Philodemus' bare outline of a reply suggests that, while he concedes that the sage will feel profound gratitude towards his teachers, he refuses to accept the inference that the sage will also feel intense anger. An obvious reason is that the analogy between gratitude and anger does not hold in respect of philosophical wisdom, since it is a uniquely valuable gift to which no harm can correspond. Moreover, no other good can be compared with it in terms of value. Philodemus ends his reply with

[109] According to Indelli (1988: 247), Philodemus imagines that an objection of this sort could be raised by his rivals. The same holds for the interjection in XLVIII. 24–8.

[110] Armstrong (cf. n. 1) suggests that these 'certain other things' (XLVIII. 26–7) are the goods that we receive from the standard list of our greatest benefactors, notably the gods, our parents, and the *polis*.

sarcasm. '"But he (sc. the sage) is enormously thankful, not just to those who made him wise, but also to those who procured certain other things for him." But if someone will claim that the wise man acts in this manner thinking chiefly of their (good) intentions, then obviously he will accept the same conclusion in respect of anger' (XLVIII. 24–32). The benefactor's intent (cf. *προαίρεσιν*: XLVIII. 29) is of course important, since we do not normally feel gratitude for unintentional benefactions resulting from accident or chance. But it is less essential than the value of the gift itself, at least regarding the intensity of our response. The sage feels deeply grateful to his teachers not for their intention to give him wisdom, but mainly for the wisdom itself and other great goods, such as friendship and community life. Perhaps Philodemus suggests that the benefactor's intent is a necessary but not a sufficient condition for (great) gratitude. If so, he adumbrates his line of response against the third *epilogismos* as well.

The second *epilogismos* is not preserved in its entirety, but on the basis of the extant remains, it can be reconstructed as follows. Assuming that drunkenness is comparable to anger, if the sage is susceptible to getting drunk, he is also susceptible to feeling angry. But he is naturally susceptible to the former, therefore he is naturally affected by the latter.

Just as we encounter many people who, whenever they drink wine, get drunk—[not] just fools but sensible people too, and the former no more than the latter—we come to understand that getting drunk happens not only in a folly, but, if even the wise [get drunk], [in wisdom as well];[111] [so also it is obvious] that not only [worthless people], when they are intentionally injured by someone, [are liable <to anger, but also> wise men]. [For this reason], we shall claim that [just as the wise man] can get drunk according to nature, so also [anger] must happen to him [because of the same] cause.

(XLVI. 40–XLVII. 18)

Like the previous *epilogismos*, this too has elements that Philodemus seems unwilling to challenge. Several ancient authors employ the analogy between drunkenness and anger for different purposes,[112] and Philodemus does not object to its use by his Epicurean opponents. Moreover, the argument as

[111] From this point onwards, the text is terribly damaged. I provisionally follow Indelli, who prints Philippson's restoration of XLVI. 10–17.

[112] e.g., Aristotle appeals to both drunkenness and anger in order to illustrate the point that acting *through* ignorance seems different from acting *in* ignorance (*Eth. Nic.* III. 1, 1110^{b}24 ff.). Cicero says that, if he has acted bravely in public life, he certainly has not acted in anger, for anger is as irrelevant

it stands rests on a premiss first accepted by Epicurus, that the sage will get drunk, and reaches the conclusion that Philodemus has defended in his own right: namely, that the sage will get angry. On the other hand, Philodemus' rivals state also that sensible people (cf. *συνετοῖς*: XLVII. 3) get drunk *no less* than fools (XLVII. 2–5), and they suggest that the same holds for the sages: according to nature (*κατὰ φύσιν*: XLVII. 15), sages get drunk *just as much* as other people or even more so (XLIX. 19–22), and they get drunk in the same manner as other people do (XLIX. 25–6).

In fact, Philodemus appears to address a stronger version of the original *epilogismos*, which incorporates these theses and runs roughly along the following lines. If the sage gets drunk *to the same degree and in the same way* as the fool, then he gets angry *with the same intensity and in the same manner* as the fool; i.e., he experiences the kind of anger that Philodemus calls *thymos*, empty anger. This version too can draw support from Epicurus' writings, and in particular from his claim in the *Symposium* that the wise man will be uninhibited when he is drunk (D.L. X. 119).[113] Part of Philodemus' reply is contained in the following passage:

> Indeed, we should consider this second argument stupid. For regarding the claim that even the wise man will get drunk, if by the phrase the good men too get drunk they mean Epicurus, they are talking nonsense, but if they mean themselves, [obviously] it is absurd to reason from them to the wise man. One could go on in a similar fashion to demonstrate that the wise man will also seek glory and will [fall in love] and [be liable to] countless other passions, [if indeed others among truly good men experience continual troubles] ... and we would have to accept that the wise man is more prone to outbursts of anger than some fools are, and that he feels them no less than the fools, since he gets drunk no less than they do according to the sense in which they use the expression 'to get drunk'.
>
> (XLVIII. 36–XLIX. 26)

Although part of this passage is heavily restored, and part of Philodemus' reply is missing (XLIX. 13–19), his main argument seems to go as

to bravery as drunkenness and insanity are (*Tusc.* IV. 52). Seneca makes a similar point: anger does not make people brave, for, by that reasoning, drunkenness would too (*De ir.* I. 13).

[113] Concerning the MSS reading of this passage, I follow Usener. However, on any of the proposed readings, one could interpret Epicurus as saying that the sage will get *very* drunk (e.g., he talks as foolishly as non-sages, or acts as insolently as they do, or surrenders his vigilance as they do, etc.). I have learned a lot from Sanders' discussion of different MSS readings.

follows. First of all, his opponents do not clarify who the good men are (cf. χα[ρ]ίεν[τας]: XLIX. 1) when they contend that even good men get drunk. If they refer to Epicurus and his associates, their claim is absurd. On the other hand, if they speak about themselves, they merely project their own passions on to the sage. Philodemus' attack is *ad hominem*. For he intimates that the authors of the *epilogismoi* are not only ignorant about how to construe a valid argument, but also susceptible to many passions, including outbursts of violent anger (cf. ὀργάς: XLIX. 22)—i.e., the emotion that they attribute to the sage on fallacious grounds.[114] Furthermore, they fail to distinguish between different senses of the expression 'to get drunk', and, consequently, taint with ambiguity the analogy between drunkenness and anger. Presumably, Philodemus' point is that, if 'getting drunk' means getting tipsy and behaving in the way in which a sage would, one could infer that the sage will also get angry in the same way: namely, he will experience anger according to nature (XLVII. 15) and usually in moderation. However, if 'getting drunk' means drinking as much as fools would and behaving in the way in which they would, the sage will probably drink less than they do and act differently from them; likewise, he will get angry both less and differently from how fools do. So, Philodemus turns the tables on his opponents. He exploits the analogy between drunkenness and anger both to refute them and to reinforce his own claim that the sage will experience only natural anger.

The third *epilogismos* once again turns on an analogy[115] and involves comparative judgements concerning the anger experienced, respectively, by the fool and the sage.

Of course, it is not because he has been hit by lightning that the fool is subject to foolish outbursts of anger, but rather because of antecedent beliefs. One man is convinced that he has been harmed, another (that he has been harmed) and greatly, [getting from some (circumstances)] no such beliefs but getting them from other (circumstances), he is unangered in the one case but beside himself in the other. So that if being roused to anger commonly follows on beliefs, and if the

[114] Philodemus' *ad hominem* argument may indicate that his opponents are maximalists: self-indulgence like theirs could justify anything, including violent anger. Compare his sarcasm against the minimalist Nicasicrates, who thought that, although anger was natural, it could be prevented: 'he himself, to the extent that he shares in human nature, cannot escape anger entirely, but is certainly susceptible to some form of it' (XL. 22–6).

[115] Cf. Schofield 1996: 227.

wise man, having been harmed by someone [intentionally], believes correctly that he has been harmed but only to the extent to which he has actually been harmed, then he will certainly become angry, but briefly, because he never receives an impression of suffering great harm since he does not consider any external thing very important. However, some (philosophers) have also used these same considerations in connection with the claim that the wise man will experience rage.

(XLVII. 18–XLVIII. 3)

According to this passage, Philodemus' opponents argue that if anger requires the presence of antecedent beliefs, and if even the fool gets angry not unaccountably but only when he has formed the belief that he has been intentionally injured, then the sage too will be angry (ὀργισθήσεται: XLVII. 36–7) only when he believes that he has been harmed to the extent to which he has in truth been harmed. Yet again, Philodemus does not take issue with either the premisses or the conclusion of the original argument, since they accord with his own position. However, after presenting his opponents' reasoning, he stresses that the wise man will not be angry for long, because he will not believe himself to be very much harmed (XLVII. 37–41); in this respect, he differs from the fool, who will occasionally think that he has suffered great harm (cf. XLVII. 24–5). In the final sentence of the passage cited above, Philodemus alludes to a stronger version of the *epilogismos*. If the sage perceives himself as being harmed greatly, he will be angered greatly (θυμωθήσε[σ]θαι: XLVIII. 1–2), just like the fool (cf. ματαίοις ὀργαῖς: XLVII. 19); and since the antecedent holds, the conclusion follows. At first, Philodemus appears inclined to reply that if the sage will not believe himself to be greatly injured, he will not be greatly angry. Assuming that the former is the case, the latter is also the case: the sage feels only a brief and, presumably, mild form of anger, not the great anger (*thymos*) also experienced by the fool.

However, when Philodemus undertakes to give a detailed answer to the third *epilogismos*, he does not pursue that line of attack. Instead, he concentrates on the issue whether the beliefs concerning an anger-provoking situation are both necessary and sufficient conditions for the sage to feel *orgē*.[116]

[116] Most recently, Sanders has read the papyrus and has made a new proposal concerning the text and the content of Philodemus' answer to the last *epilogismos*. I am very grateful to him for sending me the last version of his work on that subject. However, since Sanders' text is not yet published, and

'The last argument is inconclusive, because from the premisses 'anger (ὀρ[γ]ήν: XLIX. 29) does not occur without the belief that one has been harmed' and 'the sage is intentionally harmed', it infers 'the sage does also feel angry' ([ὀ]ργίζεσ[θ]αι: XLIX. 32–3). For just as one cannot become wise without learning the alphabet, but it will not follow that if someone has learned the alphabet, that person is also wise, so the philosopher who has postulated that anger (ὀργήν: L. 1) is consequent upon the belief of having been harmed and cannot occur otherwise is not in a position to infer that the man who has got the impression that he has been harmed will [necessarily][117] become angry (ὀ[ργ]ισθήσεσ[θ]αι: L. 3), unless one can demonstrate [also][118] that the belief that one has been harmed is an efficient cause of anger (ὀργῆς: L. 7).

(XLIX. 27–L. 8)

There is disagreement concerning the interpretation of this argument, and especially the meaning of *orgē* and its cognates. One possibility is that '*orgē*' here means natural anger as opposed to *thymos*, empty anger. If so, Philodemus argues that the sage's belief that he has been harmed is a necessary but not sufficient condition for the sage to feel natural anger. This option might appear to contradict Philodemus' claim that anger is unavoidable. However, Philodemus does not hold the view that antecedent beliefs are always sufficient conditions for anger. In fact, the alphabet analogy indicates that they are not. Just as lots of other things besides learning the alphabet are required for wisdom, so lots of other things besides the belief that one has been harmed are involved in the arousal of the sage's anger. Natural anger is inescapable for the sage in the sense that the sage is bound to experience it *sometime*—he cannot avoid it altogether. But it does not follow that the sage will feel it *every time* that he correctly believes himself to have been harmed. In fact, many things may impede the sage from anger on such an occasion: for instance, the triviality of the offence, the unworthiness of the offender, and also elements of his disposition, temperament, and upbringing (cf. *De lib. dic.* Va. 3–10, VIb. 8–15). Generally speaking, the sage's occasional outbursts of natural anger should be assessed in the light of several factors which are jointly sufficient for an emotion of this kind. Truly believing oneself to have been harmed

since I have not checked his proposed readings against the papyrus, I prefer to use the text of Indelli, who restores the disputed passages following Gomperz and Wilke.

[117] L. 2–3 τὸ [πά]ντως Indelli following Wilke.

[118] L. 6: κ[αί] Indelli following Gomperz.

is one of these factors and, moreover, is a necessary condition of natural anger. Another possible interpretation of Philodemus' answer to the third *epilogismos* is this. Philodemus uses '*orgē*' in the same sense as his opponents to mean *thymos*, empty anger.[119] He bypasses the issue whether belief is both a necessary and sufficient condition of *natural* anger, but remarks that his opponents have not demonstrated belief to be a condition both necessary and sufficient of *empty* anger. Therefore, they have failed to establish their desired conclusion, that the sage will be angry as much and in the same way as the common man.

The close of *On Anger* may leave us with the feeling that we have been let down. In fact, commentators often complain about Philodemus' summary treatment of the *epilogismoi* and his hurried and slapdash prose. Whatever the verdict on this matter, we shall gain much from a closer examination of the form as well as the content of the *epilogismoi*, especially in connection with what precedes them in the treatise. For they address an important theoretical question. They occupy a central place in the elaborate dialectic of *On Anger*. As examples of the procedure of *epilogismos*, they throw considerable light on the Epicurean conception of argument and reason. Moreover, the last *epilogismos* invites us to think harder about central issues in moral psychology: what conditions are logically equivalent to an occurrence of anger, exactly what role do beliefs play in the arousal of anger, and, in general, what are the relationships between emotion and belief.

[119] This interpretation is based on Indelli's text.

10

The Fear of Death

Philodemus' treatise *On Death*, Περὶ θανάτου, may have constituted an independent project, or it may have belonged to the ensemble *On the Passions*.[1] What survives of Book IV of the treatise (*De mort.*; PHerc. 1050)[2] has been considered for good reason 'a jewel of thought and style'.[3] As the title suggests,[4] its subject is death and the fear of death, which, according to the Epicureans, is the most powerful and fundamental emotion of human pathology.[5] We do not know anything about the contents of the lost books of the work. It seems likely that in those books Philodemus rehearsed well-known Epicurean arguments to the effect that 'death is nothing to us' (cf. Epicurus, *ad Men.* 124, *KD* 2). He may also have discussed at some length fears related to superstition, and in particular to the belief that the gods reward or punish us after death.[6] In any case, in the remaining

[1] Kuiper (1925) contains an edition of the entire surviving text of Book IV of *On Death* with Dutch translation and commentary. Gigante (1983*d*) has edited the badly damaged opening columns of the fragment (I–IX) as well as the well-preserved last three columns (XXXVII–XXXIX), with Italian translation and commentary. There is a new edition and English translation of the whole text in preparation by David Armstrong and Ben Henry, which will be published in the series 'Writings from the Greco-Roman World' of the Society of Biblical Literature as a companion volume to *On Anger*. I am very grateful to David Armstrong for having made available to me earlier drafts of his splendid translation, which I have consulted throughout. Also, I should like to thank warmly both David Armstrong and Ben Henry for sending me the latest version of their work.

[2] PHerc. 189 and PHerc. 807 have no substantial content.

[3] Gigante 1995: 43.

[4] The title is entirely preserved in the *subscriptio* of Book IV, which is probably the last book of the treatise.

[5] Notably, Epicurus claims that the fear of death poses the greatest threat to a peaceful and happy life. Also, Lucretius suggests that the fear of death nourishes several vicious traits which, at first glance, might appear entirely unrelated to it. These include greed and blind ambition, envy and malicious joy, love of glory, and also acts of dishonour, disloyalty, and injustice, and even the weariness of living and of beholding the day (*DRN* III. 60–88). However, it seems that such 'sources of evil' are less basic than the emotion from which they spring: e.g., people perceive humiliation and poverty as foretastes of death, and they try to flee them by means of evil deeds precisely because they perceive them as such (III. 60 ff.). The fear of death, then, is 'the greatest terror', 'a darkness of the soul' (III. 91) far more damaging than any other emotion, and therefore the primary object of Epicurean therapy.

[6] In *De elect.* VII. 9–11, X. 2–15, IX. 14–20, XII. 8–9, XVII. 1–XVIII. 19, and other passages, Philodemus highlights the relationship between superstition and the fear of death and shows how

parts of Book IV he assumes some familiarity with Epicurean doctrine and relies on distinctly Epicurean theses,[7] notably those concerning the loss of perception and identity that comes with death, the mortality of the soul, the limits of pleasure (cf. *De mort.* III. 32–IIIa. 1), and the Epicurean conception of the complete life. At the same time, Philodemus tries to cast his net as widely as possible. For many arguments of *On Death*[8] will have an impact whether or not one is an Epicurean. In fact, the intended audience[9] probably consists of Epicureans and also philosophers of other schools, intellectuals and ordinary people, Romans as well as Greeks.[10] Mortality is common to all, and Philodemus composes his *consolatio mortis* in order to help all kinds of people to overcome their pain and fear and to accept death as they must.

Philodemus' manner appears adapted to that purpose.[11] Unlike many of his works, *On Death* is not written in a combative, sectarian spirit, and for the most part it does not engage in controversy with opponents outside or inside the Epicurean school. On the contrary, Philodemus generously praises Zeno of Elea, Anaxarchus, Socrates, Plato, and other philosophers as well (cf., e.g., XXXV. 31–4, XXX. 17–XXXI. 4). He is equally liberal towards people who are not philosophers, whether they are eminent or just ordinary men. In fact, he often seems to have them especially in mind: for instance, when he points to good things in their lives, recognizes virtue in their character and achievement in their actions, meditates sympathetically on their fortunes, and acknowledges the naturalness and integrity of feelings that we are all likely to experience at the thought of death.[12] The

it is relevant to moral choice: see below, pp. 244–7. Both Philodemus and Lucretius suggest that superstitious fears concerning the gods are one important reason why we fear death, but also that such fears may simply disguise the fear of death. We think that we fear death on account of the tortures that may await us in the afterlife, but, in truth, what we really fear is death itself, not anything that might happen to us after we die.

[7] Cf. Warren 2004: 143 n. 74.

[8] Henceforth *On Death* will refer to the surviving parts of Book IV of the treatise, unless I indicate otherwise.

[9] As Armstrong says (2004: 20), whether Philodemus actually delivered this peroration before a particular audience is not an important issue. The important issue is what kind of audience the reader of *On Death* is asked to imagine.

[10] Armstrong (2004) makes a convincing case for that suggestion.

[11] Armstrong (2004) offers a brilliant analysis of the rhetorical and literary features of *On Death*.

[12] Dying childless is not a misfortune. Not only Epicurus and his associates, but also many laymen (cf. ἰδιωτῶν: XXIII. 9) have had friends worth having, who have cared for them and defended their memory (XXIII. 8–15). Dying unjustly has been faced with utter courage not just by philosophers, but also by warriors like Palamedes (XXXIV. 3–4) and even ordinary men (cf. ἰδιωτῶ[ν]: XXXV. 28).

style in which Philodemus chooses to express himself has been described as a masterpiece of epideictic rhetoric.[13] Especially in the peroration, 'Philodemus achieves a solemn, religious eloquence—unconventional, original, and deeply emotional, yet consciously literary.'[14] Belle-lettristic elegance, brilliant imagery, touches of gentleness and sympathy, and also of humour and satire, as well as an impressive arsenal of arguments are all put to work in this remarkable text.

A word about the structure of the fragment and Philodemus' therapeutic tactics. The argument can be read as being developed in two distinct but related phases. The first (*De mort.* I–IX) focuses on the questions whether death entails that the dead are deprived of goods, and whether dying is always *physically* painful. The second and longer part (XII–XXXIX) treats cases in which death is regarded as *emotionally* very painful and harmful. Throughout the discussion, Philodemus shows himself aware of the immense complexity of the psychological states that he proposes to treat. On the one hand, he shares the Epicurean intellectualist stance on the emotions, and places a great deal of confidence in rational argument. In addition to the traditional arguments of his school, he uses many others that are novel and recognizably his own, and he also brings up common-sense considerations for therapeutic purposes. All these types of arguments aim to eradicate the empty beliefs on account of which we view death as supremely evil and to replace them, where possible, with true beliefs about the phenomenon. Moreover, Philodemus clearly makes the cognitivist presupposition that such changes in one's belief system eventually modify one's feelings and place death and its implications in a full and proper context. On the other hand, in *On Death*, more perhaps than anywhere else, Philodemus implicitly acknowledges the essential role of the emotions and imagination in therapy.[15] His abundant use of rhetorical and poetic artifice suggests that it is necessary to engage these faculties, as well as reason,

The idea of an inglorious death will not trouble us if we remember that successful statesmen like Themistocles and Pericles died in their beds (XXIX. 5–8), and that the same holds for philosophers like Epicurus and Metrodorus, who lived more naturally than those politicians (XXIX. 5–11). Laymen and intellectuals alike are susceptible to the natural 'bite' of grief when faced with death. More on these subjects below.

[13] Cf. Armstrong 2004: 20.

[14] Ibid. 19. On the other hand, in the surviving peroration of a different kind of text (*De elect.* VII–X, XVI–XX) Philodemus speaks about the fear of death deriving from superstition in his 'gayest utilitarian prose from beginning to end' (Armstrong 2004: 27).

[15] Warren (2004: 219–21) and Armstrong (2004) differ on this point.

in order to eradicate the fear of death from one's soul.[16] Depending on the case, he scolds, ridicules, admonishes, or consoles those who fear some specific kind of death, in a harsher or gentler tone and with the aid of vivid depictions which 'set-before-the-eyes' the evil at hand. On account of both form and content, *On Death* can be read as an excellent exemplification of *parrhēsia* taken generically:[17] a very powerful piece of moral persuasion which delivers to the public 'the medicines bringing salvation'.[18] If we fully assimilate them,[19] we neutralize a major source of anxiety and suffering, and take an essential step towards attaining the supreme good: pleasure or the absence of pain.

In Section I of this chapter, I shall outline the essential features of the Epicurean position on the fear of death, and I shall point out Philodemus' contributions to that topic. That section will serve, then, as a theoretical introduction to the contents of *On Death*. It will also draw attention to certain passages of [*On Choices and Avoidances*] (*De elect.*; PHerc. 1251) which examine the fear of death in relation to superstition. Section II discusses Philodemus' treatment of specific cases in which death appears particularly fearful and hard to accept. These concern the process of dying and the moment of separation of the soul from the body; premature death; dying and leaving behind enemies who will triumph over one's death; dying without direct issue; dying in the knowledge that one's loved ones will suffer emotionally and materially because of one's death; dying abroad, or ingloriously, or violently and unjustly; drowning in the sea or perishing

[16] The reason why rational argument is insufficient must be that, according to Philodemus, the emotions have non-rational aspects. However, there is no evidence that he would place the fear of death at the level of the subconscious or unconscious. Segal (1990) makes that suggestion about Lucretius, but it is controversial.

[17] As I have suggested (p. 78), *parrhēsia* can be perceived as a generic method of moral correction, of which *parrhēsia* in a narrow technical sense (viz., the method exercised live between members of Epicurean schools) is a species. The main exegetical pay-off for thinking of the rhetoric and argument of *On Death* as a kind of *parrhēsia* is that this interpretation best accounts for the pedagogic and therapeutic aspects of that treatise.

[18] Cf. the passage from Diogenes of Oenoanda cited at p. 78 n. 16.

[19] Although Philodemus appears to concede that the most gifted natures learn philosophy quickly (*De mort.* XVIII. 1–9), his manner and style in *On Death* indicate that he believes, like Epicurus (cf. *ad Men.* 124), that it is difficult in principle to assimilate the portion of Epicureanism concerning the fear of death. One constantly needs to practise the relevant arguments, rehearse and memorize them, until one fully integrates them into one's own outlook. Warren (2004: 212–21) suggests that this could be the Epicurean answer to the complaint expressed in the pseudo-Platonic *Axiochus* (a work heavily indebted to Epicureanism) by the old Axiochus, that the arguments that he has heard against the fear of death do not manage to relieve his woes (369d ff.). Axiochus has not truly understood these arguments; he has not taken them in. If he had, he would have found solace.

in some other undesirable manner; anticipating the decomposition of one's corpse and the disposition of one's remains; facing the prospect of leaving behind a bad memory of oneself or no memory at all. Section III will study the main themes of the peroration, the grand and solemn ending of the treatise: our vulnerability to death, the ephemeral character of human existence, the sage's daily contemplation of death itself, his preparedness to die at any time, but also his supreme capacity to enjoy life. To conclude, I shall briefly speculate about a reference at the very end of the treatise to what looks like an all-important spiritual act, a brief and clear focusing on the value of life and the truth of death, which enables the sage to depart from life at once with serenity and contentment.

I

The eradication of the fear of death lies at the heart of the Epicurean ethical project. According to Epicurus and his followers, the moral end (τέλος) is pleasure or the absence of pain, but the fear of death is the source of the most disturbing kind of pain and anxiety. Removing it is, then, an essential step towards the achievement of the τέλος, and viewing death in the right way is a very important part of the good life. In fact, there are different kinds of fears involving the thought of death,[20] which are distinct[21] but often related to each other. The fear of being dead rests on the belief that that state is bad for the deceased. The fear of mortality can be described as anxiety and distress at the thought that one is going to die sometime. The fear of dying too soon typically involves the thought that one's life may be too short and/or incomplete. The fear of dying concerns the process of passing from being alive to being dead, as well as the actual moment when death occurs.

Arguably, Epicurus and his followers address all four of these fears.[22] They offer not a single argument, but a whole armoury of arguments aimed at establishing the conclusion that death is in no case an evil. The state

[20] Cf. Warren 2004: 1–6.

[21] Both the Epicureans and other ancient authors recognize that there are distinct ways in which one may fear death: see, e.g., Cicero, *Tusc.* I. 14.

[22] The Epicureans have been accused in the literature of neglecting to address the deepest and most disturbing of these fears: viz., the fear of mortality: cf. Segal 1990. Warren (2004) and Tsouna (2006*b*) argue to the opposite conclusion.

of being dead is not bad for one; nor is it bad that death is inevitably in one's future; nor is it bad to die sooner rather than later; nor is it bad to be dying. Moreover, the Epicureans pre-empt the objections that the fear of death is basic and ineradicable, and also that it is beneficial and useful for survival. In their view, what is indelible and useful is our natural aversion to pain. But death does not involve pain—at least, it does not involve literally intolerable pain. If such pain occurs, it destroys us quickly; whereas if the pain is endurable, we can handle it using the resources of Epicurean philosophy, following the example of Epicurus on his deathbed. In the surviving part of *On Death*, and also in the peroration of [*On Choices and Avoidances*], Philodemus develops and enriches that approach. One characteristic feature of his treatment is that, where this is relevant, he takes very seriously the possibility that death might involve violent physical pain. Consequently, he clarifies the relationship between these two things and establishes that, while physical pain is a perfectly legitimate concern, death itself is not.

At the outset, I should like to talk about a special category of fears about the state of being dead: fears deriving from superstition, and in particular empty beliefs about the gods and the rewards or punishments that they administer to us after death. Epicurus and his followers address these fears principally by producing an account of the divine that is both rationally plausible and consistent with other parts of their system,[23] in particular with their atomism. Whether the gods are objectively existing entities or mental constructs, their main features include that they are imperishable (ἄφθαρτον) and supremely blessed (μακάριον), and they do not interfere with the workings of the universe or the affairs of men. Although there is no sense in which we can *see* the gods,[24] we are equipped to acquire clear knowledge of their attributes (γνῶσις ἐναργής) by means of thought. Specifically, our preconceptions (προλήψεις) or correct concepts (ὀρθαὶ ἔννοιαι) of the gods yield infallible access to the divine,[25] and lead to the acquisition of genuine moral knowledge. Therefore, it is essential to keep

[23] This is standard practice among Hellenistic philosophical schools: cf. Sextus, *M*. 9. 13.

[24] Even on the realistic interpretation of Epicurean gods, they are not the kinds of compounds which can be perceived directly by the senses.

[25] Recall that preconception (πρόληψις, translit. *prolēpsis*) is one of the Epicurean criteria of truth. On the standard interpretation, we acquire correct concepts (which I take to be equivalent to preconceptions) about the gods by receiving a constant stream of very fine films of atoms (εἴδωλα), which get imprinted on the mind.

our thoughts about them pure and unimpaired, in order to achieve serenity and pleasure and live the good life.

Philodemus develops and defends Epicurus' theological theses in his treatises *On Piety*[26] and *On the Gods*. Particularly relevant to our subject are Philodemus' claims in the first part of *On Piety* that the gods must have a perfect disposition (ἕξις) in accordance with our pure conceptions of them (ἐννοήματα: *De piet.* 5. 131–44, Obbink),[27] precisely because they are capable of having perception and pleasure; they cannot partake of pains, for if they could, they would be weak and imperfect (7. 189–201); since they are immune to disturbance, they must be indifferent towards human affairs; and since they have these characteristics, we should not fear them. Following Epicurus, Philodemus provides an informative contrast between such notions and the distorted concepts that most men have, and he gives reasons why men came to attribute to the gods features incompatible with their blessedness. Either because they thought on their own that the gods must be subject to pain and disturbance like every other animal (9. 234–43), or because they were manipulated by their leaders to entertain such thoughts (11. 294 ff.), they came to fear the gods and their hostility both in life and after death. Moreover, Philodemus explains the sense in which the gods can harm or benefit us, clarifying Polyaenus' claim[28] 'that divine nature is the cause (αἰτία) for us' (38. 1096–7) of goods and evils.[29]

[26] The first part of *On Piety* (*De piet.*; PHerc. 1077, 1098, 229, 437, 452, 247, 242, 1610, 1788, 1428) is now available in a superb edition, with English translation and commentary by Obbink (1996). In the introduction, Obbink offers an authoritative account of Epicurean theology, while in the bibliography he includes virtually every important reference on that subject. As Obbink remarks, Philodemus' exposition of Epicurus' theological beliefs and attitudes has a new spin: to refute the challenge, probably raised by the Academics and the Stoics, that Epicurus was an atheist, either in the sense that he denied the existence of the gods outright (cf. Cicero, *De nat. deor.* I. 123) or in the sense that he denied it implicitly by disregarding religious cult. It is important to stress that on the Epicurean view as presented by Philodemus, atheism may not be as actively harmful as superstition; nonetheless, it too implies wrong attitudes towards the gods and death.

[27] Cf. Obbink's καθ[θ]αρὰ[ς ἐν]νο[ίας] in 9. 242–3.

[28] Polyaenus makes this claim in the first book of his writing *Against Aristotle's On Philosophy*: 38. 1092–5.

[29] His argument is intricate and occasionally obscure because of textual problems, and it cannot be discussed here in any detail. However, its main thrust seems to me to be this. Philodemus chiefly addresses two types of opponents: on the one hand, theologians and philosophers, who 'observed that evil deeds were held in check by the myths about the gods because foreboding (sc. of divine punishment) hung over the more foolish of mankind' (*De piet.* 42. 1205–14), and who claimed, therefore, that the divinities intentionally cause harm or benefit to us according to our deserts; and on the other hand, the Stoics, who reject such 'base conceptions' (41. 1180–2) but maintain that the gods cause no harm or benefit at all. Philodemus advances the Epicurean view as a reasonable compromise

Although the gods do not actually *do* or *give* goods and evils to men,[30] nonetheless, they are responsible (αἴτιοι) *in a way* and only partially, not wholly.[31] Good and evil influences 'result' (παρακολουθεῖν: PHerc. 1428, XII. 23)[32] or come to fruition (περαίνεσθαι) or are invited upon men (ἐπάγονται: D.L. X. 124) by divinities.[33] But they are not caused because these divinities act like moral agents. In truth, they are caused, importantly, by oneself. 'Those who keep their oaths and are just are moved by the most virtuous influences both from their own selves and from those' (sc. the gods: 38. 1082–7). Thus, true piety involves guarding one's intellect against defilement, attributing to the divine only qualities compatible with blessedness (44. 1266–75), and realizing that the good and ill sent to us by the gods come without anger or benevolence (40. 1138–55).[34] The opposite beliefs are incoherent as well as blasphemous (ibid.), and they fuel some of our worst fears, notably fears of unfathomable torture awaiting us in the other world.

Such beliefs precisely mark the superstitious way of thinking denounced in [*On Choices and Avoidances*]. Assuming that Philodemus is the author of this work, he there examines further the assumptions of mindless men (cf. *De elect.* IX. 6–7), shows how they influence the attitudes and actions of these people, and makes explicit their relevance to the fear of death. According to his account, in addition to beliefs concerning the nature of the gods and their active interference in human affairs, superstition centrally involves belief in determinism and providence. It is a way of thinking that one finds in both philosophers, especially the Stoics, and in ordinary men.[35]

between extremes. *Contra* the Stoics, Epicurus and his associates assert that the gods do have harmful or beneficial influences on us. But unlike those thinkers who considered it expedient to preserve in the masses false notions about the divine, the early Epicureans contend that genuine piety, not fear, is what makes people just.

[30] By contrast, the gods of the myths act in precisely that way. The second part of *On Piety* contains Philodemus' attack on myth.

[31] Obbink (1996) outlines two possible interpretations of the relevant passages of *On Piety*. The first suggests that the gods are responsible for harm and benefit to men by being implicated in various physical processes of causation, while the second posits that our *ideas* of the gods function as direct causes of harm and benefit for people.

[32] Cf. Obbink 1996: 462.

[33] As Obbink (ibid. 464), suggests, such expressions serve to qualify the Epicurean claim.

[34] These features justify the role of the gods as moral ideals, individual as well as social and civic: cf. *De piet.* 45. 1281–92, 47. 1338–44, and, concerning Epicurus, 51. 1468–76 and 53. 1508 ff. The commentary of Obbink (1996) is particularly enlightening with regard to these passages.

[35] e.g., Philodemus says that superstitious men, 'if they are not compelled by the plausibility of things, or indeed if the omens do not agree by sheer chance with what ought to happen, as they are

In the mind of superstitious people, since the gods are 'the most blessed beings' (*De elect.* VII. 10–11), they must have 'supreme power over them (sc. men) for ever' (VII. 9–11). They are 'the cause of both death and life' (X. 12–15). They can decree torture for the dead and ensure that the pains inflicted on them are truly 'intolerable' (XII. 8–9). 'What occurs through the agency of the gods and the other powers will perpetually cause for the dead evils incomparably greater than the goods which it may bring to the living in their lifetime' (IX. 14–20).[36] In that picture, then, the gods rule supreme in a providential universe in which 'nothing depends on man, but everything is controlled by the divine' (VII. 17–20). As for human beings, they are aware of their own helplessness, and therefore relinquish every effort to shape their own future and affect the lives of others.[37]

Philodemus highlights additional links between superstition and the fear of death by describing two conflicting attitudes towards death, both of which have superstitious beliefs or fears as their essential components. On the one hand, some people develop a *carpe diem* mentality as a result of thinking about death frequently and in the wrong manner, and consequently of becoming convinced that life is too short for anything except the egocentric pursuit of pleasure; as to the needs of others, the gods are supposed to provide for them (*De elect.* XVII. 1–20). Sybarites of this sort are illiberal and 'indifferent[38] towards all things' (XVII. 19–20), and also ungrateful to everyone who benefits them (XVII. 15–16). On the other hand, there are those who court death in the belief that if they abstain from all pleasure and comfort, they will get their reward in the afterlife.[39] They too are reluctant to bestow favours (XX. 8–10) or

held back and procrastinate because of their apprehension against doing anything contrary to the will of the gods, they fail to act' (*De elect.* VIII. 10–19). His remark applies to the Stoics who do believe in divination, and also to ordinary people such as Nicias, the leader of the Sicilian expedition, who delayed the departure of the Athenian army from Sicily because of a bad omen, and so lost both the army and his own life (Thucydides, *Hist.* VII. 50. 4).

[36] Discussion of these beliefs is found in Indelli and Tsouna-McKirahan 1995: 143–60.

[37] e.g., the superstitious man does not 'take advice from anybody about anything at all' (*De elect.* VII. 16–17), does not think and plan anything in advance (cf. ἀπροβ[ου]λευ[σ]ία: VII. 21–2), procrastinates or fails altogether to act (VIII. 11–19), and does not give anyone benefits or help 'on the grounds that this ought to be done by the immortals' (XVII. 10–13).

[38] On the meaning of ἀνεπίστρεπτος, see Indelli and Tsouna-McKirahan 1995: 200.

[39] 'They exclaim: "Pray, do I not live decently and justly? Or do I not live in accordance with the laws applying to men? Then, when I shall die, I shall be immortal." And they are cut off from everything by means of which they would have a better life, exactly like men who are sentenced to death. What is more, they neglect what contributes to health, adding: "How many evils shall I endure

show ingratitude. Besides, they are afflicted by avarice,[40] 'engage in wrath and hatred which do not befit humans, and become arrogant in their announcements, commands, or threats; and they lack pity and sympathy towards their kindred' (XX. 12–20).[41] To conclude, the lens of superstition usually makes the state of being dead appear as a frightful evil—an eternity of insufferable pain in Hades.

However, the Epicurean position concerning the fear of death is developed in the main independently of Epicurean theology. Epicurus and his followers notoriously advance two major arguments in support of the position that death is nothing to us, the so-called non-perception (ἀναισθησία, translit. *anaisthēsia*) and the non-identity arguments. Although they are often combined in the Epicurean literature (e.g., Lucretius, *DRN* III. 870 ff.),[42] they can be seen as independent of each other: if either of them obtains, death cannot be a harm and ought not to concern us. The non-perception, or *anaisthēsia*, argument is roughly this. Death is the dispersion of the compound constituted by one's soul atoms and one's body atoms. What is dispersed does not perceive, but the only way in which one can be harmed is through perception. Since death entails complete loss of perception, it is nothing to us (cf. Epicurus, *KD* 2 and *ad Men.* 124). The non-identity argument puts the emphasis elsewhere: the disappearance of the person who is wrongly supposed to be harmed by death. A person is a combination of soul and body, and death is the destruction of that combination; when death is present, the person is no more. But if something is to be bad for us, we must exist at the time when the bad thing or event occurs. Hence death is nothing to us (*ad Men.* 125). Severally, as well as jointly, these two arguments undermine the idea that death entails deprivation of any sort. To be deprived of something, one must have a desire for that thing, and be aware of the fact that one's desire remains unfulfilled; but *anaisthēsia* makes such awareness impossible. Moreover, to be deprived of something, one must have the relevant desire, but in death there is no one who has that

if I live luxuriously for three seasons?" ... And on account of projecting everlasting evils on to the time when they are dead, they are afflicted by immeasurable troubles' (*De elect.* XVIII. 1–19).

[40] 'When they lose money, they suffer the pains of hell' (XX. 10–12).

[41] The complete list of the vices associated with superstition in [*On Choices and Avoidances*] overlaps considerably with Lucretius' catalogue of vices related to the fear of death (*DRN* III. 60 ff.).

[42] Cf. Warren 2004: 21.

desire—there is no person, therefore there are no desires, and *a fortiori* no unfulfilled desires attached to a certain person.[43]

In the fragment of *On Death*, Philodemus strengthens the premiss of the *anaisthēsia* argument most attacked by modern critics, that what is not perceived is nothing to us.[44] He also expands the scope of the *anaisthēsia* thesis and makes it more nuanced. For instance, he suggests that the *anaisthēsia* argument should cover conditions of diminished consciousness as well as of total unconsciousness to treat the fear of dying, in addition to the fear of being dead (cf. V. 1–4, IX. 1–12). He uses the *anaisthēsia* thesis in combination with the Epicurean view about the limits of pleasure to establish that death does not imply deprivation of any sort (cf. III. 30–6). And, most importantly, he applies the non-perception argument to 'hard cases', cases in which death is considered particularly frightful. The childless man must not worry about who will bury and remember him, because he will feel nothing (XXII. 30–3). One should not pursue a glorious death for the sake of posthumous reputation, because in death there is no consciousness of one's past achievements (XXVIII. 32–6). And so on.

Turning now to Philodemus' use of the non-identity argument, we find that it does a lot of the work necessary for the therapy of the hard cases. The standard version of the argument relies partly on the premiss that the person and the harm that death is supposed to inflict must coincide temporally; since death entails the destruction of the person,[45] that condition can never be satisfied. Like Epicurus and Lucretius, Philodemus takes for granted the truth of that premiss, perhaps for the reason that it seems impossible to deny

[43] Warren (ibid. 39 ff.) remarks that, according to Lucretius, death does not entail deprivation, because of both non-perception and non-identity (*DRN* III. 894–9, 900–3; cf. also *DRN* III. 912–30). If non-identity obtains, non-perception becomes a secondary consideration. Since there is no subject, there is no loss; moreover, the dead are not aware of any loss.

[44] Nagel (1979) notoriously attacks the non-perception argument by denying that there are no unperceived harms. As Warren (2004: 24 ff.) indicates, one main challenge that Nagel and others must face is to specify the exact sense in which one can be harmed but not recognize or be aware of that fact. Feldman (1992) draws a distinction between intrinsic and extrinsic harms (respectively, harms directly or indirectly felt by the subject) and claims that in fact Epicurus believes that there are extrinsic harms and trades on ambiguity. When he says that death is not evil, he means intrinsically evil; but, nonetheless, death could be extrinsically evil. However, there is an answer available to Epicurus: viz., that extrinsic evils affect one's well-being only to the extent that they produce the only intrinsic evil, physical or mental pain. Warren (2004: 28–34) offers insightful comments on Feldman 1992 and generally on comparative and counterfactual accounts purporting to explain why death is harmful.

[45] Death here refers to the period of time after life has ceased. Most modern critics of the Epicurean position that death is nothing to us would concede, nonetheless, that death is the destruction of the person, that we do not in any sense survive our own death.

it without self-contradiction.[46] Moreover, he implicitly rules out various options as to how to locate temporally the harm that death is supposed to inflict.[47] For instance, he refutes the contention that the harm occurs during the process of dying or at the very moment when one dies. Often he relies on the non-identity argument alone to drive his point home: we should not grieve on account of having no tomb, because we shall not exist then (XXXII. 1 ff.?); there will be no subject who will be left unburied; etc. Like Lucretius, Philodemus frequently uses the non-identity argument in combination with the non-perception argument. We must not worry about our enemies mocking us after death, because we shall not be there to perceive them doing so (XX. 5 ff.).[48] Nor ought we to prefer certain causes of death over others, except on hedonic grounds, for death brings both unconsciousness and non-existence (XXVIII. 14–20). Nor must we wish for an expensive grave, because what waits for all is 'perfect unconsciousness or rather non-existence' (cf. XXX. 7–20). The formulation of this last statement may indicate that Philodemus considers the extinction of identity a stronger or more fundamental argument than *anaisthēsia*. If so, he is probably right. References of this sort to perception, awareness, consciousness, and their opposites seem to require a subject: *someone* is no longer able to perceive his foes triumphant, the cause of his death, his conspicuous grave, etc. Besides, as things stand at present, it seems to me that the Epicurean claim that there are no unperceived harms, which is essential to the non-perception argument, has robust opposition. On the other hand, the contention that if death is a harm, there should be someone who is harmed is more difficult to resist.

Another argument which has attracted much attention in the literature has become known as the Symmetry Argument, which Lucretius is the first known Epicurean author to use. It is found in two passages of his poem (*DRN* III. 832–42, 972–5) that invoke a symmetry between the past and the future to conclude that when we will not exist any more, we shall

[46] Cf. Cicero, *Tusc.* I. 3, discussed by Warren (2004: 44–6).

[47] Modern philosophers have tried in various ways to answer the question: if death is an evil, just when does it happen to one? Many of them suggest that death is a relational or a comparative harm, which cannot be located either in space or in time. Cf., e.g., Nagel 1979; Levenbook 1984: 410 ff.; Feldman 1992; discussed most recently by Warren (2004: 41–50). Mitsis (1996) offers a particularly enlightening discussion of Feldman 1992.

[48] I take it that Philodemus here emphasizes both that we shall not exist at that time and that we shall then be unable to perceive anything.

not be able to feel or be affected by anything (*DRN* III. 838–42). Just as the infinity of time preceding our birth has been nothing to us, so the stretch of time after our death will also be nothing to us (*DRN* III. 972–5). There is disagreement about the exact content of Lucretius' argument. Two main options are available in the literature, the one factual, the other normative.[49] According to the first, Lucretius asserts something about the state of affairs after our death, that our post-mortem non-existence will be nothing to us. According to the second, he makes a claim about our attitude at a given point within a lifetime: as we look forward in the present to a future time when we shall be dead, we should feel no distress about the fact that we shall not then be alive. Thus, on the one hand, the factual form of the argument can be considered a restatement of Epicurus' thesis that death is nothing to us (cf. *KD* 2). Lucretius defends it on different grounds from Epicurus: the postulated symmetry between prenatal and post-mortem time. Our non-existence will be as complete after our death as it was before our birth, and is as irrelevant to us in the one case as in the other.[50] On the other hand, the normative version implies that Lucretius offers an explicit reason why we should not have the fear of mortality.

Many commentators attribute to Lucretius the normative form of the argument,[51] precisely because it could answer the criticism that the Epicureans fail to recognize the most fundamental sense in which people fear death. The objection goes that people do not necessarily fear the state of being dead, because they may be convinced that they will be both non-existent and unconscious. However, they may still be distressed at the thought that there will come a point in time in which their life will cease. The focus of their emotion is the very prospect of unconsciousness and the annihilation of the self, not false assumptions about post-mortem sensation or some sort of personal survival. On either interpretation, what is stated about prenatal non-existence is uncontroversial. At the time before our birth our non-existence was nothing to us, and also, looking back to that time

[49] Warren (2004: 60–2) formulates and clearly distinguishes these two versions of the argument. See also Sorabji 1983: 174 ff.; Furley 1986; and Nussbaum 1994: 202 ff.

[50] Cf. Furley 1986: 76. Warren (2004: 57 ff.) also favours that interpretation and, moreover, argues that we can deduce the normative from the factual form of the argument by appealing to the principle that whatever causes no pain when present, causes only empty distress when anticipated.

[51] Cf. Warren 2004: 57 ff. That group of commentators includes Belshaw 1993; Feldman 1990; Kamm 1993; Mitsis 1988*b*; Rosenbaum 1989; and others. It should be noted that commentators interpret both the normative and the descriptive versions of the Symmetry Argument in different ways.

from a given point in the present, our prenatal non-existence is nothing to us; we do not feel distress at the fact that our life did not begin earlier than it did. The controversial features of Lucretius' argument have to do mainly with the alleged symmetrical relationship between past and future. To give an indication of its potential weaknesses, it is useful to outline two influential lines of criticism. They underscore different approaches to the fear of death, and they may bear on Philodemus' attitude towards the Symmetry Argument.

The first line of criticism strikes at both the descriptive and the normative forms of the argument. Its central contention is that the time of birth is a necessary condition of personal identity, whereas the time of death is not. We have good reason *not* to think it a misfortune that we were not born before the time when we were actually born, but, on the other hand, to consider a misfortune the fact that we are dying now rather than in a few years' time. For since each person gets identified by reference to his history and possibilities, he can be identified as the subject who has been deprived of the time *after* his death, whereas he cannot be identified as that subject at a time *prior* to his birth. In this picture, the direction of time is absolutely crucial for assigning to an individual such possibilities, and in particular the possibility that he might have lived longer.[52] Although this group of critics makes assumptions about personal identity that can be questioned,[53] they seem to be on relatively strong ground. For there is intuitive plausibility to the claim that before birth there is no subject to have been deprived of goods that might have been enjoyed if one had been born earlier, whereas, concerning post-mortem time, there is a subject that death deprives of goods that one would have enjoyed if one had died later; while death is not an evil in the former case, it is an evil in the latter.[54]

[52] The classic formulation of this criticism is found in Nagel 1979, who appears to rely on Saul Kripke's doctrine of the essentiality of origins (Kripke 1980: 110 ff.). It is debatable whether Kripke would agree with such an application of the essentiality of origins doctrine. Moreover, Nagel (1986) questions it. However, several philosophers attempt to defend Nagel's original approach. For instance, Kaufman (1999) introduces a psychologically richer concept of the self, and argues that on that understanding of the self one could not have been born earlier than one actually was. Similar lines of criticism are developed also by Brueckner and Fischer 1998; Glannon 1994; Williams 1995; and others.

[53] Cf. Warren 2004: 80–1.

[54] Warren (ibid. 81–2) is right to point out that the Epicureans have proved on grounds other than the Symmetry Argument that death involves no deprivation. However, he seems to play down the importance of the criticisms of Nagel (1979) and others. The Epicurean assertion that 'it is not possible to be born twice' (*SV* 14) points in a direction that Nagel may have welcomed.

A different line of criticism consists in pointing out that our attitudes towards past and future experiences are inevitably asymmetrical.[55] If this objection is relevant to the Symmetry Argument,[56] it concerns only the normative version of it. On a standard interpretation, the case of 'Parfit's patient' suggests that the direction of time is an ethically important factor when it comes to experiencing pleasure or pain. *When* the pleasure or pain is to occur matters greatly. We always prefer pleasures to be in the future and pains in the past, not the other way around. Therefore, concerning Lucretius' argument, our attitude to prenatal non-existence cannot be symmetrical to our attitude to future non-existence, simply because the former is in the past, while the latter is in the future, and we have a bias towards the future.[57] A particularly interesting feature of this discussion is the question whether a symmetrical attitude would be better for us. Suppose that there exists a person who has no intuitive temporal bias and who is psychologically detached from his future life.[58] From a hedonistic perspective, it would seem that such a person would lose some advantages—e.g., he would not feel relief at the thought that bad things are in the past—but also would gain some things, especially when faced with ageing and death. However, one wonders whether such a person would be happier overall than the rest of us or, in important respects, more miserable. This is a pressing issue regarding the Epicureans. For Epicurus' attitude on his deathbed can be interpreted as showing no bias towards the future.[59] And that ideal may appear inherent in Lucretius' Symmetry Argument.

Whatever the answer may be concerning the other members of the school, Philodemus does not explicitly confront objections to the Symmetry

[55] This objection was first developed by Parfit (1984: esp. 149–86) in the context of examining a hedonist version of self-interest theories (what he calls 'S' theories).

[56] The example of 'Parfit's patient' concerns pleasures and pains that we experience, whereas the Symmetry Argument refers to two stretches of time (before one's birth and after one's death) in which experience is absent. Cf. Warren 2004: 90–1.

[57] That bias can be accounted for in a number of different ways. There are evolutionary and prudential reasons why we are biased in that direction. It is not possible to affect the past, while it is possible to shape the future. The difference in our attitudes towards past and future, and especially towards prenatal and post-mortem non-existence, reflects a real difference in the distinctive features of the relevant times (Warren (2004: 86) calls the relevant distinctive features 'pastness' and 'futurity'). The difference in our attitudes reveals or justifies the value that we ascribe to their objects: post-mortem non-existence is more valuable than prenatal non-existence to the extent that we care more about it. Concerning this issue, see the brief and excellent comments of Warren (ibid. 86–7) on Brueckner and Fischer 1993 and Cockburn 1997.

[58] Parfit's Timeless: cf. esp. Parfit 1984: 174 ff.

[59] Warren (2004: 92) entertains that thought.

Argument. However, he may forestall some of them implicitly.[60] In any case, he advances three considerations of symmetry between past and future in ways that are strikingly novel. First, addressing the fear that we may receive no burial, he points to our attitude towards people who have been in that position and who have lived sometime in the distant past. One way of understanding his argument is this. As we do not think that anything evil has happened to a person who has died long ago and whose bones get unearthed, so we should not think that any evil has happened to someone whom we have known and who remained unburied or that any evil will affect us if we do not have a tomb (XXII. 24–8).[61] Second, when he treats the fear of dying childless and the related fear of having no one to remember us after death, he argues that such things will not matter to us in the future after we are dead any more than they matter to people who have lived in the past, in prehistoric times (XXIII. 37–XXIV. 5).[62] Third, Philodemus appeals to some kind of symmetry between the distant past and the infinite future, in order to dispel the fear that one will not be remembered after death (XXXVI. 17–25).[63] I postpone detailed discussion of these reasonings to the next section. Here, it is worth noting that in all three cases Philodemus uses other arguments in addition to symmetry arguments to console his patients. This may indicate some diffidence concerning the therapeutic value of symmetry arguments if they are taken by themselves. Moreover, it seems significant that Philodemus addresses the fear of mortality in ways totally independent of considerations of symmetry between the past and the future. Notably, reflection on the naturalness and the omnipresence of death, as well as the daily contemplation of death in an intense and uninterrupted manner, as Philodemus hopes, will help us accept our mortality.

As mentioned, the fear of premature death is distinct from both the fear of being dead and the fear that we are going to die sometime. It can be interpreted either as the fear that our life will be too short or, more likely, that it will be incomplete.[64] Most competing conceptions of the completeness of a life contain the intuition that lives should exhibit a

[60] Cf. Armstrong 2004. [61] The context of this argument is also discussed below, pp. 280–5.

[62] On the actual point of the symmetry between the past and the future in this case, and how we should interpret Philodemus' reference to prehistoric men, see below, pp. 282–3.

[63] Cf. below, p. 301.

[64] In the first case the issue is duration, whereas in the second the issue is the completeness of a life. Striker (1988) draws that distinction, and compares living a life to seeing an opera: the important thing

correct shape, they should be arranged in the right way, they ought to have something comparable to a plot or a perfected narrative structure.[65] On this model, premature death is an evil to the extent that it can alter the shape of a life which might otherwise have become complete.[66] It can cut off the plot before it gets resolved in an appropriate and satisfactory manner.

Epicurus does not explicitly address the problem of premature death in his surviving work. However, he suggests an alternative model of a life's completeness in which premature death is not regarded as a harmful thing. This model is based on the central thesis of Epicurus' hedonism, that the supreme good is pleasure or the absence of pain (ἀπονία), and that once it is reached, it cannot be increased but only varied (Cicero, *De fin.* I. 38). Accordingly, the main concern of the sage is how to enjoy not the longest, but the pleasantest, life (*ad Men.* 126). For reasons mentioned earlier, additional time for more pleasures does not increase the value of a life: infinite time contains no more pleasure than a finite time, if it is measured by reason (*KD* 19); the mind has the capacity to make life complete (cf. παντελής: *KD* 21) and no longer in need of infinite time; the mind achieves this result by resisting the irrational tendency of the flesh to experience ever more pleasure, removing the desire for immortality (cf. *KD* 20) and getting to know the limits of life, and therefore the way to attain the highest good (*KD* 21). Taken together, these tenets strongly suggest that duration is of little or no importance,[67] and that a longer life does not necessarily exceed a shorter one in value.[68]

To summarize, not only does Epicurus maintain that a correct understanding of death makes our mortal life enjoyable (*ad Men.* 124), and that there is nothing desirable about immortality (*ad Men.* 124),[69] but he also

is not how long the opera lasts, but whether we shall be able to see the whole opera, not only part of it. For discussion of Striker 1988 see, most recently, Warren 2004: 116 ff.

[65] Warren (2004: 122) calls this the Narrative Model. [66] Cf. ibid. 121.

[67] Epicurus leaves the role of duration underdetermined. According to one interpretation, longer and shorter lives do not differ at all in value; as soon as the highest pleasure is achieved, duration adds nothing (cf. Epicurus, *ad Men.* 128, *KD* 18; Cicero, *De fin.* II. 88). On another interpretation, however, the value of life is maximally increased only if a certain finite time is granted *after* one has achieved the greatest good; only beyond that point is the value of life complete. Both interpretations are presented and discussed by Warren (2004: 130 ff.).

[68] See the excellent discussion in Warren 2004: 124–35.

[69] Williams (1973) suggests that even if immortality were a possibility for us, it would not be a desirable thing. For an everlasting life cannot contain the kind of desires which give us reasons for continuing to live (he calls these desires 'categorical').

suggests that, for the person who thinks correctly, death can never be premature. Following in Epicurus' footsteps, Lucretius contrasts, on the one hand, satisfiable desire and the completeness of a life and, on the other hand, unsatisfiable desire and a life's incompleteness (cf. *DRN* III. 933–49, 955–62).[70] He indicates that the main reason for thirsting to prolong life is one's perpetual and self-defeating attempt to fill the 'cracked vessel'[71] of empty desires (cf. *DRN* III. 1076–84). On the contrary, the correct understanding of pleasure and its limits allows one to satisfy one's natural desires, live a complete life, and depart when one must like a well-fed guest. Again, Lucretius does not explicitly mention premature death. But his examples of people complaining that they are going to die (*DRN* III. 933–49, 955–62) suggest that such people would always consider death premature regardless of when it comes.

In *On Death*, Philodemus integrates these themes into the most sustained discussion of premature death that survives in the Epicurean literature. His treatment of that fear is grounded on the theses that if one understands the limits of pleasure, a small amount of time[72] naturally suffices in order to produce it (*De mort.* III. 33–6), and that the flesh very quickly[73] achieves as much pleasure as can be provided by an infinite time (III. 37–9). He rejects the maximalist conception of pleasure, which he perhaps considers[74] as the reason why fools fear an untimely death (cf. ἄωρον τελε[υτήν]: XII. 1). Also, like Epicurus and Lucretius, he seems to think that the Epicurean conception of a complete life is consistent, whereas the maximalist model is internally inconsistent. The correct understanding of the nature and limits of pleasure is related to the satisfaction of one's natural desires and one's capacity to enjoy a complete life. On the other hand, maximalist thinking leads to the search for unattainable objects of desire and to the inability to feel any pleasure at all. Philodemus highlights these relationships by drawing a contrast between a wise youth like Pythocles, whose complete happiness cannot be diminished by early death, and an old fool, whose

[70] Discussion of these passages in connection with the topic of premature death is found in Warren 2004: 135 ff.

[71] The metaphor concerns the cracked and leaking vessels of the Danaïds (cf. Lucretius, *DRN* III. 1003–10). An interesting analysis is found in Nussbaum 1994: 220–2.

[72] Cf. Armstrong's rendering of ὁπόσος χρόνος (*De mort.* III. 34) as 'so small a time'.

[73] I follow Armstrong's translation of εὐθύς (*De mort.* III. 37), as opposed to Warren's 'immediately' (cf. Warren 2004: 143).

[74] In *De mort.* XII. 1, [ὡς κακόν] is a conjecture.

life will always be curtailed prematurely because he will not be content at any point (XII. 26 ff.).[75] However, as we shall see in detail later, Philodemus makes two important concessions regarding the role of the duration of life and the significance of premature death. While Epicurus leaves underdetermined the exact relevance of duration to the value of one's life, Philodemus shows a clear preference for some duration: a finite length of time is desirable both before and after one reaches the highest good (cf. XIII. 3–6, XIII. 36–XIV. 10).[76] He also acknowledges that it is reasonable to wish life to last longer in order to perfect one's Epicurean way of life (XIII. 36–XIV. 10) and to feel a 'bite' of pain if one is hindered from doing so by an early death (XVII. 32–6). More on these topics below.

Epicurus and most of his followers have surprisingly little to say about fears focused on the process of dying or on the moment at which death occurs. From their point of view, it might seem rational to fear death in that sense, since it can involve severe and relatively prolonged pain. However, the story of Epicurus' death (D.L. X. 22; cf. also X. 15–16) is precisely intended to illustrate that it is possible to remain happy in the face of an excruciatingly painful terminal disease. After fourteen days of illness, on the day that Epicurus knew to be his last, he was able to counteract the pains of dying and fill his soul with joy by recollecting past discussions with his friends. It is less clear why Lucretius describes painful ways of dying in shocking and almost obsessive detail (e.g., *DRN* V. 988–93).[77] Since he also stresses the fragility of the union between the soul and the body (which indicates that dying must be a quick process), the message may be one of hope: Epicureanism can help deal with even the most painful manner of death, let alone with normal cases of dying in which the process is usually much easier on us. While these themes also emerge in *On Death*, Philodemus is the first known Epicurean to refute explicitly the suggestion that the process of dying as well as the actual time when a person expires must involve great physical pain. His arguments point to the weakened or pleasant sensations that often accompany dying, the mobility of the soul particles, the ease with which they leave the body, and the speed with which that separation becomes complete. His general attitude

[75] Warren (2004: 147) remarks that Philodemus reverses the comparison drawn in *SV* 17.

[76] On this point, see Armstrong 2004: 35–8; Warren 2004: 148–50; and my discussion below, pp. 269–77.

[77] Cf. Segal 1990: *passim*.

may be compared with that of Lucretius. Although dying can be painful or lingering, it need not be so, and it could even be pleasant. Even in the worst-case scenario, Epicureanism promises that our suffering must end soon and unconsciousness must follow.

Enough has been said, I hope, to establish that Philodemus addresses different kinds of fears of death, using both the standard Epicurean arguments and many new ones. His consolations are varied and original, and are adapted to each specific type of case. In fact, he usually proposes more than one medicine for each type of disease, perhaps to allow for theoretical as well as idiosyncratic differences between patients. If one line of argument does not work, another might. As mentioned in earlier chapters, one general feature of his treatment is the concession that in certain circumstances it is natural to feel 'bites' of pain at the thought of death. There are many reasons why Philodemus may have introduced 'bites' in *On Death*: for instance, out of sensitivity to the human condition or because of his wish to appeal to a broad audience. In any case, he and his teachers could defend the legitimacy of these experiences by appealing to the writings of Epicurus. Recall Epicurus' saying that the wise man will be more susceptible to emotion than other people (D.L. X. 117) and, specifically, that he will feel sorrow (D.L. X. 119). One could suppose, then, that the sorrow in question is caused by the thought of death, and that Epicurus perceives it as a natural, unperverted reaction compatible with the wise man's happiness.[78] The analysis of specific cases in which people commonly feel great grief at the prospect of death will show that, like the 'bites' of anger (*orgē*), the 'bites' of distress about death are genuine emotions based on true beliefs and perfectly appropriate in respect of the situation at hand.[79] They are natural, probably in senses similar to those in which *orgē* is natural.[80] In fact, Philodemus seems to think that experiencing sometimes natural 'bites'

[78] Armstrong (2004: 54 n. 69) attributes this view to Epicurus partly on the basis of a parallel with Epicurus' well-known contention that the wise man is happy even on the rack. Just as the sage can cry and groan on the rack and yet be happy, so he can grieve and shed tears for whatever damage death may cause to the community of friends, but nonetheless have complete happiness. In both cases, the pain is natural and right. And its expression is beneficial, since it gives relief.

[79] Cf. also pp. 46–51.

[80] i.e., they are beneficial to the extent that they constitute a protective mechanism or that their expression gives relief. They involve an accurate understanding of the nature of things, i.e., the grief-provoking situation of someone's death. They constitute unperverted, unmediated reactions to what has happened or is bound to happen. And they are unavoidable at least at the beginning, although eventually they can be influenced and even eradicated by reasoning. Cf. pp. 224–5 and n. 93 of Chapter 9.

of distress at the prospect of death is part of functioning properly as a human being.[81]

As in the case of anger, so in the case of sorrow about death, 'bites' are contrasted with 'empty' versions of the emotion. The latter consist in grieving excessively for the wrong reasons and on the basis of the wrong values. Thus, 'bites' caused by early death (*De mort.* XX. 1–3), the frustration of the natural desire to study philosophy and be wise (XIV. 2–10), the damage that our loved ones will suffer from our loss (XXV. 2–10), the prospect of dying among foreigners (XXV. 37–XXVI. 6), and that of dying unjustly at the hands of a corrupt jury or a tyrant (XXXIII. 37–XXXV. 34) are understandable and forgivable forms of pain (cf. XX. 1–3). On the other hand, true despair is not justified in these cases. Also, grief at the thought that one's death will give an easy triumph to one's enemies is 'unforgivable folly' (XX. 4–5), and so is pain about dying childless (XXII. 9 ff.), about the condition or disposition of one's corpse (XXI. 35–XXII. 4), etc.[82] In *On Death*, Philodemus uses sharp language against those who suffer from empty fears and grief, whereas he offers sympathy and gentle consolation to people affected by natural sorrow. In the peroration of [*On Choices and Avoidances*] there is no mention of 'bites' at all.[83]

However, the presence of 'bites' in the doctrine cannot neutralize the charge sometimes levelled against the Epicureans: that, in theory if not in practice, their attitude towards death precludes living a recognizably human life. In particular, their critics accuse them of being inconsistent, because while on the one hand, they proclaim that death is nothing to us, on the other hand, they write wills probably intended to secure certain post-mortem results (cf. Cicero, *De fin.* II. 101).[84] Also, it might seem

[81] Cf. Armstrong 2004. Presumably, different sages are more or less prone to natural 'bites' of sorrow, just as they are more or less prone to feeling the 'bite' of natural anger. But it would seem that one cannot be recognizably human if one never feels any such 'bites' at all. On the other hand, it is also part of being a rational human being to be able eventually to attenuate or even eliminate the 'bite' with the help of Epicurean rhetoric and argument.

[82] It is not the case that for every scenario of death which could cause excessive grief, there is also an approved reaction in the form of a 'bite'. In fact, there are some commonly feared cases of death which are never capable of causing a 'bite' to the sage. This is as it should be, for if the sage felt 'bites' at all times about everything that greatly distresses the fool, his serenity would be shattered.

[83] Perhaps it is significant that [*On Choices and Avoidances*] appears to be a sectarian treatise intended for a different audience from *On Death*. Armstrong (2004: 27) makes much of the stylistic differences between these two works.

[84] Warren 2004: 162–99 discusses this issue in great detail. Important objections to Warren's argument are raised by Armstrong 2006.

that by insisting that death and even premature death are not evils, the Epicureans have few resources left to explain why life is a good, and why someone who has attained a complete life should wish to continue living.[85]

It seems beyond reasonable doubt that Epicurus wrote a will and made an effort to ensure its preservation (cf. D.L. X. 16; Cicero, *De fin.* II. 96–101). The provisions of the will concerning Epicurus' friends, the celebration of his birthday, etc., would seem to imply that certain post-mortem events have value for the subject, even though he will not exist or perceive anything when these events take place. The same holds for other acts of benevolence as well, when they are motivated by an Epicurean's desire to affect the course of things after his death.[86] In particular, one could press the question why it matters to an Epicurean that his friends will be well provided for after his death and that they will retain a good memory of him, since what happens after death is nothing to us. Two alternative courses of explanation have been considered in the literature,[87] the one focusing on the pleasure that one feels at the thought of certain post-mortem events independently of the thought that these events will come about in the future, the other seeking some altruistic motive on account of which an Epicurean tries to promote the benefit of others (friends, descendants, fellow citizens, future generations, etc.), while he knows that he himself has no post-mortem interests invested in their pleasure. If disinterested concern for others could be made to fit into the Epicurean doctrine,[88] the second option would be clearly preferable. For it would solve the problem of the alleged incompatibility between (on the one side) an Epicurean's knowledge that he won't be there to experience anything after he is dead and (on the other side) his desire to provide for others after his death by

[85] Again, see Warren 2004: 199–212, which also mentions the relevant literature, and Armstrong 2006, which attacks Warren's position on good grounds. Important contributions to the topic include Silverstein 1980; Luper-Foy 1987; McMahan 1988; and Rosenbaum 1989.

[86] Recall, e.g., that Diogenes of Oenoanda began the erection of his monumental inscription in the full knowledge that he was close to his death. The explanation that he gives for his concern for future generations is found in fr. 3, IV. 13–V. 8, Smith.

[87] Warren (2004: 173–91) outlines and discusses both of them, and also gives the relevant references of secondary literature.

[88] On this point, see pp. 27–31; the notes contain bibliographical references relevant to the topic under discussion. Borrowing the terminology of Partridge 1981, Warren (2004: 180 ff.) suggests that an Epicurean has 'the capacity for moral abstraction': i.e., the ability to contemplate events which transcend his own temporal and physical limits and will not be experienced by himself, but which, nevertheless, matter to him. In Warren's view, Diogenes' order of an inscription which would not be to his own advantage but to the advantage of a group presupposes that capacity.

writing a will or in some other way. Your friendship and love for others makes you desire and try to do good things for them, even though when they materialize, you will not exist or feel anything at all.

Whether or not Epicurus would have chosen it, that line of argument seems appropriate for Philodemus. I maintained earlier[89] that, of the three theories of friendship outlined by Torquatus (Cicero, *De fin.* I. 65–70), Philodemus probably holds the second, according to which pleasure is the original motivation for forming attachments, but intimacy subsequently leads to disinterested friendship and love (*De fin.* I. 69). If this hypothesis is correct, there seems to be room in his doctrine for 'moral abstraction' and genuine concern for others.[90] Philodemus recommends that one should provide for one's friends both when one is alive and after one's death, and, moreover, he seems to approve of the writing of wills. For instance, he suggests that the claims of friendship determine the extent to which the philosophically inclined property manager saves with a view to the future.[91] Presumably, one way in which the Epicurean manager transmits his savings to his friends after his death is by leaving a will. Moreover, Philodemus concedes that any intelligent, sensitive person naturally feels 'bites' of pain at the thought that his relatives and friends will suffer material hardships as a result of his death (*De mort.* XXV. 2–10). Hence it seems natural to infer that a person in that condition will do what he can to procure life's necessities for his loved ones after he is dead,[92] and an obvious way to do so is by writing a will.

[89] Cf. pp. 29–31.

[90] The objection that generosity to others after one's death may have no place in a system which denies the possibility of post-mortem benefit and harm to the agent (cf. Warren 2004: 189) does not seem to me decisive. For Philodemus' analyses of the relationships of benefit and gratitude suggest that he does not view them on a *do-ut-des* basis. A good person benefits his friends out of good will, not because he expects to receive gratitude in return. Of course, assuming that his friends are also good people, he will receive their gratitude and will be pleased to do so. But their gratitude is not the reason why he benefits them, but the natural consequence of his benefaction. His good disposition prompts him to benefit his friends through provisions in his will, although when that benefaction occurs, there will be no possibility of reciprocation.

[91] 'If one has friends, one must save more in order that they may have [means of maintaining themselves] even after one's death, and one must regard them as one's children. On the other hand, if one does not have friends, [one must relax] not only the practice of saving money, but also the more parsimonious administration of property' (*De oec.* XXVII. 5–12).

[92] Warren (2004: 195) takes 'bites' to provide an unsatisfactory explanation of why Epicureans write wills, because the concept of 'bites' is not endorsed by every Epicurean faction, and also because it is not clear to Warren why the sage would indulge in such feelings and write a will. Since my own concern is Philodemus alone, and 'bites' are present in his doctrine, it is irrelevant whether his rivals also use that concept. Also, there is no evidence that 'bites' are intended to supply a sufficient explanation of the

Wills are also relevant to Philodemus' argument against the fear of dying childless, and in particular the fear that one's property will pass to people outside one's direct lineage (*De mort.* XXIII. 33–XXIV. 17, XXIV. 31–8). Philodemus addresses that fear, on the one hand, by emphasizing that we cannot totally control such matters and, on the other hand, by suggesting that we leave (presumably in our will) our property to 'noble friends'. Wills and every other measure about the future are ineffective against chance. Provided that a person understands that, he will compose his will in the proper spirit.[93] In it he expresses natural but not necessary post-mortem desires, and has only reasonable expectations that they may be fulfilled, benefiting his excellent friends after his death. Besides, wills reappear in the peroration of *On Death* (XXXIX. 9–15), when Philodemus contrasts the attitude of fools to that of people who have fully assimilated the truth about death. On my interpretation of the relevant passage,[94] there is something positive implied about wills. Fools caught unprepared by death are totally paralysed to the point of being unable even to compose a will (cf. XXXIX. 6–15). But presumably that would have been the right thing to do when death became imminent, if not long before. One might wonder whether the attitude of Philodemus and, generally, of the Epicureans towards will-writing may not indicate some concern after all for the Narrative Model of a complete life.[95] Writing a will for the right reasons and in the right spirit makes an appropriate end to one's life story. Circumstances permitting, one ties up the loose ends, resolves the plot, and signs the script as one's own.

Let us now turn to the second criticism of the Epicurean position, that since duration is more or less irrelevant to a life's completeness, and since death detracts nothing from a life's value, it is hard to see why the sage would judge it worthwhile to continue living. The Epicureans do not face this challenge explicitly, because in all probability they assume

writing of wills. The sage writes his will not because of 'an occasional concern' in which he indulges, but because of genuine affection for others.

[93] In short, Philodemus' argument could be this. If I am an Epicurean, I am writing a will because I feel pleasure at the thought of providing for my friends after my death, or because I wish to relieve my anxiety about what might happen to them after I die. At the same time, I recognize that my efforts may be thwarted by factors beyond my control. I am rational in trying to do what I can to secure the benefit of those whose well-being I value. But I would be irrational if I worried about not being able to achieve the impossible: viz., to guarantee the success of my efforts.

[94] Cf. my discussion of the peroration, pp. 302–11.

[95] Armstrong (2006) briefly entertains that possibility.

that there is no need to do so. There is disagreement as to how to understand the relevant evidence. However, the following outline seems plausible.[96] According to both Epicurus and Lucretius, death implies not only the absence of pain but also the absence of pleasure. Although it is not an evil, it is not a good either. Therefore, death is not intrinsically choiceworthy, although there are circumstances in which on balance it is better to die than to live. On the other hand, once a person has become free of fears and illusions, especially concerning the gods and death, he discovers supreme pleasure in living and tastes the love of life (cf. Lucretius, *DRN* V. 177–80). Whenever death comes, it does not affect the happiness that has already been attained.[97] Until then, however, the liberated person wishes to continue to live, not because of mere inertia,[98] but because the pleasure of living constitutes a very strong motivation for remaining alive. Philodemus makes decisive contributions to that topic. He explains why the removal of the fear of death does not undermine the desire to live, and he identifies important features of the sage's love of life.

In addition to conceding in his treatment of premature death that it is natural and proper to wish to live as long as possible (XIII. 38–XIV. 10),[99] Philodemus maintains that many concerns and activities of the sage derive, precisely, from his love of life and his desire to continue living as long as circumstances permit. While he is not at all afraid of death, nonetheless, he tries to avoid a careless end (*De elect.* XXII. 4–5). When he is ill, he spares no effort that could lead to an improvement in his condition (XXIII. 3–13). He takes the greatest care of his health (XXIII. 7–9), with the result that he often has a long life (cf. *πολυχρόνιον ζωήν*: XXII. 9–10; XXIII. 2). Even when he is subject to severe physical pain, he is not inclined to commit suicide except perhaps in extreme circumstances. For it seems that, for Philodemus, as for Epicurus, well-thinking people are able to counteract most pains and find pleasure in conditions unendurable to others.[100] Moreover, 'since he (sc. the sage) does not cut short the long

[96] I am indebted to David Armstrong and Michael Wigodsky for their thoughts on this point.

[97] Hence duration does not play any important role, and death, including premature death, is not an evil.

[98] *Pace* Warren (2004: 210), who suggests that the Epicureans appear to offer as a reason for continuing to live merely the fact that there is no reason to curtail a pleasant life.

[99] Cf. below, pp. 275–6.

[100] Compare also Lucretius, *DRN* III. 79–82. According to Philodemus, suicide is often an irrational course of action prompted by the fear of death (cf. *De elect.* XVI. 18 ff.) as well as by other passions:

extent of his life, he always begins new activities and friendly attachments' (XXII. 8–11) which give him ever more reasons to continue living.

Recall that the sage makes future-directed commitments keeping the reality of death always in mind. Therefore one might object that the sage can be only superficially involved with them, since he is prepared to give them up at any time and without any regret.[101] However, there is evidence that Philodemus advocates not that we should not care very much about future-directed activities and attachments, but that we should invest in them in the right way. He says emphatically that a person with true understanding will feel the 'bite' of pain and shed tears uniquely and most of all other men (*μόνον ἢ μάλιστα*: *De mort.* XXV. 10).[102] Not only is such a person recognizably human, but in fact he has deeper attachments than most of us. Is Philodemus' position paradoxical? Perhaps not. His insight seems to be that as the sage's understanding of death enhances his appreciation of life so it adds depth and value to his relationships and activities. Contrary to those who might claim that the Stoic sage is better off because he is imperturbable, Philodemus suggests that emotional sensitivity is essential to our humanity and to the Epicurean ideal of the good life.

II

With this theoretical background in mind, I shall now take a closer look at the arguments of *On Death*. Following the order of the fragment, I shall try to reconstruct them, provide short commentaries to the main issues, and assess the value of Philodemus' consolations and refutations. I have already indicated that there are many original and important elements in his approach. Philosophically, its strongest features include the application of the traditional Epicurean arguments (i.e., the loss of perception, the destruction of personal identity, and the Symmetry Argument) to specific scenarios of death, which are commonly considered exceptionally fearful; the explicit recognition and treatment of the fear of dying; the extensive

e.g., anger (*De ir.* XVI. 25–34; cf. also XXVI. 25–34). On the other hand, Philodemus suggests that the sage may choose under certain circumstances to commit suicide: see p. 291 and n. 161 below.

[101] Warren (2004: 211–12) raises this issue.

[102] Armstrong (2006) rightly emphasizes this point.

discussion of the fear of premature death; and the ways in which Philodemus addresses the fear of mortality in the peroration of the treatise.

1. As mentioned, Philodemus is the first Epicurean to have taken seriously fears concerning the last stages of the dying process and to have addressed them by means of arguments. In fact, the opening columns (I–IX) of the fragment of *On Death* deal precisely with such fears. Typically, they are based on the conviction that dying always involves bodily pain. In consequence, the debate between Philodemus and his rivals focuses to a large extent on that belief: Philodemus denies its truth, whereas his opponents (whoever they may be) maintain it. Some parts of the text are very corrupt, and therefore leave it uncertain whose views these are. Provisionally, however, the dialectic of the passage seems to develop as follows.

At the outset, Philodemus rehearses one of Epicurus' main consolations (cf. [πα]ραμύθιον: *De mort.* I. 2–3) concerning the fear of being dead.[103] Death is nothing to us, since it is accompanied by loss of perception (cf. μετ' ἀναισθησ[ίας]: I. 9). Being unable to have good things when alive is not at all the same thing as not enjoying them when dead (cf. I. 11–12). The reason is that we feel the deprivation in the first case but not in the second (cf. II. 3 ff.).[104] Indeed, the dead are not conscious of being deprived of any goods (cf. I. 8–9). Philodemus emphasizes further the total absence of consciousness in death, as well as the immunity of the dead to any kind of harm. While a healthy person may fall ill, and a rich one may fall into poverty, no such troubles can affect the dead, since they lack perception (cf. II. 7 ff.).[105] Also, fools cry at the thought that they will be deprived of goods when they are dead, because they fallaciously project such experiences to the time when their bodies will be dissolved (III. 30–1). They imagine that they will *miss* things when they are dead, on the grounds of what deprivation feels like when one is alive.

To allay such fears, Philodemus uses an argument that, as we shall see, he will develop further in connection with the fear of dying prematurely. Death does not deprive us of anything, not only because we cannot desire or miss anything after we die, but also because usually we have enjoyed

[103] The perfect infinitive τεθνάναι (*De mort.* I. 6) indicates that this is the kind of fear in question.

[104] The text of cols. I and II is doubtful, and much is restored *exempli gratia* by all editors.

[105] This seems to be the main point of col. II, which is very badly damaged.

all the pleasure there is while still alive. 'Do let us pour libations to Zeus Soter [for the reasons already stated, namely] for how (little) time (ὁπόσος χρόνος)[106] a person naturally needs in order to secure pleasure, once one understands its limits' (III. 32–6). These are located in the body and are attained, if not immediately, in a very small time. 'The flesh very quickly (εὐθύς)[107] achieves the infinite magnitude of pleasure, [even if] infinite time has produced it' (III. 37–9). Since we have the capacity to reach quickly the supreme good during our lifetime, and since it cannot become more or less once we have reached it, it follows that death cannot deprive us of anything valuable, no matter when it happens. As I suggested, the basic idea underlying this argument is that if we thoroughly understand the nature and limits of pleasure, we ensure the satisfaction of our natural desires and a complete life. The temporal duration of our life is relatively (or totally) unimportant to the accomplishment of these goals.

However, there is still room for fears concerning the stages immediately preceding one's death. For while, on the Epicurean view, the condition of being dead precludes the presence of sensation, certain unnamed opponents object that the process of dying does not. 'It is possible for one [as one is expiring ([ἐκπνέον]τι) to have some perception (ἀν[τίληψιν])], just as it is also possible for films of atoms (εἴδωλ') to be taken in through the same [pores] as he explains they do' (IV. 2–5). According to these adversaries, then, expiring involves sensation for physiological reasons: films of atoms are coming in through the pores of the body at the same time as the atoms of the soul are getting out through them. Evidence for this thesis is sought in cases of people who have died feeling pleasure during sexual intercourse (V. 7–11) and others who have expired in great pain—for instance, hanging themselves or deliberately starving themselves (V. 10–13). Since some sensation is probably present during the process of dying, and since that sensation can be terribly painful, it would seem rational to fear dying.

It is difficult to reconstruct Philodemus' refutation of this challenge because of the poor condition of the text. So far as I can tell, it consists of several dialectical moves, some of which are more successful than others. First, he appeals to 'what has been previously said about the present topic' (IV. 6–7), in order to reject the suggestion that the pores through which

[106] Cf. p. 256 n. 72. [107] Cf. p. 256 n. 73.

the soul atoms leave the body also serve, simultaneously, as passages through which simulacra affect the sense-organs of the dying man. However, we do not know just what Philodemus has previously said, or how he uses it to refute his opponents' claim. Perhaps he had shown that, in fact, expiring and perceiving cannot take place through the same pores at the same time, but this is only a guess. Furthermore, he suggests that in the few moments of transition from life to death consciousness is drastically diminished or almost extinct. For instance, some people fade away painlessly under the influence of drugs, while others die in their sleep (V. 1–4). One might retort that those who die hanging or starving themselves, far from having diminished consciousness, are in real agony. Philodemus deals with these counterexamples in an interesting way. The pain experienced in such cases is not related to the natural process of dying, but 'is the effect of a diseased imagination' (V. 13–14), which presumably involves empty beliefs. How is this supposed to help us remove the fear of dying? Probably, by reminding us of the fact that the truly dreadful pain comes from a source which can be neutralized; for it is up to us to get rid of our empty beliefs. In the close of this phase of the debate, Philodemus and his rivals appear to occupy equally strong positions. Philodemus has made a plausible case for the thesis that the stages immediately preceding death *usually* do not involve intense suffering. But he has not attempted to demonstrate that such suffering cannot occur. Therefore, his opponents are still in a position to hold their ground: that is, to insist that it is rational to fear death in that sense.

In fact, assuming that the restoration of the text is correct, they press the issue much further. They concede the Epicurean premisses that the soul and the body are closely interdependent and interconnected, and they infer on the strength of these premisses that the process of dying, and in particular the actual separation between the soul and the body, must be very painful in every case. '[All] deaths [are accompanied by] extreme pain since, as they (sc. some group of opponents) claim, [it is impossible that] the closest of all natural unions can be dissolved without the greatest of all anguish' (VIII. 1–5). Again, Philodemus' reply is complex and develops in successive steps.

We shall of course acknowledge the sympathy (cf. συμπάθειαν) of the soul with the body even if it is, for the most part, the cause of [illness] [often] accompanied by pain, since it either abnormally [condenses] or swells the [limbs] of living things. Nonetheless, we shall not [declare it] impossible that that sympathy should somehow be dissolved [for the reason that it undergoes] some alteration [different from that which was] the cause [of pain of some sort to the sick man]. For the soul, composed as it is of tiny and exceedingly mobile particles, and also not [imprisoned in our body parts which consist] neither of the smallest, nor of the smoothest and roundest atoms, makes us wonder why it (sc. the soul) does not just fly out through [the many, indeed ten thousand,] pores that are in the body (ready for that purpose). But even if we concede that (the sympathy of the soul with the body) is a cause [of pain], for just what reason do we [greatly] fear the separation [of such elements from each other, since we shall be unconscious immediately after its completion?]

(VIII. 6–24)

As I understand it, Philodemus' chief move in this passage consists in detaching the pain that often accompanies (terminal) illness from the actual cause of the ill person's death. On the one hand, he acknowledges the symbiotic relationship between the soul and the body as well as the fact that pain often occurs as a result of that relationship. On the other hand, he denies that the dissolution of that union is necessarily painful, and that (in cases in which death finally happens) the cause of the pain preceding it and the cause of death itself need to be the same. Death occurs for a variety of reasons, and pain may be only one of them (if it is a cause of death at all). Just what does Philodemus have to gain by making this suggestion? Mainly, I think, he wants to point out that the relationship between pain and death is contingent, but there is no necessary connection between them. Trying to avoid the former does not mean that we should fear the latter, and even in cases in which death is painful, we should try to keep these two things separate in our mind. We should keep telling ourselves that although the pain that we are feeling is an evil, our death is not. Epicurean philosophy supplies us with the resources for dealing with this kind of condition, as the example of Epicurus has shown.

An alternative dialectical manoeuvre is less accommodating to Philodemus' opponents. In fact, it seems likely that death should be painless or even pleasurable,[108] because of the fineness and mobility of the soul atoms as well as the facility with which they can leave the body through its many passages (cf. VIII. 30–7). This argument has plausibility mainly for those who endorse atomism, but the next one has a broader appeal.

[108] If the conjecture [ἐνίοτε] (VIII. 35) is correct, the argument establishes that dying comes with pleasure sometimes, but not always or necessarily.

In fact, after certain instances of drunkenness and banquets, [the great change (sc. the transition from life to death) happens to people in their old age as painlessly as our growth] from children to [maturity] and our entire gradual decline from maturity to old age. And sometimes young men suffer the great change through irregular [motions] as if they sink into a sleep produced by [opium]. But, in fact, even the occurrence of violent separations of soul from body, as well as the very great alteration that follows for that reason (sc. the violent separation), [will attenuate the faculty of perception].

(IX. 1–12)

Here Philodemus modifies the *anaisthēsia* thesis in order for it to apply to both the state of death itself and several conditions immediately preceding it. Although transitions from life to death do not happen in total unconsciousness, it is not unusual for them to occur while one's sensory capacities are greatly diminished. And this holds not only for obvious cases—e.g., older persons, whose perceptual faculties are weakened because of too much wine or food—but also for cases of early or violent death. For there too the capacity to perceive and feel weakens considerably, precisely because of the extreme and abrupt change in one's constitution. It follows that we should not fear dying or, in particular, the moment when death actually occurs, since we may feel very little at that time.

To conclude, Philodemus' argumentation is not decisive, but, nevertheless, has a cumulative effect. It leads one to think about dying in a different light, not as a difficult and painful process but, most of the time, as a natural and smooth transition from being alive to being dead. In the worst-case scenario, when dying involves a lot of pain, one may seek comfort in the hope that one will soon become unconscious, certainly after or even before death occurs. On the other hand, there are negative aspects of the treatment. Philodemus relies too much on premisses drawn from Epicurean atomism, and therefore some of his arguments have no impact for those who do not espouse it.

2. Premature death is another source of fear and emotional distress. Philodemus gives us the fullest treatment of the subject found in Epicurean authors, and also one which explicitly problematizes the issue of whether the duration of one's life has any moral significance at all. Certain aspects of his account are mainly of historical interest (e.g., Philodemus' interpretation and refutation of the views of Plato and his followers). Others, however,

profoundly challenge the ways in which people commonly think about what constitutes a complete and perfect life, what impact the length of one's life has on one's happiness, and how important it is to accomplish one's plans before dying. Of particular interest are Philodemus' concessions that it is natural to feel a 'bite' of pain when confronted with premature death, and that, after all, we have some good reasons to prefer a longer to a shorter life.

According to Philodemus, the main reason why most people perceive premature death as an evil lies in their mistaken opinions about what constitutes a happy life, and especially the prevailing maximalist belief that the more time one has to enjoy more goods, the better. Also, the maximalists' preference for duration is related to their desire to live a complete life. They typically assume that the completeness of someone's life in the end depends on duration. A longer life enables us, they think, to enjoy a greater number of pleasures, satisfy our desires, and achieve something good (or the good), whereas the early curtailment of our life often entails the opposite. 'Some regard untimely death with aversion [as an evil], hoping that they will acquire the possession of many goods in a longer [lifetime], goods which without genuine wisdom cannot [be got] even in a dream. For this same reason youth [is despised] by most men, since they consider a very long life to be an accumulation of [goods],[109] in a way by their own argument.[110] For measuring [the goods] by time they obviously will not achieve anything great' (XII. 1–13). Philodemus calls this kind of reasoning empty (cf. κενῶς: XII. 14), and suggests that the main mistake lies in measuring goods by time and thinking incorrectly about both the present and the future (cf. XII. 11–15).[111] On one possible reconstruction of his argument,[112] those who agree that a longer life is a more pleasant life, and that its pleasantness consists in a greater number of accumulated pleasures, look always to the future in order to pursue new goods and achieve the greatest pleasure. But their efforts are self-defeating. They are unable ever to achieve and enjoy the greatest pleasure, precisely because they misunderstand what it is. They constantly defer it to the future, whereas it is quickly acquired and then

[109] XII. 9 ἀγαθῶν Warren. Kuiper, followed by Armstrong, supplements σοφίας.

[110] Cf. Warren's translation of XII. 10–11.

[111] XII. 13–15 are heavily supplemented lines, and any interpretation of them must be tentative.

[112] See Warren 2004: 145 ff.

available in the present. Their desires are empty and never-ending, for their objects cannot be attained. This holds for all maximalist desires, crude or sophisticated. An example of the second kind is the irrational desire to live longer in order to acquire more and more factual knowledge (XIV. 10–14).[113]

Compare now the Epicurean view, according to which philosophy ensures the achievement of the highest good, pleasure or the absence of pain (ἀπονία), especially in so far as it determines the limits of pleasure and supplies materials for rejecting maximalism. As mentioned, towards the beginning of the fragment of *On Death* Philodemus reformulates the theses first advanced by Epicurus, that provided one recognizes pleasure's limits, one needs very little time to achieve pleasure (III. 32–6), and also that the pleasure quickly achieved in a very short time is equal to the pleasure provided by infinite time (III. 37–9).[114] The conclusion that death cannot deprive us of anything valuable also applies to premature death. Philosophical wisdom entails that we are able to assess correctly the limits of pleasure and understand why the temporal duration of a life should not be the criterion of its completeness and happiness. Ἀπονία can be attained very quickly, once reached it cannot be increased, and from that point onwards death cannot affect the completeness of our life no matter how early it comes. The possessor of such wisdom enjoys the highest pleasure so long as he lives, finding completeness at every moment and thinking about the future in the right way: it offers the chance of prolonging one's happiness to the extent that will be permitted, but does not hold the promise of fulfilment as yet unattained.

Philodemus illustrates the contrast between maximalists and right-thinking persons by drawing contrasting portraits of a foolish old man whose life will be incomplete and his end premature no matter when he dies, and a wise youth, who could soon die content. Pythocles, a talented young Epicurean prodigiously praised by Epicurus (Plutarch, *Adv. Col.* 1124C), represents the kind of person who needed little time to achieve the

[113] Cf. p. 273 n. 117 below.

[114] Cf. above, pp. 256–7. As mentioned, there is disagreement about how strong Philodemus' claim is. On one interpretation, it is not very different from Epicurus' contention that finite and infinite time contain equal amounts of pleasure. On another (cf. Warren 2004: 144 ff.), Philodemus advances the much stronger position that the flesh can *immediately* receive the same amount of pleasure as is offered by infinite time. My own approach favours the weaker version of the argument.

highest good and, were he to die early, would not lose anything through his death.

[The young man who cannot even remember how many good things] he experienced because he lived [according to philosophical wisdom] is not pitiable, but rather the old man who has not yet found any thing that is naturally good, and yet [has convinced himself that in the future] all his wishes will be fulfilled. For how is it possible to feel pity for a young man [when one considers] how much can be [inferred from] what Pythocles has achieved by doing what Metrodorus recommends? Although he was not yet eighteen, he did not live [a fool's] life and had no concerns about losing all his beauty.[115] But [since it is possible] to both achieve and enjoy the greatest [of goods] in a certain period of time, as I have shown, will any young man in his senses [desire] to live any longer and even endless time, let alone aim at the old man's (length of) life? While still a youth he will acquire plenty of (good things), so as to depart glowing with joy and even be said to have lived more of a life than those who did not enjoy [however many years they have lived].

(XII. 26–XIII. 13)

Here Philodemus offers a powerful counterexample to the objection that a longer life has more chances to attain satisfaction and completeness than a life curtailed by death at an early age. In fact, any right-thinking young person can achieve the highest good even before the age of 18, just like Pythocles, and can be considered on that account to have lived a complete and most pleasant life. If death were to come then, it would do no harm at all. The youth would not wish for extra time hoping to fulfil his desires, for he would have fulfilled them already. He would meet his death joyfully (cf. *γεγανωμένος*: XIII. 10–11), not in the sense that he longs for it, but in the sense that death finds him in a joyful condition, free of pain and serene (cf. XIV. 6–9). On the other hand, the foolish old man has failed to achieve in his long life the good that the young man has grasped and enjoyed. Blind to the truth of Epicurean philosophy and his own limitations, he deludes himself into thinking that, if he lives a little bit more, he will get what he desires and be happy. For such a person death would be premature at any time, for it would put an end to a life that has not yet achieved completeness. In a sarcastic afterthought, Philodemus adds that it might be better for men of that sort to die earlier rather than later.

[115] For XII. 30–XIII. 3 I primarily use the text proposed by Sedley (1976*b*: 44), and I have consulted the translations by Armstrong and Warren (2004: 146).

For since they are bound to be unhappy anyway, a shorter period of misery should be preferable for them to a more prolonged one (XIII. 13–17; cf. also XIX. 33–8).[116]

So far, the role of duration remains undetermined. However, several passages suggest that Pythocles' likes need time both to attain ἀπονία and to enjoy it after they have achieved it. In the first place, according to Philodemus, the one good reason for trying to live longer is the assimilation of Epicurean philosophy. Since it is necessary (and even sufficient) to master Epicureanism in order to satisfy our natural desires and become free of all pain, and since temporal duration is relevant to that endeavour, we have adequate grounds for wishing to live more time. On the other hand, we might call the death of young persons who have not achieved that goal premature, and we might even regret it (cf. XIII. 36–XIV. 2).

It is [reasonable] to endeavour [for this cause] to live as long as possible and to think that some people who die young are for this reason miserable. For it is proper for any intelligent human being to wish to live for a certain additional period of time in order to fulfil his innate and natural desires and acquire an entire way of life as appropriate for himself as possible, so as to be filled with good things and cast out every disturbance caused by his desires, receiving tranquillity. But (to wish to live longer) in order to [amass factual knowledge] ([ἱστορ]ίας: XIV.11),[117] really how many [extra years will one have to live], as though it were possible anyway to [hold] the limitless [universe] in the storehouse of [one's mind]?

(XIII. 36–XIV. 14)

In the second place, Philodemus suggests that time plays a part *after* one has achieved the supreme good. He mentions two conditions both of which should be fulfilled to secure perfect happiness: a person should become wise, and he should spend some additional time in that state before he can truly be said to have reached absolute fulfilment. From this perspective too, then, duration appears ethically relevant, although it is not yet clear to what extent. 'As things are, the greatest good has been grasped by him (sc. the sage) after he has become wise and has lived a certain additional time (ποσ[ὸ]ν χρόνο[ν]: XIX. 1–2). Once his journey has achieved balance and consistency, it would be perfectly appropriate for him to proceed on it

[116] Cf. the discussion of *De mort.* XII. 26–XIII. 15 in Warren 2004: 147–8.

[117] Warren (2004: 149 n. 85) plausibly suggests that Philodemus here opposes a kind of knowledge that consists in the accumulation of facts to the wisdom of Epicurean philosophy.

forever, if that were possible. But if the removal of his happiness comes to pass, it is not of the happiness that has been, but rather a prevention of its further presence. However, neither will be any perception of the fact that it is [no longer] there' (XIX. 1–11).[118] Philodemus makes another important move in the same direction. '[Regarding the person] to whom being snatched away is [fearsome], because it would be possible for him to make progress in philosophy if he remained alive, it is on the one hand natural for such a person to feel pain' (XVIII. 32–6). According to this passage, then, it is acceptable to feel some pain on account of duration, in particular on account of the short length of one's life. However, this natural kind of pain is only a 'bite' or 'pang' (cf. [ν]ύττεσ[θ]α[ι]: XVII. 35). Philodemus will clarify later why that kind of pain is forgivable, and how it differs from irrational grief. The main point is that, unlike the grief and despair caused by empty beliefs about death and dying, the corresponding 'bites' derive from legitimate causes. In the case of untimely death, the 'bite' in question is caused by the true belief that death will interrupt one's progress in Epicureanism and one's effort to achieve the best possible life.

But even if the prospect of dying too early to perfect one's Epicurean life causes 'bites' of pain, nonetheless, that kind of pain admits of consolation.[119] With warmth and sympathy, Philodemus offers the following comforting thoughts to those who suffer. The person who made considerable progress in philosophy, but had still some way to go when death ended it all, achieved much greater goods than common men, and is therefore admirable on that account (XVII. 38–9). He is a benefactor and can be called a teacher of an infinite number of people, to the extent that he lived his life setting an example for others to imitate (XVII. 36–40). In fact, however, it is improbable that someone with a philosophical disposition would die too early to attain an absolutely complete life (XVIII. 1–9). The argument seems to be that, since one can achieve very quickly the exact same amount of pleasure as is contained in an infinite time (cf. III. 37–9), and since souls susceptible to philosophy are particularly apt to secure valuable goods both quickly and firmly (XVIII. 1–5),[120] people with such souls, who have also become familiar with philosophical reasoning, are very likely 'to grasp so

[118] The passage is cited and translated by Warren (2004: 150). My interpretation owes much to both Warren and Armstrong.

[119] Cf. Armstrong 2004.

[120] Cf. the conjectures ϵ[ὐθέ]ως (XVIII. 3) and ἠ[ρ]ματίσθαι (XVIII. 4–5).

wonderful a good as to depart full of joy' (XVIII. 7–9; cf. XVIII. 5 ff.). Of course, it is much better (cf. *πο[λὺ] κρεῖττο[ν]*: XVIII. 9) for a young person to complete his progress in philosophy and thus to reach 'the most powerful happiness [there can be]' (XVIII. 11–12). In other words, there is a strong preference for a certain duration, for the sake of both attaining the supreme good and enjoying it for a while. However, we should also be deeply grateful if we achieve the condition which approximates, but is not identical with, 'the most powerful happiness' (XVIII. 12–14). For that too preserves its value regardless of time,[121] and cannot be taken away by premature death.

Compare the empty consolations related to the false view that death, and in particular premature death, is something good or indifferent. Philodemus suggests that such beliefs were held by Plato's Socrates and his followers, while versions of them can also be traced to later Platonists, the Pythagoreans, and the Orphics. Only the body dies, while the soul is immortal (XIV. 37–XV. 1);[122] one should be concerned with nothing but dying (XVI. 1–4);[123] it is preferable to die as quickly as possible, because the separation of the soul from the body is better for the soul (XVI. 37–XVII. 3);[124] early death is undesirable only because it may occur before one has had the time to remove the evils of this life from his soul (XVII. 3–6) and thus appear clean before the judges of the underworld (cf. XVII. 8–9). The fragmentary text does not preserve Philodemus' entire refutation of these ideas. One of his replies seems to be that in fact a later rather than an earlier death profits those who have not yet made enough progress in philosophy, because it enables them to attain the highest pleasure in life (XV. 4–7).[125] Another reply is that to think constantly about death (in the wrong manner) and even to be delighted with dying is totally ridiculous (XVI. 7–10). In fact, it counteracts one's natural impulse, and is due to false opinions and empty words (XVI. 4–7). Here again Philodemus can be taken to rely on his own theses, that the natural tendency of human beings including the

[121] This seems to be the meaning of the lacunose lines XVIII. 14–16.

[122] XIV. 14 f. reads TONO.ΦAI/. According to Armstrong, this could be a specific reference to the *Phaedo*, namely [Πλά]τωνο[ς] Φαί[δων], or a general reference to Socrates or Plato's view.

[123] These lines are heavily supplemented, and therefore I cannot be sure that there is a specific reference to Plato's *Phaedo*, in which Socrates talks (cf. the conjecture [διαλεγόμενος] in XVI. 1) of nothing at all but dying (cf. Kuiper's edn. of XVI. 1–30).

[124] If the supplementation *τοῦ σο[φοῦ] λόγου* (XVI. 37) is correct, and Philodemus calls this 'a wise argument', he means it ironically.

[125] Here Philodemus implicitly reaffirms his position that duration plays a part in the achievement of a complete life.

sage is to love life and shrink from death, and that, always bearing in mind one's mortality, one should try to preserve one's health and prolong one's life as long as possible (cf. *De elect.* XXII. 4–5, 9–10; XXIII. 2–13).

Concerning the refutation of 'the wise argument', according to which we should wish for a later death for the reason that dying prematurely may impede the soul's purification in this life, Philodemus construes it in a dialectical manner. If we accept that the soul gets purified and that the judges of the underworld perform this function, it would seem better to die earlier rather than later, because then the soul would be cleansed faster (XVII. 3–9). On the other hand, if the soul does not receive purification for some reason, then it should not make any difference whether death comes later or earlier (XVII. 9–11). But even supposing that the soul does submit to purification after death, the time and also the manner of death seem irrelevant to that procedure, which takes place after death (XVII. 11–16).[126] On balance, Philodemus succeeds in casting doubt on the coherence of these views, as well as on their plausibility.

To conclude, Philodemus makes a powerful and arresting case against the fear that life may end too soon and, I think, undermines to some extent the force of the maximalist contention that one's life will become better if it lasts longer and accumulates more goods. He grounds his argument in basic elements of Epicurean hedonism: the definition of the highest pleasure in terms of the total absence of pain (*ἀπονία*) and the Epicurean conception of a complete life. However, pressed by the objections of rivals, he nuances the canonical position of his school and makes it more palatable. For he grants, first, that duration is of some importance to the attainment of perfect happiness and, second, that in certain circumstances it is natural and forgivable to feel a 'bite' of pain at the prospect of dying prematurely. On the other hand, he can be blamed for leaving unsolved certain tensions and unclarities peculiar to his approach.

For instance, he tells us that a youth like Pythocles has no reason at all to desire to live any longer, for he has both reached the supreme good and kept it for a while (cf. XII. 26–XIII. 13). He has truly lived (cf. *βεβιωκέναι*: XIII. 12) with enjoyment (*ἀπόλαυσις*), and has not merely got through life (cf. [*διέ*]*ζων*: XIII. 13), without any enjoyment

[126] Here the papyrus is very damaged. My interpretation is based on Kuiper's supplementation, which, however, may be revised in the future.

whatever (cf. ἀναπόλαυσ[τ]ον: XIII. 12–13). But what are the criteria for drawing the line between the perfect happiness of those like Pythocles and the happiness of students who are still making progress towards sane living when death occurs? Hence, one problem derives from the pressure to distinguish between different levels or degrees of completeness and happiness. Philodemus resists drawing such distinctions explicitly, and he also shies away from agreeing that premature death is an evil if it prevents one from completing one's philosophical progress. Yet he says that Epicureans who are making progress and whose lives are curtailed by an early death have a happiness that is 'less powerful' (cf. XVIII. 11–12), a second-best condition of sorts (cf. γει[τνιῶ]ν: XVIII. 13), and this might suggest the existence of degrees after all. Furthermore, if an untimely death causes one to have lived a less complete life than, say, Pythocles or Epicurus, is it not reasonable to consider that a harm,[127] and to fear early death accordingly? Besides, Philodemus does not take a position regarding people born with a philosophical nature who, nonetheless, die in childhood before they can begin to study philosophy. But it would seem that, from an Epicurean perspective, premature death should count as a great evil in such cases. In sum, even granting the controversial premisses of Philodemus's argument and overlooking possible inconsistencies in his position, there remain residual reasons why it might be rational to fear dying too soon.

3. Turning to another objection to the Epicurean thesis that death can do no harm, Philodemus addresses those who are grieved at the thought that their death will give an easy triumph to their enemies. Like other negative attitudes towards death and dying, this reaction too belongs to the Greek ethical tradition, and is paradigmatically illustrated by heroes of the Homeric poems.[128] Moreover, allowing for differences in times and

[127] As the following passage is restored, it states the contrary: '[The young man who dies ever achieving another step towards sane living is not even slightly unfortunate]' (XII. 17–19). However, the passage is heavily supplemented, and the immediate context is missing. Armstrong points out that further emendation is needed.

[128] In Homer, the dead are, on the one hand, 'burnt-out wraiths of mortal men' (*Od.* 11. 540), shades, phantoms, ghosts who are breathless (*Od.* 11. 558) and senseless (*Od.* 11. 540). On the other hand, they retain human features, and in particular the identity, behaviour, and emotions that each of them had when he was alive. In his descent to Hades, Odysseus encounters hordes of people who preserve their identity and history: brides, youths, old men, anonymous soldiers, and also famous men and women. After drinking the blood of the sacrificed victims, they are able to communicate with Odysseus, and they reassume, albeit briefly, the personas and roles that they held in life. Much of what they say indicates that they feel intense emotions resulting from memories and experiences that

cultures, the fears discussed below also mark our own outlook, just like fears about dying and premature death. To the extent that they do so, Philodemus' analyses and therapies have some philosophical interest for us.

Substantiating the contrast between natural and unnatural, forgivable and unforgivable feelings of pain about death, Philodemus suggests that, unlike natural 'bites', the pain that a person feels when he anticipates the joy of his enemies at his own death, is an empty emotion. For that emotion involves empty beliefs: notably, that a dead person somehow continues to exist and hence is aware of his foes' spiteful exultation.[129] 'Anyway, this part of one's pains (sc. 'bites' at the thought that untimely death will stop one's progress in philosophy) is easily forgivable (*συνγνωστόν*: XX. 3). What is unforgivably vain is the part concerning how one's enemies will rejoice. For no one will perceive them rejoicing, since one will have completely [vanished]' (XX. 1–7). To this unnatural sort of pain there is a counterpart: namely, a natural kind of annoyance (cf. *ἐνοχλεῖ φυσικῶ[ς]*: XX. 7–8) comparable to the natural 'bite' at the prospect of early death (cf. XVII. 35). So long as we are alive, we are entitled to feel upset when an enemy is mocking us, both because we are aware that we are being ridiculed and because we may suffer additional evils besides (XX. 7–11).[130] While the malicious joy of our foes cannot hurt or harm us after death, it can do so to some extent in life. Assuming that our attitudes ought to be determined by

they had during their lives. Anticleia's expressions of love and tenderness towards her son and her painful longing for him in Hades (*Od.* 11. 94 ff.) count amongst the most moving lines of the *Odyssey*. The same holds for Agamemnon's haunting remembrance of the death-shriek of Cassandra as she was slaughtered over his fallen body—the most pitiful thing he ever heard (*Od.* 11. 447). Achilles retains in Hades both his passion for glory and his disillusionment with the human condition. He longs to last out his fury and make his invincible hand the terror of his old father's enemies (*Od.* 11. 570 ff.). He is anxious about the fate of his comrades and the achievements of his son. And when Odysseus satisfies him on that score, he leaves 'loping with long strides across the fields of asphodel triumphant' (*Od.* 11. 615–16). As to Ajax, he keeps away, still raging at Odysseus for the harm that he inflicted on his honour. In all these cases, there seems to be a kind of survival after death, emphasized when the dead heroes comment on the deprivation caused by death and the dreariness of their underworld existence. Achilles says that he would far prefer to be a slave to the living than to lord it over the dead (*Od.* 11. 547–53). And it is he, Achilles, who feels that way, not a ghost with no sensation and no self-awareness. In general, although the dead in Homer possess properties that normal human beings do not possess (e.g., mentally, some of them have limited knowledge of the future, and, physically, the dead do not have sinews which bind the flesh and bones together), nonetheless, they are recognizably ghosts of *themselves*, i.e., of the men and women that they were in life.

[129] XX. 5–7 makes combined use of the non-perception and the non-identity arguments.

[130] The fear that our enemies will laugh at us after our death is not the same as the fear that they will mock us while we are alive. However, these two fears (the one unnatural, the other natural) are closely related in so far as they are both about some perceived harm that our enemies may inflict on us.

these truths, we should not be troubled about the former case, but we may feel some concern about the latter. However, that concern ought not to be very great. 'To the man who is good in character, no one is an enemy, once he has got to know him, (and it is those who know us) whose hatred [would be] painful for us' (XX. 11–14).

One might object that in fact the exultation of our enemies could harm us after our death by damaging our future reputation.[131] But it is absurd to worry for this reason. 'If, when we have acquired this [depth] of tranquillity, we should be dying [but were still uneasy about our future fame], we should need to worry about what this flock of locusts will experience at our death' (XX. 34–XXI. 3).[132] If the text is correctly restored,[133] Philodemus' main point seems to be this. It is irrational for a person to have achieved perfect happiness, yet be concerned about an unimportant thing: namely, how others will think of him after his death. All the more irrational because those who triumph over the dead and attempt to sully one's memory are lower, repulsive creatures—like locusts, who move together in swarms and destroy. Someone who has attained *ἀπονία* through and through could not be grieved, surely, by their feelings! In fact, the joy they take at another's death is just as empty as the dying person's grief on their account. If they laugh at the fact that we have had no happiness, they do not realize that death will be a welcome release from our evils (XXI. 3–6). But if they rejoice because death will deprive us of goods, they fool themselves that we would sense the deprivation when we are dead (XXI. 6–8). In any case, there is no way in which we (sc. the morally good persons) would die badly, so our enemies have no reason to rejoice on that score either (cf. XXI. 8–9).[134] To sum up, the beliefs involved in rejoicing at someone's end are both false and harmful, and they reveal a total incomprehension of the nature and implications of death. Hector need not have grieved about Achilles' triumph over his fallen body. Not only would Hector soon not be there to see that triumph, but also his death would have been easier for him if he had perceived Achilles' act for what it was, the act of a manic fool (cf. XXI. 5, 10–12). In general, rejoicing over the death of anyone is not an

[131] XX. 34–XXI. 3, which seems to contain part of Philodemus' answer to that objection, indicates that the objection itself was raised in the missing lines immediately preceding that passage.

[132] I follow Armstrong's translation of this passage.

[133] Both [*βά*]*θος* (XX. 35) and [*ὑστεροφημίας*] (XX. 36) are conjectures.

[134] I take it that Philodemus is being sarcastic in these lines.

attitude ever found in a good man, let alone a wise man (cf. XXII. 5–9).[135] And it should not in the least disturb us.

4. Another objection is that dying childless is particularly bad and worth grieving about (cf. XXII. 9 ff.). Several reasons are mentioned in the text as it is restored: namely, one's lineage and family name will disappear, and one's dead ancestors will somehow be hurt (XXII. 12 ff., XXIII. 33–6); there will be no children to care for one while one is still alive and to honour one's memory after death (XXII. 37 ff.); moreover, the childless person must leave his hard-earned property to people outside his direct line (XXIV. 5 ff.), and in many cases to those whom he does not wish to have as his heirs (XXIV. 31 ff.). Philodemus' rebuttal is of some interest both philosophically, because of the pertinence of these concerns,[136] and historically, because it contains an original version of the Symmetry Argument as well as enlightening references or allusions to post-mortem desires and will-writing. There is room for disagreement about the general strategy of his defence. One possibility is that his argument is *ad hominem* against an opponent who believes that it is good to die leaving children behind, but bad to die childless. If so, Philodemus aims to equate what, according to his rival, is bad with what isn't.[137] Another possibility, which I find more likely, is this: the objector assumes that to die is bad, but to die without children is even worse,[138] and focuses on the harder case. Philodemus, then, tries to show that there is no good reason why we should consider this second condition particularly evil, and that, as far as matters of inheritance are concerned, there is no evaluative difference between the two conditions.[139]

[135] There are several missing lines (XXI. 14–35), in which Philodemus probably hammered home certain consequences of the non-perception argument. This is indicated by the contents of the heavily conjectured passage XXI. 35–XXII. 5.

[136] To appreciate the urgency and poignancy of such feelings, consider the social pressure that certain cultures or environments exercise on young brides who are not expecting a child, and especially a son, within a year of their marriage.

[137] Cf. Warren 2004: 198–9. According to Warren, Philodemus' argument must be *ad hominem* because, if it were not, it might imply that there are two sources of anxiety and not just one: it is as bad to die with children as it is to die childless.

[138] Philodemus repeatedly suggests that false beliefs tend to form clusters, and the same holds for the harmful emotions to which they give rise. If a person is so misguided as to fear dying childless for the reasons mentioned, it would seem natural for such a person also to be misguided generally about death and fear it as an evil.

[139] Moreover, Philodemus believes that matters of property and inheritance should not concern us excessively, and that therefore we should not feel anxiety or sorrow on their account, whether or not we have offspring.

Philodemus dismisses outright this kind of grief, to which no natural counterpart seems to exist, as empty or vain ($\mu\acute{\alpha}\tau\alpha\iota[o]\nu$: XXII. 9).[140] He treats it by addressing in turn each consideration raised by the objectors. First of all, if we think about the continuation of our family name in an objective and impersonal manner, we shall realize that nothing hangs upon bequeathing it ourselves to the next generation. For there is an indefinitely large number of people who do or will bear the same name, and whether there is one more or less makes no difference (XXII. 12–16). Concerning whatever guilt the childless may feel towards their ancestors, they should be comforted by the thought that 'those who no longer exist have [no] perception and that fact [does not change] by having dear children' (XXII. 30–3). Even assuming that one were cutting short one's line of succession,[141] one's dead forefathers don't feel any distress about it; nor do they feel any pleasure if their line survives (XXIII. 33–6).

Moreover, the childless should not worry about having nobody to care for them and honour their memory. Initially, Philodemus leaves unquestioned the legitimacy of these desires. He concedes for the sake of the argument that they may be natural and understandable, but he denies that having children is essential to their fulfilment.

> The [childless man] will have plenty of caregivers and people to defend his memory. And if we may judge by results, who had such people to care for them as Polyaenus and Metrodorus and Leonteus and Epicurus himself from the day of their death till now, and in a word all those who made progress in our sect? And we also see among laymen many who obtained absolutely all the honour that is customary and natural from friends whose goodwill was worth having, much more than the founders of [the race of] Danaus and his brother, or of [Cadmus], or of Heracles.
>
> (XXII. 37–XXIII. 15)

Assuming that one has lived the life of a good person, one will almost inevitably[142] be cared for and then remembered after one's death. For in the ordinary course of things a good person has friends who love him

[140] Compare the use of the same adjective at XVI. 6–7.

[141] As Armstrong points out, in the gap preceding XXIII. 33 Philodemus may have noted that our ancestors must have many descendants in addition to ourselves, and so, even if we have not carried on their line of succession, others probably have.

[142] Philodemus contemplates the possibility that a person may have lived well and won many friends, but then be deprived of everyone he knows through some misfortune (XXXV. 39–XXXVI. 2). On this point, see below, p. 300 and n. 172.

and will cherish his memory after he dies if they live longer than he does. As Philodemus will make explicit later on, this is not a principal or even a secondary aim of friendship, but it may nevertheless reasonably be expected to happen.[143] Observation (cf. ὁρῶμεν: XXIII. 8) confirms that laymen often receive such services from their friends, but tells against the contention that they are always cared for and remembered by their children and other relatives. As for the members of the Epicurean community, it should be inferred that they emulate the example of the school's authorities who, according to the sources, took loving care of each other in sickness and death,[144] honoured each other's memory,[145] and had all of them been commemorated to Philodemus' day in festivals celebrating the example of their philosophical lives.[146] Philodemus emphasizes, precisely, that this memory has been long-lasting, and also that one's Epicurean friends are people of the highest moral calibre, including, first and foremost, the founders of the school.

However, already in this section Philodemus indicates that it is not rational to desire to be remembered and honoured after one's death or, at least, to wish for these things *per se*. He defends this suggestion by appealing both to the non-perception argument and to considerations of symmetry between the past and the future. 'To summarize ... I claim that whether or not we leave children behind us, and whether or not they are the ones to carry out the duties that we asked them in advance to carry out, or some sort of foreigners do that, or nobody at all, it will not matter to us any more than it did among those living in the time of Phoroneus' (XXIII. 37–XXIV. 5). Since death entails total loss of consciousness, it is nothing to us whether anyone will be concerned with us after our death (caring for our remains, guarding our good reputation, etc.) or who that would be. It is not clear why Philodemus refers to men born in the mythological time of Phoroneus. On one interpretation, Philodemus argues that 'the world that we leave behind at death will be no more of concern to us than was the world in the time of Phoroneus'.[147] If I understand correctly, the point in that case is that the future after our death is just as irrelevant to us as the very distant past before our birth. According to another interpretation, the *remote*

[143] Armstrong (2006) convincingly argues this point.

[144] See Clay 1998: 62 ff.

[145] The order in which Philodemus cites the early authorities of the school is probably identical with the chronological order of their deaths.

[146] See Clay 1998: 75–102.

[147] Cf. Warren 2004: 197.

future after our death is of no more concern to us than the *very distant* past. If so, Philodemus relies on the intuition that the *remote* past and the *remote* future are equally indifferent to us, whereas that symmetry breaks down as we come closer to our own lifetime. We are indifferent towards the time immediately preceding our birth, but not towards the time that will immediately follow our death.[148] Yet another possible interpretation, I suggest, is this. Whether or not anyone cares for us and remembers us in the future after our death matters to us as little as these things have mattered to men who have lived in prehistoric times. Just as they are not conscious whether anyone cared for them and preserved their reputation, so we will not be either.[149]

As to the idea that dying childless is an evil because one's property will pass outside one's direct line, Philodemus tries different argumentative strategies. One consolation is that even people who have children are often forced anyway to leave their trees, crops, etc. to heirs other than their children (XXIV. 5–10). Childlessness is by no means the only circumstance necessitating that kind of thing. Other such circumstances include, for instance, that one's children may die, get exiled, live far away, or be disinclined to get tied to their parents' property. In this respect, then, the childless are not worse off (or better off) than those who have children. Considerations of this sort give comfort by inducing one to enlarge one's individual viewpoint and accept the course of things.[150]

The quality of one's heirs is another matter, and its therapeutic treatment bears on the topic of wills. 'Besides, the heirs are not always bad or unworthy people, and if they are bad, it is possible to take precautions against that [by leaving one's property] to good [men] who are one's friends; and if one does not have them, he should be pitied for that, not because [these heirs of his] are bad' (XXIV. 10–17). Even though one's heirs are not one's children, if they are good persons, a well-thinking man should find consolation in the prospect that the inheritance will be passed on to them. Why so? Not, I think, because they will preserve and increase his property, but because they will administer it and dispose parts of it according to the right ethical values.[151] If, on the other hand, one's prospective heirs are

[148] Cf. Armstrong 2004: 33.

[149] Different interpretations of the argument are discussed in some detail in Tsouna 2006*b*: 90–2.

[150] On this type of therapeutic approach, see pp. 80–1.

[151] Philodemus' views in *On Property Management* point in that direction.

corrupt, Philodemus encourages people of understanding to guard against leaving their property to those that will use it badly. The way to transmit the property to better heirs is, presumably, by writing a will.

Two features of the text deserve attention in this connection. Philodemus says that 'it is possible to take precautions' (*προφυλάξεσθ[αι] δυνατόν*: XXIV. 13–14) against unworthy persons inheriting; but he does not claim that this can be achieved with certainty through a will. Moreover, he emphasizes that the absence of good friends is bad because of what it means for one's life, not for one's testament. Conversely, we may infer, good friends are important because of the happiness they bring to us when we are alive, not because of the fact that they are good prospective heirs. At the same time, there is nothing wrong with taking post-mortem precautions on behalf of our friends. At the end of this section Philodemus suggests how to do so and generally how to think about wills and inheritance in the proper spirit. 'As for those [who lament] over just this, that people whom they do not want will command their [property], it is just as possible to weep even though they have children living, [since] fortune, the mistress [of all men], is quite capable of tearing from them (sc. their children) their inheritance and throwing it at the feet of whomsoever she will' (XXIV. 31–XXV. 2). Once again we are asked to rise above our individual perspective and reflect on the impact of luck. Although we may have desires concerning states of affairs after our death, and in particular desires of the kind expressed in a will, we must always keep in mind that their fulfilment depends ultimately on fortune. We cannot guard against it, whether we have direct heirs or indirect heirs, good ones or bad ones. Those with children are just as vulnerable as the childless, and if fortune so pleases, those who do leave a will are just as helpless to influence the course of things as those who do not. The take-home message is not, I think, that we shouldn't form post-mortem desires or leave instructions concerning the disposition of our property after death,[152] but rather that we

[152] In any case, the passage referring to good and noble heirs (XXIV. 10–17) flatly contradicts this suggestion. Warren (2004: 198) claims that the concession contained in that passage, that not all heirs are bad and that we can try to take measures so that our own heirs are good, belongs to the objector; for it is inconsistent with Philodemus' thesis that the way in which our heirs will treat the property that they have inherited is nothing to us. On the contrary, I have attributed the concession in question to Philodemus, and take it to be one therapeutic argument among others. As I suggested, a hallmark of Philodemus' therapeutics is to advance several separate considerations in order to treat the same emotion or moral flaw.

should realize the utter vulnerability of our plans to the turns of fortune. It is acceptable that childless people make an honest effort to bequeath their property to good friends, provided that they do so on the basis of correct understanding. But the desire to truly control the outcome of such efforts is empty, and struggling to fulfil it is vain.

5. Philodemus gives considerable credit to the next objection: that our death matters to us to the extent that it causes difficulties for our loved ones. His treatment of this kind of fear lends support to the suggestion that his ethics leaves room for genuine affection and concern for others. But he also uses a therapeutic argument which might seem to rely on the uncompromising egoism often attributed to Epicurus.[153] 'To be sure, leaving behind parents or children or a spouse or any other dear ones who will be in difficulties or even will lack the necessities of life because of one's death, that produces a most natural bite and gives rise especially in the thoughtful man to flows of tears in a way in which nothing else can' (XXV. 2–10). In this case too, then, we feel a 'bite' of pain which is 'most natural' (cf. *φυσικώτατον δηγμόν*: XXV. 8), presumably, in the four senses indicated earlier: it is spontaneous, initially irrepressible, beneficial, and rationally justifiable. Moreover, Philodemus strongly suggests that this 'bite' has a normative character. For not only does he emphasize its naturalness,[154] he also says that the 'bite' is experienced most of all by the thoughtful person or even the wise man (cf. *νοῦν ἔχοντ[ι]*: XXV. 9).[155] His idea therefore seems to be that we *ought to* feel pain at the thought that our friends and relatives are bound to suffer from our death, assuming that we have a steady and profound commitment to their well-being. If this is right, the cognitive basis of the 'bite' consists of both the judgement that our death will deprive our dear ones of the necessities of life and the judgement that it is appropriate to feel pain in that regard. Philodemus explicitly claims, at least, that the first of these two judgements, which he takes to be true, is responsible for producing the 'bite' (cf. *ἐγείρει*: XXV. 9). Although he does not clarify just how this happens, it seems reasonable to infer that the judgement in question precedes the 'bite' causally as well as

[153] Cf. pp. 27–9 and notes.

[154] Note the use of the superlative '*φυσικώτατον*' (XXV. 8).

[155] Armstrong favours the first, broader interpretation of the Greek, whereas Warren (2004: 194) takes it to refer in particular to the wise man. Recall Epicurus' claims that the wise man will be more susceptible than other people to emotion (D.L. X. 117), and that he will feel sorrow (D.L. X. 119).

temporally, and also tells us what the 'bite' is about. Concerning its affective content, this 'bite' of pain is quite sharp. It induces the thoughtful man to shed 'floods of tears' (XXV. 8–9), whereas natural 'pangs' aroused by other circumstances seem to be less deeply felt (XXXIV. 11–12, 25–6).[156]

What can one say in consolation? It is impossible to reconstruct Philodemus' arguments with any degree of certainty, because the relevant passage is lacunose. As restored, it advances several considerations of unequal worth. The dying might find comfort in the thought that their dear ones will become good persons and have a good life, in which they will remember and emulate their dead (XXV. 30–3). One can deal with the pain of leaving one's loved ones defenceless, precisely by convincing oneself that whatever hardships his loved ones may have to suffer will not impede their happiness. Moreover, it may help to try to detach oneself from the particular situation at hand and reflect generally on the human losses that everyone must sustain. One's relatives and friends will have to bear the death of many dear people (XXV. 33–4), as has had to do oneself. Besides, it is always helpful to recall that death entails total unconsciousness. When we die, we shall feel pain no more, and we shall not be aware of the difficulties of others. Since their problems will be of no concern to us then, we ought not to feel grief on their account now (cf. XXV. 35–7).[157]

The next argument, however, has an entirely different tone. 'It is folly having fled one's own [sufferings], [still] to deplore the sufferings of others' (XXV. 35–6). As restored, this passage might appear to advocate a standpoint both egoistic and cynical. In fact, it might be taken as evidence that Philodemus does not believe in genuine affection and other-concern, and that he does not seriously mean to concede that 'bites' of pain on behalf of one's loved ones are natural and unavoidable. However, there are good reasons for resisting these inferences. The crucial passage is badly preserved. Philodemus' commitment to altruistic feelings of friendship and love is well attested in many places, as I have argued. Also, the first line

[156] As Philodemus suggests, the natural 'bites' caused by the thought of how our death will affect our loved ones are especially intense, whereas the natural 'bites' which derive from thinking about how death will affect ourselves are usually moderate.

[157] Since we shall not perceive and shall not feel any pain from the sufferings of our loved ones after our death, the grief that we feel when we anticipate their sufferings is empty or pointless (cf. Cicero, *Tusc.* I. 16).

of consolation (that our dear ones will be excellent and happy despite whatever difficulties they encounter because of our own death) works only on the assumption that we have legitimate post-mortem desires concerning others, whose fulfilment after our death cannot possibly be of benefit to ourselves. Consequently, I prefer to interpret this last argument as a dialectical manoeuvre which Philodemus ought to have avoided.

In general, Philodemus' treatment of the objection that our death is an evil to the extent that it can hurt our loved ones seems to me somewhat disappointing. On the one hand, he substantially clarifies the concept of natural 'bites' and the extent to which even the wise man is susceptible to such emotion. On the other hand, he misses an opportunity to articulate issues of altruism and concern for others in connection with these natural emotions.

6. Philodemus was an intellectual who lived most of his life abroad, and had every reason to anticipate that he would also die there. It seems likely that he had family and friends whom, after he emigrated, he did not expect to see again. Therefore, he probably had first-hand acquaintance with the kind of pain which constitutes his next topic: pain at the prospect of dying in a foreign country in the absence of relatives to care for one on one's deathbed and to bury one. Philodemus may well refer to his own experience when he says that scholars (cf. *φιλολόγοις*: XXVI. 1) are susceptible to this sorrow,[158] and he may have found solace in the remedies that he proposes. 'When death occurs in a foreign land, it is natural for scholars to feel a bite, especially if they leave parents or other relatives behind in their native country, but (of such a kind) as to give them only a pang, not to bring on grief, and in particular this great grief, to people who are subject to the difficulties that follow upon living in a foreign land'

[158] We might gain insight into the precise content of this emotion by looking at a genre of songs belonging to the modern Greek folk tradition, the so-called demotic songs (the standard edition is by Nikolaos Politis), specifically songs referring to one's death in a foreign land. (The modern Greek term for it is *τὰ ξένα* (neuter plural) and *ἡ ξενητειά* (feminine singular). Compare Philodemus' [ἐ]πὶ ξένης [γῆ]ς: XXVI. 7.) The narrator usually speaks in the first person from the depths of his grave. He laments that he was alone on his deathbed without the comforting presence of blood relatives; that no one washed him, dressed him, or kept vigil next to him after he expired; that he went to his grave unaccompanied by the tears of his relatives and the rites of his religion; most importantly, that the earth which covers him now is cold, hard, and heavy, in contrast to the warmth and lightness of his native soil. He grieves, then, not so much about death itself, but about its unfamiliar trappings: about the cultural alienation and personal solitude that, according to the proverbial saying, turn death abroad into a double death.

(XXV. 37–XXVI. 7). Here again Philodemus contrasts the natural 'bite' or pang (cf. δη[χθῆ]ναι: XXV. 38–XXVI. 1; νύττειν: XXVI. 3), which is acceptable and forgivable, with great grief (λύπην μεγάλην: XXVI. 4), which is an impermissible emotion, and he justifies the contrast on cognitive grounds. Although he does not specifically identify the beliefs involved in the natural form of the emotion, he strongly suggests that many of them concern parents and other kin from whom the emigrant has been separated. The 'bite' of sorrow could be about them or about oneself. For instance, one could be sad about the fact that one's parents will not have the practical assistance and emotional support of their child as they are growing old, or about the fact that one will not be able to share important moments in one's life with one's closest relatives, or both. Philodemus appears to assume that beliefs of this sort are true and adequately justify the occurrence of the natural 'bite'.

Moreover, he identifies and refutes the false beliefs on account of which people are deeply grieved about dying abroad. This kind of death does not matter to us, since death entails loss of perception, and there is no awareness that one's remains are lying in a foreign land (XXVI. 7–11). There is nothing intrinsically bad about dying away from home (XXVI. 11–13). For the same reason, there is nothing valuable about dying at home *per se* (XXVI. 13–14). It is not the case that one's reputation is better served at home than abroad, because of the care of one's relatives. In fact, we can be treated with the greatest affection and reverence by our friends in a foreign country, both before and after we die. Like the childless (XXIII. 2–8), those dying abroad should comfort themselves by recalling the behaviour of Epicurus and his early associates. 'Every reasonable man will admit that it was finer for their reputation, and also for themselves and for Leonteus and for Metrodorus, as they were taken care of by each other and all of them took care of Epicurus; and for Hermarchus, who wrapped (Epicurus) in his shroud and watched over his corpse' (XXVII. 1–8).

Once again, it turns out that the important thing is not whether one dies at home or abroad, but whether one has lived a life enhanced by the pleasures of friendship. The early authorities of the school illustrate just how friends care for each other and for the remains and memory of the dead. Hermarchus' loving attendance of the corpse of Epicurus constitutes an excellent paradigm of the spirit in which such actions should be performed and the therapeutic impact that the prospect of them should have. They are motivated by reverence, and are carried out with pangs of sadness, not desperate grief. They show how friendship counterbalances the sorrows of living abroad and how it renders the prospect of dying there immaterial to one's happiness. Although several lines of text are missing, it is reasonably clear that Philodemus also touches upon a point made earlier in connection with the fear of dying childless: that desires concerning one's remains and one's reputation after death are empty desires often deriving from superstition. His therapeutic strategy in this case consists in using strong language, which can be described as bitter *parrhēsia*, to bring-before-the-eyes the equality that all human beings must share regarding death. 'They (sc. believers in myths: XXVII. 8–9) forget in their stupidity that the [way] to Hades from wherever it began is of equal length and equally direct' (XXVII. 12–15).

7. Another group of objections to the effect that death can be a great evil has to do with certain causes of death, the disfigurement and decomposition of one's corpse, and the disposition of one's remains. People commonly fear death in these cases, it seems, because they assume that features of their life, such as power and wealth, accompany them to the world of the dead, and also because they desire posthumous glory and reputation. Their attitudes indicate that they have not realized the extent to which death implies absolute nothingness. Consequently, Philodemus' main therapeutic aim is to drive that truth home. Predominant features of his treatment include the following. He uses both the non-perception and the non-identity arguments, jointly as well as severally. He often argues dialectically, shifting perspective on the same subject, and thus aiming to appeal to different sensitivities and belief systems. For instance, sometimes he concedes that post-mortem remembrance has some value, whereas other times he suggests that it is morally irrelevant (anticipating his definitive position on the subject, which he will defend later on in the text).

In addition, in this section he clearly intends to address as broad an audience as possible. This is indicated by his liberalism towards the virtues of ordinary people and philosophers of other schools. Not just an Epicurean, but any intelligent person can become convinced that there is nothing particularly good or glorious about dying on the battlefield (XXVIII. 14–15). Every reasonable man can be brought to believe that politicians like

Themistocles and Pericles, who did not die in battle, are better remembered than those who did (XXIX. 2–8), and that most philosophers, including Epicurus and Metrodorus, have been more memorable than anyone else (XXXIX. 8–12). Epicurus and Plato too lived better than Hephaestion, and did not request or receive nearly as lavish a funeral as he did (XXX. 36–XXXI. 1). Lawgivers and even laymen have also shown preference for simpler rather than more elaborate burials (XXXI. 4–14). No man of good sense (cf. XXXII. 11, 19–20) would blame or pity those who happen to remain unburied, or would take account of people who consider that an evil (XXXII. 11–15). And everyone can be persuaded that 'both those properly laid out and [those] who are unburied will all dissolve into whatever he believes to be their elements' (XXXII. 28–31). This last phrase is especially revealing as to how far Philodemus intends to cast his net. One does not even need to be an atomist to understand that the burial of one's corpse does not matter to the dead and does not alter the process of decomposition which is bound to happen.[159] Finally, it is worth noting that in this section there is no mention of 'bites'. Philodemus considers groundless the fears that one will die unknown, be buried plainly or not at all, and decompose. He views the pain caused by these thoughts as an empty emotion that has no natural counterpart,[160] and he attempts to eradicate it using what seems like bitter parrhesiastic speech.

Concerning the predominant fear of Homeric heroes, that one will not be remembered for having done great deeds (typically in battle), but will die an unworthy death 'like a beached ship in one's bed and in the manner of an old woman' (XVIII. 1–2), it would have been justified only if the dead had perception and an afterlife reflecting their status when they were alive (XXVIII. 5–8). However, since death implies complete unconsciousness (cf. *ἀναισθησίαν παντελῆ*: XXVIII. 11) and non-existence (cf. *ἀνυπαρξίαν*: XXVIII. 16), that fear is irrational. More generally, the only legitimate basis for distinguishing between different causes of death is hedonic, and concerns the process of dying rather than the actual condition of being dead. 'No man of sense distinguishes between

[159] Armstrong (2004: 31) offers this passage as conclusive proof that Philodemus addresses a mixed audience of Epicureans, followers of other schools who have different convictions about elements of things, and also people who have no special beliefs about the nature of matter.

[160] Cf. the comment in n. 82 above to the effect that not all fears have natural counterparts, but only some do.

the causes of death, since all of them lead to unconsciousness and non-existence in a similar manner, except in so far as they give us before [we die] greater or lesser pain or perfect painlessness' (XXVIII. 14–20). For instance, it is a defensible choice to expose oneself to the enemy's sword thinking that that kind of death will be quick and painless, or even to commit suicide by some suitable means rather than go through a long and painful illness (XXVIII. 20–7).[161]

Nonetheless, later in the argument, Philodemus withdraws part of that concession. For he argues that dying sword in hand is not a preferable end to one's life, since it typically involves greater pains than those experienced during a long illness and among one's friends (XXVIII. 27–32). It really does not seem so bad to die in one's own bed in peace and tranquillity (ἡσυχίας: XXVIII. 28), especially when we recall the horrible wounds of those who die for glory 'slashed with ruthless bronze'. As mentioned, moreover, the best leaders of the Athenian democracy are remembered even though they did not fall in the battlefield, and the same holds for philosophers, and above all the authorities of the Epicurean school (cf. XXIX. 2–12). Besides, Philodemus points to a pragmatic consideration whose grim cynicism reflects a strong anti-war sentiment. Great military deeds are not the lot of many, but only of very few; most soldiers 'are killed in the ranks, like farm animals' (XXVIII. 37–XXIX. 2). Because they were in the ranks, they will not be remembered by future generations (cf. XXIX. 2–4), whereas their generals just might. In truth, there is an unimaginable number of people who have fought brilliantly, yet no one knows how they died (XXIX. 12–15). By stressing that post-mortem glory is rare and difficult to achieve, Philodemus invites us to reconsider the kind of desire that motivates us to seek such glory. It cannot be a natural desire since, according to Epicurean doctrine, natural desires are easily satisfied. Rather, it is an empty desire for something that is almost always unattainable. In the few cases in which it is attained, it does not matter to the hero who has gained it, for he is dead.

The non-perception argument is also an important therapeutic means of removing fears about the decomposition and disfigurement of one's body (XXIX. 27 ff.). These overlap to some extent with concerns about the

[161] Although Philodemus does not explicitly mention suicide, he seems to have that possibility in mind in XXVIII. 23–7.

manner of one's death and what happens subsequently to one's remains. Although part of the text is missing, it seems that Philodemus first treats the emotion of those who worry that they will look and smell bad as the moment of their death approaches. The reference to Democritus (XXIX. 28), whose body was allegedly decomposed in part during the last months of his life, points to people anxious that they will meet their end already disfigured by disease. But the dead perceive none of these things. Moreover, we should reflect on the naturalness and inevitability of the process of dissolution into the primary elements (whatever we take them to be). Whether one dies with one's appearance already altered or 'well-muscled and with beauty' (XXIX. 32), 'they all in a little while become skeletons and are finally dissolved into their primal natures' (XXX. 1–5). In this as in other cases, consolation will be found if we detach ourselves from our subjective and emotional viewpoint and perceive death as a natural phenomenon to which all men are subject.

In addition, Philodemus addresses people troubled by the prospect that they may die in a manner precluding that their bodies will be entombed (XXXII. 2 ff.). They too have morbid thoughts concerning what will happen to their remains, and feel fear and anxiety for that reason. A particularly acute fear of this kind is about dying at sea. Again, illustration is found in a Homeric hero, Odysseus, who bemoans that he is fated, as he thinks, to suffer that 'horrible' death (*Od.* 5. 306–12, cited in XXXIII. 10–14). Indeed, drowning in a shipwreck in the course of a voyage undertaken for military, political,[162] commercial, or private purposes was a very real possibility in ancient times (cf. XXXIII. 23–30). Dread of it must have been quite common, so it is not surprising that Philodemus treats it as a separate object of therapy. He may have drawn inspiration from writings describing Epicurus' own shipwreck[163] and his miraculous escape from death. There is evidence that, according to Epicurus' own vivid description of his adventure,[164] he felt no particular grief about his

[162] Philodemus may allude to people sent into exile when he refers to 'those who sail because of unavoidable necessities, yet run into unexpected ill fortune' (XXXIII. 31–4).

[163] Epicurus probably recorded his experience of the shipwreck in one of his letters. Both Plutarch (*Non posse* 1090e) and Diogenes of Oenoanda (fr. 72, Smith = NF 7) probably draw their information about that event from the same source. See Clay 1998: 189–206.

[164] On the close parallels between Epicurus' description of his shipwreck and Odysseus' accounts of being washed up on the island of Scheria (*Od.* 5.367–463) and of nearly being swallowed by Charybdis (*Od.* 12. 235 ff.), see Clay 1998: 189–99.

imminent death, and, after he was saved, he turned the evil that happened to him into a good: namely, pleasure at the thought of his salvation.[165] In a similar spirit, Philodemus claims that there is nothing evil about drowning at sea.[166] He relies mainly on the non-perception and the non-identity arguments, but adduces other considerations as well.

Addressing the more general worry that our corpse may not be buried, he repeats at the outset that all that matters is what happens in life, not after death. 'When someone has lived well and has had friends worthy of himself but by fortune or the wickedness of men is prevented from receiving burial, he will not suffer the least grief, because he reasons with himself that he will not even exist. For at that point he does not have the thing to which the painful event will happen, but rather everything is quite the opposite' (XXXII. 1–9). Since death implies that one does not exist any more, there is no subject to feel pain as a result of events affecting one's remains. Nor is there a subject to perceive the reactions of the living to the fact that one has remained unburied (XXII. 12–15). And they would not matter in any case, since only fools would consider the fact that one has no grave an evil thing. Sensible people (and not just philosophers) would not attach any moral value to it, and would not pay any attention to those who do (cf. XXXII. 11–20, 28–31). To drive this point home, Philodemus draws an analogy between events that happen at two different temporal modes and our respective attitudes towards them. People whom, presumably, we have not known and who have died long ago do not suffer any evil by having their bones unearthed, and we do not perceive them as suffering any evil. Likewise, those whom we have known and who are not buried or get unburied do not suffer any evil, and it is irrational to perceive them as if they did. If this reconstruction of the argument is correct, it strengthens the suggestion that Philodemus relies, both here and elsewhere (cf. the argument concerning the time of Phoroneus, XXIII. 37–XXIV. 5), on the intuition that we are indifferent towards remote times and events but become less so as we approach our

165 On the other hand, Plutarch views Epicurus' shipwreck as an unforeseen event which refutes the philosopher's thesis that one can nourish confident and steadfast hopes about life: *Non posse* 1090a.

166 Philodemus does not preclude that we should normally feel relief at our salvation, e.g., from a shipwreck. However, assuming that he remains faithful to the spirit of Epicurus, he would probably claim that the relief should concern one's escape not from death *at sea*, but from death *simpliciter*. Recall that in his view it is natural to wish to live and not to die so long as one still has the capacity to find pleasure.

own lifetime.[167] Consolation may also be found in reckoning that not having a grave is not a rare misfortune but a common occurrence shared by many men alike, including people worthy and powerful (XXXII. 16–20). The therapeutic functions of this last reasoning could be to familiarize us with the prospect of remaining unburied, and also to make the point that such a turn of things would subtract nothing from the happiness we have had in life, as it has not subtracted anything from the virtue, wealth, or power of many eminent dead.

Concerning specifically the fear of dying at sea, Philodemus tries to shock us into accepting that being drowned in the ocean is neither better nor worse than other manners of death, and that being eaten by fish is neither more nor less preferable than traditional methods of burial like entombment or cremation. The main reason given is, again, the non-perception argument.

> It is an empty emotion (*κενόν*) therefore, to feel horror about death in the sea more than [in a marsh-pond] or in a river, and about losing one's life there more than in (a barrel of) [unmixed wine]. For [it is always just the same] wet stuff. [Nor is being devoured by fishes any worse for us] than being eaten by maggots and worms deep into the ground, or being consumed by fire above ground. When the corpse has no perception of the one thing or the other, why must one differentiate? It is equally pointless to exaggerate exclaiming 'on the sea and, what is more, the Libyan sea!', when in fact one drowns, necessarily, by swallowing three or four gulps of water, and this could happen even in a bathtub.
>
> (XXXII. 31–XXXIII. 9)

So, fear about this kind of death is empty, because it involves false judgements both absolute and comparative.[168] Since we perceive nothing after we die, we have no criteria for ascribing different values to different causes of death and to different ways of having one's corpse disposed of.

Philodemus' sarcastic comparison of death in the ocean with death in one's bathtub aims to trivialize the former and ridicule epic and tragic reactions to it (cf. also XXXIII. 11–14). If I understand the text correctly,

[167] Note, however, that this argument does not appeal to the symmetry of past and future, but rather to a symmetry between a nearer and a more remote past: viz., we move from unconcern about the distant future to unconcern about the proximate future. I am grateful to István Bodnar for his comments on this point.

[168] They include the judgements that dying in the ocean is particularly painful, that it is more painful than other manners of drowning, and that it is appropriate to be horrified at the prospect of perishing in this manner.

another remedy consists in alluding to the anti-patriotic implications of fearing death at sea. Playing to his Roman readers, Philodemus points out that Odysseus and his likes implicitly reject the value of dying in sea battles in defence of one's homeland (XXXIII. 9–19). Moreover, assuming that they are concerned about what happens to their remains, their preference for dying in a land battle over dying at sea cannot be accounted for. For there they run the risk of becoming food for birds and dogs, perhaps even more so than the sea fighters risk becoming food for fishes (XXXIII. 19–23). But in truth none of these things matters, since corpses have no perception. Again, all that is important concerns the life one has lived, not the death one dies. The non-existence argument also points to that conclusion. 'By Zeus, it is actually natural both to blame and to consider miserable those who spend their whole life on the seas for love of gain and are at last, for the sake of it, sunk into waves. But it is their life that is pitiable, not their death, since they are no longer there' (XXXIII. 25–31).

Moreover, both the unconsciousness and the non-existence accompanying death constitute reasons for dismissing the pain people commonly feel when they anticipate for themselves a plain and cheap burial (XXX. 7 ff.). Philodemus calls this pain 'utterly empty' ([κε]νότατον: XXX. 7–8) and emphasizes how false are the beliefs from which it derives. 'For this is as if, when they die, there would be waiting in [Hades] for some of them rich things and for others poor, for some glory and for others ill repute. But they forget that all (dead people) are perfectly unconscious or rather do not even exist and, moreover, that of the things which are put into the graves, some are [burnt up] right then, while others [buried together with the bones become dust]' (XXX. 11–20). Alexander, who prepared a magnificent funeral for Hephaestion and wanted to honour him as a god, has merely '[the pride] of a miserable man' (XXXI. 2–3). On the contrary, as mentioned, great philosophers, legislators, and even the most virtuous laymen have preferred the simplest funerals, 'ordaining things naturally and well' (XXXI. 6). Philodemus presents them as examples for emulation, suggesting that they are motivated by generosity and concern for the resources left to the living, as opposed to those who wish to take their wealth with them to the grave (XXX. 6–11). In this case too, it is worth noting the close association between, on the one hand, empty distress and vice, and, on the other hand, 'natural' attitudes and virtue.

8. Philodemus explores this last connection further when he addresses yet another objection which, like the previous one, represents a very real possibility: that it is particularly evil for a good person to die as a result of an unjust condemnation, as many philosophers and many virtuous laymen have (XXXIII. 37). In this section too he speaks to a wide audience. Also, he allows for the natural pain of both ordinary decent people and wise men, and he attempts to console them both. An important feature of this section is that it lends considerable support to the suggestion that the 'bites' are genuine emotions rather than non-cognitive preludes to them.

Again, it might seem forgivable to be grieved if one is going to die violently, having been condemned by a jury or a tyrant, as were Palamedes, Socrates, and Kallisthenes. For this is certainly one of those things that are totally irrational and very rare concerning wise men, not (merely), indeed, because they (sc. wise men) do not perform any one of the actions which lead to this end, but because they do not even have any common points (with those who do perform such actions). But precisely because it is not impossible for this to happen, so much more since they (sc. wise men) are not among those in power,[169] to feel no bite at all is not easy but, nevertheless, it is possible to endure the entire situation with courage and to be troubled very moderately by it because of such considerations as follow.

(XXXIII. 37–XXXIV. 15)

Why is grief at the prospect of an unjust and violent death forgivable, then? Why is it difficult if not unavoidable to feel a 'bite' of pain (cf. ἀδήκτως ἔχειν: XXXIV. 11)? The passage cited above establishes that the justification lies in certain objective features of the situation and in the true beliefs that the condemned person holds about it. The victim is confronted with circumstances which he rightly considers very unusual because they are both rare and absurd (XXXIV. 5–9). He knows himself to have done nothing to deserve or even appear to deserve execution. At the same time, he is aware of the weakness of his position and the incapacity to save himself (XXXIV. 9–11). And so on. Such beliefs seem to be at least necessary conditions for one's distress (cf. XXXIII. 37–XXXIV. 3) or even constituents of it.

Concerning the affective quality of the 'bite', Philodemus initially speaks about being grieved, using a term which might give rise to the idea that

[169] Cf. Armstrong's translation of τελείων (XXXIV. 10).

the grief in question can be quite intense (λυπεῖσθαι: XXXIV. 1).[170] Later on, however, he specifies that the trouble experienced by the condemned person is very moderate in its intensity (cf. *πάνυ μετρίως*: XXXIV. 13). Also, he echoes Plato's Socrates and meets the Stoics halfway by making the following assertion. 'But when someone [has lived] well and in a manner [clean] of all stain and then is bitten by some such misfortune because of envy, slander or [conspiracies] of thoroughly wicked men, he will see that the pains, if they come, disturb him [no] more than in illness; and he already [knows] this, that even if [he were to lose everything], he shall be superior to them in his moral strength' (XXXIV. 21–9). According to this passage, the good person feels a 'bite' (cf. δ[η]χθείς: XXXIV. 25) which is only moderately disturbing. For he knows that his unjust death cannot affect the goodness that he has already achieved (XXXIV. 27–9). One conclusion that we are invited to draw is distinctly Epicurean: in this, as in every other case, the important thing is the life that one has lived, not the cause and manner of one's death. Conversely, a similar moral applies to those who are guilty as charged. They are miserable not on account of the way in which they die, but rather because they have lived in the fear of being caught and punished (XXXIV. 15–19).

Philodemus' therapeutic arguments are many and varied. They are based on true judgements, which are intended to fortify the sufferer against fearing an unjust condemnation and grieving too much at that prospect. Many of them also point to corresponding false judgements which must be rejected on account of their falsehood and the inappropriateness of the emotion to which they give rise. In addition to recollecting that one's enemies cannot destroy the virtue and happiness that have been in one's life (cf. XXXIV. 21 ff.), the person who faces the prospect of an unjust condemnation should be brought to realize that dying unjustly is a moral indifferent: it does not have moral value *per se* or because of what other people think about it (XXXIV. 29–32). In any case, sensible people do not consider an unjust death dishonourable, but even if everyone did, this could not be an obstacle to the happiness that the innocent victim has

[170] Dealing with pain about dying abroad, he contrasts one's natural and forgivable 'bite' or pang (cf. δη[χθῆ]ναι: XXV. 38–XXVI. 1; *νύττειν*: XXVI. 3) with great grief (*λύπην μεγάλην*: XXVI. 4), a harmful emotion. Note that the noun which denotes that unacceptable kind of grief (cf. *λύπη*) and the verb that refers to forgivable grief at the prospect of being executed unjustly (cf. *λυπεῖσθαι*: XXXIV. 1) are cognates.

already enjoyed (XXXIV. 34–9). According to Philodemus' argument, the idea that an unjust death will impeach our honour is wrong-headed, and the grief that we may experience for that reason is groundless. Recall that Philodemus has suggested that the concern for our post-mortem reputation is altogether empty. Consider, moreover, that he has advanced a distinctly Epicurean version of what may be recognized as a Socratic and Stoic ideal (cf. XXXIV. 21 ff.), that goodness once achieved cannot be lost.

To counter our frustration at the thought that we alone are subject to the misfortune of an unjust end (cf. XXXIV. 38–9), Philodemus recommends that we take a look at the history of humanity. In fact, many good people have been put to death violently and unjustly by all sorts of rulers and in all sorts of polities (XXXV. 1–5). Although this therapeutic move appears inconsistent with Philodemus' earlier assertion that death by unjust condemnation is a rare event, and even more so for wise men (XXXIV. 6), that inconsistency can be explained away. Such deaths may be rare within one's lifetime, but in the course of human history many have occurred. Or, they may rarely befall philosophers, but may much more frequently happen to virtuous people who are not philosophers, nobles as well as laymen. There is also another cause of pain to a person in such a situation: namely, anger at those who condemned him. The proposed remedy makes sense if we remember Philodemus' distinction between unnatural rage (*thymos*) and natural anger (*orgē*), the former entailing the empty desire for revenge, the latter accompanied by the natural desire to have the offender properly punished. Addressing the victim of injustice here, Philodemus tries to assuage the feelings of anger which that person may have by suggesting to him that his enemies, in fact, will receive full punishment. 'He gets convinced both that those who condemned him have been punished in their entire life through the evil inside themselves and that they will suffer many pangs of repentance on his account, and perhaps will also be punished more harshly by others' (XXXV. 6–11). Despite the odd syntactical structure that follows (XXXV. 11–25), we can see how Philodemus completes his thought in an almost Socratic spirit. No evil person can really be happy (cf. XXXV. 15–17), and conversely, no truly sensible person can really be miserable (cf. XXXV. 19–21). The victim of injustice should be able to draw comfort from both these convictions and gain strength from another element that can be traced back to Plato's Socrates: a profound contempt for those willing to kill an innocent person—not good men, but beasts (XXXV. 13–15). Concluding, Philodemus pays appropriate tribute to those who serve as moral paradigms, having endured unjust deaths with nobility and courage, laymen and philosophers alike (XXXV. 25–34). Reflecting on their attitude and attempting to emulate it is a very efficient therapeutic practice.

9. We have seen by now that, according to Philodemus' diagnosis, the desire to be remembered after death, as well as the corresponding fear that this may not happen, constitute reasons why people perceive death as a particularly great evil in certain circumstances: when we have enemies ready to debase us after death, when we are childless, when we anticipate dying abroad, and also when we face the prospect of perishing ingloriously and violently or unjustly (XXXVI. 31–7). Although Philodemus has advanced different arguments for each of these cases, nevertheless he has consistently maintained that post-mortem remembrance and good reputation are not valuable in themselves; that they cannot affect the dead, because the dead have no perception; but also, that our memory after death is ordinarily held dear by our friends, assuming that we have been good persons. Philodemus develops these contentions further in a separate section, which is devoted to the objection that death is harmful, and the prospect of it painful, when we anticipate that no one will remember us after we die. This section is important because it wraps up what Philodemus has to say about this topic, and also because it has an impact on issues concerning the prioritization of values and the status of post-mortem desires.

> It seems natural to feel a bite at the thought that no one at all will ever remember us, because this is sometimes the result of a friendless life and one that has had nothing good about it. But if someone who has lived well and has had the privilege of people's good will encounters some misfortune that whisks away those whom he knows, he will not lose anything in the large scheme of things. For we need these concomitant things (sc. to be remembered by one's friends) not for their own sake, but for the sake of the good life, to which they naturally appear as additions. And therefore, when that life is completed, why shall we care about that which is nothing to us even as a thought?
>
> (XXXV. 34–XXXVI. 8)

Here Philodemus evokes the distinction between natural and empty emotions to suggest that it may be permissible to feel a 'bite' of pain (cf. δηγμ[ὸν] φυσικ[όν]: XXXV. 36) when we anticipate that people will not hold us in their memory after we die. However, the natural 'bite' concerns a fact about one's life, not a state of affairs obtaining after one's death. It is a proper reaction to the absence of something very valuable, friendship, as opposed to post-mortem memory and reputation, which is totally useless to the dead. Hence there is no inconsistency with Philodemus' previous suggestion that post-mortem desires concerning one's reputation and remembrance are empty, and their fulfilment is nothing to us.

On the other hand, if we have fulfilled the natural desire to have friends and have enjoyed the pleasures of friendship, our friends will remember us after we die. In normal circumstances, their good memory of us is a natural by-product of friendship. Coining a new word for it, Philodemus calls it one of 'the concomitant things' (cf. *συνεκπτωμάτων*: XXXVI. 3), things that naturally appear in addition to (cf. *ἐπιγίγνεσθα*[*ι*]: XXXVI. 5) the good life of which friendship is an essential component. Moreover, he alludes to a distinction found also in Stoic texts, between things we pursue for their own sake and others which naturally, but not coincidentally, accompany those goods. And he maintains that friendship belongs to the former category, whereas our friends' good memory of us after we die belongs to the latter. Their memory of us can also be interpreted as an epiphenomenon of friendship, and a proof that the dead person has won and enjoyed the affection of genuine friends while he was alive. To the extent that it accompanies friendship, then, post-mortem remembrance is a pleasant prospect, whether or not circumstances will permit that it exists after one is dead. However, considered in itself and regardless of friendship, it has no value whatsoever.[171]

To argue this point, Philodemus first contemplates the case of someone who has achieved a complete life and won the love of friends, but subsequently found himself in some extreme situation deprived of everyone he knows (XXXV. 39–XXXVI. 2).[172] Since he has reached perfect happiness, death cannot deprive him of anything, even though he will die unknown

[171] As Armstrong (2006) argues (against Warren 2004), friendship is so important that it is worth our while to pursue even 'the concomitant things' for its sake. One way of doing so is to provide for our friends by writing a will. We should do so and with care, if the length and circumstances of our life allow. The goal of making such provisions in our will is to care for our friends, not to make them remember us after we die. However, the 'concomitant' result of our act will be that they will remember us with gratitude and love, and we have no reason, of course, to try to keep them from remembering us in that way.

[172] Armstrong (2006) remarks that the fact that Philodemus considers such a possibility shows how harsh life could be in the ancient world.

and will not be remembered (XXXV. 39–XXXVI. 42, XXXVI. 5–8). The triviality of a good reputation is shown by means of a thought experiment. Suppose that posterity believes someone to have been a happy man, whereas in fact he lived a miserable life. His posthumous reputation will not have made the least difference to the wretchedness of his life (XXXVI. 27–31). Besides, Philodemus points to the absurdities entailed by the ideas that commemoration after death is essential to happiness, but that forgetfulness affects it adversely. 'In truth, if it is a great misfortune not to be remembered, we must consider wretched most people who have lived since the time, [whatever that was], when things were recorded, and also all men who lived before that time, [since no one] recorded in historical documents anything at all [about them]. Or why would we not reach the point of calling wretched [simply everybody] who has been born or [even] will be born in the world since, when it gets destroyed, nobody will remember them, [for the whole world will be out of existence]?' (XXXVI. 17–26). This argument appeals to some kind of symmetry between the distant past and the infinite future, and has the structure of a *reductio*. If not to be remembered were a great evil, then everybody born in prehistoric times, as well as most people born in historic times, would have been subject to that evil and declared miserable. Likewise, everybody who has been born and everybody who will be born any time in the future will also become miserable, for eventually the world will be destroyed, and nobody will be left to remember anyone at all. Just as oblivion has marked those who lived before one's birth, so it will accompany oneself and those who will live after one's death. In short, anonymity in death is the common lot of human beings, the necessary outcome of both social and natural processes. We had better accept that fact, for the alternative of considering miserable everybody who has ever lived or will ever live is absurd.

A reasonable question to ask is why people often place such a high value on being remembered and having a good reputation after they die. Philodemus' plausible answer is, first, that they frequently project what certain things feel like in life on to the condition of being dead, and, second, that they confuse memory of past pleasures, which is essential to the good life, with post-mortem remembrance, which cannot affect the moral quality of the life that one has lived and is irrelevant after one is dead. 'They seem to think that they will consider not being talked about a painful thing after their life has ended, when they do not exist, because they turn their thoughts to what it is like to be neglected by men during life. And they rave aimlessly, calling blessed the memory which follows on whatever things attract the admiration of men and accompany unhappy lives, and not (calling blessed) just the memory which follows on the good things that one has enjoyed' (XXXVI. 8–16). The most effective means of correcting the first of these mistakes is the combined use of the non-identity and the non-perception arguments. Death implies that one does not exist any more (XXXVI. 10) and does not perceive anything, including whether one is remembered by posterity. Contrast a living man's painful awareness that he is being unnoticed or neglected. The second mistake is cured, at least in part, by a shift of focus. We should stop thinking about post-mortem remembrance, but turn our attention instead to the pleasures that we have had. When we realize that our life is complete on account of these pleasures, we shall get rid of empty emotions concerning a future state of affairs which will be nothing to us because then we shall be dead (cf. XXXVI. 5–8).

III

As suggested earlier in this chapter, both ancient and modern authors have notoriously accused the Epicurean philosophers of failing to identify and address the deepest fear concerning death: that we are going to die sometime, that we are mortal.[173] It is true, I think, that Epicurus and most of his followers do not explicitly refer to the fear of mortality, and do not directly confront it. However, they appear to recognize it as a distinct kind of fear which requires special treatment. Epicurus makes a gesture in that direction when he admonishes Menoeceus to practise (*πράττειν*) and run over in his mind (*μελετᾶν*) the precepts of the good life (D.L. X. 123), and to get used to the thought (cf. *συνέθιζε*: D.L. X. 124) that death is nothing to us. Philodemus gives a brilliant example of how this can be done in

[173] One such line of criticism concerning Epicurus is that the non-perception and the non-identity arguments are inefficient and even harmful with regard to the fear of mortality, because what we fear is precisely the experiential blank and the nothingness of death. Another line of criticism aimed at Lucretius is that, if the Symmetry Argument is intended to remove the fear of mortality, it fails, because the postulated symmetry in our attitudes towards prenatal and post-mortem non-existence is problematic; and even if that symmetry were to obtain, it is still questionable that it would remove distress at the thought that our life will sometime come to an end.

the peroration of *On Death* (XXXVII. 18 ff.). Developing the strategy first suggested by Epicurus, he shows us how a continual *meditatio mortis*, the day-to-day contemplation of death itself, enables us to 'get used to' (to understand and accept) the truth about death, reconcile ourselves with our human condition, and even make our mortality something enjoyable.[174]

Philodemus' style suits his purpose. He writes in a way strongly reminiscent of the so-called grand style of speaking, common to numerous literary and religious movements of the Hellenistic and Roman world, and developed further by Christian authors with the dual purpose of both instructing and moving the audience.[175] His sentences are long, dense, and unadorned, striving for sincerity and passion, taking on their solemn beauty from 'the force of the thought rather than the desire for decoration' (St Augustine, *Doct. Chr.* 4. 118).[176] They clothe a message worthy of their grandeur and simplicity which, if assimilated, should enable one to both live in happiness and die in serenity. Philodemus delivers it by bringing gradually to culmination the systematic contrast between sages and fools, people who have been initiated into Epicurean philosophy and those who have not. Let us now take a look at the contents of the peroration and reflect on the efficiency of Philodemus' philosophical rhetoric.

One main theme is the perception that many people have of imminent death as a paradoxical thing about which one has had little or no warning (XXXVII. 18–21). Although Philodemus concedes that in some cases death comes more unexpectedly than in others (XXXIX. 15–18), nonetheless he uses all the means in his power to imprint in our minds the truths that death is the rule and life the exception, and that we should not assume that we shall reach old age but, at most, hope that we might.

At any rate, to be caught unprepared when death falls upon us as if something unexpected and paradoxical were meeting us, (this) does [not] happen [to us], but it does happen to most people because they do not recognize that every human

[174] Tsouna 2006*b*: 103–14, contains an earlier discussion of the peroration of *On Death* and concludes that, although Philodemus' rhetoric may help to attenuate the fear of mortality, it does not prove that that fear is irrational.

[175] On the development and characteristics of the grand style, see Shuger 1988. It is controversial whether St Augustine, following Cicero and also St Paul, associates the grand style principally with the aim to influence the emotions of the audience, or sees it as serving the goals of both intellectual and emotional persuasion. On this see Shuger 1988: 42 ff. and the comments of Yunis 1996: 231–2.

[176] The text is cited and briefly discussed by Yunis (1996: 231 ff.). An interesting analysis of St Augustine's attitude to figurative language and rhetoric is found in Swearingen 1991: 174–214.

being, even if he were stronger than the Giants, is ephemeral concerning life and death, and that it is not just tomorrow that [is uncertain] but this very moment. For in respect of death we all inhabit 'an unwalled [city]' [and everything] is full of its causes both on account of our physical constitution, since we are so weak and the soul has so many passages totally ready to let it expire, and because the world that contains us generates innumerable causes of our dissolution as swift as chance and often as swift as thought,[177] and (because there is) the wickedness of men which brings on these things (sc. the causes of death mentioned above) and others impossible [for themselves] to guess and very many. Therefore, unless one is totally stupid, one will believe that the absurd and paradoxical thing is not that one should die, but that one should remain alive for some time, and that lasting until old age is the greatest wonder.

(XXXVII. 18–XXXVIII. 3)

Unlike people of Epicurean persuasion (cf. ἡμ[εῖ]ν: XXXVII. 21), then, ordinary men and philosophers too (cf. XXXVIII. 5–6) lose their composure at the approach of death because they have refused to recognize that they are mortal. Just what does this mean? Among other things, it implies that at least superficially fools assume or believe that there are ways of protecting oneself against death: for instance, by becoming more powerful, wealthier, etc. (XXXVII. 24). Moreover, locating the possibility of dying only in the future, they view the present as a time in which one can live with one's certitudes. On the other hand, opposing that way of thinking, Philodemus advocates a complete conversion, a fresh and informed perspective on life and death. The metaphor of the unwalled city, probably used first by Epicurus or Metrodorus, captures in a haunting manner the utter weakness and vulnerability of the *homo humanus*.[178] There is no protection against death. It can be anywhere and everywhere, both inside and outside, in one's constitution as much as in physical and social reality. It is a natural and usual thing that we should expect to happen to us and accept. The odds are that it will happen sooner rather than later, and we must acknowledge that probability as well. In the opposite case, the extra time that one is allowed should be seen as nothing short of a miracle (cf. τερατωδέστατον: XXXVIII. 3).[179] Of course, one is appropriately grateful for enjoying life some additional time (XXXVIII. 22–5). However, a

[177] Cf. Armstrong's translation of XXXVII. 34–6.

[178] See Gigante 1983*b*: 178–9.

[179] Philodemus' timing seems excellent. Presumably, he saves this truth until the end of the treatise, because he wishes to eradicate beforehand every residue of the fear of death. So long as we have such

person of understanding does not bank on a miracle. He does not make plans in the hope that a miracle may occur. In fact, he does not need one, for he can achieve happiness anyway, as the sequence of the systematic opposition between the sage and the fool aims to establish.

However, some have lived like such strangers to human life, and not just common people but also some of those who are called philosophers at any rate, that they determine to spend so many years in Athens for love of learning, so many years seeing Greece and what is accessible of foreign lands, so many years back home engaging in philosophical conversations, and the rest with their relatives and friends. 'But suddenly' Necessity 'steps forward unnoticed severing our long hopes'.[180] On the other hand, the sensible person, once he has realized that he can achieve everything sufficient in itself for a happy life, from that point onwards walks about like someone already laid out for burial in his shroud[181] and enjoys every single day as if it were an eternity. And when it is taken away from him [he steps forward] (to meet his death) without moaning about the possibility that he is joining (the company of the dead) missing in that manner something that belongs to the best life. Moreover, having received the additional time (allowed to him) in an appropriate way, as one who has encountered an unexpected piece of good fortune, he is thankful in this respect too to the nature of things.

(XXXVIII. 14–25)

So, according to Philodemus, the fools' status as aliens (cf. *παρω-<ι>κηκότες*: XXXVIII. 4) to life has to do with their attitudes towards the future. However, it is not clear just what is wrong in planning to devote a certain amount of time to each of several activities. The problem cannot be that one simply has future desires and plans. For instance, both the performance of the hedonistic calculus and the Epicurean practice of will-writing presuppose that an Epicurean has wishes and makes plans to the best of his ability about a number of things with a view to the future. Rather, the problem seems to be that many people form future-directed attitudes and projects without taking properly into account their

residues, we may not be ready to face the fact that death is everywhere and can strike at any time. In fact, we might become terrified at that thought, and that might delay the course of the therapy.

[180] On the provenance of these verses and Philodemus' substitution of 'Necessity' (*τὸ χρεών*: XXXVIII. 14) for 'Hades' (*Ἅιδης*: fr. 6, Schramm = 3 Nauck, 2nd edn.) in the original Hellenistic tragedy whose title is unknown, see Gigante 1983*b*: 206–13. The citation is well chosen by Philodemus, especially if it is true that the verses were cited before Philip II of Macedon shortly before he was murdered.

[181] Cf. Armstrong's wonderful translation of *ἐντεταφιασμένος περιπατεῖ*: XXXVIII. 17–18.

own mortality. Death can come at any time, including when it is least expected. But this truth is disregarded by those who assume that their life will have considerable duration and that, towards its end, it should exhibit a recognizably finished structure or a complete life story. The foolishness of a person who, like Cicero or Atticus, divides his life up into temporal phases of studying, travelling, returning home to practice philosophy, etc., consists, then, not in the intrinsic unworthiness of these objectives, but in the spirit in which he pursues them. Forgetting the ever-presence of death, he gives value to the realization of a life plan which is itself dependent on temporal duration. And he perceives his life as complete if that plan gets fulfilled, but incomplete if it does not.

On the other hand, a sensible person and, in particular, the sage rejects this kind of narrative approach to life and considers duration to have a small impact on life's completeness and happiness. Although there is room for pursuing future-directed plans in the right manner, the essential thing for one's happiness is not the fulfilment of these plans but the attainment of ἀπονία, complete freedom from disturbance and pain. As Philodemus suggested earlier, duration plays only a small role in achieving and enjoying ἀπονία, and once this happens, the sage's happiness is perfect and his life complete. In terms of quantity or quality, there is nothing valuable that life can add to or subtract from him at this point. A striking metaphor renders what the Epicureans, and paradigmatically the sage, experience on a regular basis. They walk about always wearing their death (cf. the metaphor of walking about like someone 'already laid out for burial in his shroud', ἐντεταφιασμένος περιπατεῖ, XXXVIII. 17–18),[182] and that perpetual symbiosis with death is the real source of their strength. It constitutes the foundation of both their preparedness to meet death and their perception of every single day as an eternity. This last claim indicates that the Epicureans perceive the pleasure deriving from a single day not as lasting longer for them, but as being as perfect and complete as it would be if it had lasted an eternity (cf. Epicurus, *KD* 19–21).

It is important not to confuse this day-to-day exquisite enjoyment of life with an obsessive kind of *carpe diem*, living in the present without any further

[182] According to Armstrong (2004: 49), Philodemus evokes here the imagery of death and resurrection, used in mystery religions in connection with rituals of initiation. Armstrong points out that similar images are used by Christian authors to render the unique eschatological experience of Jesus.

consideration or concern. The former kind of enjoyment derives from the constant contemplation of death itself, whereas the latter is an irrational reaction to the reality of death when one vainly tries to brush it aside (cf. *De elect.* XVII. 3–10).[183] The objection has been raised that the attitude advocated by Philodemus, and in particular the day-to-day attainment of perfect happiness, may be incoherent or psychologically impossible. For in fact most people's lives are characterized by long-term goals which constitute both projects and reasons for wishing to continue to live.[184] On the one hand, it is true that Philodemus does not offer arguments to defend his claim that people wrapped up in the contemplation of their mortality are able to enjoy each day as if it were an age. On the other hand, if my interpretation of the relevant passages is correct, Philodemus' position has more plausibility than it is given credit for. He does not urge us to avoid setting goals whose completion lies somewhere in the future, but only to bear in mind that their fulfilment is both contingent and unimportant for the happiness we have. Besides, he implicitly warns us to avoid seeing the satisfaction of such goals as a main reason for desiring to live more, since the pleasures of a fully realized life supply sufficient motivation for wishing to do so.

The contrast between the fool and the sage becomes sharper when Philodemus turns to the case of an old man who remains obstinately oblivious to his own mortality despite the many reminders that he receives, and who undertakes projects revealing the empty desire to prolong his life indeterminately into the future or even to live for ever (XXXVIII. 25 ff.). He refuses to recognize that a longer life is a rare gift (XXXVIII. 28–31), and that he has been lucky to receive it. He undertakes projects impossible to complete within his own lifetime—for instance, planting cypresses and expecting them to grow, or laying foundations for buildings which would take several generations to finish (XXXVIII. 35–XXXIX. 1). He is tortured by avarice and greed, which, according to both Lucretius and Philodemus,[185] are masks of the fear of death (XXXVIII. 36–7),[186] whereas liberality and a reasonable attitude to money indicate that one does not have that fear. Perhaps more than other fools, the old 'drone of a man'

[183] On Philodemus' criticisms of *carpe diem*, see Indelli and Tsouna-McKirahan 1995: 195–200.

[184] Warren 2004: 152–3.

[185] Cf. *De elect.* XIX. 12–16, XX. 6–12.

[186] Cf. also *De ir.* XV. 21; *De elect.* XX. 9–11. On this last passage, see the commentary of Gigante 1983*d*: 268–73.

(κηφηνώδης: XXXVIII. 26) is terrorized by death and tries hard not to think about it. To be exact, Philodemus says that such people 'push away even the focusings on it' (XXXIX. 8–9). The term rendered as focusing is 'ἐπιβολάς' (XXXIX. 8), and it occurs again in the very last line of the treatise, where it refers to the sage's constant contemplation of death (cf. XXXIX. 25). In both contexts ἐπιβολή seems to be shorthand for one of the Epicurean criteria of truth: namely, φανταστικὴ ἐπιβολὴ τῆς διανοίας (cf. D.L. X. 31), 'the focusing of thought into an impression'[187] or 'an act of focusing the mind on an object or state of affairs which leads to a sense-impression'.[188] So, Philodemus' point seems to be this. The old fool is forced into a state of denial. He shrinks away from his own ἐπιβολαί, sense-like mental impressions yielding self-evident truths about death. Therefore, he is totally taken aback 'when the vision of death becomes clear' (XXXIX. 9–10).

Philodemus dwells at length on this point: i.e., what one does at the very moment when one realizes that one's death is imminent and cannot be evaded. In fact, it is an essential element of the contrast between the fool and the sage and is the theme with which the treatise ends. The old fool, when faced with imminent death, is paralysed or becomes totally inconsistent in word and deed.[189] The kind of thinking that leads him to such extremes is like 'believing that glass and pottery vessels which collide repeatedly with other vessels made of adamant steel will remain unbroken' (XXXIX. 2–6). He reacts as if the human constitution were immortal and imperishable (cf. XXXVIII. 27–8), whereas, in fact, human beings are utterly vulnerable and fragile for reasons already mentioned. They cannot last long against the attack of the numerous causes of death, as fragile objects cannot survive collision with very hard substances. The metaphor highlights the utter irrationality of the old fool, and also prepares the ground for Philodemus' final move.

'On the other hand, the sensible men, [even if for] some compelling reason they did not suspect that the paragraph mark and limit of their life was already approaching, when it comes into actual view, after they have surveyed in their thought systematically and with the greatest clarity, in a way that cannot be explained to the ignorant, their perfect enjoyment

[187] Cf. Long and Sedley 1987: 87–90. [188] Striker 1974: 36.

[189] Cf. 'They are forced "to be in two minds" as Democritus says' (XXXIX. 13–15). On the interpretation of the phrase, see Gigante 1983*b*: 226–33.

of every thing and the utter unconsciousness that will come over them, they breathe their last as calmly as if they had never lost their focusing even for an instant' (XXXIX. 15–25). Using a well-chosen literary pun, Philodemus now turns to those who have understood the truth about life and death and who are near 'the paragraph mark and limit' of their life (cf. *παράγραφον*: XXXIX. 18), and he invites us to reflect on their attitude before we ourselves reach the paragraph mark signalling the end of the treatise.[190] There are two main points of contrast with the old fool: one concerning the kind of mental training required in order to be prepared to face imminent death, the other concerning the very last mental act of enlightened people just before they expire.

Unlike fools, these last are prepared to meet their death regardless of how suddenly it might come. What enables them to do so is, as we have been told, that they have always lived as if they were wearing their shroud ready to be entombed (XXXVIII. 17–18). The final lines of the treatise (XXXIX. 24–5), however, suggest what that metaphor means in epistemological terms. Sensible people have lived attending to their every *ἐπιβολή* about death (cf. *ἐπιβολήν*: XXXIX. 25), contemplating the reality of death in their imagination and thought. The conclusion that they expire as serenely as they would have if they had not interrupted their *ἐπιβολή* for a single moment (XXXIX. 24–5) implies that there are occasional lapses of *ἐπιβολή*, and also that such interruptions do not matter at all. But it seems to me that they would matter, if *ἐπιβολή* were a mere focusing of attention. Rather, *ἐπιβολή* should be interpreted as an intense and comprehensive mental act[191] which supports one's acceptance of one's own mortality, much as one's *ἐπιβολή* of past, present, and future pleasures fortifies one's piety towards the gods (*De dis* III. 2. 23–7).[192] We cannot be thinking literally all the time about death or about the gods, and we do not need to. It is sufficient for our peace of mind to direct our thought to these subjects as continually as we can, in a sustained and intelligent manner.

Great emphasis is now placed on a last difference between fools and sensible persons, related to the ability to compose oneself when death comes into full view. Fools are dragged out of life in mental and emotional disarray (cf. XXXIX. 6–15), because they have refused to accept the reality

[190] Cf. Armstrong 2004: 51–2.

[191] Cf. Bailey 1926: 259 ff.

[192] The first to note this parallel is Armstrong (2004: 50–1).

of death and, consequently, have been devastated by its sudden approach. Unlike them, people of genuine understanding are always ready to leave life without moaning and without particular regret (cf. XXXVIII. 20–1), and they can do so even when they have least expected to die. The ultimate manifestation of their composure is the systematicity (cf. περ[ι]οδεύσαντες: XXXIX. 19) and clarity (ὀξύτα[τ]α: XXXIX. 20) with which they sum up in their mind the morally valuable features of the life that they have lived and the death that lies ahead: immediately before they die, they go systematically through the pleasures that they have enjoyed in life and contemplate the total unconsciousness that will come (XXXIX. 19–23). Philodemus emphatically declares that only those who have understanding can perform this mental act, whereas ignorant people cannot—in fact, it is a total mystery to them (XXXIX. 19–20). He also suggests that the serenity of the dying person is due both to his previous preparation for death and to this last mental presentation of his past and of the future. However, Philodemus does not explain why he attributes so much importance to the mental act under discussion. Perhaps it is a literary τόπος that he uses for rhetorical effect. Or, as I am inclined to think, that mental act may have moral and aesthetic dimensions. The dying sage surveys in his imagination the life that he has lived and the nothingness that will determine its limit, and he contemplates that image with pleasure as a perfect work of art.

To conclude, we should try to assess the therapeutic impact of the peroration of *On Death* and ascertain to what extent it can cure our fear that we will die sometime. Since it appears intended to wrap up the main themes of the fragment, it can be read as addressing all kinds of fears, and not only the fear of mortality; and reflections about the therapeutic value of the peroration may pertain to some extent to the entire treatise *On Death*.

Philodemus' superb fusion of form and content, of rhetoric and argument, will be more effective with some people than with others. However, I think that Philodemus largely succeeds in emphasizing the precariousness of human existence and disposing us to accept what mortality implies. It seems true that an adequate preparation for death requires considerable mental training, and that the sustained contemplation of the reality and inevitability of death should be an important part of that training. Philodemus' related suggestion, that our attitude towards future plans and projects should be determined by the awareness of our own mortality, is also intuitively plausible; regarding that point, the competing portraits of the old fool and the sage have a great deal of compelling force.

Less convincing, however, are Philodemus' further claims that death is the rule, but life the exception, and that we are all equally vulnerable to destruction at all times and to the same extent. The same holds for the ideas that the person of understanding attributes little or no value to the fulfilment of future desires and the completion of a life plan, but is prepared to die and, at the same time, able to enjoy life to the utmost on a daily basis. For this attitude could be psychologically unsustainable.[193] And it also depends on the controversial and peculiarly Epicurean view as to what constitutes life's perfection and completeness. An additional difficulty for Philodemus' therapeutics is that, unlike other fears concerning death, the fear of mortality has nothing to do with concrete circumstances concerning one's death. For instance, it does not depend on whether one's death will be painful, or whether it will come too soon, or whether one will be buried, remembered, etc., after death. It is a fear whose cognitive grounds are very hard to pin down and decide whether they are true or false. Moreover, as both Lucretius and Philodemus recognize, it is a vague and elusive kind of fear, in the sense that it becomes manifest in different ways (as ambition, lust, avarice, and so on) and moves from one psychological context to another. For these reasons we cannot tell for certain whether Philodemus is able fully to address it. On balance, however, I think that Philodemus is a successful therapist. If he does not altogether cure the fear of mortality, he offers powerful consolations to attenuate it. The same holds for other kinds of fears that he discusses in *On Death*, especially those whose circumstances can cause the sage to feel a natural 'bite' of pain: dying too early or too soon, knowing that our loved ones will suffer from our death, dying abroad among foreigners, and dying violently and unjustly. Yet other fears he demonstrates to be empty, and those who entertain them to be utter fools. One take-home message is perfectly clear: even though we may have natural post-mortem desires, all that truly matters lies in life, not in death. Philodemus argues case by case in order to imprint this Epicurean truth on our souls, and enable us, as he believes, to both live and die well.

[193] Cf. p. 264.

References and Select Bibliography

Acosta Méndez, E. (1983), 'PHerc. 1089: Filodemo "Sobre la adulacion"', *CErc* 13: 121–38.

——— and Angeli, A. (1992), *Testimonianze su Socrate* (Naples).

Adams, R. (1984), 'The Virtue of Faith', *Faith and Philosophy* 1: 3–15.

Adkins, A. W. H. (1969), 'Threatening, Abusing and Feeling Angry in the Homeric Poems', *Journal of Hellenic Studies* 89: 7–21.

Algra, K., *et al.* (1999), *The Cambridge History of Hellenistic Philosophy* (Cambridge).

Amoroso, F. (1975), 'Filodemo Sulla Conversazione', *CErc* 5: 63–76.

Angeli, A. (1994), 'Lo svolgimento dei papyri carbonizzati', in *Il rotolo librario: fabbricazione, restauro, organizzazione interna, Papyrologica Lupiensia* 3: 37–104.

——— and Colaizzo, M. (1979), 'I frammenti di Zenone Sidonio', *CErc* 9: 47–133.

Annas, J. (1989), 'Epicurean Emotions', *Greek, Roman and Byzantine Studies* 30: 145–64.

——— (1992), *Hellenistic Philosophy of Mind* (Berkeley and Los Angeles).

——— (1993), *The Morality of Happiness* (Oxford).

Armstrong, D. (2004), 'All Things to All Men: Philodemus' Model of Therapy and the Audience of *De morte*', in Fitzgerald *et al.* (eds.) (2004), *Philodemus and the New Testament* (Leiden), 15–54.

——— (2006), Review of Warren 2004, *Philosophical Quarterly* 56: 294–7.

——— and Henry, B. (unpublished, *a*), Text and translation of Philodemus *On Anger*.

——— ——— (unpublished, *b*), Text and translation of Philodemus, *On Death*.

Asmis, E. (1984), *Epicurus' Scientific Theory* (Ithaca, NY).

——— (1990), 'Philodemus' Epicureanism', *Aufstieg und Niedergang der römischen Welt*, II 36. 4: 2369–2406.

Auvray-Assayas, C., and Delattre, D. (2001) (eds.), *Cicéron et Philodème: La polémique en philosophie* (Paris).

Baier, A. (1986), 'Trust and Antitrust', *Ethics* 96: 231–60.

Bailey, C. (1926), *Epicurus: The Extant Remains* (Oxford).

——— (1928), *The Greek Atomists and Epicurus* (Oxford).

Baker, J. (1987), 'Trust and Rationality', *APQ* 68: 1–13.

Barnes, J. (1982), 'Medicine, Experience, and Logic', in Barnes *et al.* 1982: 24–68.

—— (1988), 'Epicurean Signs', *OSAP* suppl. vol. 1988: 91–134.

—— *et al.* (1982), *Science and Speculation* (Cambridge and Paris).

Becker, L. C. (1996), 'Trust as Noncognitive Security about Motives', *Ethics* 1996: 43–61.

Belshaw, C. (1993), 'Asymmetry and Non-existence', *Philosophical Studies* 70: 103–16.

Berger, F. (1975), 'Gratitude', *Ethics* 85: 298–309.

Betensky, A. (1980), 'Lucretius and Love', *Classical World* 73: 291–9.

Blank, D. (1985), 'Socratics versus Sophists on Payment for Teaching', *Classical Antiquity* 4: 1–49.

—— (1995), 'Philodemus on the Technicity of Rhetoric', in Obbink 1995: 178–88.

—— (2001), 'La philologie comme arme philosophique: la connaissance technique de la rhétorique dans l'épicurisme', in Auvray-Assayas and Delattre 2001: 241–57.

Blum, L. A. (1980), *Friendship, Altruism and Morality* (London).

Blundell, M. (1989), *Helping Friends and Harming Enemies: A Study in Sophocles and Greek Ethics* (Cambridge).

Bollack, J. (1975), *La pensée du plaisir: Épicure: textes moraux, commentaires* (Paris).

Braund, S. M., and Gill, C. (1997) (eds.), *The Passions in Roman Thought and Practice* (Cambridge).

Brown, E. (2002), 'Epicurus on the Value of Friendship (*Sententia Vaticana* 23)', *CP* 97. 1: 68–80.

Brown, R. D. (1987), *Lucretius on Love and Sex* (Leiden).

Brueckner, A., and Fischer, J. M. (1986): 'Why is Death Bad?', *Philosophical Studies* 50: 213–21.

—— —— (1993), 'Death's Badness', *PPQ* 74: 37–45.

—— —— (1998), 'Being Born Earlier', *Australasian Journal of Philosophy* 76: 110–14.

Brunschwig, J., and Nussbaum, M. C. (1993) (eds.), *Passions and Perceptions* (Cambridge).

Caini, C. (1939): *Sui papiri ercolanesi 222, 223, e 1082 (Filodemo Περὶ κολακείας)* (Naples).

Calhoun, C., and Solomon, R. C. (1984), *What Is an Emotion?* (New York).

Capasso, M. (1979), 'Il presunto Papiro di Fania', *CErc* 9: 156–8.

—— (1995), *Volumen: Aspetti della tipologia del rotolo librario antico* (Naples).

—— (2001), 'Les livres sur la flatterie dans le *De vitiis* de Philodème', in Auvray-Assayas and Delattre 2001: 179–94.

Card, C. (1988), 'Gratitude and Obligation', *APQ* 25. 2: 115–27.

Cavallo, G. (1983), *Libri scritture scribi a Ercolano*, *CErc* 13 suppl. i.

Clay, D. (1983), *Lucretius and Epicurus* (Ithaca, NY).

——(1996), 'Deep Therapy', Review of Nussbaum 1994, *Philosophy and Literature* 20: 501–5.

——(1998), *Paradosis and Survival* (Ann Arbor).

Cockburn, D. (1997), *Other Times: Philosophical Perspectives on Past, Present, and Future* (Cambridge).

Coleman, J. S. (1990), *Foundations of Social Theory* (Cambridge, Mass).

Considine, P. (1966), 'Some Homeric Terms for Anger', *Acta Classica* 9: 15–25.

Cooper, J. M. (1993), 'Rhetoric, Dialectic, and the Passions', *OSAP* 11: 175–98.

——(1998*a*), 'Pleasure and Desire in Epicurus', in Cooper 1998*b*: 485–514.

——(1998*b*), *Reason and Emotion: Essays on Ancient Moral Psychology and Ethical Theory* (Princeton).

——(1998*c*), 'Posidonius on Emotions', in Sihvola and Engberg-Pedersen 1998: 71–111; repr. in Cooper 1998*b*: 449–84.

Croenert, W. (1906), *Kolotes und Menedemos* (Leipzig).

Dauer, F. W. (1988), 'The Picture as the Medium of Humorous Incongruity', *APQ* 25. 3: 241–51.

——(1993), 'Between Belief and Fantasy: A Study of the Imagination', in P. Guyer and H. Putnam (eds.) (1993), *The Pursuit of Reason: Essays in Honor of Stanley Cavell* (Lubbock, Tex.), 265–90.

Davidson, D. (1976), 'Hume's Cognitive Theory of Pride', *JP* 73. 19: 744–57.

De Falco, V. (1926), 'Appunti sul περὶ κολακείας di Filodemo, Pap. Herc. 1675', *RIGI* 10: 15–26.

De Lacy, P. (1972–89), *Galen: On the Doctrines of Hippocrates and Plato*, 3 vols. Text with English translation and commentary (Corpus Medicorum Graecorum; Berlin).

——and De Lacy, E. (1958), 'Epicurean ἐπιλογισμός', *American Journal of Philology* 79: 179–83.

————(1978), *Philodemus: On Methods of Inference*, 2nd edn. (Naples).

De Witt, N. W. (1954), *Epicurus and his Philosophy* (Minneapolis).

Deichgraeber, K. (1930), *Die griechische Empirikerschule* (Berlin and Zurich).

Deigh, J. (1994), 'Cognitivism in the Theory of Emotions', *Ethics* 104. 4: 825–54.

Delattre, D. (2003), 'Les figures du sage et du philosophe au travers de quatre livres éthiques de Philodème', *CErc* 33: 229–41.

Edelstein, L., and Kidd, I. (1972–89) (eds.), *Posidonius*, 2 vols. (Cambridge).

Erler, M. (1992), 'Der Zorn des Helden: Philodems "De ira" und Vergils Konzept des Zorns in der "Aeneis" ', *Grazer Beiträge* 18: 103–26.

Everson, S. (1998) (ed.), *Ethics* (Cambridge).

Feldman, F. (1990), 'F. M. Kamm and the Mirror of Time', *Pacific Philosophical Quarterly* 71: 23–7.

—— (1992), *Confrontations with the Reaper: A Philosophical Study of the Nature and Value of Death* (Oxford).

Fillion-Lahille, J. (1970), 'La colère chez Aristote', *Revue des Études Anciennes* 72: 46–79.

—— (1984), *Le De ira de Sénèque et la philosophie stoïcienne des passions* (Paris).

Findlay, J. N. (1954), 'The Justification of Attitudes', *Mind* 63: 145–61.

Fingarette, H. (1979), 'Feeling Guilty', *APQ* 16. 2: 159–64.

Fish, J. (2004), 'Anger, Philodemus' Good King, and the Helen Episode of *Aeneid* 2. 567–589: A New Proof of Authenticity from Herculaneum', in D. Armstrong *et al.* (eds.) (2004), *Vergil, Philodemus, and the Augustans* (Austin, Tex.), 111–38.

Fitzgerald, J. T. (1996) (ed.), *Friendship, Flattery, and Frankness of Speech: Studies on Friendship in the New Testament World* (Leiden).

Fitzgerald, W. (1984), 'Lucretius' Cure for Love in the *De rerum natura*', *Classical World* 78: 73–86.

Fortenbaugh W. W. (1970), 'Aristotle's *Rhetoric* on Emotions', *Archiv für Geschichte der Philosophie* 52: 40–70.

—— and White, S. A. (2006) (eds.), *Aristo of Ceos: Text, Translation, and Discussion* (Studies in Classical Humanities 13; New Brunswick, NJ and London).

Fosse, B., Kleve, K., and Stormer, F. (1984), 'Unrolling the Herculaneum papyri', *BCPE* 14: 9–15.

Foucault, M. (1984), *Histoire de la sexualité*, iii: *Le Souci de soi* (Paris).

Fowler, D. (1997), 'Epicurean Anger', in Braund and Gill 1997: 16–35.

Frede, M. (1986), 'The Stoic Doctrine of the Affections of the Soul', in Schofield and Striker 1986: 93–110.

—— (1987*a*), 'The Ancient Empiricists', in Frede 1987*b*: 243–60.

—— (1987*b*), *Essays in Ancient Philosophy* (Oxford).

—— (1987*c*), 'Philosophy and Medicine in Antiquity', in Frede 1987*b*: 225–42.

—— and Striker, G. (1996) (eds.), *Rationality in Greek Thought* (Oxford).

Frischer, B. (1982), *The Sculpted Word* (Berkeley).

Furley, D. J. (1986), 'Nothing to Us?', in Schofield and Striker 1986: 75–91.

Gaines, R. N. (1982), 'Qualities of Rhetorical Expression in Philodemus', *Transactions of the American Philological Association* 112: 71–81.

Gargiulo, T. (1981), 'PHerc. 222: Filodemo sull'adulazione', *CErc* 11: 103–27.

Giannantoni, G., and Gigante, M. (1996) (eds.), *Epicureismo Greco e Romano*, 3 vols. (Naples).

Gigante, M. (1975), ' "Philosophia medicans" in Filodemo', *CErc* 5: 53–61.

—— (1983*a*), 'Filodemo sulla libertà di parola', in Gigante 1983*d*: 55–114.

Gigante, M. (1983*b*), 'La chiusa del quarto libro *Della morte* di Filodemo', in Gigante 1983*d*: 163–234.

——(1983*c*), 'L'inizio del quarto libro *Della morte* di Filodemo', in Gigante 1983*d*: 115–62.

——(1983*d*), *Ricerche Filodemee*, 2nd edn. (Naples).

——(1992), *Cinismo e Epicureismo* (Naples).

——(1995), *Philodemus in Italy: The Books from Herculaneum*, trans. D. Obbink (Ann Arbor).

——(1997), 'Atakta XVI', *CErc* 27: 151–6.

——(2000), 'Libri morali di Filodemo', *CErc* 30: 125–30.

——and Indelli, G. (1978), 'Bione e l'epicureismo', *CErc* 8: 124–31.

Gill, C. (1996), *Personality in Greek Epic, Tragedy, and Philosophy: The Self in Dialogue* (Oxford).

Glannon, W. (1994), 'Temporal Asymmetry, Life and Death', *APQ* 31: 235–44.

Gomperz, T. (1864), *Philodemi Epicurei De ira liber* (Leipzig).

Goulet-Cazé, M.-O. (1986), *L'Ascèse cynique* (Paris).

Griffiths, P. E. (1997), *What Emotions Really Are: The Problem of Psychological Categories* (Chicago and London).

Hadot, P. (1995), *Philosophy as a Way of Life*, trans. M. Chase (Oxford).

Hahm, D. (2006), 'In Search of Aristo of Ceos', in Fortenbaugh and White 2006: 179–215.

Hankinson, J. (1993), 'Actions and Passions: Affection, Emotion and Moral Self-management in Galen's Philosophical Psychology', in Brunschwig and Nussbaum 1993: 184–222.

Hanser, M. (1998), 'A Puzzle about Beneficence', *Analysis* 58. 2: 159–65.

Harris, W. V. (2001), *Restraining Rage: The Ideology of Anger Control in Classical Antiquity* (Cambridge, Mass).

Hunt, L. H. (1975), 'Generosity', *APQ* 12. 3: 235–44.

——(1978), 'Character and Thought', *APQ* 15. 3: 177–86.

Ierodiakonou, K. (1995), 'Alexander of Aphrodisias on Medicine as a Stochastic Art', in P. van der Eijk (ed.) (1995), *Ancient Medicine in its Sociocultural Context* (Amsterdam and Atlanta), 473–85.

Indelli, G. (1988), *Filodemo, L'ira* (Naples).

——(2001), 'Per una nuova edizione del PHerc. 1008 (Filodemo, *I vizi*, libro X)', in *Atti del XXII Congresso Internazionale di Papirologia* (Florence), 693–8.

——and Tsouna-McKirahan, V. (1995), *[Philodemus] [On Choices and Avoidances]* (Naples).

Inwood, B. (1985), *Ethics and Human Action in Early Stoicism* (Oxford).

—— (1993), 'Seneca and Psychological Dualism', in Brunschwig and Nussbaum 1993: 150–83.

Ioppolo, A. M. (1980), *Aristone di Chio e lo Stoicismo antiquo* (Naples).

—— (1996), 'Il Περὶ τοῦ κουφίζειν ὑπερηφανίας: una polemica antiscettica in Filodemo?', in Giannantonni and Gigante 1996: 715–34.

—— and Sedley, D. N. (2006), *Philosophers, Politicians, and Patrons* (Rome).

Janko, R. (2000), *Philodemus: On Poems Book I* (Oxford).

Jensen, C. (1907), *Philodemi Περὶ οἰκονομίας qui dicitur libellus* (Leipzig).

—— (1911), *Philodemi Περὶ κακιῶν liber decimus* (Leipzig).

—— (1933), *Ein neuer Brief Epikurs* (Berlin).

Jones, K. (1996), 'Trust as an Affective Attitude', *Ethics* 107: 4–25.

Kamm, F. (1993), *Morality, Mortality*, i: *Death and Whom to Save from It* (Oxford).

Karamanolis, G. (2005), 'Philodemus, Περὶ ὕβρεως? (PHerc. 1017): New Readings and the Philodemean Conception of *hybris*', *CErc* 35: 103–10.

Kaufman, F. (1999), 'Pre-vital and Post-mortem Non-existence', *APQ* 36: 1–19.

Klein, I. (1865), *Vocum Hippocraticarum collectio* (Leipzig).

Kleve, K. (1983), 'Scurra Atticus: The Epicurean View of Socrates', in *Syzetesis: Studi sull'epicureismo greco e romano offerti a Marcello Gigante*, 2 vols. (Naples), i. 226–53.

Kondo, E. (1974), 'Per l'interpretazione del pensiero filodemeo sulla adulazione nel PHerc. 1457', *CErc* 4: 43–56.

Konstan, D. (1995), 'Patrons and Friends', *CP* 90: 328–42.

—— (1996*a*), 'Friendship from Epicurus to Philodemus', in Giannantoni and Gigante 1996, i. 387–96.

—— (1996*b*), 'Greek Friendship', *American Journal of Philology* 117: 71–94.

—— (1997), *Friendship in the Classical World* (Cambridge).

—— *et al.* (1998), *Philodemus on Frank Criticism: Introduction, Translation, and Notes* (Albany, NY, and New York).

Kripke, S. (1980), *Naming and Necessity* (Princeton).

Kuiper, T. (1925), *Philodemus Over den Dood* (Amsterdam).

Laurenti, R. (1973), *Filodemo e il pensiero economico degli Epicurei* (Milan).

Leighton, S. R. (1985), 'A New View of Emotion', *APQ* 22. 2: 133–41.

Levenbook, B. B. (1984), 'Harming Someone after his Death', *Ethics* 94: 407–19.

Long, A. A. (1971), '*Aisthēsis, prolēpsis* and Linguistic Theory in Epicurus', *Bulletin of the Institute of Classical Studies* 18: 114–33.

—— (1986), 'Pleasure and Social Utility—The Virtues of Being Epicurean', in H. Flashar and O. Gigon (eds.) (1986), *Aspects de la philosophie hellénistique* (Entretiens sur l'antiquité classique 32; Geneva), 283–324.

Long, A. A. and Sedley, D. N. (1987), *The Hellenistic Philosophers*, 2 vols. (Cambridge).

Longo Auricchio, F. (1971), 'Aspetti e problemi della dissidenza epicurea', *CErc* 11: 25–40.

——(1977), Φιλοδήμου Περὶ ῥητορικῆς *libros primum et secundum* (Ricerche sui Papiri ercolanesi a cura di F. Sbordone 3; Naples).

——(1986), 'Sulla concezione filodemea dell'adulazione', *CErc* 16: 79–91.

——and Capasso, M. (1987), 'I rotolli della villa Ercolanese: dislocazione e ritrovamento', *CErc* 17: 37–47.

——and Tepedino Guerra, A. (1982), 'Chi è Timasagora?', in *La regione sotterrata dal Vesuvio: Studi e prospettive* (Naples), 405–13.

Luper-Foy, S. (1987), 'Annihilation', *Philosophical Quarterly* 37: 233–52.

Mancini Concolino, A. (1976), 'Sulle opere polemiche di Colote', *CErc* 6: 61–7.

Mangoni, C. (1993), *Filodemo: Il quinto libro della poetica* (Naples), trans. D. Armstrong, in Obbink 1995: 255–69.

McMahan, J. (1988), 'Death and the Value of Life', *Ethics* 99: 32–61.

Meikle, S. (1995), *Aristotle's Economic Thought* (Oxford).

Miller, C. L. (1976), 'Ironic or Not?', *APQ* 13. 4: 309–13.

Milo, R. D. (1983), 'Wickedness', *APQ* 20. 1: 69–79.

Mitsis, P. (1988*a*), *Epicurus' Ethical Theory: The Pleasures of Invulnerability* (Ithaca, NY).

——(1988*b*), 'Epicurus on Death and Duration', *Proceedings of the Boston Area Colloquium for Ancient Philosophy* 4: 303–22.

——(1996), 'Epicureans on Death and the Deprivations of Death', in Giannantoni and Gigante 1996: 805–12.

Momigliano, A. (1973–4), 'Freedom of Speech in Antiquity', in P. P. Wiener (ed.) (1973–4), *Dictionary of the History of Ideas: Studies in Selected Pivotal Ideas* (New York), ii. 259.

Monet, A. (2001), 'La *Flatterie* de Philodème et l'organisation des *Vices*: réponse à Mario Capasso', in Auvray-Assayas and Delattre 2001: 195–202.

Murphy, L. B. (1993), 'The Demands of Beneficence', *PPA* 22. 4: 267–92.

Murray, O. (1965), 'Philodemus on the Good King according to Homer', *Journal of Roman Studies* 55: 161–82.

Nagel, T. (1979), 'Death', in his *Mortal Questions* (Cambridge), 1–10.

——(1986), *The View from Nowhere* (Oxford).

Natali, C. (1995), '*Oikonomia* in Hellenistic Political Thought', in A. Laks and M. Schofield (eds.) (1995), *Justice and Generosity* (Cambridge), 95–128.

Nehamas, A. (1992), 'Pity and Fear in the *Rhetoric* and the *Poetics*', in A. O. Rorty (ed.) (1992), *Essays on Aristotle's Poetics* (Princeton), 291–314.

——(1998), *The Art of Living* (Berkeley).

Neubecker, A. J. (1986), *Philodem: Über die Musik, Viertes Buch* (Naples).

Nussbaum, M. (1994), *The Therapy of Desire* (Princeton).

O'Connor, D. K. (1989), 'The Invulnerable Pleasures of Epicurean Friendship', *Greek, Roman and Byzantine Studies* 30: 165–86.

O'Keefe, T. (2001), 'Is Epicurean Friendship Altruistic?', *Apeiron* 34. 4: 269–305.

Obbink, D. (1995) (ed.), *Philodemus and Poetry* (Oxford).

—— (1996), *Philodemus, On Piety Part I* (Oxford).

Olivieri, A. (1914), *Philodemi Περὶ παρρησίας libellus* (Leipzig); repr. in D. Konstan *et al.* 1998.

Parfit, D. (1984), *Reasons and Persons* (Oxford).

Partridge, E. (1981), 'Posthumous Interests and Posthumous Respect', *Ethics* 91: 243–64.

Ponczoch, J. (unpublished), edition, translation, and commentary of PHerc. 1570.

Procopé, J. (1993), 'Epicureans on Anger', in Sihvola and Engberg-Pedersen 1998: 171–96.

Puglia, E. (1988), *Demetrio Lacone: Aporie testuali ed esegetiche in Epicuro (PHerc. 1012)* (Naples).

Ranocchia, G. (2001), 'Filodemo e il Περὶ τοῦ κουφίζειν ὑπερηφανίας: contributo ad una nuova edizione del PHerc. 1008', *Papyrologica Lupiensia* 10: 233–63.

—— (2006), 'L'autore del Περὶ τοῦ κουφίζειν ὑπερηφανίας: un problema riaperto', in Fortenbaugh and White 2006: 239–59.

Rawson, E. (1985), *Intellectual Life in the Late Roman Republic* (London).

Renehan, R. (1963), 'Aristotle's Definition of Anger', *Philologus* 107: 61–76.

Ringeltaube, H. (1913), *Quaestiones ad veterum philosophorum de affectibus doctrinam pertinentes* (Göttingen).

Rist, J. M. (1980), *Epicurus on Friendship, CP* 75: 121–9.

Roberts, C. R. (1991), 'What is Wrong with Wicked Feelings', *APQ* 28. 1: 13–24.

Robin, L. (1962), *Lucrèce, De la Nature, Commentaire des livres III–IV* (Paris; orig. pub. 1926).

Romeo, C. (1988), *Demetrio Lacone: Sulla Poesia* (Naples).

Rorty Oksenberg, A. (1980), *Explaining Emotions* (Berkeley).

—— (1987), *The Rationality of Emotion* (Cambridge, Mass.).

Rosenbaum, S. E. (1989), 'The Symmetry Argument: Lucretius against the Fear of Death', *Philosophy and Phenomenological Research* 50: 353–73.

Salomon, R. C. (1988), 'On Emotions as Judgments', *APQ* 25. 2: 183–91.

Sanders, K. (unpublished), 'The Conclusion of Philodemus' *De ira*'.

Santoro, M. (2000), *[Demetrio Lacone], [La forma del dio] (PHerc. 1055)* (Naples).

Schofield, M. (1996), ''Επιλογισμός: An Appraisal', in Frede and Striker 1996: 221–37.

Schofield, M. and Striker, G. (1986) (eds.), *The Norms of Nature: Studies in Hellenistic Ethics* (Paris and Cambridge).

Schrijvers, P. H. (1970), *Horror ac Divina Voluptas: Études sur la poétique et la poésie de Lucrèce* (Amsterdam).

Scully, S. (1984), 'The Language of Achilles: The ὀχθήσας Formulas', *Transactions of the American Philological Association* 114: 11–27.

Sedley, D. N. (1973), 'Epicurus *On Nature* Book XXVIII', *CErc* 3: 5–83.

—— (1976*a*), 'Epicurus and his Professional Rivals', *Cahiers de philologie publiés par le Centre de Recherche de l'Université de Lille* 1: 121–59.

—— (1976*b*), 'Epicurus and the Mathematicians of Cyzicus', *CErc* 6: 23–54.

—— (1982), 'On Signs', in Barnes *et al.* 1982: 239–72.

—— (1989), 'Philosophical Allegiance in the Greco-Roman World', in M. Griffin and J. Barnes (eds.) (1989), *Philosophia Togata*, i (New York), 97–119.

—— (1996), 'The Inferential Foundations of Epicurean Ethics', in Giannantoni and Gigante 1996: 313–40.

—— (1998), *Lucretius and the Transformation of Greek Wisdom* (Cambridge).

—— (1999), Review of Nussbaum 1994, *Times Literary Supplement*, 24 June.

—— (2003), 'Philodemus and the Decentralisation of Philosophy', *CErc* 33: 31–41.

Segal, C. P. (1990), *Lucretius on Death and Anxiety* (Princeton).

Shuger, D. K. (1988), *Sacred Rhetoric: The Christian Grand Style in the English Renaissance* (Princeton).

Sider, D. (1997), *The Epigrams of Philodemos* (New York and Oxford).

Sihvola, J., and Engberg-Pedersen, T. (1998) (eds.), *The Emotions in Hellenistic Philosophy* (Dordrecht, Boston, and London).

Silverstein, H. (1980), 'The Evil of Death', *Journal of Philosophy* 77: 401–24.

Smith, M. F. (1993), *Diogenes of Oinoanda: The Epicurean Inscription* (Naples).

Snyder, H. G. (2000), *Teachers and Texts in the Ancient World* (London and New York).

Sorabji, R. (1983), *Time, Creation and the Continuum* (London).

—— (2000), *Emotions and Peace of Mind* (Oxford).

Staden, H. von (1975), 'Experiment and Experience in Hellenistic Medicine', *Bulletin of the Institute of Classical Studies* 22: 178–99.

Stoker, M. (1987), 'Emotional Thoughts', *APQ* 24. 1: 59–69.

Stork, P., *et al.* (2006), 'Aristo of Ceos: The Sources, Text and Translation', in Fortenbaugh and White 2006: 1–177.

Striker, G. (1974), 'Κριτήριον τῆς ἀληθείας', *Nachrichten der Akademie der Wissenshaften zu Goettingen*, I. Phil.- Hist. Klasse II: 48–110; repr. in Striker 1996: 22–76.

—— (1977), 'Epicurus on the Truth of Sense-Impressions', *Archiv für Geschichte der Philosophie* 59: 125–42; repr. in Striker 1996: 77–91.

—— (1988), Comments on P. Mitsis, 'Epicurus on Death and Duration', *Proceedings of the Boston Area Colloquium in Ancient Philosophy* 4: 322–8.

—— (1996), *Essays in Hellenistic Epistemology and Ethics* (Cambridge).

Sudhaus, S. (1896), *Philodemi Volumina Rhetorica*, 2 vols. (Leipzig; repr. 1964, Amsterdam).

Sullivan, S. D. (1993), 'Person and θυμός in the Poetry of Hesiod', *Emerita* 61: 15–40.

Swearingen, C. J. (1991), *Rhetoric and Irony: Western Literacy and Western Lies* (Oxford).

Tepedino Guerra, A. (1977), 'Filodemo sulla gratitudine', *CErc* 7: 96–113.

—— (1978), 'Il primo libro sulla riccheza di Filodemo', *CErc* 8: 52–95.

—— (1985), 'Il PHerc. 1678: Filodemo sull'invidia?', *CErc* 15: 113–25.

—— (1994), 'L'opera filodemea *Su Epicuro* (PHerc. 1232, 1289b)', *CErc* 24: 5–53.

Tiberius, V. and Walker, J. D. (1998), 'Arrogance', *APQ* 35. 4: 379–90.

Trianosky, G. W. (1988), 'Rightly Ordered Appetites: How to Live Morally and Live Well', *APQ* 25. 1: 1–12.

Tsouna-McKirahan, V. (1996), 'Epicurean Attitudes to Management and Finance', in Giannantoni and Gigante 1996: 701–14.

Tsouna, V. (2001*a*), 'Cicéron et Philodème: quelques considerations sur l'éthique', in Auvray-Assayas and Delattre 2001: 159–72.

—— (2001*b*), 'Philodemus on the Therapy of Vice', *OSAP* 21: 233–58.

—— (2003), ' "Portare davanti agli occhi": una tecnica retorica nelle opere morali di Filodemo', *CErc* 33: 243–8.

—— (2006*a*), 'Aristo on Blends of Arrogance', in Fortenbaugh and White 2006: 279–92.

—— (2006*b*), 'Irrationality and the Fear of Death in Epicurean Philosophy', *Rhizai* 3. 1: 79–117.

—— (2006*c*), 'Philodemus on Ethics and Moral Psychology', in R. Sorabji and R. Sharples (eds.) (2006), *Greek and Roman Philosophy 100 BC to 200 AD, Bulletin of the Institute of Classical Studies*.

—— (2007), 'Philodemus and the Epicurean Tradition', in Ioppolo and Sedley 2007.

Vogt, S. (2006), 'Characters in Aristo', in Fortenbaugh and White 2006: 261–78.

Warren, J. (2004), *Facing Death* (Oxford).

Wellman, C. H. (1999), 'Gratitude as a Virtue', *PPQ* 80: 284–300.

Wilke, K. (1914), *Philodemi Epicurei De ira liber* (Leipzig).

Williams, B. (1973), 'The Makropoulos Case: Reflections on the Tedium of Immortality', in his *Problems of the Self* (Cambridge), 82–100.

—— (1985), *Ethics and the Limits of Philosophy* (London).

—— (1995), 'Resenting One's own Existence', in his *Making Sense of Humanity* (Cambridge), 224–32.

Yunis, H. (1996), *Taming Democracy: Models of Political Rhetoric in Classical Athens* (Ithaca, NY).

Index

Index of Names

Index Locorum